John Lovell

Lovell's historic report of census of Montreal, taken in January,

1891.

John Lovell

Lovell's historic report of census of Montreal, taken in January, 1891.

ISBN/EAN: 9783337872991

Printed in Europe, USA, Canada, Australia, Japan

Cover: Foto ©ninafisch / pixelio.de

More available books at **www.hansebooks.com**

LOVELL'S

HISTORIC REPORT

of

CENSUS OF MONTREAL

TAKEN IN

JANUARY, 1891.

COMPILED BY JOHN LOVELL.

FOUNDERS OF CANADA.

Engraved for Lovell's Gazetteer and History of Canada, in Eleven Volumes.

1596-1676.   1500-1560.   1567-1635.

PAUL CHOMEDEY DE MAI-   JACQUES CARTIER, born at St.   SAMUEL DE CHAMPLAIN, born
SONNEUVE, born about 1596, in   Malo, Brittany, in 1500; first   at Brouage, Saintonge, France,
Champagne, France; founded   crossed the Atlantic in 1534; vi-   in 1567; first ascended River St.
Ville Marie, May 17, 1642;   sited Hochelaga in October, 1535;   Lawrence in 1603; founded
died at Paris, Sept. 19, 1676.   died in 1560.   Quebec in 1608; died in 1635.

MAYORS OF MONTREAL

Engraved expressly for Lovell's Historic Report of Census of Montreal.

1787-1858.

1789-1860.

1823-1891.

JACQUES VIGER, Commander of St. Sylvestre, born at Montreal, May 7, 1787; first mayor of Montreal, 1833; died Dec. 12, 1858.

HON. PETER McGILL, born at Cree Bridge, Wigtownshire, Scotland, in August, 1789; first English-speaking mayor of Montreal, 1840; died September 28, 1860.

JACQUES GRENIER, born at Berthier en Haut, January 20, 1823; first elected to City Council in 1857; mayor of Montreal, 1889-90.

CORPORATION OF THE CITY OF MONTREAL.

1890.

HIS WORSHIP MAYOR JACQUES GRENIER.

ALDERMEN.

J. D. Rolland,	Geo. W. Stephens,	Daniel Wilson,	James McBride,
R. Préfontaine,	J. O. Villeneuve,	William Kennedy,	W. H. Cunningham,
H. Jeannotte,	Arthur Dubuc,	Jos. Brunet,	L. H. Boisseau,
A. A. Stevenson,	Jérémie Perrault,	F. Martineau,	Vital Grenier,
Thomas Conroy,	W. Clendinneng,	Patrick Kennedy,	Dennis Tansey,
M. Malone,	James Griffin,	J. R. Savignac,	J. M. Dufresne,
H. B. Rainville,	N. A. Hurteau,	Pierre Dubuc,	Hollis Shorey,
Edwin Thompson,	J. C. Robert,	Alex. Germain,	A. Lamarche,
A. S. Hamelin,	J. B. R. Dufresne,	W. Farrell,	Thomas Gauthier.

WARDS REPRESENTED.

East..........J. M. Dufresne, J. B. R. Dufresne, Perreault.

Centre........Farrell, Hamelin, Rainville.

West..........McBride, Stephens, Stevenson...

St. Ann's.....Malone, P. Kennedy, Conroy.

St. Antoine...Shorey, Wilson, Clendinneng.

St. Lawrence..Cunningham, W. Kennedy, Griffin.

St. Louis........Boisseau, Savignac, A. Dubuc.

St. James........Lamarche, Brunet, Hurteau.

St. Mary's.......Jeannotte, Martineau, Robert.

Hochelaga.......Gauthier, Rolland, Préfontaine.

St. Jean Baptiste..Grenier, Villeneuve, Germain.

St. Gabriel......Tansey, P. Dubuc, Thompson.

OFFICERS.

B. A. T. de Montigny, City Recorder.
Roger Roy, Q.C., City Attorney.
Chs. Glackmeyer, City Clerk.
William Robb, City Treasurer.
P. W. St.George, City Surveyor.
B. D. McConnell, Superintendent Water Works.
Lieut. Col. George A. Hughes, Chief of Police.
—— City Comptroller.
O. Dufresne, City Auditor.
Z. Benoit, Chief Engineer Fire Department.
P. Lacroix, Inspector of Buildings.
E. O. Champagne, Inspector of Boilers.
F. H. Badger, Superintendent Telegraph Department.
Louis Laberge, M.D., Medical Health Officer.
Alphonse Gosselin, Assistant City Clerk
Léandre J. Ethier, Q.C., Assistant City Attorney.
W. H. McDonnough, City Accountant.
S. Caravan, Cashier.
F. B. Lavallée, Deputy City Surveyor.
J. O. E. Laforest, Assistant Supt. Water Works.
A. Britain, Assistant Surveyor, City Surveyor's Office.
Charles Arnoldi, Accountant Arrears Department.

F. X. Castonguay, Receiver Revenue Department.
Napoleon Lesage, Accountant Water Revenue Dept.
P. O. Reilly, Secretary.
James Lowe, Sewer Inspector.
J. P. Flynn, Street Inspector Road Department.
I. C. Radford, Sanitary Inspector.
Joseph I. Flynn, Secretary and Clerk of Statistics.
V. H. Lefebvre, Accountant.
George Fullum and A. Hamall, Meat Inspectors.
F. X. Gauthier, Assistant Supt. Telegraph Dept.
Wm. McGibbon, Superintendent Mount Royal Park.
W. B. Desmarteau, Supt. St. Helen's Island Park.
J. Perrigo, Clerk Bonsecours Market.
J. N. Duhamel, Clerk St. Ann's Market.
Elzéar Derome, Clerk Eastern Abattoir Market.
M. Groulx, Clerk Viger Market.
Z. C. Jolicœur, Clerk St. Lawrence Market.
W. J. Page, Acting Clerk St. Gabriel Market.
G. Tessier, Clerk St. Antoine Market.
T. Giroux, Clerk St. James Market.
J. M. Coté, Clerk Hochelaga Market.
A. Normandin, Clerk St. Jean Baptiste Market.

BOARD OF ASSESSORS.

J. T. Dillon, Chairman.	Richard Thomas.	George B. Muir.
P. H. Morin.	J. W. Grose.	A. Hamilton.

CITY POLICE FORCE.

1 Chief,	1 Chief Detective,	26 Acting Sergeants,
3 Sub Chiefs,	1 Secretary,	329 Sub Constables,
1 Accountant,	7 Detectives,	1 Drill Instructor,
1 Assistant Accountant,	12 Sergeants,	1 Police Matron.

MONTREAL FIRE DEPARTMENT.

1 Chief,	15 Captains,	3 Foremen of Chemical Engines,
3 Assistant Chiefs,	2 Foremen of Salvage,	1 Hose and Harness Repairer,
1 Supply Officer,	8 Engineers,	70 First-class Firemen,
1 Secretary.	4 Foremen of Ladders,	38 Second-class Firemen,

15 Fire Stations.

1891.

LOVELL'S HISTORIC REPORT

OF

CENSUS OF MONTREAL,

Taken in January, 1891.

Population—110,098 Females ; 104,204 Males ; 155,511 Catholics ; 55,835 Protestants ; ⎱ 214,302
28 Chinese ; 923 Jewesses ; 1005 Jews.............. .... ⎰

OR

TOWN OF ST. HENRY.

Bordering on Limits of City of Montreal.

Population—5,995 Females ; 5,719 Males ; 10,950 Catholics ; 764 Protestants 11,714

OR

CITY OF ST. CUNEGONDE.

Bordering on Limits of City of Montreal.

Population—4,104 Females ; 4,055 Males ; 7,089 Catholics ; 1,065 Protestants ; 5 Jews.. 8,159

OR

ST. LOUIS OF MILE END,

Bordering on Limits of City of Montreal.

Population—1,723 Females ; 1,726 Males ; 3,319 Catholics ; 130 Protestants........... 3,449

OR

COTEAU ST. LOUIS,

Bordering on Limits of City of Montreal.

Population—1,389 Females ; 1,464 Males ; 2,600 Catholics ; 253 Protestants........... 2,853

OR

TOWN OF NOTRE DAME DES NEIGES.

Bordering on Limits of City of Montreal.

Population—385 Females ; 388 Males ; 637 Catholics ; 136 Protestants............. 773

OR

OUTREMONT.

Bordering on Limits of City of Montreal.

Population—173 Females ; 190 Males ; 98 Catholics ; 265 Protestants............... 363

Montreal:
PRINTED BY JOHN LOVELL & SON,
23 AND 25 ST. NICHOLAS STREET.

* I appealed to seventeen Municipalities in the neighborhood of Montreal to aid me to take the Census of each separately, by subscribing for fifty copies of LOVELL'S HISTORIC REPORT OF CENSUS OF MONTREAL at 50 cents each. It is distressing to say that only six consented.

JOHN LOVELL, *Compiler*

POPULATION OF MONTREAL IN JANUARY, 1891: **211,302**.

Nationalities and Religions
on
Page 21.

Nationalities
on
Pages 22 and 23.

> Entered, according to Act of Parliament of Canada, by JOHN LOVELL, in the year one thousand eight hundred and ninety-one, in the Office of the Minister of Agriculture.

Historical Sketch
of
Montreal:
1535–1642
on
Pages 25–44.

THIS HISTORIC REPORT

OF THE

CENSUS OF MONTREAL

IS

VERY RESPECTFULLY, BUT WITHOUT THEIR KNOWLEDGE,

Dedicated

TO

Andrew F. Gault, Esquire,

MERCHANT,

AND TO

Hugh Graham, Esquire,

PROPRIETOR OF THE DAILY STAR,

AS THE

ACTUAL PROMOTERS OF THE WORK;

WITHOUT THEIR COUNTENANCE AND FINANCIAL AID,

AND, I MAY ADD, THE

CONTRIBUTIONS OF PATRIOTIC LINE CONTRIBUTORS,

This Work,

CHEERFULLY AND HOPEFULLY UNDERTAKEN,

COULD NOT HAVE BEEN PROSECUTED TO A SUCCESSFUL CONCLUSION,

BY THEIR HUMBLE SERVANT,

JOHN LOVELL, *Compiler*

MONTREAL, January, 1891.

VICTORIA BRIDGE, MONTREAL.

Engraved for Lovell's Gazetteer and History of Canada.

INDEX TO CONTENTS.

THE CARNIVAL AT MONTREAL, 1885.—THE ICE PALACE.
Engraved for Lovell's projected Gazetteer and History of Canada, in Eleven Volumes.

INDEX TO MONTREAL LINE CONTRIBUTORS

IN

LOVELL'S CENSUS REPORT OF MONTREAL.

Recapitulation by Nationalities and Religions, page.... 21

Nationalities on pages ....22 and 23.

Municipalities on pages........................133 to 149

PLACE D'ARMES, MONTREAL.

VICTORIA SQUARE, MONTREAL.

Engraved for Lovell's projected Gazetteer and History of Canadian. Eleven Volumes.

HON. JAMES McSHANE. MAYOR OF MONTREAL.

CHARLES GLACKMEYER. CITY CLERK.

WILLIAM ROBB. CITY TREASURER.

CHARLES GLACKMEYER, born in Montreal, 1820; Entered the Corporation 1847.

HON. JAMES McSHANE, born in Montreal, in 1834; made Justice of the Peace, 1864. City Councillor 1867, returned to Legislative Assembly, 1878. Minister of Public Works, 1887.

WILLIAM ROBB, born at Aberdeen, Scotland, 1817; came to Canada, 1854; Entered the Corporation 1865.

INDEX TO BUSINESS HEADS OF LINE CONTRIBUTORS.

4

PUBLISHER'S PREFACE.

EVERY possible means has been taken to insure a reliable CENSUS OF MONTREAL. To those who really desire the Census I have to say that they are mainly indebted to ANDREW F. GAULT, Esq., and to HUGH GRAHAM, Esq., for the undertaking and completion of it. At the request of the former and after consultation with the latter of these gentlemen, I decided to undertake a Census of Montreal. I then prepared a Prospectus and commenced a canvass for subscriptions; but after an urgent appeal I soon saw that sufficient subscribers, at 50c. each, could not be secured to meet half the cost of publication. This being the case I applied to patriotic citizens to aid me by becoming 50c. Line Contributors, and thereby save me from serious loss, as otherwise I should be forced to abandon the work I had so cheerfully undertaken, and to disappoint my generous and true friends. I am proud to say that 50c. Line Contributors enabled me to put sixty Sworn Enumerators on the Streets, Squares, etc., of the City, to look for and obtain the actual number sleeping in each house, or other building, their sex, religion and calling; and at the request of the Finance Committee of the Corporation, to take the Nationalities, Forms for which were prepared with studied care and in the belief that they would be acceptable. But, no! A few gentlemen were annoyed because I had no heading or column for *English* Canadians! Well, I fancied I had several headings for English Canadians; that is, I had a heading for English, English born in Canada; Irish, Irish born in Canada; Scotch, Scotch born in Canada, and so on; these headings enabled me to make a Recapitulation of Nationalities, printed on page 21. It will, I trust, satisfy the most fastidious. The sixty sworn Enumerators did not hear of complaints about the Nationalities. I may add that each Enumerator spoke and understood French and English. Their returns show a population, within City limits, of 110,098 females; 101,204 males; 81,189 Catholic females; 74,322 Catholic males; 27,896 Protestant females; 25,939 Protestant males; 28 Chinese; 923 Jewesses; 1005 Jews; or, a total population of 211,302.

The Nationalities are printed on pages 22 and 23; with the Recapitulation on page 21.

In this matter of Nationalities the Enumerators had much to contend with, in trying to explain to unwilling citizens the object of taking them. A few would not listen to reason but abruptly declined giving any information relative to their Nationality. Yet it is pleasing to state that a very large number of the population were glad to give all required information. At times six or eight different Nationalities were found in a single dwelling, causing great delay in securing complete and accurate returns.

My HISTORIC REPORT OF CENSUS OF MONTREAL is given in the honest belief and conviction that it will be found as correct as the means available would allow.

My sincere thanks are tendered to the several Religious, Benevolent and Charitable Institutions for satisfactory answers to direct questions, and especially to the Ladies of the Grey Nunnery, for devoting five hours of their valuable time to the task of verifying the statistics relative to their institution. The Lady Superioress, without a moment's hesitation, authorized two of the Reverend Sisters to give me all the information I wanted.   They accordingly went to their vaults in search of records, papers and books that contained dates and other information, now printed in this Historic Report as a correct statement to January, 1891.   I might single out other institutions, but where all were desirous of giving full and unreserved details, my sincere thanks are tendered to all.

To the writer of the able and interesting " HISTORICAL SKETCH OF MONTREAL," I beg to offer my sincere and heartfelt thanks.

To CHARLES GLACKMEYER, Esq., our estimable and obliging City Clerk, and to WILLIAM ROBB, Esq., our able and worthy City Treasurer, I am indebted for valuable data relative to Municipal affairs and the City's Financial position.

I am deeply indebted to my old friend, PETER CROSSBY, for his careful and trust-worthy account of the Port of Montreal.

To ALEXANDER ROBERTSON, Esquire, Secretary of the Harbor Commissioners, I cheeringly offer my thanks for statements and figures which give additional value to Mr. Crossby's sketch.

To Mr. E. J. GOLLIFER, my indefatigable and trustworthy assistant, for collecting information from Religious, Benevolent and Charitable Institutions, my best thanks are offered.

To the energetic, painstaking and intelligent staff of SIXTY ENUMERATORS I have pleasure in saying that they worthily earned my confidence and esteem.

To my OFFICE STAFF of twelve intelligent and painstaking YOUNG GIRLS, and to two first-class ARITHMETICIANS, JOSEPH L. SMITH and EMILE HANDCOCK, from whom I received constant and able assistance, thanks are also due.   Their task was to examine and arrange 2771 sheets of 524 Streets, Squares, etc., returned by the Enumerators.

To reduce to alphabetical order, and secure uniformity and accuracy, the column of clerical, legal and medical professions, mercantile and other callings, and trades, or as the case might be, had to be copied and collated three different times.   The additions and checking were most arduous, but the work had to be done.   2771 sheets of 11 columns each with 17 lines on the sheet, gave a total addition of 30,481 columns, and, consequently, a like quantity of checking.   In addition to these, 30 Nationalities contained in 412 Forms, and arranged under 212 separate headings, were compared, copied and checked, the result being the totals as found on pages 22 and 23 of this work.

The anxious labor and effectiveness of all who were engaged on the work are worthy of all praise.

These details are given as a reasonable cause of delay in the issue of this Census Report.   Some extra copies have been printed, with the hope that they may be sold for transmission to friends in the Mother Country and elsewhere.   For myself I will send one thousand copies to THE PRESS of this Canada of ours ; to leading papers in New York, Boston, Philadelphia, Baltimore, New Orleans, Richmond, Chicago, Buffalo, and Detroit ; to some leading papers in England, Scotland, and Ireland, as well as to journals in France, Germany, and Belgium.

To THE PRESS of this City I am deeply indebted for the public spirited and kindly manner in which they noticed the Prospectus of this work.

                                                        JOHN LOVELL, *Publisher.*

MONTREAL, January, 1891.

MONTREAL is represented at Ottawa, in the Dominion Parliament, by three members :

> THE HONORABLE SIR DONALD A. SMITH, K.C.M.G., LL.D., M.P., president
> of the Bank of Montreal ; president and chancellor of McGill University.
> JOHN J. CURRAN, Q.C., LL.D.
> ALPHONSE T. LEPINE, newspaper proprietor, and book and job printer.

MONTREAL has 25 Catholic Churches ; 33 Catholic Chapels.

> 151,720 total congregations, as returned by clergymen.

MONTREAL has 58 Protestant Churches ; 39 Protestant Chapels, or Meeting Rooms.

> 49,520 total congregations, as returned by clergymen.

MONTREAL has 4 Jewish Synagogues, and 1 Meeting Room.

> 1125 total Sabbath attendants, as returned by Rabbis.

MONTREAL has 23 Convents and Monasteries :—

> 820 sisters ; 184 novices ; 130 sister teachers ; 1853 pupils.

MONTREAL has 4 Catholic Hospitals :—

> 9 resident and attendant physicians ; 19 visiting physicians ; 116 nuns as
> nurses : 139 female employees; 54 male employees.

MONTREAL has 7 Protestant Hospitals ;

> 151 female patients ; 122 male patients ; 18 resident and attendant phy-
> sicians ; 26 visiting physicians ; 52 female nurses ; 18 male attendants ;
> 40 female employees ; 56 male employees.

RECAPITULATION OF POPULATION BY NATIONALITIES AND RELIGIONS.

Born in Canada.		Born in		Catholics.	Protestants.	Total.
French Canadian..	120,121			117,498	 2,623	120,121
English............	16,376	England ...	13,309	 3,164	 27,121	 30,285
Irish..............	22,369	Ireland..........	15,129	 20,531	 7,458	 37,389
Scotch...........	7,775	Scotland......	5,253	 897	 12,131	 13,028
Welsh............	174	Wales..........	109	 32	 251	 283
Newfoundlanders..	197	Newfoundland....	524	 620	 401	 1,021
Australian........	7	Australia..........	14	 8	 13	 21
East Indian.......	7	East Indies........	20	 9	 18	 27
West Indian.......	29	West Indies	16	 14	 31	 45
Br. Poss. colored..	31	Br. Possessions ...	9	 16	 24	 40
U. S. of America..	601	U. S. of America..	2,069	 978	 1,692	 2,670
French, France....	259	France............	896	 1,001	 151	 1,155
Belgian...........	90	Belgium	207	 224	 73	 297
Dutch	38	Holland	42	 9	 71	 80
Italian...........	197	Italy	429	 511	 115	 626
German.	500	Germany	592	 300	 792	 1,092
Austrian....	17	Austria....	29	 31	 15	 46
Polish	28	Poland...........	43	 7	 64	 71
Swiss............	39	Switzerland	44	 33	 50	 83
Norwegian.... ...	108	Norway..........	162	 39	 231	 270
Swedish...........	48	Sweden..........	166	 23	 131	 157
Danish	42	Denmark..........	70	 25	 87	 112
Hungarian	7	Hungary	13	 7	 13	 20
Russian...........	13	Russia.... ...	23	 11	 25	 36
U.S. Colored,.....	63	U.S. of America..	110	 13	 160	 173
Chinese...........		China............	28	....	 28	 28
Other Nations.....	70	Others............	126	 110	 88	 198
	169,007		40,277	155,511	 53,863	209,374
Jewesses.... 304		Judea, etc... 619				
Jews........ 373		" ... 632				
	677		1,251	....	....	 1,928
	169,774		41,528		Total population ...	211,302

NATIONALITIES.

Montreal—Fr. Canadian Catholic females.... 60,871
" " " " males 56,627
           117,498
" " " Protestant females .. 1,343
" " " " males..... 1,280
           2,623

England—English Catholic females........... 584
" " " males............... 537
          1,121
" " " females, { born in { 981
" " " males, { Canada { 1,062
          2,043
" " Protestant females........... 6,490
" " " males........... 6,298
          12,788
" " " females, { born in { 7,444
" " " males, { Canada { 6,889
          14,333

Ireland—Irish Catholic females............. 6,144
" " " males............. 5,612
          11,756
" " " females, { born in { 9,392
" " " males, { Canada { 8,783
          18,175
" " Protestant females... 1,749
" " " males............ 1,624
          3,373
" " " females, { born in { 2,114
" " " males, { Canada { 1,981
          4,085

Scotland—Scotch Catholic females........... 196
" " " males 146
          342
" " " females, { born in { 326
" " " males, { Canada { 229
          555
" " Protestant females........ 2,332
" " " males........... 2,579
          4,911
" " " females, { born in { 3,956
" " " males, { Canada { 3,264
          7,220

Wales—Welsh Catholic females........... 9
" " " males............... 7
          16
" " " females, { born in { 5
" " " males, { Canada { 11
          16
" " Protestant females........... 39
" " " males............... 54
          93
" " " females, { born in { 75
" " " males, { Canada { 83
          158

Newfoundland Catholic females........... 261
" " males........... 238
          499
" " females, { born in { 58
" " males, { Canada { 63
          121
" Protestant females........... 157
" " males........... 168
          325
" " females, { born in { 41
" " males, { Canada { 35
          76

Australia—Australian Catholic females........... 4
" " " males......... 4
          8
" " " females, { born in {
" " " males, { Canada {

    Carried forward........ 202,135

    Brought forward........ 202,135
Australia—Australian Protestant females..... 4
" " " males......... 2
          6
" " " females, { born in { 5
" " " males, { Canada { 2
          7

E. Ind.—E. Indian Catholic females........... 3
" " " males........... 4
          7
" " " females, { born in { 1
" " " males, { Canada { 1
          2
" " Protestant females........... 6
" " " males........... 7
          13
" " " females, { born in { 2
" " " males, { Canada { 3
          5

W. Ind.—W. Indian Catholic females........... 1
" " " males........... 4
          5
" " " females, { born in { 4
" " " males, { Canada { 5
          9
" " Protestant females........... 4
" " " males 7
          11
" " " females, { born in { 2
" " " males, { Canada { 8
          20

Br. Poss'ns—Colored Catholic females...........
" " " males........... 2
          2
" " " females, { born in { 7
" " " males, { Canada { 7
          14
" " Protestant females........ 2
" " " males........... 5
          7
" " " females, { born in { 12
" " " males, { Canada { 5
          17

U. S.—American Catholic females........... 399
" " " males........... 370
          769
" " " females, { born in { 104
" " " males, { Canada { 105
          209
" " Protestant females 696
" " " males........... 604
          1,300
" " " females, { born in { 193
" " " males, { Canada { 197
          390

France—French Catholic females........... 315
" " " males........... 457
          772
" " " females, { born in { 101
" " " males, { Canada { 128
          229
" " Protestant females 46
" " " males 78
          124
" " " females, { born in { 12
" " " males, { Canada { 18
          30

Belgium—Belgian Catholic females........... 67
" " " males........... 103
          170
" " " females, { born in { 20
" " " males, { Canada { 34
          54
" " Protestant females........... 12
" " " males........... 25
          37
" " " females, { born in { 23
" " " males, { Canada { 13
          36

    Carried forward........ 205,382

Brought forward......	205,382		
Holland—Dutch Catholic females, ...	2		
" " " males	3		
			5
" " " females, { born in }	3		
" " " males, { Canada }	1		
			4
" " Protestant females..........	14		
" " " males...	23		
			37
" " " females, { born in }	15		
" " " males, { Canada }	19		
			34
Italy—Italian Catholic females..............	135		
" " " males	233		
			368
" " " females, { born in }	72		
" " " males, { Canada }	71		
			143
" " Protestant females.............	22		
" " " males.............	39		
			61
" " " females, { born in }	27		
" " " males, { Canada }	27		
			54
Germany—German Catholic females...........	49		
" " " males...........	90		
			139
" " " females, { born in }	82		
" " " males, { Canada }	79		
			161
" " Protestant females..... ...	215		
" " " males.............	238		
			453
" " " females, { born in }	179		
" " " males, { Canada }	160		
			339
Austria—Austrian Catholic females.............	5		
" " " males	11		
			16
" " " females, { born in }	6		
" " " males, { Canada }	9		
			15
" " Protestant females.............	5		
" " " males.............	8		
			13
" " " females, { born in }	1		
" " " males, { Canada }	1		
			2
Poland—Polish Catholic females..........	1		
" " " males	1		
			2
" " " females, { born in }	2		
" " " males, { Canada }	3		
			5
" " Protestant females.............	18		
" " " males.............	23		
			41
" " " females, { born in }	12		
" " " males, { Canada }	11		
			23
Switzerland—Swiss Catholic females...........	11		
" " " males........	8		
			19
" " " females, { born in }	6		
" " " males, { Canada }	8		
			14
" " Protestant females	10		
" " " males.............	15		
			25
" " " females, { born in }	13		
" " " males, { Canada }	12		
			25
Norway—Norwegian Catholic females	12		
" " " males............	10		
			22
" " " females, { born in }	2		
" " " males, { Canada }	5		
			17
" " Protestant females.........	57		
" " " males......... ..	83		
			140
" " " females, { born in }	50		
" " " males, { Canada }	41		
			91
Sweden—Swedish Catholic females..........	4		
" " " males............	11		
			15
" " " females, { born in }	3		
" " " males, { Canada }	5		
			8
Carried forward........	207,673		

Brought forward........	207,673	
Sweden—Swedish Protestant females.....	37	
" " " males........	57	
		94
" " " females, { born in }	21	
" " " males, { Canada }	19	
		40
Denmark—Danish Catholic females	3	
" " " males	7	
		10
" " " females, { born in }	8	
" " " males, { Canada }	7	
		15
" " Protestant females	21	
" " " males......... ...	39	
		60
" " " females, { born in }	15	
" " " males, { Canada }	12	
		27
Hungary—Hungarian Catholic females..........	2	
" " " males	2	
		4
" " " fem., { born in }	1	
" " " males, { Canada }	2	
		3
" " Protestant females..........	5	
" " " males.............	4	
		9
" " " females, { born in }	1	
" " " males, { Canada }	3	
		4
Russia—Russian Catholic females	2	
" " " males.........	3	
		5
" " " females, { born in }	3	
" " " males, { Canada }	3	
		6
" " Protestant females	7	
" " " males	11	
		18
" " " females, { born in }	5	
" " " males, { Canada }	2	
		7
Other Nationalities, Catholic females..........	34	
" " " males..........	38	
		72
" " " females, { born in }	24	
" " " males, { Canada }	14	
		38
" " Protestant females..........	22	
" " " males.............	34	
		56
" " " females, { born in }	17	
" " " males, { Canada }	15	
		32
Colored from the United States and elsewhere :		
Catholic females.........	5	
" males.......	6	
		11
" females, { born in }	1	
" males, { Canada }	1	
		2
Protestant females........... ...	42	
" males.........	57	
		99
" females, { born in }	29	
" males, { Canada }	32	
		61
Chinese, males....................	28	
Jews from Judea and elsewhere :		
Jewesses..............	619	
Jews....................	632	
		1,251
Jewesses, { born in }	304	
Jews, { Canada }	373	
		677
Total............		211,302

RECAPITULATION.		HOUSES IN MONTREAL.	
Catholics...........	155,511	Brick...........	25,774
Protestants.........	52,863	Dashed...........	81
Jewesses ...	923 }	Stone............	5,482
Jews ...... 1,005 }	1,928	Wood............	3,118
Population : 211,302		**Houses : 34,455**	

MONTREAL.

Engraved for Lovell's projected Gazetteer and History of Canada, in Eleven Volumes.

1535-1642.

HISTORICAL SKETCH OF MONTREAL:
THE STORY OF ITS FOUNDATION.

WRITTEN EXPRESSLY FOR LOVELL'S HISTORIC REPORT OF CENSUS OF MONTREAL.

NEXT YEAR (1892) Americans of every name will be commemorating, as is most meet, the discovery of this western hemisphere by Columbus, four hundred years before. In the same year the people of Montreal will also be celebrating the two hundred and fiftieth anniversary of the foundation of their city by De Maisonneuve. But its antiquity ought not really to be bounded by that formal act. Even if we pass over the fact that Champlain had actually, in 1611, begun the work of clearing and building on the very point that De Maisonneuve subsequently selected for his fortress and habitation—giving it the very name, *Place Royale*, which it bore long afterwards,—it must not be forgotten that Montreal is one of the rare instances of a European city having been superimposed upon an Indian town. More than a hundred years before De Maisonneuve, with the solemn rites of the Church, consecrated to the Virgin Mother the capital of his colony, a fortified *bourgade* stood at the base of the trappean hill, from which Montreal receives its name. How long it had occupied that position of pre-eminence we can only conjecture. But the fact, that in the early part of the sixteenth century it was the strong dwelling-place of an apparently thriving community, shows that its admirable natural advantages had been recognized even by the rude predecessors of its civilized inhabitants. The sight that greeted the eyes of the hardy mariner of St. Malo and his brave companions was an augury of the greatness and prosperity of Montreal in days to come, when the din of strife should have been succeeded by the sounds of manifold industry.

It was a happy instinct which impelled the children of the forest to make a stronghold of Hochelaga. For security, for shelter, for convenience of *rendezvous*, no point could present better facilities, so that its choice by those rude warriors and hunters was an unconscious forecast of its remoter and grander destinies. By patient, far-seeing nature those destinies had, indeed, been marked out in the very dawn of time. The slow preparation for fulfilment began when the primeval germ of the continent rose, bleak and lifeless, above the archæan sea. By the unhurrying action of mighty forces, below and above, its foundations had been laid deep and solid. The throes of the volcano raised aloft its mountain bulwark. True father of waters, the yet nameless St. Lawrence, first born of American rivers, had indicated it as the *entrepôt* of mighty nations ere yet the Mississippi Valley had emerged from the primal ocean.

Evidently, therefore, the history of Montreal embraces three successive periods,—the Aboriginal, the French, and the British. The first of these divisions, though it admits of voluminous treatment, involving, as it necessarily does, a question of the utmost value to ethnologists, is mainly interesting to the general reader for its association with Jacques Cartier. The story of that explorer's visit to Hochelaga has been told by many writers, and is familiar to every Canadian school boy. He was born at St. Malo, in Brittany, in the year 1500. In 1534 he first crossed the Atlantic, the route being already frequented by Basque and Breton fishermen, and, having entered the Gulf, named the Baie des Chaleurs, made acquaintance with the natives of our coast land, and set up a cross with a French escutcheon ; he returned to France with a couple of Indians, who afterwards served him as interpreters. Next year (1535) he again entered our great water-way, to which he gave the name which it has ever since been proud to bear. His squadron consisted of *La Grande Hermine* (from 100 to 120 tons burden), which he commanded in person ; *La Petite Hermine* (of 60 tons), in command of Macé Jalobert, Cartier's brother-in-law ; and the *Emerillon* (of 40 tons), in charge of Guillaume Le Breton. Accompanying the leader of the expedition were several persons of note, members of noble families, such as Claude de Pontbriand, son of the Seigneur de Montreuil, and cup bearer to the Dauphin ; Charles de la Pommeraye and Jehan Poullet ; the names of the crews have also been preserved in the archives of St. Malo. The total enumeration comprises 74 names. Reaching Stadacona (Quebec), Cartier was cordially received by Donnacona, the chief of the tribes which had their headquarters at that place. But when it was perceived that the strangers purposed advancing still further up the river, all kinds of dissuasive arguments were employed to deter the daring explorer from such an attempt.   The chiefs, finding their oratorical powers unavailing, had recourse (says the record) to a *ruse*, by which, if possible, to arouse the superstitious fears of the adventurers. Cartier, however, was not to be diverted from his course ; on the 17th of September he began the arduous ascent, and on the 2nd of October he reached the site of Canada's future metropolis.

What ensued may be fitly described in the ancient mariner's own language* as urned into English by the Rev. Richard Hakluyt :—

" The captaine the next day very earely in the morning, having attired himselfe, caused all his company to be set in order to go to see the towne and habitation of those people, and a certaine mountaine that is neere the citie ; with whom went also the gentlemen and twenty mariners, leaving the rest to keepe and looke to our boates : we tooke with us three men of Hochelaga to bring us to the place.

* In order that the French reader, or the English reader, who is a student of the French language and literature, may have an opportunity of contrasting Jacques Cartier's speech with the modern tongue, an extract from the original of the passage quoted is here appended :—

Le lendemain au plus matin, le Capitaine s'accoustra, et fist mettre ses gens en ordre pour aller voir la ville et demeurance du dit peuple, et une montagne qui est jacente à la dite ville, où allèrent avecque le dit Capitaine les gentils-hommes, et vingt mariniers, et laissa le parsus pour la garde des barques, et prit trois hommes de la dite ville de *Hochelaga* pour les mener et conduire au dit lieu. Et nous estans en chemin, le trouvasmes aussi battu qu'il soit possible de voir, en la plus belle terre et meilleure plaine : des chênes aussi beaux qu'il y en ait en forêt de France, sous lesquels estoit toute la terre couverte de glands. Et nous, ayant fait environ une lieu et demie, (*) trouvasmes sur le chemin l'un des principaux de la dite ville de *Hochelaga*, avecque plusieurs personnes, lequel nous fist signe qu'il se falloit reposer au dit lieu près un feu qu'ils avoient fait au dit chemin. Et lors commença le dit Seigneur à faire un sermon et preschement, comme ci-devant est dit être leur coutume de faire joye et connoissance, en faisant celui Seigneur chère au dit Capitaine et sa compagnie ; lequel Capitaine lui donna une couple de haches et une couple de couteaux, avec une Croix et remembrance du Crucifix qu'il lui fist baiser, et lui pendit au col : de quoi il rendit grâces au dit Capitaine. Ce fait, marchames plus outre, et environ demie lieue de là commençames à trouver les terres labourées, et belles grandes campagnes pleines de blé de leurs terres, qui est comme mil de Bresil, aussi gros ou plus que pois, (†) duquel ils vivent, ainsi que nous faisons de froment. Et au parmi d'icelles campagnes est située et assise la dite ville de *Hochelaga*, (‡) près et joignante une montagne qui est à l'entour d'icelle, bien labourée et fort fertile : de dessus laquelle on voit fort loin. Nous nommasmes icelle montagne le *Mont Royal.*

(*) Ce qui fait voir, que Quartier aurait pris terre au-dessous du Courant de Ste. Marie. (†) Bled d'Inde. (‡) Montréal.

All along as we went we found the way as well beaten and frequented as can be, the fairest and best country that possibly can be scene, full of as goodly great okes as are in any wood in France, under which the ground was all covered over with faire akornes. After we had gone about league and a half we met by the way one of the chiefest lords of the citie, accompanied with many moe, who so soone as he sawe us beckned and made signes upon us, that we must rest in that place where they had a great fire, and so we did. Then the said lord began to make a long discourse, even as we have saide above, they are accustomed to doe in signe of mirth and friendship, shewing our captaine and all his company a joyful countenance and good will; who gave him two hatchets, a paire of knives and a crucifix, which he made him to kisse, and then put it about his necke, for which he gave our captaine heartie thankes. This done, we went along, and about half a league farther, we began to finde goodly and large cultivated fieldes, full of such corne as the countrie yeeldeth. It is even as the millet of Bresil, as great and somewhat bigger than small peason, wherewith they live even as we doe with our wheat. In the midst of those fields is the citie of Hochelaga, placed neere, and as it were joyned to a great mountaine, that is tilled round about, very fertill, on the top of which you may see very farre. We named it Mount Roiall. The citie of Hochelaga is round, compassed about with timber, with three course of rampires, one within another framed like a sharp spire, or pyramid, but laid acrosse above. The middlemost of them is perpendiculer. The rampires are framed and fashioned with pieces of timber layd along very well and cunningly joyned togither after their fashion. This enclosure is in height about two rods. It hath but one gate or entrie thereat, which is shut with piles, stakes and barres. Over it, and also in many places of the wall, there is a kind of gallery to runne along, and ladders to get up, all full of stones and pebbles for the defence of it. There are in the towne about fiftie houses, at the utmost about fiftie paces long, and twelve or fifteen broad, built all of wood, covered over with the barke of the wood, as broad as any boord, very finely and cunningly joyned togither according to their fashion. Within the said houses, there are many roomes. In the midest of every one there is a great hall in the middle whereof they make their fire. They live in common togither: then doe the husbands, wives and children each one retire themselves to their chambers. They have also on the top of their houses certaine granaries, wherein they keepe their corne to make their bread withall; they call it Caracony, which they make as hereafter shall follow. They have certaine peeces of wood, like those whereon we beat our hempe, and with certain beetles of wood they beat their corne to powder; then they make paste of it, and of the paste, cakes or wreathes, then they lay them on a broad and hote stone, and then cover it with hote pebbles, and so they bake their bread instead of ovens. They make also sundry sorts of pottage with the said corne and also of peas and beanes, whereof they have great store, as also with other fruits, great cowcumbers and other fruits. They have also in their houses certaine vessels as bigge as any But or Tun, wherein they keepe their fish, causing the same in sommer to be dried in the smoke, and live therewith in winter, whereof they make great provision, as we by experience have seene. All their viands and meats are without any taste or savour of salt at all. They sleepe upon barkes of trees laid all along upon the ground, being over-spread with the skinnes of certaine wilde Beastes, wherewith they also clothe and cover themselves, namely, of the Dormouse, Beaver, Martin, Fox, Wild Cat, Deer, Stag, and other wild beasts, but the greater part of them go almost naked (during the sommer). The thing most precious that they have in all the world they call Esurgny,[*] which is white, and which they take in the said river in Cornibots, in the manner following: When any one hath deserved death, or that they take any of their enemies in warres, first they kill him, then with certaine knives they give great slashes and strokes upon their buttocks, flankes, thighs and shoulders; then they cast the same bodie so mangled downe to the bottome of the river, in a place where the said Esurgny is, and there leave it ten or twelve houres, then they take it up againe, and in the cuts find the said esurgny or cornibots. Of them they make beads, and use them even as we doe gold and silver, accounting it the preciousest thing in the world. They have this vertue in them, they will stop or stench bleeding at the nose, for we proved it. These people are given to no other exercise, but onely to husbandrie and fishing for their sustenance: they have no care of any other wealth or commoditie in this world, for they have no knowledge of it, and never travell an l go out of their country, as those of Canada and Saguenay doe, albeit the Canadians with eight or nine villages more alongst that rive be subject unto them.

---

[*] Wampum.

"So soone as we were come neere the towne, a great number of the inhabitants thereof came to present themselves before us, after their fashion, making very much of us : we were by our guides brought into the middest of the towne. They have in the middlemost part of their towne a large square place, being from side to side a good stone cast, whither we were brought, and there with signes were commanded to stay, and so we did : then suddenly all the women and maidens of the towne gathered themselves together, part of which had their armes full of young children, and as many as could came to kiss our faces, our armes, and what part of the bodie soever they could touch, weeping for very joy that they saw us, shewing us the best countenance that possibly they could, desiring us with their signes, that it would please us to touch their children. That done, the men caused the women to withdraw themselves backe, then they every one sate down on the ground round about us, as if we would have shewen and rehearsed some comedie or other shew : then presently came the women againe, every one bringing a fouresquare matte in manner of carpets, and spreading them abroad on the ground in that place, they caused us to sit upon them. That done, the lord and king of the country was brought upon nine or ten men's shoulders (whom in their tongue they called Agouhanna), sitting upon a great stagge's skinne, and they laid him downe upon the foresaid mattes neere to the captaine, every one beckning unto us that hee was their lord. This Agouhanna was a man about fiftie yeeres old ; he was no whit better apparelled than any of the rest, onely excepted that he had a certaine thing around his head made of the skinnes of hedgehogs* like a red wreath. He was full of the palsie, and his members shronke together. After he had with certaine signes saluted our captaine and all his companie, and by manifest tokens bid all welcome, he shewed his legges and armes to our captaine, and with signes, desired him to touch them, and so he did, rubbing them with his own hands : then did Agouhanna take the wreath or crowne he had about his head, and gave it unto our captaine ; that done they brought before him diverse diseased men, some blinde, some criple, some lame and impotent, and some so old that the haire of their eyelids came downe and covered their cheekes, and layd them all along before our captaine, to the end they might of him be touched ; for it seemed unto them that God was descended and come down from heaven to heale them. Our captaine, seeing the misery and devotion of this poore people, recited the Gospel of St. John, that is to say, 'In the beginning was the Word, making the signe of the cross upon the poor sick ones, praying to God that it would please him to open the hearts of this poore people, and to make them know our holy faith, and that they might receive baptisme and christendome ; that done, he took a service-booke in his hand, and with a loud voice read all the passion of Christ, word by word, that all the standers by might beare him, all which while this poore people kept silence, and were marvellously attentive, looking up to heaven, and imitating us in gestures. Then he caused the men all orderly to be set on one side, the women on another, and likewise the children on another, and to the chiefest of them he gave hatchets, to the other knives, and to the women beads and such other small trifles. Then whereby children were he cast rings, counters and broaches made of tin,† whereat they seemed to be very glad. That done, our captaine commanded trumpets and other musicall instruments to be sounded, which when they heard they were very merie. Then we took our leave and went away ; the women seeing that put themselves before to stay us, and brought us out of their meates that they had made readie for us, as fish, pottage, beanes, and such other things, thinking to make us eate and dine in that place ; but because the meates were not to our taste we liked them not but thanked them, and with signes gave to understand that we had no neede to eate. When we were out of the towne, diverse of the men and women followed us, and brought us to the toppe of the foresaid mountaine, which wee named Mount Roiall, it is about a quarter of a league from the towne. When as we were on the toppe of it, we might discerne and plainly see thirtie leagues about. On the north side of it there are many hilles to be seene running west and east, and as many more on the south, amongst and betweene the which the countrey is as faire and as pleasant as possible can be seene, being levell, smooth, and very plaine, fit to be husbanded and tilled, and in the middest of those fieldes we saw the river further up a great way than where we had left our boates, where was the greatest and the swiftest fall of water that any where hath beene seene which we could not pass, and the said river as great, wide and large as our sight might discerne, going southwest along three fair and round mountaines that we sawe, as we judged about fifteen leagues from us. Those which brought us thither tolde and shewed us, that in the sayd river there were three such falles of water more as that was where we had left our boates ; but we could not understand how farre they were one from another. Moreover,

---

* Hérissons.　† In the original : "Petites bagues et *Agnus Dei* d'étain."

they shewed us with signes, that the said three falles being past, a man might sayle the space of three months more alongst that river, and that along the hills that are on the north side there is a great river, which (even as the other) cometh from the west. We thought it to be the river that runneth through the countrey of Saguenay. Then, without any signe or question mooved or asked of them, they tooke the chayne of our captaine's whistle, which was of silver, and the dagger-haft of one of our fellow mariners hanging on his side, being of yellow copper gilt, and shewed us that such stuffe came from the said river, and that there be Agojudas, that is as much to say, an evill people, who goe all armed even to their fingers' ends. Also they shewed us the manner of their armour; they are made of cordes and wood, finely and cunningly wrought together. They gave us also to understande that those Agojudas doe continually warre one against another ; but because we did not understand them well, we could not perceive how farre it was to that countrey. Our captaine shewde them redde copper, which in their language they call Caquedazé, and looking towarde that countrey, with signes asked them if any came from thence, they shaking their heads answered no ; but they shewed us that it came from Saguenay, and that lyeth cleane contrary to the other. After we had heard and seene these things of them, we drewe to our boates accompanied with a great multitude of those people ; some of them, when they sawe any of our fellowes weary, would take them up on their shoulders, and carry them as on horseback."

Such is the account that the great navigator has left us of his memorable visit to Hochelaga. Many attempts have been made to identify the native tribe by which he was so cordially received, and it is now generally admitted that the little settlement was of the great Huron-Iroquois family, with both branches of which the early colonists of New France were so closely, though diversely, associated. This conclusion has been reached by a comparison of Cartier's vocabularies with the language spoken at a later date by the confederate Iroquois and their Huron kinsmen. When, in the early years of the 17th century, Samuel de Champlain visited the scene of their sojourn, all traces of the little town and its occupants had disappeared. The founder of Quebec was not unaware of the importance of the locality. On his second visit in 1811 he selected and cleared a space of ground, near the mouth of a small stream that entered the St. Lawrence at *Pointe à Callières*, where the Custom House now stands ; and, in order to test the effects of the ice-shove, he erected a river wall with bricks made out of clay found in the vicinity. It was on the very same spot that De Maisonneuve, thirty-one years later, landed with his devoted companions, and laid, in humble faith, the foundations of Ville Marie. The impulse which moved that pious and intrepid company to establish in an unknown wilderness in the New World a centre of evangelization—a veritable *civitas Dei*, as the more sanguine were fain to believe—has been laid bare in recent years by the researches of Abbé Verreau. Without consulting the writings of that learned historian, especially his annotated reproduction of the *Véritables Motifs de Messieurs et Dames de Montréal*, it is impossible to have an adequate appreciation of the aims and aspirations of that pious band. According to the record from which Mr. Verreau's diligence has raised the veil of two centuries and a half of silence (for it was virtually out of print), the motives which led the *Société de Notre Dame de Montréal* to undertake its apostolic task were all of a spiritual and religious character—a fact which gives the beginnings of Montreal an exceptional interest in the history of colonization. The visions and revelations that preceded and prompted the enterprise may have a basis which modern historical criticism may find insufficient, and Mr. Verreau reminds his readers that in such matters the Church has always maintained a judicious reserve. But that the mission was due to strong religious convictions, and was characterized by an extraordinary share of that faith which, as we are told on good authority, can remove mountains, no one can deny.

It was on the 18th of May, 1642, that Paul de Chomedy, Sieur de Maisonneuve (whose life, with its trials and triumphs and melancholy close, has been written by Abbé Rousseau, P.S.S.), planted, as Father Vimont said, the grain of mustard seed that was destined to take root, to grow up, and to overshadow the land. M. de Montmagny, having in vain tried to dissuade M. de Maisonneuve from his resolution, at last gracefully yielded, and accompanied the pioneers up the river, so as to instal the first governor of Montreal in his office. Leaping ashore, M. de Maisonneuve and his companions fell on their knees, and with hymns of praise returned thanks to Providence for having guided them to the land of promise. An altar was erected and adorned by the pious hands of Madame de la Peltrie and Mademoiselle Mance. Father Vimont intoned the *Veni Creator Spiritus*, and celebrated the sacrifice of the mass, and then pronounced a benediction on the great work thus inaugurated. It is noteworthy that, instead of candle or lamp, a white glass bottle filled with fire-flies was suspended before the Eucharist, and Sister Morin has recorded that the light thus afforded was equal to that of several tapers.

Around the stately figure of De Maisonneuve there gathered men and women, whose names should not be forgotten. Among them were Father Poncet, M. de Puiseaux, Mlle. Mance, Mdme. de la Peltrie, Mlle. Catherine Barré, Jean Gorry, Jean Robelin, Augustin Hebert, Antoine Damien, Jean Caillot, Pierre Laimery, Nicholas Godé and François Gadois, with his wife and their four children. All these were in Montreal in the summer of 1642. During the succeeding twelve months (1642-43) the following additions were made to the population :—

Gilbert Barbier, J. B. Legardeur de Repentigny, Guillaume Boissier, Bernard Berté, Pierre Laforest, Henri ——, César Leger, Jean Caron, Léonard Lucot dit Barbeau, Jacques Haudebert, Jean Massé, Mathurin Serrurier, Jean Bte. Damien, Jacques Boni, Jean Philippes, Pierre Didier, Pierre Quesnel, Julien Pothier, —— Bellanger. Louis Godé, Louis d'Ailleboust and Barbe de Boullogne, his wife, Mlle. Philippine de Boullogne, Catherine Lezeau, Jean Matiemalle, Pierre Bigot, Guillaume Lebeau, M. David de la Touze, Fathers Joseph Imbert Duperron, Ambroise Davoust and Gabriel Dreuillettes.

The dwellings of the little community were clustered together, the whole settlement being surrounded by palisades of wood and stone. The whole group of habitations was known as the Fort and Chateau of Ville Marie. The scene with which the first new comers made acquaintance in the season of luxuriant vegetation was one of exceeding beauty. Away behind rose Mount Royal, clad in budding verdure, while past the little fortress village swept the grand St. Lawrence—both in their names recalling the visit of Jacques Cartier, as St. Helen's recalls Champlain (whose wife's name it bears) and St. Paul's does honor to De Maisonneuve himself. But the beauty of their surroundings could not make the pioneers forget the lurking peril of the thick forest that almost encircled them.

It was not, however, from that source that the first ordeal through which they were called to pass had its origin. Against the raids of the Iroquois all due precautions had been taken, but there was another foe against whose encroachments no thought of defence had as yet occurred to the settlers. "In the month of December, 1642," writes Abbé Faillon in his *Histoire de la Colonie Française*, "an unforeseen event that overtook the pious colonists increased their confidence in the divine goodness. Nor, if we judge by the results which followed, can we help thinking that God only permitted it in order to give them a fresh mark of His fatherly care. When M. de Maisonneuve selected the Place Royale as the site of the fort of Ville Marie, the locality, as already mentioned, seemed to offer many advantages. But, not having yet resided in the country, he did not foresee that the River St. Lawrence, notwithstanding its breadth, which is some three-quarters of a league at that point, might leave its bed and inundate the neighboring grounds. In the month of December, in the same year, 1642, it overflowed its banks to an extraordinary degree, and in a few moments covered all the environs of the Fort. At last as the flood augmented more and more, everyone retired within that place of safety and had recourse to prayer to turn aside so disastrous a visitation. The little stream on the bank of which the Fort had been built had already begun to overflow, when M. de Maisonneuve, moved by a lively sentiment of faith and trust, conceived the design of planting a cross on the bank of the river, so that it might please God to keep it within its bounds, if it were for His glory, or that He might make known His will, if He wished to be served in some other part of the island, in case the lately erected habitation should be overwhelmed by the waters. He declared his purpose to the Jesuit Fathers, who approved of it, and also made it publicly known to the colonists, who, aware of the purity of his intentions, were of one heart with him as to the religious act which he had determined on. He accordingly set up the cross, at the same time making a solemn promise to God to carry another cross to the summit of the mountain if his prayer should be heard. But it was God's will to purify the faith of those zealous colonists as He had formerly perfected Abraham by the trials to which He exposed him. The waters still rose, rolling in great waves, till they had filled up the ditches of the Fort, approaching even to the threshold, and menacing with their fury the buildings in which were stored the munitions of war and the provisions for the subsistence of the colony. Nevertheless, alarming though the spectacle was, none murmured at the dispensation, which they accepted without fear and even without disquietude, though it was midwinter, even the day of the Lord's Nativity. M. de Maisonneuve was especially courageous, hoping that in good time his prayer would be heard. And that is just what happened, for the waters, having lingered a while at the gate of the Fort, without passing further, gradually retired, and thus freed the colony from the threatened danger."

M. de Maisonneuve, in his gratitude at so signal a deliverance, was not forgetful of his vow. Workmen were employed to clear a path up the mountain, while the great cross was being hewed into shape, and on the 6th of January (Epiphany), 1643, all being in readiness, the cross was solemnly blessed, and the procession set out on its journey up the mountain. M. de Maisonneuve bore the cross himself, though it was of no light weight and though the road was rough. An altar was duly erected on the mountain, and Mr. Duperron celebrated mass, Madame de la Peltrie being the first to communicate. For long afterwards the cross was the destination of pious pilgrimages. So ended the first Montreal flood of which history has preserved the record.

The Iroquois, whose notice the settlers had happily escaped during the first few months, no sooner saw what was taking place, than they put forth all their ingenuity and malice in their efforts to undo the work and to exterminate the workers.

Some Algonquins, having slain an Iroquois, sought refuge within the walls of the Fort from the tribesmen who undertook to avenge his death. The pursuers saw the fugitives enter the gates, but not being numerous enough to assail the colony, they contented themselves with a stealthy examination of the defences against their return in stronger force. It was not long till the murdered Iroquois was more than avenged. In June, 1643, sixty Hurons, proceeding from their country with letters from the Jesuit Fathers, came upon a band of Iroquois near the place now well-known as Lachine, to whom, in order to secure immunity for themselves, they treacherously suggested an attack on Ville Marie. The Iroquois accepted the advice, and detailed forty of their number, all picked warriors, to carry out the raid. It so happened that just then six Frenchmen were engaged in building at some distance from the Fort, and these, by a feigned retreat, were decoyed into the hands of the enemy. Three met their fate on the spot. The other three were taken prisoners. As no danger had been apprehended to these workmen—the scene of their labors being only about two hundred feet from the Fort itself,—it was not till they failed to make their appearance at the usual hour for their return that any anxiety was felt for their safety. The fears of the governor and his companions were soon realized. The lifeless body of Guillaume Boissier, bearing the marks of fierce struggle and triumphant savage ferocity, was a silent but eloquent witness of Ville Marie's initial tragedy. Sadly and reverently the remains of the dead pioneer were borne back within the precincts of the town, and on the same day were solemnly laid to rest in a small enclosure set apart for a burying-ground, *ad confluxum magni et parvi fluminis.**

A few days later, the bodies of two of his companions, Bernard Berté and Pierre Laforest, generally called *l'Auvergnat*, were discovered in the bush. Of the three taken prisoners, one escaped ; the others were tortured and burned by the Iroquois. After that display of savage enmity the hostile Indians seldom ceased infesting Ville-Marie.

Meanwhile, M. de Maisonneuve kept on the defensive. The consciousness that on his prudence and judgment the safety of the infant colony depended made him careful not to provoke an encounter with the savages. Again and again he resisted the demands of the bolder spirits of his small garrison, sensible of the fearful risks of their situation, should the Iroquois determine to assail the colony *en masse*. Fearless on his own account, he had not dreamed that his policy of self-restraint would incur the imputation of lack of courage. But when, after the loss of five of their number, the colonists became more and more importunate in their appeals to him to lead them against the foe, it began to dawn upon him that his motives were liable to be misunderstood, and that the only way to convince the impatient of the wisdom of his course was to give them, under his own leadership, an opportunity of testing their exuberant bravery. Hitherto, his plans for the protection of the settlement had been admirably devised. Those whose duties made it necessary that they should pass daily beyond the environs of the Fort had been drilled to set out and return at the sound of the bell, so as to guard against surprise from the Indians who were wont to conceal themselves in the underwood. Another effective source of protection consisted in a number of well-trained dogs, whose instinct enabled them to scent the Iroquois.

---

* This first cemetery, a small triangular area of the extremity of *Pointe à Callières*, was used until 1654, when that of the Hotel-Dieu succeeded it. The reflection that the spot was devoted to such a purpose, and that it received the dust and ashes of Ville-Marie's first dead, is another added to the many claims which this earliest nucleus of their city has upon the people of Montreal. See *Bibliography*, pages 43, 44.

Every morning regularly, these sagacious animals, headed by a bitch of rare endowments, well-named Pilot, formed themselves into a patrol and made a reconnoitring tour all over the town. Pilot was a veritable martinet, and allowed no skulking or lagging on the part of her canine brigade. Her own young she trained to be genuine dogs of war, administering discipline, when they disobeyed orders, by cuffs and bites, and never forgetting to punish in due time those who misbehaved while on duty. On perceiving any traces of the Iroquois, she turned back promptly and made straight for the Fort, uttering her warning bay to intimate that danger was nigh. But even the soldierly qualities of Pilot, and the faithful services that she rendered, only made the malcontents more dissatisfied, as they saw the honors of war carried off by a dog. To no purpose De Maisonneuve counselled delay, representing that they were far too few to expose themselves to the multitude of the enemy, by whom a loss that to them would be destruction would hardly be felt. At last the governor received a hint that his protective policy had been misconstrued, and though to such a man any insinuation of cowardice could in itself have seemed merely worthy of contempt, it was of the utmost importance that no doubt on such a subject should impair his influence with his people. He resolved, therefore, to set the question finally at rest by leading his ardent militia forth against the foe. The 30th of March, 1644, was a day that the colonists had cause to remember long afterwards, for it was then that the champions of Montreal had their first serious brush with the Iroquois. The scene, as tradition has placed it before us, stands out in such salient contrast to the Montreal of to-day that it is not easy to conjure up the picture. The whole stage on which the drama was enacted, Fort, town, bush, combatants on both sides, lay well within the limits of the present city, and even of its business portion. The dogs howled their deep notes of alarm, the soldiers flew to their arms, every loophole in the little fortress was manned, and every adit covered with the guns. There stood the governor, cool and tranquil as ever, giving his directions for the defence. But suddenly his countenance seemed to change, the exultant radiance of the warrior overspread it, the statesman was transformed into the soldier. "Yes," he replied to those who clamored for battle, "I shall lead you to the fray myself." It was near the close of winter, but the snow was still deep; walking was difficult, and the supply of snow-shoes was defective, but De Maisonneuve marshalled his men and made the best of what equipment he had. Leaving M. d'Ailleboust (who had arrived some time before) in command of the Fort, M. de Maisonneuve marched out with a company of thirty men against, as we are told, from eighty to two hundred Iroquois. The latter, seeing the French issue forth, separated into three bands and lay in wait to receive them. The Montrealers soon suffered from their ignorance of woodcraft and lack of experience of Indian warfare. M. de Maisonneuve's chief trouble was to prevent them exposing themselves to the sweeping fire of the savages, by which three were killed and many wounded. At last he got them under cover, and they retaliated so vigorously that in a short time their ammunition was all spent. Nothing then could save them but a skilful retreat. The only path of safety was the *traineau* road that had been levelled to cart timber for the hospital, and thither M. de Maisonneuve directed his imperilled company. Once there, locomotion would be comparatively easy, as snow-shoes would no longer be required. In their actual position they were, as an old writer quaintly says, like ill-furnished infantry against well-mounted dragoons. The soldiers obeyed those instructions readily enough—too readily, indeed, for their withdrawal was much more preci-

pitate than their commander desired, and than became men who had burned so long
to meet the Iroquois face to face. The consequence was that the cool, courageous
governor was soon left alone in the presence of the blood-thirsty savages. Armed
with two pistols, he kept facing the foe and at the same time retreating. That he
was in deadly peril, he knew, had the Iroquois aimed only at taking his life. But, as
the leader of the French nation, they wished to have the satisfaction of taking him
alive, carrying him home in triumph, and torturing him. They made way for their
own chief that he might have the distinction of such a capture, and the savage had
almost effected his purpose, when M. de Maisonneuve turned and fired. The first
shot missed, a second was more successful, and the third laid the pursuer dead, and
gave the governor time to escape. For the savages, dreading lest reinforcements
arriving should wrest the corpse from their possession, gave themselves up to the
task of rescuing it, and no longer troubled themselves with M. de Maisonneuve.
Meanwhile, the more hasty flight of his men had very nearly ended in a wholesale
disaster. For, marking the speed with which they made for the Fort, the guards
thought they were Indians, and prepared to deal with them as such. One soldier,
with more dispatch than judgment, attempted to discharge a canon that covered the
traineau road, to the imminent jeopardy of the approaching fugitives who looked for a
very different reception. Happily dampness prevented the fuse igniting; otherwise
a most deplorable catastrophe would have closed that eventful day. One important
result of that first engagement was that thereafter the cautious policy of M. de Maisonneuve was never called in question. A great historian has well said, in connection
with this event, that " Samuel de Champlain and Chomedy de Maisonneuve are among
the names that shine with a fair and honest lustre on the infancy of nations."

As the area of habitation enlarged, fresh means of protection were constantly
required. Like the Israelites of old, they held their building implements in one hand,
their weapons of warfare in the other. Already in 1643 the limits of the Fort were
found too narrow to accommodate the garrison and the settlers. A hospital and
attached chapel were then erected, and surrounded with walls, pierced by loopholes,
and strong enough to resist the attacks of the savages, which were renewed every
spring. The tillers of the soil were constant objects of violence or treachery. In
1648, a new redoubt was constructed to the south of the fort, which was to serve as
a mill and post of observation. In 1651, M. de Maisonneuve marked out a common
for the grazing of cattle, an arpent broad and forty arpents long, extending along the
river, where we now find Commissioners and Common streets, the latter, *rue de la
Commune*, preserving the record of the event. The area in question was gradually
resumed into the domain of the state, to be built upon as the needs of the citizens and
the requirements of the harbor demanded. In 1652, Lambert Closse, lieutenant of
De Maisonneuve, with certain followers, exterminated a band of Iroquois not far
from the foot of the present McGill street, and repulsed another band at Point St.
Charles, where a redoubt had been built.

From that date the erection of houses advanced rapidly. In 1654, Sister Bourgeois, the founder of the *Congrégation*, again set up on the mountain the cross which
had been destroyed, whether by frost or by the Iroquois. At the same time a new
cemetery was marked out, where the *Place d'Armes* is to-day. In 1656, the corner
stone of a large church was laid near the cemetery, and a redoubt was built at the

corner of Notre Dame and St. Denis streets, to protect the workmen on the Côteau St. Louis, the name of which is still preserved in St. Louis street and ward.

In 1657, Sister Bourgeois commenced building the church of Notre Dame de Bonsecours, and in the following year M. de Maisonneuve gave her the ground to build a school, which was taken possession of on the 30th of April, the day of St. Catherine of Sienna. It was also in the year 1657 that the first Sulpicians arrived. They were lodged in the hospital buildings. At the same time a new redoubt was erected at the extremity of St. Louis Côteau, where Dalhousie square now is. Later, it was augmented and furnished with bastions and intrenchments, and was called the *Citadel.*

In 1659, there were forty well built houses, isolated from each other, with thick walls and loop-holes, but close enough for defence in case of attack. By this time the bastions of the early Fort had suffered so much from the spring ice and floods as to be practically of little use. The Fort itself served still as a residence for the governor. Three new redoubts were built in this year—that of Ste. Marie, at the foot of the current which bears that name ; that of St. Gabriel, so called by Abbé Queylus in honor of his patron saint ; and, thirdly, to the north, in the St. Lawrence suburbs, another still, given by M. de Maisonneuve to his lieutenant, Lambert Closse, which stood where the Montreal General Hospital now stands. Each of these redoubts had crenelated walls for the defence of the workmen's lodges and the buildings attached to them. Closse himself left the Fort and went to live with the men in the redoubt which he had built, from which point of vantage he was able to guard all the northern part of the city.

A letter from M. d'Argenson describes the city as it was in those early and trying years: "I must," that gentleman writes, "give you some account of Montreal, of which place so much noise is made, although it is in itself but a small concern. I speak of what I know, as I was there this spring, and can assure you that if I were a painter I would not take long to depict it. Montreal is an island, rather difficult to land on, even in a boat, on account of the great currents of the St. Lawrence, especially at about a league down the river. There is a port where the boats land, but it is falling in ruins. They have begun a redoubt and a mill on an advantageous rising ground, for the defence of the habitation. There are about forty houses, almost all in sight of each other, and, in that respect, well situated for defence."

In 1660, Mademoiselle Mance asked M. de Maisonneuve for permission to build a stone barn of sixty by thirty feet in the interior of the fort, to guard the crops. At this time the Iroquois were very formidable, making frequent raids, as if they had resolved on the extermination of the French. Nevertheless, so watchful was the governor and so well-laid were his plans, that very few of the farmers fell victims to their attacks. Considerable progress had already been made in the establishment of *Domaines* and seigneuries around the city, which also served as vanguards for its defence. On the River St. Pierre was a fief of three hundred arpents, granted to Major Dupuy (whose family is still represented in the country). It was he who took Major Closse's place in the task of defence at the St. Lambert mill. The *concessionnaire* had to erect a redoubt and workmen's buildings on his land. Several fiefs were also distributed on the left bank of the St. Lawrence—that of Lachine to La Salle ; that of Gentilly, of the Courselles islands and the Bay d'Urfé, so called from Abbé d'Urfé, the missionary there. Towards the Lake of Two Mountains was the fief of

Boisbriant, and, returning by the north, other fiefs granted to different officers. Finally, on the River Des Prairies, there were two fiefs named after Messieurs *de Corion* and *de Merel*, given to those officers for the protection of the island on that side, and to prevent the savages that came by L'Assomption River from landing.

In succeeding years both sides of the river became occupied. M. de Laubia, of the de Broglie regiment, obtained two leagues of front and depth on Lake St. Peter ; his sergeant, Labadie, the neighboring district ; and Sieur de Moras, the island at the mouth of Nicolet River. M. de Normanville was given land nearer Montreal. Seigneuries were constituted at La Valtrie, de Repentigny, de Berthelot, as rewards to officers in the employ of Government. That was to fortify the north side. On the south, defence was still more needed on account of the Iroquois, who were constantly descending the Richelieu to attack Quebec, Montreal and Three Rivers. Large concessions for that purpose were made to M. de Berthier, captain in the Carignan regiment—the land opposite the Richelieu, which still bears his name, being the portion allotted to him ; while to M. du Pas was granted the island still so called. To M. de Sorel was conceded all the land on both sides of the Richelieu for two leagues in depth ; the rest of the river land being given to Messieurs St. Ours—one a captain, the other an ensign of the Carignan regiment. M. de Chambly received the fort of St. Louis and all the lands adjacent, and lands were also given to Messieurs de Contrecœur, de Varennes, de Boisbriant, Boucher de Boucherville, etc.

M. Charles Le Moyne received lands situated between the Seigneurie of M. de Boucher and the Seigneurie of La Prairie, granted to the Jesuit Fathers. The name of Longueuil was given it from the name of a seigneurie near Dieppe. Beyond La Prairie he obtained a large grant which he called Chateauguay, a name which it still bears. All these fiefs were settled by soldiers belonging to the companies of the officers who obtained them, and became the *nuclei* of towns and villages of importance, such as Sorel, Chambly, Berthier, St. Ours, Contrecœur, Verchères, La Valtrie, Varennes, Boucherville, Longueuil, La Prairie, Chateauguay, etc.

Meanwhile, as the surrounding country was being thus partitioned, and what was virtually a chain of garrisons was being established for its defence, it became necessary to draw up a plan of the city itself, for the guidance of those erecting buildings. The delicate task fell to M. Dollier de Casson, superior of the Seminary of St. Sulpice. The *procès-verbal*, drawn up in 1672, gives the following particulars :—

In the first place, M. Dollier de Casson traced through the centre of Ville Marie a long main street, to which he gave the name of Notre Dame, in honor of the blessed patroness of the city. Parallel thereto he drew a line, to which he gave the name of St. James street, in honor of the Rev. Jacques Olier, with whom the idea of the colony originated. On the other side of Notre Dame, and close to the river, stretched St. Paul street, so named from the founder Paul Chomédy de Maisonneuve. At right angles to these three principal streets extended several others—St. Peter, in honor of the Prince of the Apostles, and as a compliment to M. de Fancamp, one of the founders ; St. François, in honor of the patron saint of M. Dollier de Casson himself ; and St. Joseph, in honor of the pious husband of the Virgin Mary. St. Lambert was the fourth of these transverse streets, and so called after Captain Lambert Closse, already mentioned, lieutenant of M. de Maisonneuve. who was slain in an encounter with the Iroquois. Another was called St. Gabriel, in remembrance of M. Gabriel de Queylus and M. Gabriel Souart, his successor. The street called St. Jean Baptiste, which probably dates from about the same time, was at once a mark of reverence to Canada's great patron and an indication of esteem toward the illustrious Colbert who did so much for the colony. Another of those early streets was named St. Charles in consideration of M. Charles Le Moyne, who had rendered distinguished services to the colony, and had his residence on the site of the present Bonsecours market.

The city was thus for the most part an elevated plateau, in the shape of a parallelogram of about a mile and a half long, and about a-third of a mile in breadth. On the one side it had the river ; while the rest was almost encircled by a deep natural entrenchment, through which flowed a stream, that emptied itself into the St. Lawrence, and was susceptible, if necessary, of enlargement for defensive purposes. This stream had its course in part where Craig street is to-day.

MONTREAL : 1642-1891.

The Fort constructed by M. de Maisonneuve was mainly of wood. Not far from it stood the first mill used by the colonists. As the population increased, new structures became necessary, and before the close of the 17th century the city between Craig street and the river had taken the form which is still largely preserved. Dalhousie square is the site of the new mill and battery erected about 1682. Early in the 18th century it was deemed advisable to fortify the city by the traditional plan of circumvallation, and 300,000 livres were granted for the purpose by the King of France—arrangements being, however, made for the gradual payment of half the amount by the Seigneurs (the Seminary) and inhabitants. In the report which he forwarded to France in 1717, M. Chaussegros de Lery, to whom the task had been entrusted, described Montreal as a city of three-quarters of a league in circumference, but without any proper protection, the old enclosure being in a ruinous condition. His recommendation was to erect such a wall as would be capable of resisting English artillery. The revetment must be at least three feet thick, and a ditch would also be necessary. He began the work on the Lachine Gate, as being the side most exposed to attack. Though a start had been made with this system of fortifications before the close of 1717, nothing of much importance was effected until 1721. After that date, notwithstanding occasional interruptions from various causes, the work of strengthening the city was persevered in until it was a *fait accompli.* Fortification lane is an extant memorial of the Montreal of the great wars of the 18th century. Although the testimony of travellers and the opinion of experts leave the unavoidable impression that Montreal, as fortified by Chaussegros de Lery's plans, was a city of considerable strength, its defences proved of little avail in the hour of trial. On the 8th of September, 1760, it passed quietly into the hands of the British, and a few years later English merchants were doing business within its limits as though it had never changed its allegiance.

The hundred and eighteen years that elapsed between the arrival of De Maisonneuve and the capitulation of the city to General Amherst, were in many ways eventful. About half this period might be assigned as the heroic age of Montreal. It comprises the early struggles with the insidious Iroquois, the story of Dollard's devotion, of the dreadful massacre of Lachine, of the inception of those daring enterprises of exploration which were ultimately to find their diverse goals in the Pacific, the Gulf of Mexico and the Arctic Ocean. Then, too, were initiated those great religious, educational and charitable projects, the memory of which is cherished in many a hallowed spot within and without the line of the ancient walls. Then, too, was begun the crusade against intemperance among the Indians and that traffic which made them fiends, while zealous priests were striving to make them Christians. It was also the age of the *coureurs des bois*, the bushrangers, whose exploits are so romantic to read about, though they caused sorrow to many a home and were the object of many a weighty censure from the Church.

By the close of the 17th century a marked change began to be observable in the social, industrial and commercial conditions of the city. The system of government was already established and justice was regularly administered. While Colbert was in power, earnest efforts had been made to promote colonization, agriculture, manufactures and commerce, and although in 1701 the entire population, even including Acadia, did not reach 20,000 souls, so many outposts had been occupied that the possibilities of development were obvious to the far-seeing statesman. Iron-works, tanneries, shipbuilding, and other industries had been started, and there was a considerable trade with the Mother Country and the West Indies. Montreal had a share in this various progress—small, indeed, compared with its relative rank as a centre of business in later generations, but still sufficient to indicate what, under favorable circumstances, it was destined to become.

The erection of the improved fortifications, the nature and extent of which have just been outlined, show to what degree the authorities had recognized its advantages. Though Quebec, in point of population, and as the metropolis and chief garrison of the colony, as well as from its readier access to visitors from Europe, took precedence during the whole period of French rule, and for a considerable time after the Cession, the situation of Montreal clearly pointed it out as the great *entrepôt* between the East and West. In that sense, the naming of Lachine (China) was one of those unconscious prophecies which are sometimes met with in the pages of history.

At the time of its occupation by the British forces it contained thirty-two streets and four lanes. Notre Dame street was then the aristocratic quarter. The parish church marked its centre. The Court house and civic offices were nearly opposite the Seminary, at the corner of St. François Xavier street. The Jesuits' establishment was nearly on the site of the present Court house. The old Bonsecours Church, which had been burned in 1754, had not yet been replaced by the new one erected in 1771-73. The Recollet church, with the adjoining monastery and garden, was conspicuous in the area between Lemoine and Notre Dame streets,—the intervening Recollet street bearing witness to the fact. The citadel stood on Dalhousie square. Not far off a portion of M. de Lery's walls remained standing until 1881, when it was removed to make room for the Canadian Pacific Railway Station. The Château de Ramezay, now occupied by Laval University, is one of the most remarkable relics of old Montreal. It was built as long ago as 1704, and was long the centre of fashion and official distinction under the *ancien régime*. It is also noteworthy as having sheltered Benjamin Franklin, Samuel Chase and Charles Carroll of Carrolltown, when these celebrated men came here as emissaries from Congress to allure the Canadians from their allegiance to King George.

Montreal owes its present architectural splendor very largely to devastating fires. Both before and after the capitulation, it was often the scene of holocausts that

attracted attention in Europe as well as on this Continent. In 1765 a great part of it
fell a prey to the flames, owing to the greed and carelessness of one Livingston. Jonas
Hanway, the philanthropist, headed a subscription in England for the relief of the
sufferers. A more handsome and flourishing city rose above the ruins of the destroyed
buildings. Three years later, another fire swept away a hundred houses, and
before the new *régime* had lasted for a quarter of a century, the appearance of Montreal had been materially transformed. The year 1774 is a critical year in the history of
Canada and of all North America. It worked the inception of a new era—that of the
Quebec Act, which assured to the King's new subjects the free exercise of their religion
and the practice of their civil law, and also created a legislative council. It had hardly
gone into force when Montreal was occupied by the invading army of Congress. On
the 12th of November, 1775, the citizens saw the alien foe approaching their gates, and
as no resistance was possible, Montgomery and his troops were admitted on the
following day. On the departure of that officer for Quebec, where he was repulsed and
met his death, Wooster, who had been left in command at Montreal, subjected the
inhabitants to vexatious petty tyrannies, from which they were glad to be delivered in
the ensuing summer. The presence of the Americans in the city had one important
result—the foundation of a newspaper, the Montreal *Gazette*, which still flourishes after
a hundred and twelve years of existence. The idea originated with Joseph Fleury de
Mesplet, whom Franklin had brought with him to serve as an intermediary with the
French Canadians, and who, when his master's mission failed, cast in his lot with the
people whom he could not convert. The American Revolution had grave conse-
quences in which Montreal shared to some extent. It caused an influx of many
thousands of loyalists, who, having lost home and property in their native land, were
given an asylum in Canada, to which their advent brought a material increase of
population. Most of them settled in Western Canada and the Maritime Provinces,
but a considerable proportion chose the Quebec and Montreal districts for their permanent residence. In 1791 the province of Quebec was divided by the Constitutional
Act into Upper and Lower Canada, each with its own legislature.

In the following year the bounds of the city underwent considerable enlargement. In population it had already taken precedence of all other cities in Canada.
Beyond the walls towards the mountain there was a considerable number of villas,
with spacious gardens and orchards. The seigneurs and other gentry had capacious
stone-built houses, and how well the merchant princes of those days lived and fared we
know from abundant testimony of travellers. Some of the wealthiest of them were Nor'-
Westers. "Our dinner," writes a guest of one of these magnates, "was excellent,
served in sumptuous style. We had soup, salmon, roast beef and mutton, geese, ducks,
and pigeons, plum pudding, pies and tarts, biscuits and butter, brought from the Grand
Portage at the head of Lake Superior, several kinds of English cheese, and a dessert of
various kinds of foreign and domestic fruit. Our liquors were London porter,
bottled cider, strong ale, Madeira, port, claret and Champagne wines." The same
writer refers to his host's "extensive and well-managed garden, in which were not only
to be seen all the plants usually found in gardens here, but many exotics. Those of
milder climates are preserved in a green house. Peach and other fruit trees are
protected from the rigor of winter by a wall." Belonging to the same establishment
was "an aviary well stocked, as also deer, rabbits and other animals tamed, with
many curiosities in and about the house, which render it an interesting place to an

inquisitive mind." Of the prospect from the mountain he writes that it is " exceedingly picturesque and grand," and that " luxuriant and well cultivated fields extend to the city."

Testimony of this kind to the social habits of well-to-do people in Montreal a hundred years ago could be multiplied from the works of travellers. Nor are we without indications of other phases of life at that period. In 1783 a lottery was established for the purpose of raising money to build a new gaol—the tickets being sold for 46s. 8d., and the prizes ranging from £8 5s. to £4. The magistrates issued strict injunctions for keeping the streets in order. Every householder had to keep "free from filth, mud, dirt, rubbish, straw or hay " one-half of the street opposite his own house. The " cleanings " were to be deposited on the beach. Stray pigs could be kept by the finder, if no one turned up to claim them in twenty-four hours, and, on making himself known, the owner had to pay a fine of 10s. For a stray horse the penalty was 5s. The carters were obliged to keep the markets clean. The regulations for vehicles, slaughter-houses, side-walks, etc., were equally strict. Keepers of inns and taverns had to light the streets. Every one entering the town in a sleigh had to carry a shovel with him to level the *cahots* at any distance within three leagues of the city limits. The rates for cabs and ferry-boats were fixed with much precision. No carter was allowed to plead a prior engagement, but had to go with the person who first asked him, under a penalty of twenty shillings.

Opportunities for intellectual improvement were not wanting. Montreal had a public library before the 18th century came to an end, and some of the books that formed part of it may still be seen in the Fraser Institute.

Reference has already been made to the extensive fires which, at successive epochs, swept so much of old Montreal out of existence, and thus furnished an opportunity of building a better class of houses on the devastated areas. On the 26th of January, 1819, a great fire broke out in a store-house of pork belonging to Mr. D. W. Eager, and situated near the site of the present Custom house. When the fire brigade (then a volunteer body) arrived on the spot, the flames had gained the mastery of the upper part of the building, and all efforts to save it were paralyzed for want of water. It was impossible to break the thick ice on the river in time to be of any service, and so, though there was a multitude of willing helpers on the spot, they could render no effectual aid. Just then the happy thought occurred to Mr. Corse to attack the destroyer with snowballs. No sooner said than done. In five minutes a perfect fusillade from hundreds of brawny arms had smothered the fire with snow, which, melting, extinguished the flames. In that way some 800 barrels of pork were saved from premature and profitless consumption. Already steps had been taken to remedy the great inconvenience consequent on a deficient supply of water, and in April, 1801, an act was passed by the Legislature, constituting Joseph Frobisher and others a company, which bore the name of " Proprietors of the Montreal Water Works." It was the starting point of the grand organization which still bears that name.

As has already been mentioned, it was not long after the foundation of the city that attention was called, in a very practical manner, to its liability to devastating floods. But although from time to time the city suffered materially from this source, it was not until recently that decisive and effective protective measures were determined on. This subject is closely connected with that of harbor improvement and the removal of obstructions to navigation in Lake St. Peter channel. With these developments the commercial growth of Montreal has been intimately associated. No city in the world has proved more alive to all the great advances in every department of commerce consequent on the application of steam to the movement of vessels. The first attempt to utilize the discovery on our great central waterway was made in 1809 by the late Hon. John Molson. More than forty years intervened between that experiment and the establishment of a line of steamships to effect regular communication with Europe. Once this latter enterprise was fairly launched, the progress achieved was remarkable, and to-day Montreal's great ocean lines are among the finest, best equipped and most trustworthy in the world. Still more signal has been the extension of Montreal's opportunities for intercourse by means of railways with the rest of the world. Only those who can recall the day of small things, and can follow stage by stage in their memories the successive triumphs of the last half century, can realize what in this direction have been the gains of Montreal. The opening of the St. Lawrence and Atlantic road in 1851, for a distance of less than a hundred miles, was deemed an event of sufficient importance to justify the rejoicings of the entire community. In 1891, there is no point from the Eastern to the Western ocean, or from the sub-arctic north to the Gulf of Mexico, with which the city is not in communication, while mercantile fleets have placed it in comparative proximity to the very "ends of the earth." In solidity and beauty, in all that makes a great business centre an enjoyable dwelling-place, Montreal has at the same time been making welcome progress. The cemeteries, which were once within the city limits, are now some miles beyond it, and are laid out with a skill and taste which rob them of all but the tenderest associations. In their stead, gardens and squares afford pleasure grounds and breathing spaces to the inhabitants, while the Island and Mountain Parks are among the most deservedly admired of such attractive areas on this continent. At this moment a scheme of street enlargement and multifarious improvement is in course of being carried out, which, when completed, will make Montreal second, for architectural splendor and broad, well paved thoroughfares, to no city in the world. The suburbs are gradually embracing the most picturesque and desirable portions of the island, within a circuit of from five to seven miles, and ultimately, doubtless, the entire insular domain for which, in olden times, the Superiors of Saint Sulpice rendered homage, will be conterminous with the city.

To attempt, in this brief survey, to describe any of Montreal's great edifices would be vain, as to comprehend them all would be impossible, and to particularize a few where so many are deserving of praise would be invidious. The Roman Catholic institutions of the city would require a volume rather than a sketch for worthy treatment, while the later Protestant churches, colleges, schools and houses of charity would demand no less attention. Notre Dame, Our Lady of Lourdes, the Grey Nuns' Convent, St. Peter's, the Seminary, the Hotel-Dieu, the Gesu, among the former, and the Anglican Cathedral, St. James the Apostle, St. Paul's, St. James Methodist Church, McGill College, the Mackay Institute for Deaf-Mutes, and the General Hospital, among the latter, are among the edifices which will repay inspection. Mention has already been made of the Bonsecours Church. As holding the same venerable repute among Protestant places of worship, the St. Gabriel Street (Kirk of Scotland) church (now disused for congregational purposes) ought not to be forgotten. The history of old St. Gabriel, by the Rev. Robert Campbell, is, moreover,

a thesaurus of manifold information, touching the early religious and social history
of the English-speaking section of the population. The records of education in
Montreal cover nearly a quarter of a millennium ; the history of public instruction,
as a department of state administration, is, however, confined within half a century.
It has been a time of progress in which all the inhabitants have shared, and a visit to
the handsome school buildings erected by the Roman Catholic and Protestant
Commissioners, as well as to the Normal Schools (Jacques Cartier and McGill) for
the training of teachers, not to speak of special institutions (as the École Poly-
technique, etc.), will show that Montreal does not in this phase of development lag
behind the other great cities of the world.

There is one cluster of buildings to which the eye of the stranger on his way
round or up the mountain is sure to be attracted,—those which were erected in
view of a regular annual exhibition. For a number of years, while its facilities were
much less perfect than they are to-day for such a purpose, Montreal had its yearly
industrial and agricultural fair. Through whatever cause or causes the interruption
occurred, it is to be hoped that the efforts recently made to revive this important
institution will prove successful. More especially is it to be hoped that the year
1892, in which Montreal will have completd a quarter of a millennium of history as
habitation of civilized people, will not be allowed to pass without worthy recognition.

The Government of Montreal has undergone frequent changes. Under the Old
Regime it was placed in charge of governors, some of whom asserted, if they did
not succeed in exercising, a certain independence. The following is a list of these
functionaries from 1642 to the close of French rule :—

Paul de Chomedey, Sieur de Maisonneuve.	Louis Hector de Callières.
Etienne Pezard, Sieur de La Touche.	Philippe de Rigaud, Marquis de Vaudreuil.
Zacharie Dupuis.	Claude de Ramezay.
Dominique de Lamothe, Sieur de Lucière et de Saint-Paul.	Charles LeMoyne, 1st Baron de Longueuil.
	Jean Bouillet de la Chassaigne.
Sieur de la Fredière.	Dubois Berthelot, Chevalier de Beaucourt.
François-Marie Perrot.	J. B. Roch de Ramezay, Charles LeMoyne,
F. X. Tarien de la Naudière, Sieur de la Perade.	3rd Baron de Longueuil.
	Pierre de Rigaud de Vaudreuil, brother of
Henault de Rivaux.	the Governor-General.*

The system of local governors was continued for some years after the establish-
ment of British rule, Brigadier-General Gage being appointed by His Excellency,
General Murray, as first English governor of Montreal and the surrounding district.
He was succeeded by Col. Burton. In 1764, Civil Government succeeded to the
Régime Militaire, and Courts of Justice were established to sit regularly. The trial
of the persons accused of attempting to assassinate Mr. Thomas Walker, one of His
Majesty's Justices of the Peace for the Montreal District, in December of that year,
the documents of which have been preserved among our archives. lets in considerable
light on the political and social condition of Montreal at that early period of British
administration. From lists prepared by Governor Murray, registers of births,
marriages and deaths by Anglican clergymen, the names of jurors and signers of

* From *Histoire Populaire de Montréal.* See *Bibliography*, pages 43, 44.

petitions and other sources of knowledge, it is evident that soon after the capitulation of the city there must have been a considerable influx of British subjects from the other colonies and from the Mother Country. In these documents, moreover, are found the names of several persons who were destined to rise to positions of influence in later years. Early numbers of the Quebec and Montreal *Gazettes* convey a good deal of interesting information, regarding the course of events from the inception of Civil Government till the division of the province into Upper and Lower Canada.

* From the year 1796 to the year 1833, the municipal affairs of Montreal were administered by Justices of the Peace sitting in special sessions for that purpose. In 1832 the city was incorporated (1st William IV., chap. 59), and to that end was divided into eight wards: East, West, St. Ann, St. Joseph, St. Antoine, St. Lawrence, St. Louis and St. Mary. The first meeting of the Corporation was held on the 5th of June, 1833. On that occasion Jacques Viger, Esquire, was elected mayor, an office which he continued to hold until the new incorporation of 1840. The Corporation of 1840 was appointed by the Governor-General for a term which was to expire in December, 1842. Their successors were to be elected by the people.

From 1840 till 1852, the mayors were (with the exception of the Hon. Mr. McGill in 1840) chosen by the Council. By the Act 14 and 15 Vic., cap. 128, passed on the 31st of August, 1851, the election of the city's chief magistrate was committed to the citizens.

The following table gives the names of Montreal's Mayors during the last half century :—

Year.	Mayor.	By whom appointed or elected.	Year.	Mayor.	By whom appointed or elected.
1833.	JACQUES VIGER,	City Council.	1856.	HENRY STARNES.	By the People.
1840.	HON. PETER McGILL,	Governor-General.	1858.	C. S. RODIER,	" "
1841.	HON. PETER McGILL,	City Council.	1862.	J. L. BEAUDRY,	" "
1842.	HON. PETER McGILL,	"	1866.	HENRY STARNES,	" "
1843.	JOSEPH BOURRET,	"	1868.	WM. WORKMAN,	" "
1844.	JOSEPH BOURRET,	"	1871.	CHARLES J. COURSOL,	" "
1845.	HON. JAMES FERRIER,	"	1873.	FRANCIS CASSIDY,	" "
1846.	HON. JAMES FERRIER,	"	1874.	ALDICE BERNARD,	" "
1847.	JOHN E. MILLS,	"	1875.	W. H. HINGSTON, M.D.,	" "
1848.	JOSEPH BOURRET,	"	1877.	J. L. BEAUDRY,	" "
1849.	E. R. FABRE,	"	1885.	H. BEAUGRAND,	" "
1850.	E. R. FABRE,	"	1887.	HON. J. J. C. ABBOTT,	" "
1851.	HON. CHARLES WILSON,	"	1889.	JACQUES GRENIER,	" "
1854.	WOLFRED NELSON,	By the People.			

* For this full and interesting statement thanks are due to Mr. CHARLES GLACKMEYER, City Clerk.

BRIEF BIBLIOGRAPHY OF MONTREAL.

For the benefit of those who wish to enter into a minute study of the history of Montreal, it has been thought well to append to this sketch a brief bibliography of the subject. Like all bibliographies, it is only tentative. It has not been thought necessary to include histories of Canada, and other works, of which the authors of the books cited must have availed themselves. For information as to the industrial and commercial development of Montreal, especially in recent years, many publications of a special character (such as Board of Trade Reports, etc.) would have to be consulted, while many excellent articles as to other phases of its progress are to be found in the contributions to periodicals and newspapers.

The Iroquois Book of Rites. By H. Hale, in Brinton's Library of Aboriginal American Literature Philadelphia : 1883.

Fossil Men and their Modern Representatives. By Sir William Dawson, C.M.G., F.R.S., etc. London : 1880.

Iroquois et Algonquins, in Mélanges d'Histoire et de Littérature. By Benj. Sulte. Ottawa : 1876.

The Conquest of Canada. By George D. Warburton, edited by Eliot Warburton. London and New York : 1846-1850.

Voyages de Découverte au Canada entre les années 1534 *et* 1542. Par Jacques Cartier, etc. Reimprimés sur d'anciennes relations, et publiés sous la direction de la Société Littéraire et Historique de Québec. Quebec : 1843.

Jacques Cartier, his Life and Voyages. By Joseph Pope. Ottawa : 1890.

Jacques Cartier and his Four Voyages to Canada. By Hiram B. Stephens, B.C.L. Montreal : 1891.

Pioneers of France in the New World. By Francis Parkman. Boston : 1887.

The Old Régime in Canada. By Francis Parkman. Boston : 1885.

Histoire de la Colonie Française en Canada. By M. L'Abbé Faillon, P.S.S. Ville Marie : 1865.

Histoire et Vie de M. Paul Chomédey, Sieur de Maisonneuve. By M. l'Abbé Rousseau, P.S.S. Montreal : 1888.

Hand-Book of the Dominion of Canada. By S. E. Dawson, Docteur ès Lettres. Montreal : 1884.

Histoire Populaire de Montréal, de son origine jusqu'à nos jours. By A. Leblond de Brumath. Montreal : 1890.

Le Vieux Montréal, 1611-1803. Dessins de P. L. Morin, H. Beaugrand. Montreal : 1884.

Annuaire de Ville Marie. By L. A. Huguet Latour. Montreal : 1863-1877.

Hochelaga Depicta, or the History and Present State of the Island of Montreal. Montreal : 1839. With Addenda ; edited by Newton Bosworth, F.R.A.S. Montreal : 1846.

Ville Marie, or Sketches of Montreal, Past and Present. By Alfred Sandham. Montreal : 1870.

Montreal and its Fortifications. By Alfred Sandham. Montreal : 1874.

Reports on Canadian Archives. By Douglas Brymner, Archivist. Ottawa : 1872-1891.

Pen and Ink Sketches. By John Fraser. Montreal : 1891.

Montreal, its History, with Biographical Sketches and Portraits of its Principal Citizens. By J. Douglas Borthwick. Montreal : 1875.

The First Catholic Cemeteries of Montreal and a Guide to the present Cemetery. E. Senecal & Fils. Montreal : 1887.

History of St. Gabriel Street Church, Montreal. By the Rev. Robert Campbell, M.A. Montreal : 1887.

Picturesque Canada. Edited by the Rev. G. M. Grant, D.D. ; illustrated under the supervision of L. R. O'Brien, Pres. R. C. A. Chapter on Montreal by John Lesperance and J. C. Bray. Toronto : 1884.

MONTREAL IN JANUARY, 1894.

MONTREAL is the commercial Capital of Canada and the most populous City (211,302) of the Dominion. It is situated at the head of Sea or outward Navigation, and at the foot of the great chain of River, Lake and Canal Navigation which extends westward to Kingston, Toronto, Hamilton, Niagara, Buffalo, Detroit, Chicago and Duluth, embracing an almost unequalled extent of inland water communication. It occupies one of the most commanding positions in the Dominion, and it is on a large fertile and beautiful island of the same name, 30 miles in length by 10 miles of extreme breadth, formed by the confluence of the Ottawa and St. Lawrence Rivers, and on the north bank of the latter, thus situated near the junction of two important rivers, with a free communication seawards, though 70 miles above the influence of the tides, and 300 miles from salt water. Montreal possesses all the advantages of both an inland city and a seaport, accessible to seagoing steamships of over 5000 tons burthen. Holding, too, as it were, the navigation of the Canals and Lakes of the West, of the far west, makes it the greater centre of attraction and the COMMERCIAL EMPORIUM of the Dominion. The City is the chief seat of manufacturing operations in costly establishments, the productions of which will compare favorably with those of other cities. Among the daily increasing and prosperous undertakings are :

227 factories, employing 2996 hands ; 36 foundries, employing 1028 hands ; 77 manufactories, employing 1084 hands ; 43 mills, employing 757 hands. Other branches will be given in this Report. It may be stated that an average of 107 Railway Passenger cars, 28 Sleepers, 720 Freight and Cattle cars, arrive daily at the several railway stations.

During navigation 624 Ocean Steamships arrived in the Port of Montreal, the arrivals for last season being 746. During same season 252 Gulf and River Steamers and 5,162 Inland craft, having 966,959 tons burthen, arrived in Port : also 122 sailing ships, barques, brigs, brigantines and schooners arrived in Port of Montreal, from the Atlantic Ocean.

The wharves are on the eve of extensive and wonderful ameliorations to meet urgent business demands. The City and suburbs are fully and beautifully lit with gas and numerous electric lights.

Peace, happiness and prosperity abound, and brotherly love forms a link that might be prized in any city. The policeman is seldom needed. Intemperance is becoming a thing of the past.

Montreal has magnificent Water Works. The water is taken from the St Lawrence, a mile and a half above the Lachine Rapids, and conducted a distance of five miles through an open canal to a spacious basin, where it is, by powerful and costly machinery, forced up through the pumping main two miles and three-quarters in length, to reservoirs on the brow of the Mountain, capable of containing fifteen million gallons. This great work was undertaken and successfully completed by our eminent Civil Engineer, THOMAS C. KEEFER. Everything connected with it is kept in admirable order. Our active firemen can always depend on the extensive mains for a plentiful supply, which enables them to combat successfully and speedily accidental fires.

Our "Father of Waters," the St Lawrence, is spanned by the Victoria Bridge, the most costly and magnificent work of the kind ever erected, with its two long abutments and twenty-four piers of solid masonry ; this great tubular bridge of iron stands a monument of engineering skill, and places the name of its eminent engineer, ROBERT STEPHENSON, foremost in the ranks of Civil Engineers. The total length of the bridge is 9,184 lineal feet, with 24 spans of 242 feet each, and one (the central tube, which is 60 feet above highwater) of 330 feet. The first stone of this great work was laid on the 20th July, 1854, and the first passenger train of the Grand Trunk Railway Company passed through it on the 17th December, 1859. The Canadian Pacific Railway Bridge at Lachine is another connecting link between Montreal and the South shore. It connects the Pacific system with the Eastern States, with connections to the sea by way of Halifax and St John. These great enterprises and similar undertakings have placed Canada in a proud and prosperous position before our beloved Mother Country and the outside world.

Montreal has 51 avenues, 2 hills, 41 lanes, 2 parks, 5 places, 4 roads, 1 row, 12 squares, 381 streets, 3 terraces, 1 track ; 34,455 houses : 25,774 brick, 81 dashed, 5482 stone, 3118 wooden.

Montreal is distant from Quebec 172 miles, from Berthier 58, from Chambly 12, from Frelighsburg 62, from Melbourne 77, from Richmond 76, from Sherbrooke 101, from St Johns 27, from Three Rivers 86, from Ottawa 120, from Toronto 333, from Halifax 758, from Fredericton 437, from Charlottetown 692, from Winnipeg 1423, from Victoria 2990, from Regina 1779 ; from Boston 334, from New York 400, from Chicago 845, from Liverpool 2750 miles. Population 211,302.

FINANCES OF THE CITY OF MONTREAL,

KINDLY FURNISHED BY WILLIAM ROBB, ESQ., CITY TREASURER.

The City of Montreal was incorporated in 1832. It embraces an area of about 6,000 acres, divided into 13 wards, each returning three members to the City Council. The Mayor is elected by the suffrages of the citizens generally; and the terms of office are one year for the Mayoralty and three years for the Aldermen (one for each ward retiring annually).

The assessed value of its real estate approaches $125,000,000, of which over $20,000,000 is exempted under the following heads :—

Government property	$3,000,000	Benevolent Institutions—all others	$1,800,000
Municipal "	5,000,000	Churches and Parsonages—Roman Catholic	2,000,000
Benevolent Institutions—Roman Catholic	5,700,000	" " —all others	1,600,000
Special Business exemptions	900,000		

The valuations are made annually by a Board of Assessors, who visit every property for that purpose; and while the law directs the appraisement to be made at the actual market value, it is generally conceded to average about twenty per cent. under actual selling prices.

The rate of annual assessment is one per cent. on value, with an additional one-fifth of one per cent. for School Tax, which is levied and collected by the City but handed over to the School Commissioners, a body appointed by the Local Government and the City jointly, for administration. In addition to this one and one-fifth per cent. on Realty, there is a Water Rate, based on a sliding scale, which approximates $7\frac{1}{2}$ per cent. on annual rental values, and an assessment of seven and one-half per cent. on the rental of all business premises, which is known as the "Business Tax," beside specific licences on certain trades or professions and the usual taxes on horses, carriages, dogs, etc., which come under the head of "Personal Taxes." The City also derives a considerable revenue from its Markets, and from penalties imposed by the Recorder's Court. Street improvements are paid for by assessments on the parties benefitted, as determined by Commissioners appointed by the Courts; except in special cases where the City bears a portion of the expense. Drains are charged against the properties which they pass ($\frac{1}{2}$ on each side), with the exception of main sewers, of which the greater part of the cost is defrayed from the general funds of the City: abutting properties being charged the proportion of a small sewer only.

The present revenue from all sources is about $2,225,000, and the following figures will illustrate the more recent progress of the City:

Gross Revenue of 1850	$150,000		Gross Revenue of 1875	$1,325,000
"	1855	225,000	"	1880	1,500,000
"	1860	450,000	"	1885	1,770,000
"	1865	600,000	"	1890	2,225,000
"	1870	800,000			

The detail of its total revenue is as under:

From Assessment of 1 per cent. on Realty for Civic purposes	$750,000		From Carters' licences and dog taxes	$ 76,000
" " $\frac{1}{5}$ per cent. on Realty for School purposes	160,000		" Fines, etc., in Recorder's court	23,000
" Business duty of $7\frac{1}{2}$ per cent. on rentals of business premises and special licences	190,000		" Private butcher stalls	13,000
			" Innkeepers' licences	9,000
" Arrears of the above	172,000		" Road Department permits	5,000
" Water rates and arrears of same	637,000		" Ground rents	1,500
" Markets	83,000		" Miscellaneous items	10,500
			" Interest collected on arrears	65,000
				$2,225,000

The annual appropriations for the administration of the City's affairs are based on the actual receipts of each preceding year; five per cent. being reserved for unforeseen expenditure. Provision for the interest on its funded debt is made, by law, the first charge on its revenue.

The debt of the City, which is limited to 15 per cent. of the assessed value of its Real Estate, is now about $16,000,000, of which more than one-half is represented by *bond fide* assets in the shape of Water Works, Markets, Fire and Police Stations, City Hall, etc., which yield a revenue, directly or indirectly, equal to the interest on that portion of the debt; while its Parks, though non-revenue producing, are none the less *bond fide* assets of immense and ever-increasing value.

The credit of the City stands so high that it has been able to float its loans on the London money markets at prices comparing favorably with Government securities; and at the present day it is obtaining funds for its permanent improvements on inscribed, transferable stock at an interest cost of less than $3\frac{3}{4}$ per cent. per annum.

PORT OF MONTREAL UP TO FALL OF 1890.

WRITTEN EXPRESSLY FOR LOVELL'S HISTORIC REPORT OF CENSUS OF MONTREAL,

BY PETER CROSSBY.

IN order justly to appreciate the present importance of the PORT OF MONTREAL, it is necessary to consider from what a small beginning, and with what rapid strides, Montreal has risen to its present rank amongst the Cities of the World.

According to Garneau's History of Canada, there were only 584 persons in Montreal in the year 1666 ; and in 1734 the whole population of Canada, of European descent, amounted to 37,633 souls ; but, in 1851, there were, according to the Census of that year, 57,715 souls in Montreal alone. In 1861 the number had increased to 90,323, in 1871 to 107,225, and in 1881 to 140,747—a gain, in these successive decades, of respectively 56.15 and 31 *per cent*. Elsewhere in these pages will appear the advancement within the last decade. As early as 1861 Montreal held the tenth place among the Cities of North America, as shown by the following table :

CITIES.	POPULATION.	CITIES.	POPULATION.
New York	814,277	St. Louis	162,179
Philadelphia	568,034	Cincinnati	160,660
Brooklyn	271,425	Chicago	109,420
Baltimore	214,037	Montreal	101,602
Boston	177,392	Buffalo	81,132
New Orleans	170,766		

Montreal was merely an outpost of Quebec until 1832, when it was constituted a Port of Entry.

In the year 1800, the number of vessels cleared at the Port of Quebec was 64, and their total tonnage was 14,293 tons. They carried 20,271 barrels of flour, 217,128 bushels of wheat, 3,512 bushels of peas, 1,555 bushels of barley, and 6,896 bushels of oats.

In 1816, the number of vessels cleared had risen to 288, and their total tonnage to 61,211.

On the 17th of February of the following year (1817), as appears by the journals of the House of Parliament of Lower Canada, one François Pagé petitioned the House, representing that he had, after a long time, perfected a machine (steamboat) for navigating the St. Lawrence and other rivers ; and, considering the inclination of the House to reward public benefactors, he prayed to be granted the exclusive right to build and use such machines (steamboats) built upon the said model, which petition was deemed of so much importance, that the late Andrew Stuart, by command of the Governor, stated to the House that His Excellency, having been informed of the purport of the Petition, gave his consent to doing therewith as the House should see fit.

On the 28th day of the same month (February, 1817), John Goudie represented to the House that two American steamboats occasionally ran into that part of Lake Champlain which lies in Canadian territory, and successfully competed for Canadian trade ; and apprehending very evil results from such free intercourse, he asked the House for a monopoly of commerce by steam power in the Canadian portion of Lake Champlain.

What would have been the effect of conceding the proposed monopolies in the infancy of steam navigation on Lake Champlain, the St. Lawrence, and all its great tributaries, can only be imagined,

Fortunately wise counsels prevailed, and the Legislature displayed no tendency to a Chinese policy of exclusion and non-intercourse.

In 1833, when Montreal had become a Port of Entry, the total number of sea-going vessels which cleared from Montreal and Quebec was less than the number which had cleared from Quebec alone in the previous year, and their tonnage was also less, the number sailing from Quebec in 1832 having been 1,053, of a total burthen of 281,598 tons, against 969 in 1833, of 247,933 tons burthen, and 133 vessels from Montreal of 30,769 tons burthen ; yet, for some cause, neither the number nor the tonnage of vessels clearing from Montreal increased in 6 years following 1833 ; but the year 1840 showed a slight improvement up to 137 vessels of 31,266 tons burthen.

In 1861, the number of vessels was 3 $\frac{7}{10}$ times as many as in 1833, and the total tonnage had become 8 times as large as in that year.

In Capper's "Port and Trade of London," it is stated that in 1860, the entire Import and Export Trade of Great Britain with the North American Colonies was valued at £10,496,769 sterling; and as in that year the value of Exports, from the Port of Montreal, was $6,020,715, and the value of Imports was $15,479,453, it is obvious that the trade of the Mother Country with Montreal, at that date, was nearly half her whole trade with the British North American Provinces.

Though in 1880 the number of vessels clearing this Port was only 710, so greatly had they increased in size, that while in point of numbers the augmentation had only been 5.3 fold, the tonnage had become more than twenty times as great as in 1833. The still greater enlargement of the ships subsequently employed in the commerce of Montreal presented last year the contrast of barely 5.2 the number of vessels employed in 1833, having more than twenty-six times their capacity.

The Customs Duties collected at the Port of Montreal amounted, in 1858, to $1,673,503; in 1859, to $2,335,190; in 1862, to $2,490,025; in 1882, to $8,395,654.07; and in 1889, to $9,321,981.91, an increase of 457 *per cent.* in thirty-one years.

Probably the increase of River Craft has been in proportion to that of the Sea-going vessels.

The total estimated storage capacity of Montreal for Flour and Wheat, in 1869, was 1,680,000 bushels of wheat and 417,000 barrels of flour. Since that time several very large Elevators have been erected, so that the storage capacity is equal to any probable demand upon it.

The receipts of Flour at this Port varied but little from 1845 to 1860, inclusive; the smallest quantity received in any year, 1855, being 433,011 barrels, and the largest, in 1858, being only 669,064 barrels; but, in 1861, the quantity received reached 1,095,339, nearly double the receipts of the next previous year, which were estimated at 577,196. Although for two succeeding years the total of receipts increased, the quantity received in any subsequent year, up to 1870, did not reach one million barrels; but from 1871 to 1875, there was an average annual receipt of 1,020,661 barrels, gainst 858,839 shipped.

The total Exports of Grain from this Port, in 1887, amounted to 11,372,789 bushels.

The Export of Sawn Lumber from this Port to South America, which was previously inconsiderable, reached 1,412,128 feet in 1867, and 31,592,960 in 1873, and then diminished, because of the unsettled state of affairs in that part of the world.

In 1880-81, the total Produce of the Forests of Canada was estimated at $22,326,184, or somewhat over $30 per family of the entire Dominion.

In a country larger than the United States, but peopled by hardly one-tenth of its population, having the Ocean on two sides and Inland Seas on two others, and drawing its revenues largely from Customs Duties, which the vast extent of the country makes it possible to evade, it almost necessarily happens that Government, even when aided by the advice and active assistance of Boards of Trade and the Harbor Commission, must often disregard matters of convenience to the Public out of consideration for matters which are of vital importance. However sparsely populated a country may be, rocks in the course of its navigation must be marked by light-houses or fog signals, to save the country the reproach of inhospitably beguiling into unknown dangers foreign mariners who trustfully approach its shores. It thus happens that there always remains some boon which commerce demands, and which Government is slow to concede, because commerce declines to be adequately taxed to provide it; while, on the hand, there are imports, dues and duties of which Trade is weary, but which Government hesitates to remove until commerce is made as safe as it can possibly be.

Seeing that our great Waterway, which furnishes a natural outlet for the products of half a continent, lies in direct line between the consumers of one hemisphere and the producers of another, Government has been particularly solicitous of good capacious canals and a safe and deep channel to the Port of Montreal, which, being at the head of navigation, is the centre of the railway system, not merely of Canada, but, in part, also of the Northern and Western States, and this notwithstanding adverse legislation.

Montreal, besides its natural advantage of being central, which a city situated like New York, at the sea-board, cannot be, has the further advantage of being three hundred miles nearer Liverpool than

New York. It is nearer the latitude of Liverpool, and consequently ships sail to it upon a shorter arc, and besides being nearer to both producer and consumer, it offers natural and therefore cheaper transit for heavy merchandise than New York can boast. Indeed, the products of the wheatfields of the great West, both of Canada and the United States, come naturally to this Port by simple gravitation. It is therefore of paramount importance to the whole country that navigation throughout the River and Gulf of St Lawrence should be made safe and convenient. In this connection it is well to consider what has been done and what is being done to make this Port easily and safely accessible and as inexpensive as possible. Prior to 1851 only vessels under 400 tons and drawing not more than eleven feet of water could pass through Lake St Peter and up to the Harbor of Montreal; but as far back as 1875, vessels drawing 22 to 23½ feet of water, and being from 3500 to 4000 tons burthen, passed down to the sea. This was made possible by dredging a channel through the enlargement of the River St Lawrence, which goes by the name of Lake St Peter. This work was begun by the Harbor Commissioners of Montreal in June, 1851.

Within that year the Channel is said to have been deepened two feet for a breadth of 75 feet. In a little over two years it had been deepened more than four feet, and was one hundred and fifty feet wide; at the end of eight years it was deepened over seven feet, and was three hundred feet in width In fourteen years there was a twenty foot channel, or an improvement of nine feet, but the Harbor Commissioners had in view a twenty-five foot channel, to admit of the largest sized ships coming into Port, without lighterage. But before the Commissioners had attained the *desideratum* of a twenty-five foot channel, the increasing size of ships trading to and from this Port convinced the Commission and the public generally a depth of 27½ feet must be secured. This having now been accomplished, and the Commissioners having been relieved by Government of duties outside the Harbor, they have now turned their attention to much needed wharf extension and many other strictly Harbor Improvements.

Occasionally Bills before Parliament, or the Local Legislature, tend to interfere with free navigation; but the Harbor Commissioners and the Board of Trade have been hitherto so vigilant as to protect the Harbor and its approach. During many years the deepening and enlargement of Canals has been going on with a view to securing 14 feet depth and ample Basins.

A Hydrographic re-survey of the Gulf of St Lawrence is in progress, and is watched by British as well as Canadian Scientists and Mariners, because it is doubted whether the recent loss of a vessel was not due to an unknown current.

The opinions of captains of ships are being collated as to the points at which additional signals and lights are needed in the River and Gulf, and also in the Straits of Belleisle.

Measures are also being taken to improve the Code of Signals in use in Inland Navigation, the necessity whereof was made evident at the investigation of a recent collision near Longue Pointe.

Vessels from Montreal, landing a few passengers or goods at Quebec, have been recently relieved from paying police dues at that Port.

It is probably owing to the above mentioned difficulties, attending vast possessions, a sparse population, and the consequent financial difficulty of foregoing dues, while undertaking fresh works of great public interest, that although the Right Honorable Sir John A. Macdonald agrees with the Board of Trade that the habitual concession of a special rate of toll of two cents per ton on certain grains shipped to Montreal, or to any Port east of Montreal, loses much of its value by lacking the quality of permanence, which, in like case in the United States, has been secured by an amendment of Constitution, the reduction is still made each year at the expense of a deputation of leading men to Ottawa. Only grave reasons of State should allow the continuance of this inconvenient practice.

The Government having some time since acknowledged the principle long contended for, that the whole country should share the cost of works carried on in the general interest by the Harbor Commissioners of Montreal, and having done this Port tardy justice by assuming a portion of the Harbor Commissioners' indebtedness undertaken to improve the National Highway, it is hoped that Government, extending the application of this principle to its just limits, will acknowledge a further claim of over one million dollars outlaid by the Harbor Commission in the interest of the Commerce of the whole Country, in which case improvements in the Harbor proper, begun or proposed, including extensive wharves and graded drive-ways, may be proceeded with in the spring of 1891.

To others, as well as ship owners and navigators, the following tables will be of interest:

ARRIVALS—DEPARTURES.

Year	Opening of Navigation.	Closing of Navigation.	First Arrival from Sea.	Last Dep. for Sea.	Year.	Opening of Navigation.	Closing of Navigation.	First Arrival from Sea.	Last Dep. for Sea.
1842	April 4	Dec. 2	May 9	Nov. 18	1862	April 23	Dec. 7	April 28	Nov. 27
1843	" 30	" 6	" 7	" 16	1863	" 25	" 12	May 6	" 26
1844	" 14	" 6	" 5	" 19	1864	" 13	" 11	April 28	" 7
1845	" 13	Nov. 29	" 4	" 22	1865	" 10	" 16	May 3	" 24
1846	" 9	Dec. 6	April 27	" 21	1866	" 19	" 15	" 1	" 28
1847	May 3	" 2	May 11	" 23	1867	" 22	" 6	" 4	" 29
1848	April 12	" 22	" 3	" 20	1868	" 17	" 9	" 4	" 27
1849	" 13	" 7	" 4	" 27	1869	" 25	" 6	April 30	" 24
1850	" 15	" 6	April 25	" 29	1870	" 18	" 18	" 27	" 27
1851	" 11	" 9	" 28	" 19	1871	" 8	" 1	" 28	" 28
1852	" 25	" 18	May 2	" 27	1872	May 1	" 8	May 2	" 29
1853	" 15	" 15	April 28	" 26	1873	April 25	Nov. 26	" 4	" 21
1854	" 25	" 6	May 20	" 23	1874	" 25	Dec. 13	" 11	" 21
1855	" 28	" 12	" 9	" 20	1875	May 3	Nov. 29	" 9	" 22
1856	" 24	" 3	April 30	" 24	1876	April 27	Dec. 10	" 8	" 23
1857	" 18	" 13	May 1	" 25	1877	" 17	Jan.'78 2	April 20	" 24
1858	" 9	" 12	April 30	" 24	1878	M'ch 30	Dec. 23	" 20	" 24
1859	" 4	" 11	May 3	" 20	1879	April 24	" 10	May 1	" 24
1860	" 10	" 7	April 30	" 25	1880	" 17	" 3	" 2	" 22
1861	" 24	" 22	" 27	" 4					

Years.	Opening of Navigation.	Closing of Navigation.	First Arrival from Sea.	Last Departure for Sea.	Years.	Number of Vessels.	Tonnage.	Greatest Number in Port at one time.
1881	April 21.	Jan.2, 1882.	April 29.	Nov. 23.	1881	6,036	949,380	191 ... Nov. 4
1882	" 11.	Dec. 9.	May 6.	" 21.	1882	5,947	846,780	190 ... Sept. 29
1883	" 27.	" 16.	" 5.	" 20.	1883	5,477	764,721	174 ... " 5
1884	" 22.	" 18.	" 2.	" 20.	1884	4,808	726,015	161 ... July 9
1885	May 5.	" 7.	April 30.	" 20.	1885	5,003	724,975	142 ... Oct. 1
1886	April 24.	" 4.	May 3.	" 25.	1886	5,521	809,819	178 ... Aug. 25
1887	May 1.	" 23.	" 3.	" 28.	1887	5,567	791,452	189 ... May 31
1888	April 29.	" 14.	" 4.	" 22.	1888	5,509	863,014	163 ... Aug. 14
1889	" 14.	" 29.	April 27.	" 23.	1889	5,447	1,029,709	187 ... Aug. 15
1890	" 15.	" 3.	" 30.	" 24.	1890	5,162	966,959	167 ... Oct. 20

The total number of arrivals from sea this year has been 746, which is 21 less than in 1887, but 51 more than last year, and 91 more than in 1888. The number of arrivals of Ocean Steamships is 624. There have not been so many Sailing Ships in Port as in former years, but in these there has been almost a steady decrease since 1870, when they numbered 536 and Steamships only 114.

The total tonnage of the Ships in Port this year exceeds that of any former year. The total tonnage of the Port up to the 1st of December was 930,337. The greatest tonnage for the whole season of any previous year is only 870,773 (the tonnage of 1887).

It thus appears that the tonnage of this year exceeds that of any previous year, and was 107,222 tons more than in 1889. This increase proves that the class of vessels coming to Montreal is still rapidly improving, and, inferentially, that the business men of the world are becoming more and more aware that the relative importance of this Port, as a distributing point, is far beyond what its rank, in respect of population, would indicate.

In the season of Navigation, from 15th April to 1st December, 1890, 624 Ocean Steamships, of 889,189 tons burthen, arrived in the Port of Montreal;

During the same season, 9 ships, 33 barques, 2 brigs, 8 brigantines, and 70 schooners (from the Atlantic Ocean), with a total of 41,143 tons burthen, arrived in Port.

And, during same season: 252 Gulf and River steamers, and 5,162 Inland Craft, with 966,959 tons burthen, arrived in Port.

Of the Ocean Steamships: 20 were owned by Allan Line of Steamships, 6 by Donaldson Line of Steamships, 5 by Ross Steamship Line of Steamships, 6 by Thomson Line of Steamships, 10 by Dominion Line of Steamships, 5 by Canada Shipping Co. (Beaver Line), 7 by Hansa Steamship Co., 2 by Bossière Line.

NUMBER and TONNAGE of SEA-GOING VESSELS consigned to the following MERCHANTS, during the season of 1890:—

No.	Name of firm.	Steam.	Tonnage.	Sail.	Tonnage.	Total No. of Vessels	Total T'nnage.
1	H. & A. Allan	77	180,297	...	...	77	180,297
2	R. Reford & Co	72	121,469	...	...	72	121,469
3	D. Torrance & Co	47	107,425	...	...	47	107,425
4	Canada Shipping Co	30	73,657	...	...	30	73,657
5	Kingman, Brown & Co	64	64,052	...	...	64	64,052
6	McLean, Kennedy & Co	38	58,846	3	3,089	41	61,935
7	Carbray, Routh & Co	31	31,001	3	4,389	34	35,390
8	Mundetloh & Co	24	34,107	...	...	24	34,107
9	J. G. Sidey	28	31,659	...	...	28	31,659
10	J. & R. McLea	28	30,818	1	66	29	30,884
11	Henry Dobell & Co	36	25,010	...	...	36	25,010
12	Intercolonial Coal Co	26	24,148	...	...	26	24,148
13	H. Dobell & Co (Canal)	28	19,268	...	...	28	19,268
14	F. C. Henshaw	16	16,790	...	...	16	16,790
15	Carbray, Routh & Co. (Canal)	11	9,983	...	1,500	12	11,483
16	Anderson McKenzie	2	2,782	14	8,498	16	11,280
17	J. G. Sidey (Canal)	10	9,996	...	...	10	9,996
18	Thos. Fraser & Co	20	7,860	11	828	31	8,688
19	David Shaw	5	8,349	...	...	5	8,349
20	Kingman, Brown & Co. (Canal)	9	8,206	...	...	9	8,206
21	J. Burstall & Co	5	6,845	...	...	5	6,845
22	Anderson McKenzie (Canal)	...	...	9	3,857	9	3,857
23	Masters	2	2,092	10	1,683	12	3,775
24	W. E. Boyd	...	...	3	3,230	3	3,230
25	Imperial Government	2	3,175	...	...	2	3,175
	Eighteen others	13	11,054	67	13,993	80	25,047
		624	889,189	122	41,143	746	930,332

STATEMENT SHOWING the NUMBER and TONNAGE of OCEAN STEAMERS and SAILING VESSELS, also of INLAND VESSELS, that ARRIVED in the PORT of MONTREAL, from 1850 to 1890.

Year.	Ocean-going Steam-ships.	Tonnage of Ocean-going Steam-ships.	Ocean-going Sailing Vessels.	Tonnage of Ocean-going Sailing Vessels.	Total Tonnage of Steam-ships and Sailing Vessels.	Total No. of Steam and Sailing Vessels.	Inland Vessels.	Tonnage of Inland Vessels.	Grand Total of Ocean and Inland Tonnage.
1850	...	...	222	46,867	52,905	222	...	...	46,867
1851	...	...	275	58,605	52,905	275	...	...	58,605
1852	...	...	185	45,012	45,012	185	...	...	45,012
1853	4	1,051	245	37,752	59,703	258	...	...	59,703
1854	6	5,545	212	65,365	70,910	258	4,251	383,558	374,488
1855	...	...	197	48,154	48,154	197	7,231	312,201	360,355
1856	16	14,256	231	57,045	71,321	242	3,811	384,467	455,288
1857	9	7,541	218	60,199	67,740	227	3,725	429,532	497,272
1858	18	17,887	207	60,922	78,809	225	4,122	393,224	472,033
1859	33	43,704	195	50,956	94,660	230	4,198	459,065	553,725
1860	32	47,383	222	74,154	121,539	257	4,558	349,652	470,211
1861	40	81,298	534	180,495	261,793	574	5,247	530,224	792,017
1862	52	63,012	519	202,231	265,243	571	4,675	523,991	789,234
1863	54	56,260	450	152,762	209,222	504	4,597	534,740	743,962
1864	55	59,071	327	102,930	161,001	378	4,809	420,594	582,595
1865	63	78,015	295	74,928	152,943	358	4,771	626,550	779,493
1866	70	78,474	446	130,301	205,775	516	5,062	613,679	819,454
1867	106	87,199	358	111,854	199,053	464	5,043	744,477	943,530
1868	105	101,966	373	97,193	198,759	478	5,893	746,927	945,686
1869	117	117,565	440	141,898	259,463	557	5,866	721,324	951,237
1870	144	133,012	536	182,924	316,846	680	6,343	819,476	1,136,322
1871	147	146,927	522	204,794	351,721	669	6,878	824,787	1,176,508
1872	215	217,713	512	181,087	398,800	727	7,130	936,782	1,335,582
1873	242	245,237	460	167,241	412,478	702	6,751	933,462	1,345,934
1874	266	262,096	465	161,327	423,423	731	6,895	956,837	1,380,260
1875	256	255,435	386	130,677	386,112	642	6,178	811,410	1,197,525
1876	240	202,720	362	128,351	331,120	602	6,083	846,083	1,177,203
1877	247	240,210	266	136,650	376,859	543	6,328	847,978	1,224,837
1878	207	272,850	309	124,388	397,800	516	5,502	764,343	1,161,503
1879	289	365,463	323	139,506	504,969	612	3,696	817,743	1,324,212
1880	354	475,741	356	152,530	628,271	710	6,343	1,024,380	1,652,651
1881	323	446,457	245	85,472	531,929	568	6,030	949,280	1,481,399
1882	372	466,460	296	88,186	554,646	648	5,947	889,280	1,443,926
1883	464	605,805	196	58,458	664,263	660	5,477	764,721	1,428,984
1884	444	585,397	182	64,977	649,374	626	4,808	726,015	1,375,389
1885	441	619,647	188	64,207	683,854	629	5,093	724,975	1,408,829
1886	532	736,648	171	73,051	809,699	703	5,363	809,830	1,619,529
1887	600	807,471	167	63,302	870,773	767	5,367	791,452	1,662,225
1888	532	742,278	123	40,179	782,473	655	5,900	863,014	1,645,487
1889	522	763,783	173	59,382	823,165	695	5,837	1,069,709	1,892,874
1890	624	889,189	122	41,143	930,332	746	5,162	966,959	1,897,291

In the years 1850, 1851, 1852 and 1855, no Ocean-going Steamships arrived, 1853 being the first to witness such vessels; while for the years 1850-1853 inclusive, the figures for Inland Vessels cannot be given, owing to the records having been destroyed by a fire.

OCEAN STEAMSHIPS.

ALLAN LINE OF STEAMSHIPS,

33 Vessels of 110,420 tons burthen, from Liverpool : consigned to H. & A. Allan. Head office, 25 Common st cor St Peter st.

BEAVER LINE OF STEAMSHIPS,

Owned by the Canada Shipping Co., Limited ; sailing between Montreal and Liverpool during the summer months and between New York and Liverpool during the winter months. H. E. Murray, general manager, 1 Custom House sq.

DONALDSON LINE OF STEAMSHIPS,

Sailing between Montreal and Glasgow.
Consigned to Robert Reford & Co. Office 23 and 25 St Sacrament st.

Alcides,	3500 tons,	Captain Rolls,
Amaryathin,	4000 "	"	Crighton.
Concordia,	2600 "	"	Taylor.
Circe,	2400 "	"	Jennings
Colina,	2000 "	"	Browne.
Warwick,	2000 "	"	Coutts.

Agents in Glasgow, Donaldson Bros.

THOMSON LINE OF STEAMSHIPS,

Sailing between Montreal and London, Newcastle-on-Tyne, Dundee, Leith, Aberdeen and Mediterranean Ports
Consigned to Robert Reford & Co. Office 23 and 25 St Sacrament st.

Gerona.	3500 tons.	Captain Anderson.
Fremona,	3500 "	"	Tait.
Escalona,	2000 "	"	Cummings.
Dracona,	2000 "	"	Howick
Barcelona,	2000 "	"	Boyle.
Avlona,	2000 "	"	Yule.

Agents and owners, William Thomson & Sons, Dundee, Scotland.

ROSS LINE OF STEAMSHIPS,

Sailing between Montreal and London.
Consigned to Robert Reford & Co. Office 23 and 25 St Sacrament st.

Storm King	3500 tons,	Captain Crosby.
Ocean King,	2500 "	"	O'Toole.
Norse King,	3500 "	"	Johnston.
Erl King,	2200 "	"	James.

Agents in London, William Ross & Co., 3 East India avenue.

HANSA STEAMSHIP COMPANY OF HAMBURG,

Service by the following Steamers between Hamburg and Antwerp and Montreal :

Pickeuben,	(new)	4200	tons.
Stubbenhuk,	(new)	4200	"
Grimm,	(new)	3600	"
Steinhoft,	(new)	3500	"
Kahrwieder		3000	"
Braunwall,	(new)	4000	"
Wandrahm,	(new)	3600	"
Cremon,		2000	"
Grassbrook,		3000	"

August Bolten, Hamburg, agents :
Gristar & Marsily, Antwerp, agents :
Steinmann & Co., Antwerp, agents.
Munderloh & Co , general agents.
Montreal office 61 St Sulpice st.

DOMINION LINE OF STEAMSHIPS TO LIVERPOOL AND BRISTOL

8 Vessels of 33,200 tons burthen ; from Liverpool. Consigned to David Torrance & Co. Office 8 Hospital st.

WHITE STAR STEAMSHIP COMPANY.

B. J. Coghlin, agent, 364 St Paul st.

DOBELL LINE,

Sailing from Montreal for Newfoundland and Cape Breton. 4 steamships, 4500 tons burthen. Agents, H. Dobell & Co., 21 St Sacrament st.

BLACK DIAMOND LINE,

Sailing from Montreal to Cape Breton and Newfoundland 4 steamers of 5000 tons burthen. Kingman, Brown & Co., agents, Custom House sq.

QUEBEC STEAMSHIP COMPANY,

Sailing from Montreal to Miramichi.
1 steamer of 491 tons burthen. Thomas Fraser & Co., agents, 204 Commissioners st.

RICHELIEU HOTEL,

Established in 1871.

J. B. DUROCHER & CO., PROPRIETORS.

This Hotel has a large dining hall and 200 apartments. It will accommodate 400 guests. It has now 12 permanent guests ; 40 female employees ; 40 male employees. 45 St. Vincent Street, Montreal.

ENUMERATION OF PROFESSIONS, BUSINESS HOUSES. TRADES, Etc..

In Montreal in January, 1891.

Catholic Clerical profession and Churches:

1 archbishop of Montreal ; 1 vicar general ;
193 priests ;
25 Catholic Churches ; 33 Catholic Chapels ;
21 Convents.

Protestant Clerical profession and Churches:

1 bishop of Montreal ; 1 dean ; 1 archdeacon ;
63 ministers ; 16 assistant ministers ;
58 Protestant Churches ; 31 Mission Halls.

Jewish Clerical profession and Synagogues:

2 rabbis ; 3 ministers ;
5 Jewish Synagogues.

Legal profession :

300 advocates ; 1 clerk of appeals ; 23 judges ;
233 magistrates ; 119 notaries ; 2 police magistrates ;
1 prothonotary ; 1 recorder ; 1 sheriff ; 10 marriage license issuers.

Medical profession :

	f	m
5 aurists and oculists	5	
124 chemists and druggists	90	186
42 dentists	43	27
249 physicians	310	250
21 veterinary surgeons	9	13
3 chiropodists	4	
19 doctresses	19	

Banks:

16 Banks :—11 chartered banks, 5 branch banks ;
5 savings ; 5 private banks. *

Railway companies:

107 passenger cars arriving daily at stations.
28 sleeping and parlor cars arriving daily.
720 freight and cattle cars arriving daily at stations.

Ocean and other steamers, sailing ships, inland craft, etc.*

624 ocean steamships arrived in Port of Montreal during navigation (1890).
252 gulf, lake and river steamers.
122 sailing ships, barques, brigs, brigantines and schooners, arrived from the Atlantic Ocean.
5162 inland craft.

Printing offices:

37 newspapers and periodicals—		f	m
6 French, 4 English dailies *		149	629
8 " 14 " weeklies *		95	181
1 " 2 " fortnightlies			
7 " 11 " monthlies			
2 " annuals			
64 printers, book and job		47	100

Educational Institutions:

		f	m	f	m
34 academies	teachers	285	53	50	37
86 schools	"	210	281	47	28
10 colleges	"	3	224	26	85
3 universities.					

* See page 45 for Line Contributors in aid of cost of publication of Lovell's *Historic Report of Census of Montreal*; and page 79 for condensed detail of Banks.

Professions :

	f	m
68 accountants		97
6 adjusters		10
39 appraisers		70
73 architects		43
13 artists	5	
8 assignees		12
30 auctioneers		69
18 auditors		36
49 civil engineers		43
10 land surveyors		27

Wholesale houses :

	f	m
11 china, glass and earthenware		59
17 clothiers	120	212
8 drain pipes		11
9 druggists		15
56 dry goods	12	332
34 fancy goods	18	43
14 flour		132
20 furriers	160	180
41 grocers		467
6 haberdashers	48	44
44 hardware		229
15 jewellers	4	50
1 jute	28	20
43 leather		150
6 millinery	15	40
31 paints and oils		100
106 produce and provisions		259
11 sporting goods		30
8 tinware		30
15 varnish and paints	6	20
22 wines	17	32

Wholesale and retail houses :

	f	m
2 baby linen	10	
1 bag store		7
72 booksellers and stationers	98	182
197 boots and shoes	80	206
1 brewery supplies	1	2
38 china, glass and earthenware		76
6 church ornaments	6	11
61 clothiers	50	68
190 confectioners	166	87
175 dry goods	265	363
113 fancy goods	94	70
28 general stores	28	34
36 gents' furnishings	35	89
945 grocers	129	941
71 hardware		239
46 hatters and furriers	25	46
17 house furnishings	10	40
164 jewellers		119
18 machinery depots		39
4 machine supply stores		26
120 merchant tailors	164	369
1 mill supplies	12	20
2 mineral water depots	1	23
15 music	18	18
14 musical instruments	12	20
6 oils	3	13
20 pianos and organs	10	84
27 railway supplies		29
19 smallwares		50
53 tea		151
3 undertakers' supplies		12
2 waterproof clothing	3	20
16 woollen goods		48

Dealers :

	f	m
7 artists' materials	4	35
2 bicycle		3
32 butter and cheese		35
46 candy and fruit	46	14
6 cattle		10
3 chemical		6
96 cigars	35	102
20 coal		57
81 coal and wood		91
12 coal oil	12	4
1 fine art	2	2
30 fish	13	157
13 fishing tackle	2	13
99 flour and grain		150

DEALERS—Continued.

	f	m
110 fruit	78	100
62 furniture	22	101
46 hay and straw		75
9 hide and skin		15
7 ice		30
9 junk	3	5
43 leather		54
2 live-stock		12
50 lumber		68
12 news		24
28 oil		50
15 oyster and lobster	4	25
29 patent medicine	210	407
2 phosphate		6
12 pork		32
19 poultry, game and egg	10	31
115 produce		250
36 provision		109
45 second-hand	7	50
3 seeds, garden and field		9
35 stove		70
26 vegetable	5	17

Companies—Insurance:

	f	m
5 accident	3	30
2 boiler inspection	4	37
33 fire	5	43
1 guarantee	2	21
36 life	6	42
4 live stock	4	19
15 marine	3	7
2 plate glass	2	22
265 other different companies	272	4

Agents—Different Callings:

	f	m
10 advertising	7	12
3 book	3	6
3 commercial	3	
20 commission	18	2
11 custom house	9	2
3 dry goods	3	
9 electric light	8	
10 employment	10	2
11 express	9	4
42 financial	43	6
7 general	61	
2 immigration	2	2
86 insurance	85	8
2 machine	4	
134 manufacturers	132	7
7 mercantile	2	17
22 metal	20	4
5 millers	6	5
mineral water		2
4 news		4
1 phosplate	1	
29 produce	11	42
27 railway supply	21	40
69 real estate and house		75
21 sewing machine	16	2
25 shipping	29	13
2 steamboat	2	
17 steamship	15	2
6 telegraph	6	4
9 ticket	11	
385 without a city office	396	62

Brokers:

	f	m
11 commission		12
9 custom		12
4 exchange		8
5 freight		3
1 hardware	3	1
21 insurance	7	20
8 money	3	14
5 produce	4	2
4 ship	1	8
46 stock	22	15
6 tea	8	12

Other Callings:

	f	m
2 assistant post office inspectors	2	
1 bible depository	15	13
29 boarding houses	400	112
526 book keepers	200	
8 bridgemasters	8	
1030 cabmen with carioles, single carriages, double carriages	986	204

	f	m
16 captains		16
119 caretakers		113
2815 carters with carts and trucks, jobbing expresses, single and double	2735	220
62 charwomen		10
27 checkers		27

375 City Police force :
  1 chief ; 3 sub-chiefs ;
  1 accountant ; 1 assistant accountant ;
  1 chief detective ; 1 secretary ;
  7 detectives ; 12 serjeants ;
  26 acting serjeants ; 320 sub-constables ;
  1 drill instructor ; 1 police matron.

	f	m
1120 clerks	1740	5
11 clubs	20	49
63 collectors	59	1
425 commercial travellers	329	2
155 commission merchants	133	300
76 conductors	76	
283 contractors	287	130
1 custom house	5	224
78 customs officers	77	10
2 dancing academies		4
1 decorative art rooms		4
10 detectives	5	1
1 directory for nurses	10	30
12 draughtsmen	11	
404 engineers	400	12
2 express companies	11	110
11 farmers	13	1
1 federal telephone office	98	7
524 foremen	421	
1 gas company		155
69 grooms	69	
30 guardians	29	9
167 hotels	7800	280
1 huntsman	2	
2 immigration offices		7
21 importers	9	72
2 Indian curiosity shops	1	11
1 inland revenue office		55
102 inspectors	114	8
3 jail guards	3	
5 janitors	9	
41 journalists	47	
71 letter carriers	50	
6 librarians	6	
133 licensed billiard and pool rooms		199
12 licensed Mississippi and pigeon hole tables		28
71 licensed second-hand dealers	57	
23 licensed junk dealers	15	32
163 licensed rag pickers	25	
90 pedlars on foot	79	
12 licensed pedlars with hand carts	7	
19 licensed pedlars with horse and waggon	17	
5 licensed pawn brokers	5	
3 licensed money lenders	3	
30 livery stables	18	138
21 lunch rooms	21	9
154 managers	163	12
3 Mercantile Agencies	7	44
42 messengers	40	

153 Montreal Fire department :
  1 chief ; 3 assistant chiefs ;
  1 supply officer ; 1 secretary ;
  15 captains ; 2 foremen of salvage ;
  8 engineers ; 4 foremen of ladders ;
  3 foremen of chemical engines ;
  1 hose and harness repairer ;
  76 first class firemen ;
  38 second class firemen.

	f	m
2 news companies	6	22
8 pilots	8	
1 post office inspector		2
1 powder company		82
2082 private residences	2318	184
59 professors	63	2
1 public pound		1
310 restaurants	290	289
1 rice mill	1	2
3 rolling mills	9	675
33 sculptors	31	8
41 second-hand stores	51	13
8 solicitors of patents	8	16
5 speculators	5	
47 stenographers	18	5
1 street railway company		350
24 surveyors	3	

	f	m
14 switchmen	14	
2 telephone companies	95	43
13 warehousemen		29
2 wheel houses	2	32
1515 widows	1539	4
1421 unoccupied houses.		
327 churches, houses and buildings in course of construction—219 brick, 117 stone, to be completed during the coming summer.		

Factories:

	f	m
2 billiard table		8
3 bolt		162
22 box	19	133
84 carriage and sleigh		225
3 chair		24
2 cordage	18	60
62 furniture		600
5 horse nail		42
1 jute	25	24
4 knitting	18	34
1 mucilage	1	3
7 nail		60
5 paper box	60	20
2 paper stock	244	79
5 rubber	609	336
1 slipper	20	7
2 sugar	1	770
2 telephone		112
2 thread	45	11
1 truss		20
6 wooden ware	2	27
2 woollen	36	58

Manufactories:

	f	m
11 agricultural implement		75
2 bell		50
16 boiler		105
2 file		10
6 safe		22
3 saw		22
4 sewing machine	18	175
6 tool		30
1 wood working machinery		6

Manufacturers:

	f	m
12 account book	80	100
11 aerated water, ginger ale, cider	15	195
8 baby carriage		32
6 baking powder		34
1 basket		7
12 bedding		100
6 belt		18
8 biscuit and cracker	35	80
1 blanket	1	5
53 boot and shoe	391	579
1 brace and garter	8	6
27 brick		45
7 broom		30
8 brush		29
1 card board		10
4 card clothing		18
28 cigar and tobacco	949	1080
1 clay pipe		20
17 clothing	100	175
8 confectionery	50	100
3 cork	15	60
8 corset	20	5
2 cotton	829	561
2 cotton waste		8
17 door, sash and b'ind		205
1 dry plate	2	5
1 feather	10	15
3 felt	1	30
2 fibre	2	18
1 fringe and tassel	15	5
3 glass		404
4 glove	115	25
1 glue		35
8 grate and mantel		47
1 hat and cap block		4
3 hay press		9
2 jersey and blouse	40	7
23 jewellery		76
8 lamp		45
5 lard	5	7
8 last	2	29
4 lead pipe	17	56

	f	m
6 leather belting		60
10 mirror		40
30 moulding		125
6 office furniture		22
2 paint		30
4 oil cloth	5	21
14 paper	60	128
6 paper bag	104	50
1 paper collar	45	9
3 pickle	30	50
1 pop corn	1	
2 printers' supplies	10	20
2 rubber goods		24
1 sack	25	225
3 nail	10	23
5 scale		32
11 shirt and collar	731	60
10 soap and candle	32	84
5 spring bed	15	50
9 spring		45
12 stationery	28	38
2 straw hat	25	12
3 suspender	39	5
7 tailors' trimmings		36
4 tent and awning		9
3 thread	30	15
2 tinware		175
1 tubular lamp	24	10
6 umbrella	12	23
21 trunk and valise	22	92
9 varnish		33
2 vermicelli	87	4
6 vinegar		14
2 wall paper		106
1 wire	1	5
5 wire goods	48	22
4 wire mattress	4	10
1 wood pulp		4
1 wrench		2
1 yeast	2	7

Trades:

	f	m
2 art metal workers	2	3
53 bakeries	18	153
153 bakers	109	
165 barbers, master		199
159 barbers	98	
1 band instrument repairer	1	2
7 beer bottling	4	36
36 beer bottlers	28	
30 bell makers	23	
3 bird fanciers	2	3
64 blacksmith, master		208
208 blacksmiths	150	
23 bookbinderies	300	171
21 baggagemen	25	
54 bookbinders	30	
101 boiler makers	150	
14 brassfoundries		114
114 brassfounders	90	
3 brass polishers	1	
10 breweries		150
150 brewers	160	
129 bricklayers, master		244
244 bricklayers	240	
4 bridge builders, master		1
11 bridge builders	12	1
61 brakemen	57	
29 builders, master		24
24 builders	24	18
3 burnishers	3	
240 butchers, master		300
530 butcher stalls		765
565 butchers	750	
62 button hole makers	8	
53 cabinetmakers, master		104
104 cabinetmakers	75	
4 cap makers	9	3
2 carders	3	
102 carpenter and joiners, master		123
923 carpenters and joiners	800	
2 carpet beating companies		37
2 carpet layers	4	
68 carriage makers, master		192
192 carriage makers	88	
7 carvers and gilders		20
20 carvers	15	
8 caterers	20	50
260 compositors	180	
40 cooks	30	

TRADES—*Continued.*

Trade	f	m
16 coopers, master		296
226 coopers	120	
7 coppersmiths, master		70
79 coppersmiths	45	
2 dairymen	2	
4 die makers, master		35
35 diemakers	20	
317 dressmakers	650	
11 dye works	44	22
22 dyers and scourers	17	
61 electricians	59	4
7 electroplaters, master		10
40 electroplaters	25	
6 electro type foundries		20
29 electro-typers	12	
1 embosser	1	1
14 engineers, master		250
250 engineers	120	
34 engravers, master		60
69 engravers	40	25
7 feather cleaners and dyers	20	
4 fik makers	6	
10 florists	11	15
29 furriers, master	146	96
96 furriers	50	
6 fur dressing works	15	52
6 fur dressers		40
86 gardeners	94	1
14 gliders, master		30
20 gliders	17	
25 glass-blowers	25	
23 glass workers	16	
14 glaziers, master		42
10 glaziers	7	
2 goldsmiths	2	
6 granite works		100
100 granite workers	60	
4 gravel roofers	5	4
7 gunsmiths, master		50
50 gunsmiths	35	
3 hat bleacheries	1	3
59 hatters and furriers	67	26
71 horseshoers, master		65
20 horseshoers	10	
11 horse traders		
15 iron works		14
300 iron workers	215	500
2 japanners, master		20
4 japanners	3	
2 key makers	2	
5534 laborers	5342	
1 lard refinery		14
49 laundries	364	51
109 laundresses	122	2
72 leather cutters	50	
7 lime kilns		
6 lime burners		25
15 lithographers, master	5	32
56 lithographers	30	50
12 locksmiths, master		25
23 locksmiths	13	
35 machinists, master		254
254 machinists	200	
8 marble works		82
82 marble cutters	35	
19 masons, master	97	107
107 masons	95	
5 metal works		35
33 metal workers	20	
134 milkmen	127	11
36 millers	36	16
32 milliners	100	
6 millwrights, master		77
32 millwrights	32	
353 moulders	250	
32 musicians	34	
88 music teachers	25	
60 nail makers	45	
8 nickle platers, master		30
59 nickle platers	29	
8 nurserymen	12	25
40 oil refiners	30	
11 oil cloth workers	5	
11 opticians, master		13
18 opticians	10	
3 organ builders, master		11
11 organ builders	6	
32 packers	31	10
87 painters, master		597
597 painters	450	
128 paper workers	60	
50 paper bag makers	35	
53 paper collar makers	41	
35 pattern makers	20	
32 photographic studios	54	100
43 piano tuners	15	
30 picture framers, master		120
120 picture frame workers	80	
5 pipe layers	5	
7 plasterers, master		183
183 plasterers	120	
117 plumbers, master		722
722 plumbers	500	
1 plumbers, supplies		2
31 polishers	20	
26 porters	15	
192 pressmen	98	
2 pump works		20
29 pump makers	15	
49 roofers	42	15
709 rubber workers	600	336
42 saddlers and harnessmakers, master	3	93
93 saddlers and harnessmakers	71	
60 safe makers	40	
12 sailors	11	
73 sale-men	40	
12 sausage makers	12	
11 saw filers	11	
7 scale repairers	5	
158 seamstresses	99	
4 seed merchants	4	23
4 ship builders, master		60
69 ship builders	45	
6 ship carpenters	7	
6 ship chandlers	6	7
2 ship liners	1	4
29 shippers	29	6
851 shirt makers	791	60
1315 shoemakers	900	
1 show card writer		3
21 sign writers, master		60
69 sign writers	35	
10 silver platers, master		40
40 silver platers	25	
1 smelting work		9
9 smelters and refiners	5	
1 snuff maker	4	
soap makers, master		15
50 soap makers	35	
3 spinners	3	
42 stable men	32	
5 stained glass works		32
32 stained glass workers	29	
7 stair builders, master		17
21 stair builders	18	
62 steamfitters, masters		500
509 steamfitters	350	
4 stencil works		21
21 stencil cutters	16	
24 stevedores	18	
29 stokers	25	
178 stonecutters	125	
70 stonemasons, master		100
167 stone masons	86	
19 stone polishers	10	
289 storemen	232	
770 sugar refiners	698	
369 tailors	300	
175 tailoresses	13	
6 tanneries		250
250 tanners	210	
4 taxidermist, master		8
8 taxidermists	7	
36 telegraph operators		
2 telephone box makers	2	
84 tinsmiths, master		247
297 tinsmiths	227	
2929 tobacconists	719	1080
30 tool makers	18	
695 traders	500	
25 trunk makers	16	

		f	m
19 undertaker shops....		11	53
53 undertakers....		40	
73 upholsterers....		68	37
42 wailers....		35	
200 watch makers....		95	
4 watch case makers....		3	
105 watchmen....		8	
4 water carriers....		4	
4 wax workers....		4	
3 weight houses....			12
12 weighers....		9	
4 wheelwright shops....			13
13 wheelwrights....		5	
14 whitewashers master....			40
40 whitewashers....		40	
5 wire workers master....		5	90

		f	m
90 wire workers....		65	4
4 wood engravers master....		4	13
13 wood engravers....		8	
55 wood workers....		30	
Foundries:			
29 brass, store, etc....			648
6 iron foundries....			342
1 type foundry....		13	15
Mills:			
11 coffee and spice mills....		21	700
7 flour mills....			86
3 rolling mills....			250
20 saw and planing mills....			300
2 woolen mills....			40

CATHOLIC CHURCHES.

First Bishop of Montreal, MONSEIGNEUR JEAN JACQUES LARTIQUE.

Present Bishop (Jan., 1891) HIS GRACE MONSEIGNEUR EDOUARD CHARLES FABRE, Archbishop of Montreal.

Names of Churches.	Address.	Built of	In	Present Priest.	Assist. Priests.	Congregation.	Sittings f	m	Empty's f	m
Cathedrale St Jacques....	135 Cathedral	Brick	1822	The Archbishop	10	3000	5	11	5	4
St Patrick's Church....	731 Lagauchetiere	Stone	1846	Rev. P. Dowd	5	10,000				8
Notre Dame Parish Church	Notre Dame	Stone	1658	Rev. A.J. Sentenne	26	20,000				6
Eglise St Jean Baptiste..	743 Sanguinet	Stone	1875	Rev. M. Auclair	4	11,700			3	
Eglise St Joseph....	306 Richmond	Stone	1860	Rev. J.U. Leclerc	6	10,000				2
Eglise N.D. de Bonsecours	St Paul	Stone	1772	Rev H Lenoir	1	4000			4	1
Church of the Gesu....	144 Bleury	Stone	1865	Rev. Lewis Drummond	20	1400				
Immaculate Conception...	Papineau road	Stone	1884	Rev. S. Proulx	1	2000				
Eglise du Sacré-Coeur....	Ontario	Stone	1876	Rev. A. Dubue	6	10,000				
Notre-Dame de Lourdes..	St Catherine	Stone	1874	Rev. C. J. Maillet		2750			3	1
St Bridget's Church.....	53 Maisonneuve	Stone	1879	Rev. D J. Lonergan	4	15,000				
Notre Dame des Anges..	53 Lagauchetiere	Stone	1876	Rev. V. W. Marie		100				
Eglise St Jacques........	St Denis	Stone	1891	Rev. P. Deguire		10,000				3
Eglise de Mont St Croix..	1075 Dorchester	Stone	1878	A. Tranchemontagne	2					
Eglise St Charles........	164 Island	Wood	1883	Rev. J H. Carrières	3	6000				2
St Ann's Church........	Basin	Stone	1854	Rev. Father Catulle	11	8000				9
Our Lady of Good Counsel	401 St Denis	Stone	1851	Rev. R. G. Reid	1	200				2
Eglise St Louis de France	Laval av	Stone	1890	Rev. Chs. Larocque	2	3000				1
Eglise St Pierre........	Dorchester	Stone	1842	Rev J. Jodoin, OMI	13	3000				2
Eglise St Vincent de Paul	726 St Catherine	Stone	1876	Rev. L. Lavallée	3	8000				7
St Mary's Church........	164 Craig	Stone	1879	Rev. J. J. Salmon	2	3500				1
Eglise de la Nativité....	392 Ontario	Stone	1876	Rev. F. L. Adam	2	4500			2	1
Notre Dame de Pitié....	1652 Notre Dame	Stone	1858	Rev. V. Sorin		500			2	
St Gabriel Church.......	322 Centre	Wood	1870	Rev. Wm. O'Meara	1	3325				4
St Anthony of Padua....	Seigneurs	Stone	1890	Rev. J. H. Leclerc	2	3500				3

CATHOLIC CHAPELS.

L'Hotel Dieu.........	Pine av	Stone	1860	Rev. G. Fragesser						
Hospice St Joseph....	60 Cathedral	Stone	1862	Rev. Isidore Tallet		700				2
Notre-Dame du Sacré-Coeur	70 Notre Dame	Stone	1879	Rev. P. Valois						
Noms de Jesus et Marie	128 Notre Dame	Brick	1860	Rev.F.X. Ecrement		338				
Soeurs de la Misericorde..	326 Dorchester	Stone	1860	Rev.H.Charpentier		600				
Providence.........	St. Catherine	Stone	1885	Rev. Alf. Faubert		400				
Notre-Dame de Pitié..	1188 Mignonne	Stone	1867	Rev. Am. Therrien		356	2		1	
Chapelle de Ste Anne..	466 St Antoine	Stone	1888	Rev.E.Picotte		124			1	
Notre-Dame Sacré-Coeur..	456 St Urbain	Stone	1890	Rev.O. Hebert		13				
Chapelle du St Sacrement..	50 Mt Royal ave.	Stone	1890	Rev. P. Estevenon	3			7		
Immaculate Conception..	326 Guy	Stone	1875	L. D. A. Maréchal	2	339				
SS.Noms de Jesus et Marie	392 Rachel	Stone	1876	Father M. Auclair.		100				
St Louis de Gonzague..	105 Sherbrooke	Stone	1879							1
Our Lady of Seven Dolors	337 Centre	Brick	1882	Rev. H. Brissette		40				1
Chapelle de St Joseph..	2353 Notre Dame	Brick	1887	Rev. F. Cavanagh		20				1
Immaculate Conception..	102 McCord	Stone	1857	Rev.FatherCatulle						1
Chapelle de St Antoine...	854 Lagauchetiere	Brick	1867	Rev. F.N. Bruchési		15				1
Archbishop's Academy..	37 St Margaret	Brick	1853			7				1
Chapelle des Jeunes Gens.	103 Visitation	Stone	1842	Rev. H. Legault		750				
Chapelle de St Elouard..	160 Forfar	Brick	1888	Rev. Father Catulle		83				
Sacré-Coeur Chapel....	Sanguinet	Stone	1887	Rev. M. Auclair		1000			1	
L'Asile de la Providence..	1031 St Catherine	Stone	1843	Rev. J.A. Bertrand		400				
Chapelle Nazareth....	2021 St Catherine	Stone	1850	Rev.N.Latraverse,S.S.		400				
Rev. Peres Franciscains..	504 Richmond	Stone	1890	Father J. Baptiste	3			10		
L'Orphelinat St Alexis..	145 St Denis	Stone	18--	Rev. Jacques Palatin		200				2
Saint Coeur de Marie..	754 St Catherine	Stone	1881	Rev. L. A. Dubue		150				
Academie St Denis....	37 St Denis	Stone	1861	Rev. W. Duckett		30				2
Chapelle St Charles....	1419 Notre Dame	Stone	1877	Rev. Joseph Reid		60				
L'Hopital Notre-Dame..	1429 Notre Dame	Stone	1880	Rev. N. Latraverse		100				
St Vincent de Paul....	46 Visitation	Stone	1869	Rev. R. P. Antoine		100				
Chapelle de St Louis....	444 Sherbrooke	Stone	1887	Rev. C. Therrien		470				1
Chapelle Bethlehem....	41 Richmond sq.	Stone	1868	Father Leclaire	1	100				
Good Shepherd........	500 Sherbrooke	Stone	1844	Rev. A. Latulippe		500				

E

CATHOLIC CHURCHES.

There are twenty-five CATHOLIC CHURCHES in Montreal, January, 1891.

HIS GRACE MONSEIGNEUR EDOUARD CHARLES FABRE, *Archibishop of Montreal.*
VERY REVEREND LOUIS D. A. MARECHAL, *Vicar General;* REVEREND J. M. EMARD, *Chancellor.*

Cathedrale St. Jacques was originally built of stone in 1822 on St. Denis st cor St. Catherine st, and destroyed by fire in 1852. The present pro-cathedral was built of brick in 1853 to serve temporarily during the erection of the new Cathedrale St. Jacques, which is under course of erection (on the model of St. Peter's at Rome) on Dorchester st between Cathedral and Mansfield sts. First Bishop Right Reverend Ignace Bourget, Lord Bishop of Montreal; present Bishop His Grace Monseigneur Edouard Charles Fabre, Archbishop of Montreal; 10 assistant priests; 5 Catholic Fr. Canadian female employees; 4 Catholic Fr, Canadian male employees. Nationalities of inmates: 5 Catholic Fr. Canadian females; 11 Catholic Fr. Canadian males; 3000 congregation. 873 Lagauchetière st.

Notre Dame Parish Church, originally built of stone in 1658, on a part of Place d'Armes, facing Notre Dame street, westward, by the Reverend Sulpiciens. First superior Rev. M. de Queylus; present superior Rev. Frédéric Louis Colin; present parish priest Rev. Louis Alfred Sentenne; 26 assistant priests; 6 Catholic Fr. Canadian employees; 20,000 congregation. Notre Dame st facing Place d'Armes.

Eglise Notre Dame de Bonsecours, built of stone in 1673, being the first church built on the Island of Montreal. It was burnt in 1754, and rebuilt of stone in 1772. First priest Rev. M. Souart, S.S.; present priest Rev. H. Lenoir, S.S.; 1 assistant priest; 4 Catholic Fr. Canadian female employees; 1 Catholic Fr. Canadian male employee; 4000 congregation. St Paul st, facing Bonsecours st.

St Patrick's Church, built of stone in 1846. First and present parish priest Rev. Patrick Dowd, P.S.S.; 5 assistant priests; 8 Catholic Irish male employees. 10,000 congregation. 731 Lagauchetière cor St Alexander st.

St Bridget's Church, built of stone in 1879-80. First and present priest Rev. D. J. Lonergan; 4 assistant priests; 15,000 congregation. 53 Maisonneuve st.

Eglise St Jacques, built of stone in 1834, by Monseigneur Jacques Lartique; burnt in 1852; rebuilt of stone in 1853; burnt second time in 1859; rebuilt of stone in 1860. First priest Rev. Luc Pellissier; present priest Rev. Pierre Deguire, S.S.; 3 Catholic Fr. Canadian male employees; 10,000 congregation. Cor St Denis and St Catherine sts.

Eglise St Jean Baptiste, built of stone in 1875. First priest Rev. S. Maynard; present priest Rev. M. Auclair; 4 assistant priests; 3 Fr. Canadian female employees; 11,700 congregation. 743 Sanguinet st.

Eglise St Joseph, built of stone in 1860. First priest Rev. Father Arraud, S.S.; present priest Rev. J. L. Leclere; 6 assistant priests; 2 Catholic Fr. Canadian male employees; 10,000 congregation. 506 Richmond st.

Church of the Gesu, built of stone in 1865. First rector Rev. Louis Tache, S. J.; present rector Rev. Lewis Drummond, S.J.; 20 assistant priests; 4000 congregation. 144 Bleury st.

Eglise du Sacré Coeur de Jésus, built of stone in 1876. First and present priest Rev., A. Dubuc; 6 assistant priests; 10000 congregation. Cor Ontario and Plessis sts.

St Mary's (Our Lady of Good Counsel) Church, built of stone in 1879-80. First priest Rev. J. S. Lonergan; second parish priest Rev. S. P. Lonergan, who built the Presbytery; present priest Rev. J. J. Salmon; 2 assistant priests; 3 Catholic male employees, 3500 congregation. 164 Craig cor Panet sts.

Notre Dame de Lourdes Church, built of stone in 1874. First priest Rev. H. Lenoir, S.S.; present priest Rev. C. J. Maillet; 3 Catholic Fr. Canadian female employees; 1 Catholic Fr. Canadian male employee; 2750 congregation. St Catherine st facing Presbytère St James Church.

Church of the Immaculate Conception, built of stone in 1884. First priest Rev. P. L. Arpin, S.J.; present priest Rev. S. Proulx, S.J.; 1 assistant priest; 2000 congregation. Cor Papineau road and Rachel st.

Eglise St Charles, built of wood; founded in 1883. First priest Rev. Simeon Rouleau; present priest Rev. J. H. Carrières, P.P.; 3 assistant priests; 2 Catholic Fr. Canadian male employees; 6000 congregation. 164 Island st.

St Ann's Church, built of stone in 1851. First priest Rev. Michael O'Brien; present priest Rev. Father Catulle, C.S.S.R.; 11 assistant priests; 9 Catholic Irish male employees; 8000 congregation. Basin cor McCord st.

Eglise St Louis de France, built of stone in 1890, by the parishioners. First and present priest Rev. Charles Larocque; 2 assistant priests; 1 Catholic Fr. Canadian male employee; 3000 congregation. Cor Laval av and Roy st.

Eglise St Pierre, built of stone in 1842. First priest Rev. Jean Claude Léonard, O.M.I.; present priest Rev. Joseph Jodoin, O.M.I.; 13 assistant priests; 4 brothers; 2 Catholic Fr. Canadian employees; Nationalities of inmates: 13 Catholic Fr. Canadians; 5 Catholic French; 2 Catholic Fr. Canadian inmates. 3000 congregation. Cor Dorchester and Visitation sts.

Eglise St Vincent de Paul, built of stone in 1876. First priest Rev. Father Langlois; present priest Rev. Louis Motse Lavallée, P.P.; 3 assistant priests; 7 Catholic Fr. Canadian employees. 8000 congregation. 796 St Catherine st.

Eglise de la Nativité de la Ste Vierge d'Hochelaga, built of stone in 1876. First priest Rev. James Lonergan; present priest Rev. F. L. T. Adam; 2 assistant priests; 2 Catholic Fr. Canadian female employee; 1 Catholic Fr. Canadian male employee; 4500 congregation. 392 Ontario st bet Desery and St Germain sts.

St. Gabriel Church, built of wood in 1870. First priest Rev. J. J. Salmon, P.P.; present priest Rev. William O'Meara; 1 assistant priest; 4 Catholic male employees; 3325 congregation. 322 Centre cor St Andrew st.

St. Anthony of Padua, built of stone in 1890. First and present priest Rev. J. H. Leclerc, P.P.; 2 assistant priests; 3 Catholic male employees; 3500 congregation. Cor Seigneurs and St Antoine sts.

Eglise de Notre Dame de Pitié, built of stone in 1693; rebuilt in 1858 by the Sisters of the Congregation. Reverend V. Sorin, S.S., director; 2 nuns; 2 Catholic Fr. Canadian female employees; 500 congregation. 1652 Notre Dame st.

Our Lady of Good Counsel, built of stone in 1851. First priest Rev. F. X. Trepanier; present priest Rev. R. G. Reid; 1 assistant priest; 2 Catholic Fr. Canadian employees. 200 congregation. 401 St Denis st.

Eglise du Mont Ste Croix, built of stone in 1858. First priest Rev. Mathurin Bonissant, P.S.S.; present priest Rev. Alfred Tranchemontagne, P.S.S.; 2 assistant priests. Though strangers are allowed to visit this Church at stated hours, the services and religious ceremonies are held only for the inmates of the Institution. 1975 Dorchester st.

Notre Dame des Anges Church, built of stone in 1876. First and present priest Rev. V. W. Marre. 1000 congregation. 537 Lagauchetière st.

Seminary of St Sulpice, built of stone in 1657, on Notre Dame street, by the Reverend Sulpiciens. First superior Rev. M. de Queylus; present superior Rev. Frédéric Louis Colin. The Seminary contains 26 priests, in charge of various churches throughout the city and as assistants in churches; 15 Catholic Fr. Canadian male employees. Nationalities of inmates: 30 Fr. Canadian males; 11 French males. 1710 Notre Dame st, nearly facing Place d'Armes.

Pro-cure Office of the Seminary of St Sulpice, built of stone; established in 1657, for the management of the receipts and expenditures of the Seminary. Present procureur Rev. Jean Baptiste Larue; Gustave Adolphe Raymond, accountant; Edouard Lafleur and Joseph Bonin, notaries; Louis Barré, collector. 1710 Notre Dame st.

St Patrick's Presbytery. 3 Catholic Fr. Canadian males; 22 Irish Catholic males; 4 Irish Catholic males b in C; 1 Catholic American male. 770 Dorchester st.

St Ann's Presbytery; 8 Fr. Canadian Catholic males; 1 Irish Catholic male; 2 Irish Catholic males b in C, 9 Belgian Catholic males. 32 Basin st.

Presbytère St Vincent de Paul, 7 inmates. Nationalities of inmates: 2 Catholic Fr. Canadian females; 5 Catholic Fr. Canadian males. 796 St Catherine st.

Presbytère de St Pierre, 21 inmates, 3 Catholic Fr. Canadian females; 13 Catholic Fr. Canadian males; 5 Catholic French males. 107 Visitation st.

CATHOLIC CHAPELS.

There are thirty-three CATHOLIC CHAPELS in Montreal. January, 1891.

Chapelle de l'Hôtel-Dieu, built of stone in 1860. Present priest Rev. George Tragesser. Pine av.

Sacré Cœur Chapel, built of stone in 1887. First and present priest Rev. M. Auclair ; 1 Catholic Fr. Canadian female employee ; 1 Catholic Fr. Canadian male employee ; 1000 congregation. Sanguinet st n Rachel st.

Chapelle de l'Hospice St Joseph, built of stone in 1862 ; founded by the families of Olivier Bertheler and Alfred LaRocque. First priest Rev. Jean Baptiste Larue, P.S.S.; present priests Rev. Isidore Tallet and J. Bte. Brasseur, P.S.S. ; 2 Catholic Fr. Canadian male employees ; 700 congregation. 60 Cathedral st.

Chapelle des Sœurs de la Miséricorde, built of stone in 1860. First priest Rev. Canon Venant Pilon ; present priest Rev. Herménégilde Charpentier ; 600 congregation. 326 Dorchester n Campeau.

Chapelle de la Providence, built of stone in 1885. First and present priest Rev. Alfred Faubert, chaplain ; 400 congregation. Cor St Catherine and Fullum sts.

Chapel of the Immaculate Conception, built of stone in 1875. First Priest Rev. J. Comte, S.S.S. ; present Priest Rev. L.D.A. Maréchal, V.G., 2 assistant priests ; 339 congregation. Mount St. Mary. C.N.D., 306 Guy st.

Chapelle de l'Asile de la Providence, built of stone in 1843. First priest Rev. Monseigneur Charles Prince ; present priest Rev. J. A. Bertrand ; 400 congregation. 1631 St Catherine st.

Chapelle Nazareth, built of stone in 1870. First priest Rev. Victor Rousselot, S.S. ; present priest Rev. Narcisse Latraverse, S.S. ; 400 congregation. 2021 St Catherine st.

Notre Dame de Pitié Chapel, built of stone in 1867. First priest Rev. M. Clément ; present priest Rev. Amédée Therrien , 1 Catholic Fr. Canadian male employee ; 366 congregation. 1189 Mignonne st.

Chapelle de l'Orphelinat St Alexis, built of stone in 1887. First priest Rev. Alexis Truteau ; present priest Rev. Jacques Palatin, S.S. ; 2 Catholic Fr. Canadian male employees; 200 congregation. 145 St Denis st.

Chapelle du Saint Cœur de Marie, built of stone in 1881. First priest Rev. A. Wm. Meunier ; present priest Rev. L. A. Dubuc ; 120 congregation. 754 St Catherine st.

Chapelle des Sœurs des SS Noms de Jesus et Marie, built of stone in 1876. First priest Rev. François Xavier Ménard ; present priest Rev. Father M. Auclair ; 100 congregation. 312 Rachel st.

Chapelle des SS. Noms de Jesus et Marie, built of brick in 1860. First priest Rev. L. A. Valois ; present priest Rev. F. X. Ecrement ; 338 congregation. 128 Notre Dame st, adjoining the Convent of the Holy Names of Jesus and Mary.

Chapelle de Ste Anne, built of stone in 1884. First priest Rev. J. Fortin ; present priest Rev. E. Picotte, P.S.S.; 1 Catholic Fr. Canadian male employee ; 124 congregation. 466 St Antoine st.

Chapel of Our Lady of Seven Dolors, built of brick in 1882. First priest Rev. Jean Evangelist Salmon ; present priest Rev. Hyacinthe Brisette ; 1 Catholic Fr. Canadian male employee ; 40 congregation. 237 Centre st.

Chapelle de St Joseph, built of brick in 1887. First priest Rev. Father Pelissier , present priest Rev. Father

Felix Cavanagh ; 1 Catholic French Canadian male employee ; 20 congregation. 2353 Notre Dame st.

Chapel of the Immaculate Conception, built of stone in 1857. First priest Rev. Father O'Farrell, C.S.S.R.; present priest Rev. Father Catulle, C.S.S.R. ; 1 Catholic Fr. Canadian employee. 102 McCord st.

Chapelle de Notre Dame du Sacré Cœur, built of stone in 1875 ; founded by the Valois family. First and present chaplain, Rev. P. Valois. 70 Notre Dame n City limits.

Chapelle de Notre Dame du Sacré Cœur, built of stone ; founded in 1830, by the Reverend Sisters of the Congregation of Notre Dame. First and present priest Rev. O. Hebert, P.S.S. ; 13 congregation. 456 St Urbain st.

Chapelle du St Sacrement, built of stone in 1890. First and present priest Rev. P. Estevenon ; 3 assistant priests ; 3 brothers. Nationalities of inmates : 3 Catholic French ; 2 Catholic Fr. b in C ; 1 Catholic Dutchman ; 1 Catholic Belgian. 50 Mount Royal av.

Chapel of our Lady of the Good Shepherd, built of stone in 1844. First priest rev. Alexis F. Truteau ; present priest rev. A. Latulippe, chaplain ; 1 Catholic employee ; 500 congregation. 500 Sherbrooke st.

St. Louis de Gonzague Chapel, built of stone in 1879. 1 Catholic Fr. Canadian male employee. 405 Sherbrooke.

Chapelle de St Antoine, (private) built of brick in 1867. First priest Rev. Edmond Moreau, chaplain ; present priest Rev. P. N. Brachesi ; 1 Catholic Fr. Canadian male employee ; 15 congregation. 856 Lagauchetière st.

Chapelle des Jeunes Gens, built of stone in 1842. Director Rev. H. Legault, O.M.I. ; 750 congregation. Basement of St Peter's Church, 109 Visitation st.

Chapelle de St Edouard of the Little Sisters of the Poor, built of brick ; founded in 1888. First present priest Rev. Father Cutelle, C.S.S.R. Redemptorist Fathers of St Ann's Church assistant priests ; 83 congregation. 105 Forfar st.

Chapelle des Rev. Pères Franciscains, sous le patronage de St Joseph ; opened June, 1890, by Monseigneur Edouard Charles Fabre, Archbishop of Montreal ; Rev. Father Jean Baptiste, superior ; 3 assistant priests ; 2 brother students ; 3 penitents. Nationality of inmates : 9 French ; 1 French Canadian. 304 Richmond st.

Académie St Denis Chapel, built of stone in 1861. First priest Rev. H. Lenoir ; present priest Rev. William Dickett, S.S. ; 2 Catholic Fr. Canadian male employees ; 30 congregation. 37 St Denis st.

Chapelle St Charles, built of stone in 1877. First priest Rev. R. Rousseau, S.S. ; present priest Rev. Jos. Reail ; 50 congregation. 1413 Notre Dame st.

Chapelle de l'Hôpital Notre Dame, built of stone in 1880. First priest Rev. M. Levesque, S.S. ; present priest Rev. Narcisse Latraverse ; 60 congregation. 1423 Notre Dame st.

Chapelle Salle d'Asile St Vincent de Paul, built of stone in 1869. Rev. R. P. Antoine, O.M.I., superior ; 103 congregation. 46 Visitation st.

Chapelle de St Louis, built of stone in 1887. First and present chaplain Rev. Candide Therien ; 1 Catholic Fr. Canadian employee ; 470 congregation. 444 Sherbrooke st.

Chapelle Bethlehem, built of stone in 1868. First priest Reverend Father Arrocut, P.S.S. ; present priest Reverend Father Leclaire, P.P. ; 1 assistant priest. 100 Congregation. 1 Richmond sq.

Chapel of Archbishop's Academy, built of brick in 1833 ; served by the clergy of Cathedrale St Pierre ; 1 Fr. Canadians employee ; 7 congregation. 37 St Margaret st.

CONVENTS.

Names of Convents.	Address.	Built of	In	Present Lady Superioress.	No. of Sisters.	No. of Novices.	No. of Teachers.	No. of Pupils.
Mount St Marie Convent	326 Guy	Stone	1860	Sister Mary Josephine	30	1	30	192
Couvent de la Miséricorde	326 Dorchester	Stone	1886	Mother Marie du S. C.	60	12		
Pensionnat Noms de J.M	39 Notre Dame	Brick	1880	Mother Marie J.B.	28		28	161
Congrégation de N.D.	1051 Ontario	Brick	1877	Sister Ste Dosithée	19	2		
Couvent St Léon	150 Cadieux	Stone	1885	Sister St Gustave	10	1		
Ladies of the Sacred Heart	St Catherine	Stone	1872	Mother Schulten	37			100
Couvent Ste Marguérite	Point St Charles	Stone	1662		4			
St John the Evangelist	337 Centre	Brick	1882		12	2		
Jardin de l'Enfance	1198 Mignonne	Stone	1880	Sister Dosithée	11	3		
Pensionnat Cong. N.D.	754 St Catherine	Stone	1878	Sister St Bathélemy	16		16	700
Asile de la Providence	1631 St Catherine	Stone	1843	Sister Mary Hedwige	59			
Orphelinat St Alexis	11 St Denis	Stone	1852	Sister Dosithée	7	3		
Pensionnat Notre Dame	49 St Jean Baptiste		1857	Sister St Eulalie	66		56	350
Académie St Anne	162 McCord	Stone	1857	Sister St Alphonsus	10			350
Little Sisters of the Poor	109 Forfar	Brick	1888	Sister Domitine	9			
Couvent de Communauté	99 Notre Dame	Brick	1861	Mother Marie J.B.	123	16		
Monastery of Notre Dame	98 Notre Dame	Stone	1879	Mother Raphael	17	3		
Mount St Louis Monastery	444 Sherbrooke	Stone	1887	Rev. Brother Denis	39			
Our Lady of Charity Mon.	590 Sherbrooke	Stone	1844	St Alphonsus	74	40		
Franciscan Observants	201 Richmond	Brick	1890	Father J. Baptiste	4			
Most Blessed Sacrament M.	56 Mount Royal av	Stone	1890	Rev. P. Estevnon	4			
Couvent de l'Hotel Dieu	Pine av	Stone	1860	Sister J. Bonneau	85	11		
Couvent de l'Hôpital Gen.	390 Guy	Stone	1870	Mother P. Filiatrault	105	90		

CONVENTS.

There are twenty-one CONVENTS or SISTER-HOODS in Montreal. January, 1891.

Couvent de l'Hotel-Dieu de St Joseph de Montréal, built of stone in 1859-60; founded by Mademoiselle Jeanne Mance in 1642. Its object is the care of the sick poor and orphans. First Reverend lady superioress Reverend Sister Judith de Bresoles; present Reverend lady superioress Reverend Sister Justine Bonneau. The Hospital contains 250 beds; the Orphan Asylum contains 8 beds; 85 nuns; 11 novices. Nationalities of inmates: 1 Protestant English; 1 Protestant Irish; 1 Protestant American; 3 Catholic French; 1 Catholic English; 18 Catholic Irish; 19 Catholic Irish b in C; 2 Catholic Americans. This Institution is maintained by the rents of houses and lands bequeathed to the Hotel-Dieu. Pine av.

Couvent de l'Hopital Générale, Mother House of the Order of Grey Nuns. Originally built of stone in 1694, on Foundling street, by Rev. Charron Brothers, and received its title under Letters Patent from His Majesty Louis XIV. The Charron Institution was afterwards transferred to the Sisters of Charity, Grey Nuns, an order founded in 1738 by Madame Marie Marguerite Dufrost de la Jemmerais (widow of M. François d'Youville), the first Lady Superioress, on the 7th October, 1747, and sanctioned on the 3rd of June, 1754, under its primitive title of "General Hospital of Montreal" by Letters Patent, under the seal and signature of His Majesty Louis XV. It was twice destroyed by fire in the years 1735 and 1765, and rebuilt of stone. It was used for upwards of 160 years as an asylum for the sick, maimed, infirm, aged, insane, foundlings, and desolate of all ages and sexes. In 1863, it was found necessary to secure a more desirable locality. The same Reverend Ladies erected (in 1870) a spacious Convent and Hospital on Guy street. They are under the direction and management of the Reverend Mother Praxède Filiatrault, the present Lady Mother Superioress General of the Order; 3 assistant lady superioresses; 1 mistress and 2 sub-mistresses of novices, directresses and sub-directress of wards, ateliers, workrooms, laundries, kitchens, etc.; 105 sisters; 90 novices; 15 female employees; 3 male employees; 50 gentlemen boarders; 23 lady boarders. For Nationalities see Hopital Generale, page 64. This institution is maintained by the rents of houses and lands belonging to the Order and the united industries of the Sisterhood, Governing Body Reverend Lady Mother Superioress and her Council. The Ladies also erected a fine Church as a part of their noble Institution. 390 Guy st cor Dorchester st.

Couvent Mont Ste Marie, built of stone; founded by the Sisters of the Congregation of Notre Dame, in 1860, for the education of young ladies. It is maintained by the board and tuition fees of the pupils. First lady superioress Rev. Sister of the Nativity; present lady superioress Rev. Sister St. Mary Josephine; 30 nuns; 1 novice; 18 Catholic female employees; 2 Catholic male

employees; 192 Catholic female pupils; 3 Protestant female pupils; 2 Jewish female pupils. Nationalities of inmates: 242 Catholic Fr. Canadian females; 1 Catholic English female; 5 Catholic Irish females; 76 Catholic Irish females b in C.; 7 Catholic American females; 3 Protestant English females; 2 Protestant American females; 2 Jewish females b in C. 326 Guy st.

Couvent des Sœurs de la Congrégation de Notre Dame, built of brick in 1877. First lady superioress Reverend Sister St Athanase; present lady superioress Reverend Sister Ste Dosithée; 19 sisters; 2 novices; 2 Catholic female employees. Nationalities of inmates: 24 Catholic Fr. Canadian females. 1051 Ontario st a Church of the Sacré Cœur.

Couvent St Léon, built of stone; founded in 1885 by the ladies of the Congregation of Notre Dame. First lady superioress Reverend Sister Ste Alix; present lady superioress Reverend Sister St Gustave; 10 nuns; 1 novice; 2 Catholic Fr. Canadian female employees; 2 Catholic Fr. Canadian male employees. Nationalities of inmates: 11 Catholic Fr. Canadian females; 2 Catholic Fr. Canadian males; 1 Protestant English female; 1 Protestant American female. 115 Cadieux st.

Ladies of the Sacred Heart Convent, built of stone in 1872; addition built of stone in 1886, as a day school for girls. First lady superioress Reverend Mother Desmarquet; present lady superioress Reverend Mother Schulten; 37 sisters; 2 male employees. Nationalities of inmates: 25 Catholic Fr. Canadian females; 2 Catholic French females; 1 Catholic Belgian female; 2 Catholic German females; 2 Catholic Irish females; 5 Catholic American females. Cor St Catherine and Bleury sts.

Couvent Ste Marguerite, built of stone in 1662, by the Congregation of Notre Dame; founded by the Venerable Mother Marguerite Bourgeoys, in 1662, as a home of health; School opened in 1886; maintained by the revenue of the farm; 100 Catholic female pupils. First Reverend Superioress Venerable Mother Marguerite Bourgeoys. This Convent is dependent on the mother house; 4 nuns; 1 Catholic Fr. Canadian female employee; 5 Catholic Fr. Canadian male employees. Point St. Charles farm.

Couvent du Sacré Cœur, built of stone in 1872, founded by the Reverend Ladies of the Sacred Heart, for the education of young girls. First lady superioress Reverend Mother Desmarquet; present lady superioress Reverend Mother Schulten; 37 sisters; 2 Catholic female employees. Nationalities of inmates: 25 Catholic Fr. Canadians; 2 Catholic female Irish; 2 Catholic female French; 5 Catholic female Americans; 1 Catholic female Belgian; 2 Catholic female Germans. 2082 St Catherine st cor Bleury st.

Couvent of St John the Evangelist, built of brick in 1882, by the Reverend Sisters of the Holy Cross, for the higher education of young girls, under the control of the Catholic Board of School Commissioners. First lady superioress Reverend Sister Mary of St. Adelaide; 12 nuns; 2 novices; 1 Catholic female employee; 15 inmates. Nationalities: 15 French Canadians. 337 Centre st.

Jardin de l'Enfance Convent, built of stone in 1882; founded in 1881 by the Reverend Sisters of Charity of Providence, for the care and protection of orphans. It is self-maintained. First lady superioress Reverend Sister Marie Hedwidge; present lady superioress Reverend Sister Dosithée; 11 reverend sisters; 3 novices; 5 Catholic Fr. Canadian female employees. Nationalities: 20 Catholic Fr. Canadians. 1 Catholic female Irish. 1138 Mignonne st.

Pensionnat de la Congregation de Notre Dame Convent, built of stone in 1878; founded by the Reverend Ladies of the Congregation of Notre Dame, as a day and boarding school for girls. First lady superioress Reverend Sister St Dorothy; present lady superioress Reverend Sister St Barthelemy; 16 reverend sister teachers; 700 Catholic female pupils; 4 Catholic female employees; 1 Catholic male employee. Nationalities of inmates: 10 Catholic Fr. Canadian females; 3 Catholic English females b in C; 24 Irish females b in C. 734 St Catherine st.

Asile de la Providence Convent, built of stone in 1843; founded in 1845 by the late Bishop Bourget and Mrs. J. B. Gamelin, as an asylum and dispensary for the poor. Visits are paid to the sick, and gifts distributed to necessitous people. It is supported by different industries and by public charity. First lady superioress Reverend Sister Gamelin; present lady superioress Reverend Sister M. Hedwige; 50 reverend sisters; 55 tertiar sisters; 170 old invalid females; 16 adult boarders; 9 male employees. Nationalities of inmates: 280 Catholic Fr. Canadians; 20 Irish Catholics. 1631 St Catherine st.

Orphelinat St Alexis Convent, built of stone in 1852; founded in 1853, by Rev. A. Trudeau, as an orphelinate. It is maintained by the sisters' industry and public charity. First lady superioress Reverend Sister Charles; present lady superioress Reverend Sister Dosithée; 7 reverend sisters; 3 novices; 4 female employees; 1 male employee. 145 St Denis st.

Pensionnat Notre Dame Convent; founded in 1657, incorporated in 1671, as an educational establishment for young ladies; conducted by the Ladies of the Institution. First lady superioress Venerable Mother Bourgeoys, foundress of the Order; present lady superioress Reverend Sister St Eulalie; inmates, 66 nuns; 16 teachers; 350 female pupils; 22 female employees; 4 male employees. 45 St Jean Baptiste st.

Académie St Anne Convent, built of stone; founded in 1857 under the direction of the rev. Sisters of the Congregation of Notre Dame of Montreal as a school for girls. First lady superioress Reverend Sister St Agnes; present lady superioress Reverend Sister St Alphonsus of Ligouri; 10 nuns; 350 Catholic female pupils; 2 female Catholic employees; 1 Catholic male employee; 14 inmates. Nationalities of inmates: 2 Catholic Fr. Canadian females; 1 Catholic American male; 2 Catholic English females; 9 Irish females. 132 McCord st.

Convent of the Little Sisters of the Poor, built of brick; founded in 1888, by the Ladies of the Little Sisters of the Poor, as a home for aged and infirm poor of both sexes, who have no means of support. It is supported by the united industry of the sisterhood and contributions of the charitable. First mother superioress Rev. Sister St Germain of St Mary; present mother superioress Rev. Sister Donitine of St Mary; 2 sisters; 41 aged women; 33 aged men. Nationalities of inmates: 9 Catholic Fr. Canad an females; 32 Catholic Irish females; 2 Catholic English females; 3 Catholic French females; 1 Catholic German female; 1 Catholic Irish female b in C; 7 Catholic Fr. Canadian males; 20 Catholic Irish males; 3 Catholic French males; 1 Catholic Belgian male; 1 Catholic American male; 1 Protestant English male. 20 Fortar st, Point St Charles.

Pensionnat des Sœurs des SS. Noms de Jésus et Marie, built of brick in 1860; founded in 1843 at Longueuil; transferred to Montreal in 1864; incorporated in 1845. First Lady Superioress Reverend Mother Marie Rose; present Lady Superioress Reverend Mother Marie Jean Baptiste; 22 reverend sisters teachers; 143 Catholic female pupils; 13 Protestant female pupils. Nationalities of inmates: 124 Catholic Fr. Canadian female pupils; 28 Protestant females English b in C; 78 Catholic American female pupils. 97 Notre Dame st.

Convent du Communauté des Sœurs des Saints Noms de Jésus et de Marie, built of brick in 1862. Founded in 1843 at Longueuil, by Reverend Mother Marie Rose, for the education of young girls. Self-supported. First lady superioress Reverend Mother Marie Rose, present lady superioress Reverend Mother Marie Jean Baptiste; 123 sisters; 16 novices; 38 postulants; 8 male employees; 125 Catholic female inmates. The nationalities are: 111 Fr. Canadians; 12 Irish; 2 Scotch. 99 Notre Dame st.

Convent of the Order of the Most Blessed Sacrament, built of stone; founded in 1890, by the Rev. Fathers of the Order for the Perpetual Adoration and Exposition of the Most Blessed Sacrament. It is supported by the industries of the Fatherhood and free-will offerings of the faithful. First and present superior Rev. P. Estevenon; 4 Fathers and 3 Brothers. Nationalities of inmates: 2 Catholic Fr. Canadians; 3 Catholic French; 1 Dutchman; 1 Belgian. 50 Mount Royal avenue.

Mount St Louis Monastery, built of stone in 1887, by the Rev. Brothers of the Christian Schools. First rev. superior Rev. Brother Andrew; present rev. superior Rev. Brother Denis; 39 reverend brothers; 18 Catholic male employees. Nationalities. 444 Sherbrooke st.

Monastery of Notre Dame of the Carmelite Nuns, built of stone in 1879. The order was founded in 1875. First Lady Superioress Reverend Mother Marie Seraphin du Divin Cœur de Jésus; present Lady Superioress Reverend Mother Raphael de la Providence; 17 professed nuns; 3 novices; 3 postulants; 4 sœurs tourières; 27 inmates. Nationalities: 24 Fr. Canadians; 3 French. 98 Notre Dame n City limits.

Monastery of Franciscan Observants, under the patronage of St. Joseph, built of brick; founded by the Rev. Brothers of the Franciscan Order, in 1890, for prayer and the salvation of men. It is supported by the free-will offerings of the faithful and the industries of the brotherhood. First rev. superior Father Jean Baptiste; 4 monks; 3 lay friars; 2 students of Theology. Nationalities: 8 Catholic Fr. Canadian inmates. 304 Richmond st.

Convent de la Miséricorde, founded in 1845 by Monseigneur Ignace Bourget, Bishop of Montreal, and Madame Rosalie Jetté (Sr. M. de la Nativité), for the care and protection of unfortunate women and infant children. Mother House of the Order of the Sisters of Miséricorde. First stone building erected in 1855, completed in 1885. Present Hospital built of stone in 1886. A Gynecological Dispensary is connected with this Hospital. Five visiting physicians, one resident Chaplain. First Lady Superioress, Reverend Mother Ste. Jeanne de Chantal; present Lady Superioress Reverend Mother Marie du Sacré Cœur; 60 Sisters; 12 novices; 55 magdalens; 9 nurses; 23 Consecrated; 93 Catholic female patients; 1 Catholic male patient; 2 Protestant female patients; 23 Catholic female infants; 22 Catholic male infants; 4 Catholic male employees; 2 Catholic college students; 3 Catholic female private boarders. Nationalities of inmates: 262 Fr. Canadians; 7 Irish; 22 Irish b in C; 10 Americans; 4 English; 2 Scotch; 1 French; 2 Germans. 326 Dorchester st.

Monastery of our Lady of Charity of the Good Shepherd, built of stone in 1844, founded in Montreal in 1846, by Monseigneur Bourget and M. Arraud, for the care and reformation of unfortunate women, and for the education of young girls. It is maintained by the proceeds of daily work for the public. First lady superioress Reverend Mother Mary of Ste. Céleste; present lady superioress Reverend Mother Mary of St. Alphonsus de Ligouri; 71 reverend sisters; 40 novices; 6 postulants and out-door sisters; 120 penitents; 40 magdalens; 71 reformed children; 128 pupils of the Industrial school; 432 inmates. Nationalities of inmates: 364 Catholic Fr. Canadian females; 68 Catholic English females; 6 Catholic Irish females. 500 Sherbrooke st.

CATHOLIC HOSPITALS.

There are four CATHOLIC HOSPITALS in Montreal. January, 1891.

Les Religieuses Hospitalières de St. Joseph de l'Hôtel-Dieu de Montreal, built of stone in 1861 ; founded in 1636, by Reverend Mother Marie de la Ferres Lallèche (France). The first nuns who came to Canada in 1659, viz., Judith de Bresoles, Marie Maillet and Catherine Maci, were taken from the Maison de Laflèche in France. First lady superioress in Canada Rev. Sister Judith de Bresoles; present lady superioress Rev. Sister Justine Bonneau; 85 sisters; 11 novices; 2 teachers; 36 Catholic female pupils; 12 Catholic male pupils; 48 Catholic female employees; 28 Catholic male employees; 2 chaplains; 1 resident physician; 1 student. Nationalities of inmates: 1 Hollander; 1 Scotch; 1 American; 2 French; 1 Indian; 1 Negro; 1 Swiss; 1 Belgian; 109 Catholic Fr. Canadians; 4 Catholic French; 5 Catholic English; 1 Protestant English; 35 Catholic Irish; 21 Catholic Irish b in C; 6 Catholic Americans; 1 Protestant American; 1 Catholic German; 1 German Jew. This Institution is maintained by the rents of houses and lands bequeathed to the Order. Pine av.

Hospital Général (or Grey Nunnery), Mother House of the Order of Grey Nuns. Originally built of stone in

1634, on Foundling street, by the Rev. Charron Brothers and received its title under Letters Patent from His Majesty Louis XIV. The Charron Institution was afterwards transferred to the Sisters of Charity, Grey Nuns, an order founded in 1738, by Madame Marie Marguerite Dufrost de la Jemmerais (widow of M. Francis d'Youville), the first Lady Superioress, on the 7th October, 1747, and sanctioned on the 3rd of June, 1754, under its primitive title of "General Hospital of Montreal," by Letters Patent, under the seal and signature of His Majesty Lo in XV. It was twice destroyed by fire in the years 1755 and 1765, and rebuilt of stone. It was used for upwards of 160 years as an asylum for the sick, maimed, infirm, aged, insane, foundlings, and desolate of all ages and sexes. In 1869, it was found necessary to secure a more desirable loca ity. The same Reverend Ladies erected (in 1870) a spacious building on Guy cor Dorchester street, to be used for the same objects as was the building in 1747, except for the insane. The present hospital has over 320 rooms, and is now under the direction and management of the Reverend Mother Praxède Filiatrault, the present Lady Mother Superioress General of the Order ; 1 assistant Lady Superioresses ; 1 Mistress and 2 Sub-Mistresses of Novices, Directresses, Sub-Directress of Wards, Ateliers, Workrooms, Laundries, Kitchens, etc., 105 professed nuns; 92 novices; 77 female employees; 13 male employees; 66 infirm and aged men ; 116 aged and infirm women ; 67orphan boys ; 40 orphan girls ; 17 fo indling boys ; 25 foundling girls ; 16 male babies in the crib; 10 female babies in the crib. Nationalities: 698 Fr. Canadians; 23 Irish; 7 Americans; 3 French; 2 English ; 1 German ; 1 Belgian. This institution is maintained by : 1st, the rents of houses and lands belonging to the Order; 2nd, an annual grant of $2,340 from the Quebec Government; 3rd, the united industries of the Sisterhood; 4th, the alms and donations of visitors and other charitable persons. Governing Body : Reverend Lady Mother Superioress and her Council. 392 Guy cor Dorchester st.

Notre Dame Hospital, built of stone and founded in 1880, by the citizens of Montreal, for the relief of sick and maimed. First and present lady superioress Reverend Sister Perrin ; 16 sisters ; 24 female employees ; 13 male employees. 1492 Notre Dame st.

Hospice de la Maternité de Montréal, built of stone in 1885, founded in 1845, under the direction of the Reverend Sisters of Mercy. First lady directress Reverend Mother St. Jean de Chantal. Second lady directress Reverend Mother Marie du Sacré Cœur ; 5 visiting physicians ; 1 resident chaplain ; 19 reverend sister nurses ; 75 patients ; 24 female infants ; 19 male infants ; 134 inmates. Nationalities : 87 Catholic Fr. Canadian females; 8 Catholic English females ; 16 Catholic Irish females ; 2 Catholic American females, 3 Protestant English fem'les ; 13 Catholic Fr. Canadian males ; 4 Catholic Irish males b in C ; 2 Catholic English males b in C. 326 Dorchester st.

CATHOLIC MEDICAL DISPENSARIES.

There are two CATHOLIC MEDICAL DISPENSARIES in Montreal. January, 1891.

Pharmacie de l'Hôpital Général, built of stone, and founded in 1694, by the Ladies of the Grey Nunnery, for the dispensing of medicines and cordials to the inmates of l'Hôpital Général. In this Institution one of the Reverend Ladies is a practical dentist, by whom the teeth of the inmates are carefully and scientifically attended to. 5 Catholic female employees. 390 Guy cor Dorchester st.

St Joseph's Dispensary, built of stone ; founded in 1864, by the Reverend Gentlemen of the Seminary of St Sulpice, for the dispensing of medicines and cordials to the poor, without distinction of nationality, sex or creed. It is under the charge of Reverend Ladies of the Grey Nunnery ; 2 Catholic female employees. 56 Cathedral st.

CATHOLIC BENEVOLENT INSTITUTIONS.

There are thirteen CATHOLIC BENEVOLENT INSTITUTIONS in Montreal. January, 1891.

Nazareth Asylum and Institute for the Blind, built in 1860 by the Rev. V. Rousselot, P.S.S. First superioress Rev. Sister Marie Louise Christia. The Chapel and Home for the blind were built in 1869 by the Rev. V. Rousselot, P.S.S. First Chaplain Rev. F. Martineau, P.S.S.; present chaplain Rev. H. Bedard ; first and present superioress Reverend Sister M. H. Robin ; 18 sisters ; 46 Catholic blind females ; 28 Catholic blind boys ; 17 Catholic female employees ; 2 Catholic male employees ;

1 Catholic aged male ; 3 Catholic male students ; 8 Catholic females. Nationalities : 123 Catholic French Canadians. 2023 St Catherine st.

St Joseph's Infant School, in connection with Saint Joseph's Asylum, built of stone ; founded in 1853 by Rev. Victor Rousselot, P.S.S. It is managed by the Reverend Ladies of the Grey Nunnery. It has 4 sister teachers ; 3 Catholic female employees; 200 pupils ; 130 Catholic Fr. Canadian fem les; 70 Catholic Fr. C inadian males : Nationalities of inmates : 130 Catholic Fr. Canadian females ; 70 Catholic Fr. Canadian males. 541 St James cor Cathedral st.

St Patrick's Orphan Asylum, built of stone in 1841 ; founded in 1849, by Rev. Patrick Dowd, P.S.S., opened in 1851, for orphan girls and boys. It is under the management of the Reverend Sisters of Charity of the Grey Nunnery ; 9 sisters ; 20 Catholic female employees ; 2 Catholic Fr. Canadian m ale employees ; 67 Catholic orphan girls ; 1 Protestant orphan girl ; 82 Catholic orphan boys ; 1 Protestant orphan boy. Nationalities of inmates : 28 Irish ; 113 Irish b in C.; 13 English ; 12 Irish American ; 9 French Canadian ; 1 Scotch. Dorchester st bet St Alexander st and Beaver Hall hill.

Noviltal des Frères de St Gabriel, built of brick ; founded in 1870, by the Rev. Brothers of the Order of St Gabriel, for instructing and educating young children. First and present superior Rev. Brother Louis Bertrand ; 3 brothers ; 1 novice ; 1 postulant ; 6 inmates. Nationalities of inmates : 5 Catholic French ; 1 Catholic American. 1961 St Catherine st.

Institution des Sourdes Muettes, built of stone and founded in 1851 ; founded by the Reverend Sisters of Providence. Present lady superioress Reverend Sister St Charles de la Providence ; 43 nuns; 8 lay sisters ; 18 Catholic lady inmates ; 235 Catholic Fr. Canadian female mutes ; 6 Catholic Fr. Canadian female employees ; 8 Catholic Fr. Canadian male employees ; 2 chaplains, Rev. F. X. Trépanier and Rev. F. Reid. 401 St Denis st.

St Bridget's Home, built of stone in 1860 ; founded by Reverend Patrick Dowd, P.S.S., for aged and infirm women and men, for servant girls out of place ; also as a night refuge. It is under the direction of the Reverend Ladies of the Grey Nunnery ; Reverend Sister St James, lady superioress It has 8 sisters ; 12 Catholic female employees ; 41 Catholic aged women ; 27 Catholic aged men ; 11 Catholic servant girls out of place. Nationalities of inmates : 53 Irish. Lagauchetière n St Patrick's Church.

St Joseph's Asylum, built of stone ; founded in 1853, by Olivier Berthelet and Alfred LaRocque, for the reception of orphan girls and boys. It is under the direction of the Reverend Ladies of the Grey Nunnery ; 17 sisters ; 2 novices ; 1 visiting physician ; 85 Catholic orphan girls ; 3 Catholic orphan boys ; 5 aged Catholic infirm women; 28 Catholic female assistants ; 2 Catholic male employees. Nationalities of inmates : 140 Fr. Canadians ; 1 English and 1 Irish. 60 Cathedral st, bet St James and St Antoine sts.

Catholic Orphan Asylum, built of stone ; founded in 1832, by Madame Cotté, for training and educating Catholic orphan boys. It is under the direction of the Ladies of the Grey Nunnery. First Lady Superioress Madame Cotté ; present Lady Superioress Reverend Sister Turgeon ; 3 nuns ; 3 Catholic female employees ; 56 Catholic orphan boys ; 63 inmates. Nationalities of inmates : 62 Fr. Canadians ; 1 English. 2049 St Catherine st.

Hospice St Charles, built of brick in 1879 ; founded in 1877 by Rev. R. Rousseau, P. S. S., for the care of aged and infirm poor of both sexes. First lady superioress Reverend Sister Ste Croix ; present lady superioress Reverend Sister Labelle ; 8 sister ; 9 female emyloyees ; 2 male employees ; 70 Catholic males ; 100 Catholic females. Nationalities : 170 Fr. Canadians ; 1 English ; 20 Irish ; 5 Irish b in C ; 1 French ; 1 American ; 1 German. 1416 Notre Dame st.

Bethlehem Asylum, built of stone ; founded in 1868, by the Hon. Charles S. Rodier as an asylum for destitute young orphan children. It is under the care and direction of the Reverend Ladies of the Grey Nunnery. First lady superioress Reverend Sister Painchaud ; present lady superioress Reverend Sister St. Louis ; 8 Sisters ; 18 Catholic female employees ; 1 Catholic male employee ; 66 Catholic female orphans ; 7 Catholic male orphans. 1, 2 and 3 Richmond sq.

Orphelinat Industriel St François Xavier, built of stone ; founded in 1889 by the estate of the late F. X. Beaudry ; for the maintenance and education of Catholic orphan boys, directed by the Frères of St Gabriel. First and present Superior Rev. Brother Louis Bertrand ; 4 Catholic brother teachers ; 2 Catholic male employees ; 50 Catholic male orphans ; 57 inmates. 1961 StCatherine st.

Refuge de la Passion, built of stone ; founded in 1870, by the Sisters of Notre Dame de Lourdes, as a Refuge for friendless girls and servant girls out of place. Lady Directress Sister Sarah Octavie ; 2 sisters ; 6 servant girls out of place ; 2 Catholic female employees ; 1 Catholic male employee ; 12 inmates. Nationality of inmates : 11 Fr. Canadian females ; 1 Fr. Canadian male. Cor Lagauchetière and St Urbain st.

Home for the Aged of the Little Sisters of the Poor, founded in 1886, by Rev. F. Catulle, for aged women and men ; 8 sisters ; 2 novices ; 4 Catholic Fr. Canadian employees ; 78 inmates ; 48 Catholic Fr. Canadian women ; 30 Catholic Fr. Canadian men. 109 Forfar st.

CATHOLIC CHARITABLE SOCIETIES.

There are nine CATHOLIC CHARITABLE SOCIETIES in Montreal. January, 1891.

Living Rosary Confraternity, established in 1847. First director Rev. Patrick Dowd, P.S.S. ; present director Rev. James Callaghan, P.S.S. St Patrick's Church, cor Lagauchetière and St Alexander sts.

Leo Club, founded in 1884, by the Rev. James Callaghan, P.S.S. First president E. Leduc ; present president J. Brophy ; St Patrick's Parish Hall, 92 St Alexander st.

Society of Ladies of Charity of St Patrick's Congregation ; founded by Reverend Patrick Dowd, P.S.S., for providing clothing to poor children attending school. Present director Rev. J. A. McCallen, P.S.S. 92 St Alexander st.

Association des Enfants de Marie, founded in 1852, by the Reverend Sisters of the Congregation of Notre Dame, for religious instruction and benevolence, under the direction of the Sisters of the Congregation and a committee of ladies. 40 St Jean Baptiste st.

Bethlem Infant School, built of stone ; founded in 1868 as a school for infant children by Hon. Charles S. Rodier. It is under the direction of the Reverend Ladies of the Grey Nunnery. First lady superioress Reverend Sister St Louis ; 3 reverend sisters teachers ; 3 Catholic female teachers ; 120 Catholic female infant pupils ; 180 Catholic male infant pupils ; 3 Catholic female employees. 444 Richmond st.

Association des Enfants de Marie, Externat des Dames du Sacré Cœur; founded in 1842, by the Ladies of the Sacred Heart, for religious instruction and benevolence, under the direction of the Ladies of the Sacred Heart, and a committee of ladies. 2084 St Catherine st cor Bleury st.

Union St Joseph, built of stone ; founded in 1851 by Louis Leclaire ; incorporated in 1856, for benevolent purposes. Honorary chaplain Mgr. E. C. Fabre, Archbishop of Montreal ; Rev. J. M. Emard, chaplain. 1796 St Catherine st.

Union St Pierre, built of stone ; founded in 1859 ; incorporated in 1862, for benevolent purposes. Rev. Abbé P. N. Bruchesi, chaplain ; Joseph Contant, president ; A. Gosselin, treasurer. 1796 St Catherine st.

Union of Prayers and of Good Works ; founded in 1850 by Rev. E. Picard, to obtain a happy death and funeral service. Office at Seminary of St Sulpice, 1710 Notre-Dame st.

CATHOLIC COLLEGES.

There are four CATHOLIC COLLEGES in Montreal. January, 1891.

Grand Séminaire, built of stone, in 1857, by the Gentlemen of the Seminary of St Sulpice, for the education of young men for the clerical profession. First director Rev. P. Billodeau ; present director Rev. Charles LeCoq ; Rev. J. D. Bray, bursar. There are two communities in the building, under one director : one of theology and one of philosophy ; 9 Catholic professors of theology ; 4 Catholic professors of philosophy ; 133 Catholic theological students ; 85 Catholic students of philosophy ; 22 Catholic male employers ; 240 inmates. Nationalities : 118 Catholic Fr. Canadian males ; 100 Catholic Irish males ; 1 Catholic English male ; 10 Catholic Scotch males ; 1 Catholic French male ; 9 Catholic German males ; 1 Catholic Bohemian male. 1197 Sherbrooke st.

Montreal College.—First Sulpitian College was started at Longue Pointe, in 1737, with the Rev. T. B. Curateau as director, and under the name of *St. Raphael's College*. Having been destroyed by fire, it was rebuilt in this city, on College street ; opened in 1806 with the Rev. Jacques Roque as director. In 1870 the community was trans-

lated to the new college, built of stone, on Sherbrooke street, and adjoining the Grand Séminaire on the brow of the mountain, under the name of the Montreal College.

Montreal College, built of stone, in 1870, by the Gentlemen of the Seminary of St Sulpice, for the education of young men for the medical and legal profession, and for mercantile pursuits. First director Rev. Charles Lenoir ; present director Rev. F. Lelandais ; Rev. H. Dupret, bursar ; 22 Catholic professors ; 300 Catholic students ; 10 Catholic female employees ; 23 Catholic male employees ; 333 Catholic inmates. Nationalities : 10 Catholic Fr. Canadian females ; 223 Catholic Fr. Canadian males ; 100 Catholic Irish males. 1181 Sherbrooke st.

St Mary's or Jesuits' College, built of stone in 1850. First principal Rev. Felix Martin, S. J. ; present principal Rev. Lewis Drummond, S. J. ; 26 Catholic male professors ; 446 Catholic male pupils ; 41 male employees. Nationalities of inmates : 412 Fr. Canadian ; 67 Irish b in C ; 10 English b in C ; 12 Scotch b in C ; 14 Americans ; 12 French ; 2 Belgians ; 2 English ; 1 Irish ; 2 Germans. 142 Bleury st.

CATHOLIC ACADEMIES.

There are thirty-six CATHOLIC ACADEMIES in Montreal. January, 1891.

CATHOLIC ACADEMIES.

Archbishop's Academy, built of brick ; in 1873 ; founded in 1873, for the higher education of young men, under the direction of the Rev. Brothers of the Christian Schools. First principal Rev. Brother Servillian ; present principal Rev. Brother Marcellian ; 7 rev. brother teachers ; 240 Catholic male pupils ; 1 Fr. Canadian Catholic male employee. Nationalities of inmates : 6 Catholic Fr. Canadian males ; 1 Catholic Irish male ; 1 Catholic Irish male b in C. 35 St Margaret st.

St Gabriel Academy for boys, built of stone. It is under the direction of the Reverend Brothers of the Christian Schools. First director Rev. Brother Andaine ; present director Rev. Brother Theodulph ; 7 reverend brother teachers ; 2 secular teachers ; 3 Catholic male employees ; 412 Catholic male pupils. Nationalities : 6 Catholic Fr. Canadian males ; 2 Catholic French males ; 2 Catholic Irish males. 350 Centre st.

Academie St Denis, built of stone ; and established by the Reverend Sisters of the Congregation of Notre Dame, as a school for girls. First lady superioress Reverend Mother St Gabriel ; present lady superioress Reverend Mother Aglaé ; 18 reverend sister nuns ; 300 Catholic female pupils. Nationalities of inmates : 23 Catholic Fr. Canadian females ; 5 Catholic Irish females ; 1 Catholic Fr. Canadian male. 37 St Denis st.

Academie St Antoine, built of brick ; founded in 1857, by the Ladies of the Congregation of Notre Dame, for the higher education of young girls. First Lady Superioress Reverend Sister St Michael ; present Lady Superioress Reverend Sister Ste Marguerite-Marie ; 10 Reverend Sister teachers ; 99 Catholic Fr. Canadian female pupils ; 5 Protestant female pupils ; 2 Catholic Fr. Canadian female employees ; 1 Catholic Fr. Canadian male employee. Nationalities of inmates : 9 Catholic Fr. Canadian females ; 1 Catholic Fr. Canadian male ; 3 Protestant English females b in C. ; 1 Protestant German female b in C. 854 Lagauchetière st.

St Patrick's Academy, built of stone ; established in 1890, by the Rev. Patrick Dowd, P.S.S. It is under the direction of the Reverend Ladies of the Congregation of Notre Dame, for the education of girls ; superioress Rev. Mother St Aloysius ; 12 reverend sister teachers ; 2 Catholic female secular teachers ; 3 Catholic female employees ; 1 Catholic male employee ; 400 Catholic female day pupils ; 3 Catholic boarding pupils. Nationalities of inmates : 4 Catholic Fr. Canadian females ; 2 Catholic Irish females ; 11 Catholic Irish females b in C ; 3 Catholic English females b in C. 79 St Alexander st.

Visitation Academy, built of stone ; founded in 1833, by the Gentlemen of the Seminary of St. Sulpice, as a school for girls. It is under the direction of the Ladies of the Congregation of Notre Dame. First Lady Superioress Reverend Sister Ste Barbe ; present Lady Superioress Reverend Sister Ste Olive ; 12 sisters ; 4 novices ; 17 Catholic Fr. Canadian female teachers ; 828 Catholic Fr. Canadian female pupils ; 2 Catholic Fr. Canadian female employees ; 1 Catholic Fr. Canadian male employee. Nationalities of inmates : 17 Catholic Fr. Canadian females ; 1 Catholic Fr. Canadian male ; 2 Catholic Irish females b in C. 179 Craig st.

Académie St Ignace, built of stone; founded in 1871, by the Reverend Mère Marie de St Alphonse, to educate young girls. First Reverend Mère Supérieure Sœur de St Henri; present Reverend Mère Supérieure M. de St Charles Borromée; 4 nuns; 2 novices; 1 Catholic Fr. Canadian male employee; 3 boarders; 100 pupils. Nationalities of inmates: 109 Catholic Fr. Canadian females; 1 Catholic Fr. Canadian male. 91 St Hubert st.

Academy, built of stone; established in 1869 as a school for young ladies; conducted by Madame Marchand; 10 Catholic Fr. Canadian female teachers; 293 Catholic Fr. Canadian female pupils; 4 Protestant female pupils; 4 Catholic female employees; 1 Catholic male employee. Nationalities of inmates: 5 Catholic Fr. Canadian females; 1 Catholic Fr. Canadian male. 62 St Hubert st.

Académie du Sacré Cœur, built of stone; founded in 1858, by the Catholic Board of School Commissioners, as a school for boys, under the direction of the Rev. Brothers of the Christian Brothers Schools. First director Rev. Brother Austin; present director Rev. Brother Louis; 4 Catholic Fr. Canadian female teachers; 8 Catholic Fr. Canadian male teachers; 860 Catholic Fr. Canadian male pupils; 2 Catholic Fr. Canadian male employees. Plessis st and 380 Maisonneuve st.

Leduc's Academy, built of stone; founded in 1886 as a commercial school for ladies and gentlemen. First and present principal Zotique Leduc; 1 Catholic female teacher; 1 Catholic male teacher; 3 Catholic female pupils; 2 Protestant female pupils; 2 Catholic male pupils; 4 Protestant male pupils. Nationalities of inmates: 5 Catholic Fr. Canadian females; 1 Catholic Fr. Canadian male. 85 St Constant st.

Académie Ste Marie, built of brick; established in 1881, as a model school for girls and young boys, under the supervision of the Catholic Board of School Commissioners. First and present principal Miss Ida Labelle; 6 Catholic Fr. Canadian female teachers; 123 Catholic Fr. Canadian female pupils; 57 Catholic Fr. Canadian male pupils. Nationalities of inmates: 6 Catholic Fr. Canadian females; 4 Catholic Fr. Canadian males. 174 Amherst st.

Miss Cronin's English, French and Music Academy, built of stone; established in 1862, under the control of the Catholic School Commissioners. First and present principal Miss Anna Louisa Cronin; 3 Catholic Fr. Canadian male teachers; 47 Catholic Fr. Canadian female pupils; 61 Protestant female pupils; 38 Catholic Fr. Canadian male pupils; 1 Catholic Irish female employee. 1428 Notre Dame.

Académie Commerciale Catholique de Montréal, built of stone in 1871. First and present principal U. E. Archambault; 15 professors; 500 scholars; 4 Catholic Fr. Canadian employees. Nationalities of professors: 9 Catholic Fr. Canadian; 2 Catholic French; 3 Protestant English; 1 Catholic Irish. Plateau av, 399 St Catherine st.

Académie St Jean Baptiste, built of stone in 1884; founded by Rev. Magloire Auclair, as a commercial school for boys. It is under the direction of the Clercs of St Viateur. First and present superior Rev. Frère J. A. Desjardins; 14 brother teachers; 21 Catholic pupils as boarders; 913 pupils as day scholars; 4 Catholic employees; 40 inmates. Nationalities: 40 Fr. Canadians. 776 Sanguinet st.

Académie St Joseph, built of brick in 1882, by the Catholic School Commissioners, as a day school for boys. First director Rev. Z. N. Blais, C.S.C.; present director Rev. Brother J. Everiste, C.S.C.; 8 brother teachers; 447 Catholic male pupils; 2 Catholic female employees; 2 Catholic male employees; 36 inmates. Nationalities: 36 Fr. Canadians. 265 Dorey st.

Académie Ste Angèle, built of stone in 1888; founded by the Reverend Sisters of St Anne, as a boarding and day school for young ladies. First and present lady superioress Reverend Sister Marie Pacifique; 21 reverend sisters teachers; 96 Catholic female boarding pupils; 1 Protestant female boarding pupil; 70 Catholic female day pupils; 1 Protestant female day pupil; 4 Catholic female employees; 1 Catholic male employee. Nationalities of inmates: 112 Catholic Fr. Canadian pupils; 5 Catholic American pupils; 5 Catholic Irish pupils b in C; 1 Protestant English pupil. 466 St Antoine st.

Académie St Urbain, built of stone; founded by the Reverend Ladies of the Congregation of Notre Dame, in 1890, as a ladies' school. It is self supporting. First lady superioress Reverend Sister St Nativity of Jesus; present lady superioress Reverend Sister St Honoré; 8 nuns; 1 novice; 1 lay nun; 80 female pupils; 2 Catholic female employees. Nationality: 83 Fr. Canadians. 43 St Urbain st.

Académie St Anne, built of stone, founded in 1857 under the direction of Rev. Ladies of the Congregation of Notre

Dame of Montreal as a school for girls. First lady superioress Reverend Sister St. Agnes; present lady superioress Reverend Sister St. Alphonsus of Liguori; 10 nuns; 350 Catholic female pupils; 2 Catholic female employees; 1 Catholic male employee; 14 Catholic inmates. Nationalities: 2 Catholic Fr. Canadian females; 9 Catholic Irish Canadian females; 2 Catholic English Canadian females; 1 Catholic American female. 102 McCord st.

Académie St Joseph Convent, built of stone; founded in 1867 by Rev. Ladies of the Congregation of Notre Dame, as a high school for girls. It is supported by a small government grant and the industries of the sisterhood. First lady superioress Rev. Sister St. Calixte; present lady superioress Rev. Sister St. Mary of the Crucifix; 11 sisters; 6 novices; 2 Catholic female employees; 1 Catholic male employee; 680 Catholic female pupils; 20 Catholic inmates. Nationalities: 17 Catholic Fr. Canadian females; 2 Catholic Irish females; 1 Catholic French Canadian male. 2353 Notre Dame st.

Académie de St Louis de Gonzague, built in 1879; founded by Reverend Ladies of Charity of the Good Shepherd as a boarding and day school for girls. First lady superioress Reverend Sister St. Francis de Sales; present lady superioress Reverend Sister St. Francis de Borgia; 30 nuns; 8 Catholic female employees; 1 Catholic male employee; 99 Catholic female pupil boarders; 1 Protestant female pupil boarder; 80 Catholic female day pupils; 239 Catholic female inmates; 1 Protestant female inmate. Nationalities of inmates: 109 Catholic Fr. Canadian females; 23 Catholic English females; 6 Catholic American females; 1 Protestant English female; 1 Catholic Fr. Canadian male. 405 Sherbrooke st.

Académie St Urbain, built of stone; established in 1890 by Reverend Ladies of the Congregation of Notre Dame. First lady superioress Rev. Sister of the Nativity of Jesus; present lady superioress Rev. Sister St. Honoré; 8 rev. sister teachers; 1 novice; 1 lay sister; 80 Catholic female pupils; 4 Protestant female pupils; 2 Catholic female employees; 1 Catholic male employee. Nationalities: 22 Catholic Fr. Canadian females; 1 Catholic Fr. Canadian male. 43 St Urbain st.

Académie Bourgeois, built of brick in 1877, by the Reverend Ladies of the Congregation of Notre Dame, as a day school for young girls. First lady superioress Reverend Sister St Athanase; present lady superioress Reverend Sister St Dosithée; 13 reverend sister teachers; 2 novices; 963 Catholic Fr. Canadian female pupils; 2 Catholic Fr. Canadian female employees. Nationalities of inmates: 22 Catholic Fr. Canadians; 1 Protestant English female b in C. 1051 Ontario st.

Académie St Léon, built of stone; founded in 1885, by the Reverend Ladies of the Congregation of Notre Dame, for higher education of girls. First lady directress Reverend Sister St Alix; present lady directress Reverend Sister St Gustave; 10 reverend sister teachers; 1 novice; 188 Catholic Fr. Canadian female pupils; 2 Protestant female pupils; 2 Catholic Fr. Canadian female employees; 2 Catholic Fr. Canadian male employees. Nationalities of female inmates: 15 Catholic Fr. Canadian. 115 Cadieux st.

Académie Marie Rose, built of stone in 1876; founded by Reverend Sisters of the Holy Names of Jesus and Mary, for the higher education of young girls. First lady superioress Reverend Sister Marie Ste Apollonie; present lady superioress Reverend Sister Ste Félicité; 23 sisters; 4 lay sisters; 60 Catholic Fr. Canadian female boarders; 176 Catholic Fr. Canadian female pupils; 2 Catholic Fr. Canadian female employees; 1 Catholic Fr. Canadian male employee. Nationalities of inmates: 1 Catholic Fr. Canadian male; 3 Catholic Irish females b in C; 85 Catholic Fr. Canadian females. 390 Rachel st.

Académie St Edouard, built of brick; founded in 1885, by the Reverend Sisters of the Holy Cross, as a school for young girls. First and present lady superioress Reverend Sister Marie St Dorothy; 8 sisters; 357 Catholic Fr. Canadian female pupils. Nationalities of inmates: 11 Catholic Fr. Canadian females; 4 Protestant English females. 105 Maisonneuve st.

Académie Ville Marie, built of brick; opened in 1887, as a mixed school. First and present lady superintendent Mme Eliza Desivières; 1 Catholic female teacher; 14 Catholic female pupils; 14 Catholic male pupils. 1685 St Denis st.

Academy for Young Children, built of brick; opened in 1884, by the first and present principal, Miss McKay; 4 Catholic female teachers; 46 Catholic female pupils; 3 Protestant female pupils; 46 Catholic male pupils; 2 Protestant male pupils; 4 Jewish female pupils; 2 Jewish male pupils.

Nationalities of inmates : 1 Irish Catholic ; 4 Irish Catholics b in C ; 1 Catholic Belgian male b in C. 58 German st.

Academy for Young Girls and Boys, built of brick ; established in 1883. First and present lady principal Mme Marie Louise Gravel ; 2 Catholic Fr. Canadian female teachers ; 35 Catholic Fr. Canadian female pupils ; 28 Fr. Canadian male pupils ; 2 Protestant male pupils ; 1 Jewish male pupil ; 4 inmates ; 2 Catholic Fr. Canadian females ; 1 Catholic Fr. Canadian female employee ; 1 Catholic Fr. Canadian male employee. Nationalities of inmates : 3 Catholic Fr. Canadian females ; 1 Catholic Fr. Canadian male. 220 St Christophe st.

Couvent St Edouard Académie, foun ed in 1885 by the Reverend Ladies of the Holy Cross, for the higher education of girls. First and present lady superioress Reverend Sister Marie St Dorothy ; 9 sisters : 9 Catholic Fr. Canadian females. 103 Maisonneuve st.

Couvent Marie Rose Académie, built of stone in 1876 ; founded by the Reverend Sisters of the Holy Names of Jesus and Mary, for the higher education of young girls. First lady superioress Reverend Sister Marie St Apollonie ; present lady superioress Reverend Sister Ste Félicité ; 23 nuns ; 2 lay sisters ; 2 Catholic Fr. Canadian female employees. Nationalities of inmates : 27 Catholic Fr. Canadian females. 392 Rachel st.

Pensionnat Ste Catherine Académie, built of stone in 1879 ; founded by Reverend Ladies of the Congregation of Notre Dame, as a boarding school for young girls. Self-supporting. First lady superioress Reverend Sister Ste Dorothy ; present lady superioress Reverend Sister St Barthe'emy ; 16 nuns ; 2 Catholic fe male employees ; 1 Catholic Fr. Canadian male employee. Nationalities of inmates : 21 Catholic Fr. Canadians. 754 St Catherine st.

Mrs. Viger's Academy, built of brick ; established in 1873, as a day school for young children. First and present lady principal Mme. Maria Viger ; 2 Catholic Fr. Canadian female teachers ; 25 Catholic Fr. Canadian female pupils ; 30 Catholic Fr. Canadian male pupils ; 8 inmates ; 7 Catholic Fr. Canadian females ; 1 Catholic Fr. Canadian male. Nationalities of inmates : 1 Catholic Italian female ; 6 Catholic Fr. Canadian females ; 1 Catholic Fr. Canadian male. 87 St Christophe st.

Ladies Academy, built of brick ; established 1870. First and present principal Miss Phelonise Thibadeau ; 4 Catholic female teachers ; 110 Catholic female pupils. Nation dities of inmates : 4 Catholic Fr. Canadian females. 158 Cadieux or Roy.

French and English Academy, built of brick ; established in 1875 as a day school for young ladies. First and present principal Mademoiselle Eleanor Thibolear ; 4 Catholic female teachers ; 220 Catholic female pupils. 137 Chatham st.

Mrs. Mair's Academy, built of stone, opened in 1886, on St Antoine st, as a day school for young children. First and present principal Mrs. A. B. Mair ; 18 Protestant female pupils ; 12 Protestant male pupils ; 3 Protestant English female inmates. 151 Lusignan n St Antoine st.

Misses O'Brien & Rapetti's English and French Academy, built of stone ; established 1887. First principal Mrs. Cornwall ; present principals Miss Leonora T. O'Brien and Seraphina Rapetti ; 20 Catholic girls ; 2 Catholic boys ; 1 Protestant boy pupil ; 2 Catholic female inmates. Nationalities : 1 Catholic American Italian female ; 1 Catholic Spanish female. 272 St Antoine st n Guy st.

CATHOLIC SCHOOLS.

There are thirty-one CATHOLIC SCHOOLS in Montreal. January, 1891.

St Patrick's School, built of stone ; established in 1849, by the Gentlemen of the Seminary of St. Sulpice as a boy-school. First director Rev. Brother Adelbertus ; present director Rev. Brother Ulric ; 6 reverend brother teachers ; 350 Catholic male pupils. Nationalities of inmates : 24 reverend brothers,—13 Catholic Fr. Canadians ; 6 Irish b in C ; 2 Americans ; 1 Catholic Fr. Canadian male employee. 50 Cotté st.

St Ann's School, built of stone ; established in 1863. It is under the control of the Rev. Brothers of the Christian Schools. First director Rev. Brother Servilian ; present director Rev. Brother Arnold ; 11 reverend brother teachers ; 2 Catholic male employees ; 600 Catholic male pupils. Nationalities of inmates : 3 Catholic Fr. Canadian males ; 10 Catholic Irish males. 113 Young st.

St Lawrence School, built of stone ; established in 1837, by the Gentlemen of the Seminary of St Sulpice. It is under the direction of the Brothers of the Christian Schools. First director Rev. Brother Aidant ; present director Rev. Brother Ultric ; visitor Rev. Brother Flamian ; assistant visitor Rev. Brother Alphonsus ; procurator Rev. Brother Probotus ; 7 reverend brother teachers ; 2 male lay teachers ; 2 Catholic male employees ; 500 Catholic male pupils. 50 Cotté st.

St Jacques School, built of stone ; established in 1850, by the Gentlemen of the Seminary of St Sulpice ; directed by the Reverend Brothers of the Christian Schools. Principal Rev. Brother Richarius ; 8 resident brother teachers ; 1 Catholic male employee ; 1 Catholic female employee ; 405 Catholic male pupils. 117 St Denis st.

St Bridget's School, built of brick ; established in 1845. It is under the control of the Catholic Board of School Commissioners, directed by the Rev. Brothers of the Christian Schools. First director Rev. Brother Aidian ; present director Rev. Brother André ; 12 reverend brother teachers ; 2 Catholic male employees ; 800 Catholic male pupils. Nationalities of inmates : 10 Fr. Canadian Catholic males ; 2 Irish Catholic males ; 1 Catholic Irish male b in C. 133 Dorchester st.

Champlain School, built in 1870 ; and rebuilt of stone in 1890, by the Catholic Board of School Commissioners as a school for boys. First principal R. Martineau ; present principal H. O. Dore ; 13 Catholic male teachers ; 655 Catholic male pupils ; 2 Protestant male pupils ; 1 Catholic male employee ; 6 inmates. Nationalities : 3 Catholic Fr. Canadian females ; 3 Catholic Fr. Canadian males. 172 Fullum st.

Belmont School, built of stone and founded in 1877 by the Catholic Board of School Commissioners, as a commercial school for boys. First and present principal P. L. O'Donoughue ; 9 Catholic male teachers ; 361 Catholic and 4 Protestant male scholars ; 2 employees. Nationalities : 1 Catholic Fr. Canadian male ; 1 Catholic Fr. Canadian female. 245 Guy st.

Olier School, built of stone and founded in 1877 by the Catholic Board of School Commissioners, as a Commercial school for boys. First and present principal Louis Antoine Primeau ; 10 Catholic male teachers ; 1 Catholic male employee ; 424 Catholic male pupils ; 6 Protestant male pupils. Nationalities : 4 Catholic Fr. Canadian females ; 2 Catholic Fr. Canadian males ; 6 inmates. 24 Roy st.

Sarsfield School, built of stone ; founded in 1890 by the Catholic Board of School Commissioners, as a Commercial school for boys. First principal H. C. O'Donoghue ; present principal J. T. Anderson ; 9 Catholic male teachers ; 443 Catholic male pupils ; 37 Protestant male pupils ; 1 Catholic male employee. Nationalities : 3 Catholic Fr. Canadian females ; 3 Catholic Fr. Canadian males ; 6 inmates. Cor of Grand Trunk and Centre sts.

Sarsfield School Evening Classes, under the control of Montreal Night School Committee. Established in 1889 for evening instruction of working men and boys. First and present principal Mr. J. T. Anderson ; 13 Catholic male teachers ; 2 Protestant male teachers ; total number of pupils 467. 97 Grand Trunk st.

School of the Immaculate Conception, built of brick in 1886, by the Jesuit Fathers. The girls are under the direction of three sisters of the Holy Names of Jesus and Mary ; Reverend Sister Marie Cornélie, superioress ; 2 sisters ; 1 lay teacher ; the boys are under the direction of 4 Lamennaipian brothers, Rev. Brother Norbert, director ; 3 brothers ; 30 Catholic male pupils ; 207 Catholic female pupils. Cor Papineau road and Rachel st.

Pensionnat de la Congregation de Notre Dame, built of stone in 1887, founded by Rev. Ladies of the Congregation of Notre Dame as a day and boarding school for girls. First lady superioress Rev. Sister St Dorothy ; present lady superioress Rev. Sister St. Barthelemy ; 16 rev. sister teachers ; 4 Catholic female employees ; 1 Catholic male employee ; 700 Catholic female pupils ; 127 Catholic inmates. Nationalities : 99 Catholic Fr. Canadian females ; 1 Catholic Fr. Canadian male ; 24 Catholic Irish Canadian females ; 3 Catholic English Canadian females. 754 St Catherine st.

St Lawrence School, built of brick in 1850. It is under the direction of the Ladies of the Congregation of Notre Dame, as a school for girls. Lady superioress Reverend Sister Ste Odile ; 6 sisters ; 2 novices ; 250 Catholic Fr. Canadian female pupils ; 49 Irish Catholic female pupils in C. 1966 St Catherine st.

Montcalm School, founded in 1860, by the Catholic Board of School Commissioners. First principal Frs. Xavier Desplaines; present principal A. D. Lacroix; 9 Catholic Fr. Canadian teachers; 433 Catholic male pupils; 4 Protestant male pupils; 3 Jew male pupils; 1 Catholic employee. Nationalities of inmates: 2 Catholic Fr. Canadian females; 2 Catholic Fr. Canadian males; 1 Protestant American male; 1 Protestant Scotch male. 184 and 186 Craig st and 20 Montcalm st.

St Jean Baptiste Parochial School, built of stone in 1876; conducted by the Reverend Sisters of the Holy Names of Jesus and Mary. First and present directress Reverend Sister Ste Félicité; 7 sister teachers; 367 Catholic female pupils. 392 Rachel st.

Ecole St Pierre, built of stone in 1887, as an educational establishment for boys; conducted by Les Frères Maristes. First and present principal Rev. Brother Surius; 12 brother teachers; 350 Catholic Fr. Canadian male pupils. It is a self-supporting establishment, receiving no grant from the Government or School Commissioners. Cor St Rose and Panet sts.

St Joseph's School, built of brick in 1860 by Reverend Ladies of the Holy Names of Jesus and Mary, as a day school for young girls. First lady directress Reverend Sister St Mary Augustin; present lady directress Reverend Sister Marie Ludivine; 8 sisters; 1 Catholic male employee; 533 Catholic female pupils; 2 Protestant female pupils. 17 Desery st.

St Joseph's School, built of brick in 1873, founded by the Rev. Brothers of the Christian Schools in 1865 as a boys school. First principal Rev. Brother Conoll; present principal Rev. Brother Maurilius; 14 Rev. brother teachers; 600 Catholic male pupils. Nationalities: 8 Catholic Fr. Canadian males; 1 Catholic English male b in C.; 3 Catholic French males; 1 Catholic Irish male; 1 Catholic German male. 14 inmates. 322 Richmond and 141 St Martin sts.

Mons. Mederic Lanctot's Commercial, French, English and Spanish School, built of stone, founded in 1880. First and present principal Mons. M. Lanctot; 1 Catholic male teacher; 12 Catholic male pupils; 1 Jewish male pupil. Nationalities: 1 Catholic Fr. female; 1 Catholic Fr. male; 2 inmates. 229 St Denis st.

Miss Apolline Ethier's Model School, built of brick; established in 1889. First and present principal Miss Apolline Ethier; 1 Catholic female teacher; 3 Catholic female pupils; 15 Protestant female pupils; 2 Catholic male pupils. Nationality of inmates: 3 Catholic Fr. Canadian females; 1 Catholic Fr. Canadian male. 85 St André st.

Miss McGee's Select Private School, built of brick; established in 1881. First and present principal Miss Mary McGee; 2 Catholic female teachers; 12 Catholic female pupils; 17 Protestant male pupils; 10 Catholic male pupils; 21 Protestant male pupils. Nationalities of inmates: 7 Catholic American females; 1 Protestant English female; 1 Protestant English male. Prince Arthur bet St Hypolite and St Dominique sts.

Mount St Louis Institute, built of stone in 1887; founded by the Rev. Brothers of the Christian Brothers Schools as a commercial and scientific college. First superior Rev. Brother Andrew; present superior Rev. Brother N. Denis; 39 brother teachers; 230 Catholic Fr. Canadian male pupils; 170 English pupils; 18 Catholic Fr. Canadian male employees. 444 Sherbrooke st.

Maitrise St Pierre, built of stone in 1869; the residence of Rev. Frères Maristes. First and present Superior Rev. Brother Surias; 12 Catholic male teachers; Catholic pupils; Nationalities of inmates: 2 Catholic Fr. Canadians; 2 Catholic Irish; 8 Catholic Fr. 109 Visitation st.

St Alphonsus de Ligouri School, built of brick in 1890, for girls and boys; under direction of the Redemptorist Fathers and Ladies of the Congregation of Notre Dame. First lady directress Reverend Mother St Claude; 1 reverend sister; 1 Catholic female teacher; 22 Catholic female pupils; 12 Catholic male pupils; 1 Catholic female employee. Nationalities of inmates: 1 Catholic Fr. Canadian female; 1 Catholic Scotch female b in C; 1 Catholic Irish female; 1 Catholic Irish female b in C. 120 Conway st.

St James Christian Brothers School, Brother Richarus, principal; 8 brothers; 1 Catholic Fr. Canadian male teacher; 490 pupils. 117 St Denis st.

Christian Brothers Monastery, built of stone; founded in 1878. First rev. superior Brother Austin; present rev. superior Brother Louis; 7 brothers; 1 law teacher; a female teacher; 2 Catholic Fr. Canadian male employee. Nationalities of inmates: 9 Catholic Fr. Canadians. 383 Plessis st.

Christian Brothers School, built of stone; founded in 1879, by the Rev. Brothers of the Christian Brothers Schools for the education of young boys. First and present superior Rev. Brother Louis; 1 Catholic Fr. Canadian male teacher; 4 Catholic Fr. Canadian female teachers; 490 Catholic male pupils. 181 Lagauchetiere st.

French, English and Music Classes; founded in 1875. First and present principal Mrs. Philomene Quevillon; 28 Catholic Fr. Canadian female pupils; 6 Catholic Fr. Canadian male pupils. Nationalities of inmates: 5 Catholic Fr. Canadian females; 2 Catholic Fr. Canadian males. 472½ St Hubert st.

Montreal School of Medicine and Surgery, founded in 1843; incorporated in 1845. First president Dr. William Sutherland; present president Dr. Wm. H. Hingston; registrar Dr. L. D. Mignault. Since 1867 it has been affiliated with Victoria University of Cobourg, in virtue of which affiliation it has been enabled to give degrees of Doctor of Medicine and Master of Surgery. Recently a bill was presented in the Legislature to increase its corporative capacity and passed. The effect of this bill is to make all the members of the Laval Faculty of Medicine in Montreal members of the Corporation of the Montreal School of Medicine and Surgery, and in the session 1891-2 the Corporation will give medical teaching to all students who have or would have followed the lectures of either of the pre-existing Corporations, and the degrees in Medicine will be given by Laval University of Quebec. It has a teaching staff of 23 Catholic professors and 390 Catholic students. The Institutions controlled by these faculties are Hotel Dieu and Hôpital Notre Dame, various dispensaries and the Maternité de la Miséricorde. Nationalities of inmates: 1 Catholic Fr. Canadian female; 1 Catholic Fr. Canadian male. Pine av.

Ecole Veterinaire Laval, built of brick; founded in 1886, by V. T. Daubigny, M.D., Laval; incorporated in 1889, for the medical treatment of horses, cattle, dogs, &c. First and present director Dr. V. T. Daubigny; 6 Catholic professors; 27 Catholic pupils; 2 Catholic Fr. Canadian male employees. It is supported by an annual grant from the Quebec Government. There is a dissecting room, brick stable for 12 horses; 1 sleigh and 2 four-wheeled carriages belonging to the establishment. 378 and 380 Craig st.

Reformatory School of St Vincent de Paul, founded in 1873 by Rev. Brother Eusèbe and directed by the Brothers of Charity of St Vincent de Paul, for the reformation of youthful criminals. First superior Rev. Bro. Eusèbe; present superior Rev. Brother Hilduard; 32 Brothers; 31 Catholic male employees; 317 Catholic male inmates convicted; 2 Jewish male inmates convicted; 21 Catholic male inmates boarders. Nationalities: 274 Catholic French Canadian males; 1 Catholic French male; 4 Catholic English males; 2 Catholic Scotch males; 30 Catholic English males b in C.; 7 Catholic American males b in C.; 12 Catholic American males; 4 Catholic Irish males b in C.; 6 Catholic Irish males. Total number of inmates 403. 1189 Mignonne st.

PROTESTANT CHURCHES.

ANGLICAN CHURCHES.

No.	Name of Church.	Address.	Built of	In	Present Clergymen.	No. of Assistants	No. of Employees	No. of Congregation
1	Christ Church Cathedral	2295 St Catherine	Stone	1859	Rev. J. G. Norton, D.D.	1	3	2000
2	Trinity Church	96 St Denis	Stone	1862	Rev. Canon W. F. Mills	1	2	2250
3	St George's Church	27 Osborne	Stone	1870	Very Rev. J. Carmichael	1	3	2500
4	St Stephen's Church	391 College	Stone	1842	Ven. Lewis Evans	....	2	800
5	St James the Apostle	2359 St Catherine	Stone	1864	Rev. J. Ellegood	1	3	1000
6	St John the Evangelist	4783 Ontario	Stone	1882	Rev. E. Wood	2	2	750
7	St Luke's Church	113 Dorchester	Stone	1853	Rev. T. E. Cunningham	....	3	1225
8	St Martin's Church	472 St Urbain	Stone	1874	Rev. G. O. Troop	1	3	500
9	St Jude's Church	50 Coursol	Stone	1876	Rev. J. H. Dixon	1	2	1500
10	St Mary's Church	39 Marlborough	Stone	....	Rev A Bareham	....	1	500
11	St Mathias' Church	Churchill av	Wood	1875	Rev. E. Bushell	....	2	300
12	St Thomas Church	1636 Notre Dame	Stone	1841	Rev. Canon Henderson	....	1	250
13	L'Eglise du Redempteur	123 Chatham	Brick	1879	Rev. D. Larivière	....	1	160
14	Grace Church	458 Wellington	Brick	1870	Rev. John Ker	....	3	2000
15	All Saints Church	St Denis	Brick	1890	Rev. H. J. Evans	....	2	150
16	Rushbrook St Mission Room	Rushbrook	....	18..	Mr. Chas. Manning	....	1	100
17	Bourgeois St Mission Room	Bourgeois	....	....	Mr. W. C. Blake	....	1	100

There are fifteen ANGLICAN CHURCHES and two MISSION ROOMS in Montreal. January, 1891.

RIGHT REVEREND WILLIAM BENNETT BOND, LL.D., Lord Bishop of Montreal;

VERY REVEREND JAMES CARMICHAEL, M.A., D.C.L., Dean of Montreal, and Rector of St George's Church.

Christ Church Cathedral, originally, built of stone in 1814 on Notre Dame street. Rev. Jacob Mountain, D.D., elder brother of the Right Rev. Bishop Mountain, first minister and rector. It was destroyed by fire in 1856 and rebuilt of stone in 1859 on St Catherine street. The first congregation of the Church of England and Ireland was formed in 1789. Right Rev. Bishop Stuart was the first bishop, and was succeeded by Right Rev. Bishop Mountain, Most Rev. Francis Fulford, D.D., Lord Bishop of Montreal and Metropolitan, Right Rev. Bishop Oxenden, and the present Lord Bishop of Montreal, the Right Rev. William Bennett Bond, LL.D. The first minister and rector was Rev. John Bethune, D.D.; present minister and rector Rev. John George Norton, D.D., 1 assistant clergyman; 1 employees; 3000 congregation. St Catherine bet Union av and University st.

Trinity Church, built of stone in 1840, on St Paul near Bonsecours street, by Major Wm. Plenderleath Christie. First bishop the Right Rev. George Jehoshaphat Mountain, first minister Rev. Mark Willoughby. The Church was sold in 1859, and the present Trinity Church was built of stone commenced in 1862 and completed in 1865 on St Denis street. The Most Rev. Francis Fulford, D.D., Lord Bishop of Montreal and Metropolitan; first minister and rector Rev. Charles Bancroft, D.D., LL.D. The Right Rev. William Bennett Bond, LL.D., is the present Lord Bishop of Montreal; present minister and rector Rev. Canon W. F. Mills, B.D.; 1 assistant clergyman; 2 employees; 2250 congregation. 96 St Denis cor Dubord st facing Viger sq.

St George's Church was built of stone; opened on the 30th June, 1843, on St Joseph st, now called Notre Dame street. It was sold, and the present St George's Church built. The latter was opened on 9th October, 1870. First minister and rector Rev. William T. Leach, D.D.; he was succeeded by Rev. William Bennett Bond, now Lord Bishop of Montreal; present minister and rector Very Rev. James S. Carmichael, M.A., D.C.L., Dean of Montreal; 1 assistant minister; 1 lay assistant; 8 licensed lay readers; 3 employees; 2500 connected with the congregation. Cor Osborne and Windsor sts facing Dominion sq.

St Stephen's Church, built of stone in 1842. First minister and rector Rev. Dr. Falloon; present minister and rector Ven. Lewis Evans, M.A., Archdeacon of Montreal; 2 employees; 800 congregation. Cor College and Inspector sts.

Church of St James the Apostle, built of stone, in 1864, by Charles Phillips. First minister and rector Rev. Jacob Ellegood, M.A., Canon of Christ Church Cathedral; 1 assistant minister; 3 employees; 1000 congregation. 2359 St Catherine cor Bishop st.

St. John the Evangelist Church, built of brick in 1860, on the corner of Dorchester and St. Urbain sts. In 1882 this church was sold, and the present church was built of stone. First minister and rector Rev. Edmund Wood, M.A.; 2 assistant ministers; 2 employees; 750 congregation. Cor Ontario and St. Urbain sts.

St. Luke's Church, built of stone in 1853. First minister and rector Rev. Canon Gibson; present minister and rector Rev. T. E. Cunningham, M.A.; 2 employees; 1225 congregation. 113 Dorchester st.

St. Martin's Church, built of stone in 1874. First minister Rev. J. Philip DuMoulin, M.A.; present minister and rector, Rev. G. Osborne Troop, M.A.; 1 assistant clergyman; 3 employees; 500 congregation. 472 St Urbain cor Prince Arthur st.

St Jude's Church, built of stone in 1876. First and present minister and rector Rev. James H. Dixon; 1 assistant clergyman; 2 employees; 1500 congregation. Cor Coursol and Vinet sts.

St Mary's Church, built of stone, on Marlborough st; it was demolished in 1890, and is now in course of re-erection on a new site. First minister and rector Rev. J Douglas Borthwick; present minister and rector Rev. Arthur Bareham, B.A.; 1 employee; 500 congregation. 39 Marlborough st. Services are now held in the Mission room on Notre Dame st, bet Descry and Marlborough sts, during re-erection.

St Mathias' Church, built of wood in 1875. First minister and rector Rev. Canon Empson, M.A.; present minister and rector Rev. Edward Bushell, M.A.; 2 employees; 300 congregation. Cor Churchhill av and Cote St Antoine road.

St Thomas Church was built of stone in 1841, by Thomas Molson of Montreal. First minister and rector Rev. William Thompson. It was destroyed by fire, and rebuilt of brick by Mr. Molson. Last minister and rector the late Rev. Robert Lindsay, M.A.; present clergyman in charge Rev. Canon Henderson, D.D.; 1 Protestant male employee; 250 congregation. 1636 Notre Dame st.

L'Eglise du Redempteur, built of brick in 1879. First minister and rector Rev. Josiah J. Roy, B.A.; present minister and rector Rev. Dufard Larivière, B.A.; 1 employee; 160 congregation. 123 Chatham st.

Grace Church, built of brick in 1870. First minister Rev. Samuel Belcher; present minister Rev. John Ker, D.D.; 3 employees; 2000 congregation. 458 Wellington n Centre st.

All Saints Church, built of brick in 1890. First and present minister Rev. H. J. Evans, M.A.; 2 employees; 150 congregation. Cor St Denis and Marianne sts.

Rushbrook Street Mission Room, in connection with Grace Church, opened in 18..; conducted by Charles Manning; 1 employee; 100 congregation. Rushbrook n Hibernia st.

Bourgeois Street Mission Room, in connection with Grace Church; opened in 1890; conducted by W. C. Blake; 1 employee; 100 congregation. Bourgeois n Favard st.

PRESBYTERIAN CHURCH.

No.	Name of Church	Address.	Built	In	Present Clergyman.	Assistants	Employees.	Congregation.
1	St. Andrew's Church	Beaver Hall Hill	Stone	1851	Rev. J. Edgar Hill		3	1050

There is one KIRK OF SCOTLAND in Montreal. January, 1891.

St Andrew's Church was originally built of stone in 1810, on St Helen street. First minister Rev. Alexander Mathieson, D.D. The Church was sold in 1849, and the present St. Andrew's Church was erected in 1851, on Beaver Hall hill; Rev. Dr. Mathieson being the first minister; present minister Rev. J Edgar Hill, M.A., B.D., Edin.; 3 Protestant employees; 1050 congregation. 28 Beaver Hall hill.

CANADA PRESBYTERIAN CHURCHES.

	Name	Address	Built	In	Present Clergyman	Assistants	Employees	Congregation
1	St Paul's Church	846 Dorchester.	Stone	1868	Rev. J. Barclay		4	1450
2	St Gabriel's Church.	2148 St Catherine.	Stone	1886	Rev. R. Campbell		3	800
3	Knox Church	887 Dorchester.	Stone	1865	Rev. James Fleck		3	750
4	St John's French Pres. Ch.	1876 St Catherine.	Brick	1870	Rev. J. L. Morin	2	3	300
5	St Matthew's Church	185 Congregation	Brick	1859	Rev. W. R. Cruickshank		2	1000
6	Calvin Church	2565 Notre Dame	Brick	1862	Rev. Wm. J. Smyth		2	1100
7	Chalmers Church	504 St Lawrence.	Stone	1870	Rev. G. C. Heine		2	800
8	Taylor Pres. Church	99 Champlain.	Brick	1880	Rev. Thos. Bennett		1	625
9	St Mark's Church	128 William	Brick	1869	Rev. John Nichols		2	600
10	Stanley Street Church	41 Stanley.	Brick	1873	Rev. F. M. Dewey		2	600
11	Erskine Church	2363 St Catherine.	Stone	1866	Rev. A. J. Mowat	1	2	1050
12	Crescent Street Church	955 Dorchester.	Stone	1878	Rev. A. B. Mackay	2	2	1250
13	Eglise du Sauveur	90 Canning.	Brick	1876			2	200
14	La Croix Church	Hochelaga.	Brick	1889	Rev. P. Duclos		3	300
15	Melville Church	Cote St Ant. rd..	Wood	1886	Rev. J. MacGillivray		1	400
16	Nazareth St Mission Hall	136 Wellington.	Brick	1870			1	100
17	Italian Pres. Mission	1786 St Catherine.	Brick	1870	Rev. A. Internoscia		1	90
18	Maisonneuve Mission	150 Lecours av.	Brick	1891	Mr. E. Mackenzie.		1	75
19	St Gabriel Mission Hall	Point St. Charles		1889			1	60
20	St Henri Pres. Mission Hall.	Notre Dame	Stone	1889	Mr. W. H Pickard		1	.....
21	Victoria Mission Hall	53 Conway					1	200
22	St Jean Baptiste Mission	144 Dufferin.	Brick		Rev. G. W. Charles.		1	80

There are fifteen CANADA PRESBYTERIAN CHURCHES and seven MISSION HALLS in Montreal. January, 1891.

St. Paul's Church was formerly built of stone in 1834 on cor Recollet and Lemoine streets. It was sold in 1866, and a new church was built and completed in 1868, on Dorchester st. First minister Rev. Edward Black, D.D.; present minister Rev. James Barclay, M.A. Glasgow; 4 Protestant employees; 1450 congregation. 846 Dorchester n St Monique st.

St Gabriel Church, was built of stone, on St Gabriel st, in 1792. First minister Rev. John Young. This church was sold in 1856, and a new church bought on St Catherine st. First and present minister Rev. Robert Campbell, M.A., D.D.; 3 Protestant employees; 800 congregation. 2148 St Catherine opp City Councillors st.

Knox Church, built of stone in 1865. For seventy-three years this congregation occupied the old St Gabriel Street Church and was known first as the Scotch Presbyterian Church, later as St Gabriel St Church, and afterwards as the Knox Church Congregation. It was first formed as a congregation in 1786 by Rev. John Bethune. The first church on St. Gabriel street was built in 1792 and opened in same year, the first minister being the Rev. John Young. In 1865 the present church was built for the congregation (a new congregation being formed in the old building known as the St. Gabriel Church). Present minister Rev. James Fleck, B.A.; 3 Protestant employees; 750 congregation. 887 Dorchester cor Mansfield st.

St John's French Presbyterian Church (Russell Hall), built of brick in 1870. First minister Rev. Charles A. Doudiet; present minister Rev Joseph L. Morin; 2 assistant ministers; 3 Protestant employees; 300 congregation. 1876 St Catherine n St Constant st.

Melville Church, built of wood in 1886. First and present minister Rev. John MacGillivray; 400 congregation. Cote St Antoine road.

St Matthew's Church, built of brick in 1859. First minister Rev. James Black; present minister Rev. Wm. R. Cruickshank, B.A.; 2 Protestant employees; 1000 congregation. 185 Congregation st. St Matthew's new Church, corner Wellington and Bourgeois sts., built of stone, will be ready for occupation about June.

Calvin Church, built of brick in 1862. First minister Rev. P. D. Muir; present minister Rev. William James Smyth, D.D., B.Sc., Ph.D.; 2 Protestant employees; 1100 congregation. 2565 Notre Dame st.

Chalmers Church, built of stone in 1870. Mission formed in 1865. First minister Rev. John Jones; present minister Rev. George Colborne Heine, B.A.; 2 Protestant employees; 800 congregation. 504 St Lawrence above Sherbrooke st.

Taylor Presbyterian Church, built of brick in 1880. First minister Rev. John Jones; present minister Rev. Thomas Bennett; 1 employee; 625 congregation. 99 Champlain st.

St Mark's Church, built of brick in 1869. First minister Rev. Wm. M. Black; present minister Rev. John Nicholls; 2 Protestant employees; 600 congregation. 128 William cor Dalhousie st.

Stanley Street Church, built of brick in 1873. First minister Rev. Dr. Baxter, now in Scotland; present minister Rev. Finlay M. Dewey, M.A.; 2 Protestant employees; 600 congregation. Stanley st n Windsor Hotel.

Erskine Church was originally built of stone in 1833, on Lagauchetiere st. It was sold in 1866, and the present church was built of stone on St Catherine st. First minister Rev. Wm Taylor, D.D.; present minister Rev. A. J. Mowat; 1 assistant minister; 2 Protestant employees; 1050 congregation. 2363 St Catherine cor Peel st.

Crescent Street Church, built of stone in 1878. First and present minister Rev. A. B. Mackay, D.D.; 2 assistant ministers; 2 Protestant employees; 1250 congregation. 955 Dorchester cor Crescent st.

Eglise du Sauveur, built of brick in 1876. First minister Rev. Charles Chiniquy; present minister (no appointment); 2 Protestant employees; 200 congregation. 90 Canning st.

La Croix Church, built of brick in 1889. First and present minister Rev. P. Duclos; 3 Protestant employees; 300 congregation. Hochelaga.

Nazareth St Mission Hall, built of brick in 1870. Services are conducted by missionaries in connection with Crescent Street Presbyterian Church; 1 Protestant employee; 100 congregation. 136 Wellington cor Nazareth st.

Italian Presbyterian Mission, built of brick in 1870. First and present missionary Rev. Antonio Internoscia, 1 Protestant employee; 90 congregation. 1786 St Catherine st.

Maisonneuve, a mission of Erskine Church Congregation. The mission house is now being built of brick. Present missionary Mr. E. Mackenzie; 75 congregation. 150 Lecours av.

St Gabriel Mission Hall, in connection with St Mathew's Presbyterian Church; opened in 1889; 1 Protestant employee; 60 attending Sabbath School and Evening Service. Point St Charles.

St Henri Presbyterian Mission Hall, built of stone, founded in 1883. It is connected with Calvin Church and conducted by Mr. William H. Pickard; 1 Protestant employee. Notre Dame st n St Henri Tollgate.

Victoria Mission Hall, in connection with St Matthew's Presbyterian Church; 1 Protestant employee; 200 congregation. 53 Conway st.

St. Jean Baptiste (French Presbyterian Mission), built of brick. Present missionary G. W. Charles, B.A.; 1 Protestant employee; 80 congregation. 144 Dufferin st.

AMERICAN PRESBYTERIAN CHURCHES.

No.	Name of Church.	Address.	Built	In	Present Clergymen.	Assist-ants.	Em-ploye congregation.	Congre-gation.
1	American Pres. Church	904 Dorchester	Stone	186	Rev. Geo. H. Wells, D.D.		2	1200
2	American Pres. Chapel	75 Inspector	Stone	1870	Rev. M. Stewart Oxley		3	250

There is one AMERICAN PRESBYTERIAN CHURCH and one CHAPEL in Montreal. January, 1891.

American Presbyterian Church was originally built of stone in 1826, on the corner of St James and McGill sts. Rev. J. S. Christmas was the first minister. The church was sold in 1864, and a new church, the present one, was

erected of stone on Dorchester corner Drummond street. Present minister Rev. George H. Wells, D.D.; 2 Protestant employees; 1200 congregation. 904 Dorchester cor Drummond st.

American Presbyterian Chapel, built of stone in 1870. First and present pastor Rev. M. Stewart Oxley, B.A.; 3 Protestant employees; 250 congregation. 75 Inspector st.

METHODIST CHURCHES.

	Name	Address	Built	In	Present Clergymen			Congregation
1	St James Meth. Church	2145 St Catherine	Stone	1888	Rev. J. Henderson, M.A.	1	5	3000
2	Douglas Methodist Church	2794 St Catherine	Stone	1889	Rev. J. C. Antliff, D.D.		2	600
3	Dorchester St Meth. Church	565 Dorchester	Brick	1860	Rev. C. E. Bland, B.A.		1	400
4	Dominion Sq Meth. Church	894 Dorchester	Stone	1865	Rev. S. P. P. Rose		3	600
5	West End Meth. Church	Coursol	Stone	1890	Rev. C. R. Flanders		1	1000
6	First French Meth. Church	431 Craig	Stone	1862	Rev. E. de Grachy		2	250
7	Second Methodist Church	119 Mountain	Stone	1870	Rev. J. Tallman Pitcher	1	4	1000
8	East End Meth Church	118 Lagauchetière	Stone	1844	Rev. A. McCann		4	1000
9	Sherbrooke St Meth. Church	546 Sherbrooke	Stone	1853	Rev. T. G. Williams		2	550
10	Point St Charles Meth. Church	592 Wellington	Brick	1864	Rev. John Scanlon		3	1000
11	Eglise Evangélique Méthodiste	142½ Delisle	Brick		Rev. M. Sadler		1	200
12	Cote St Antoine Meth. Ch.	Cote St Ant. rd.	Brick	1888	Rev. F. Tripp		1	200
13	St. Henry's Meth. Church	St. Antoine	Brick	1880	Rev. Wm. Harris		1	300
14	Hoch and Cote St Louis M. Ch.	Mount Royal av.	Brick	1888	Rev. H. Walker		1	200
15	Des Rivières Street Mission	13 Des Rivières	Brick	1861				100
16	Brewery Mission	97 College						90

There are fourteen METHODIST CHURCHES and two MISSIONS in Montreal. January, 1891.

St. James Methodist Church was built of stone in 1821 on St James st. First minister Rev. Robert L. Lusher. This church was sold and a new church erected on Great St James st facing the present building of the Canada Life Assurance Co. It was also sold and another new church built of Credit Valley stone, at a cost of $320,000, on St Catherine st, St Alexander and City Councillors sts. It was completed and opened in 1889. First and present minister Rev. James Henderson, M.A.; 1 assistant minister; 5 Protestant employees; 3000 congregation. 2145 St Catherine bet St Alexander and City Councillors sts.

Douglas Methodist Church, built of stone in 1889. First and present minister Rev. J. Cooper Antliff, D.D.; 2 Protestant employees; 600 congregation. 2794 St Catherine st.

Dorchester Street Methodist Church, built of brick in 1860. First minister Rev. Andrew Henderson; present minister Rev. Charles E. Bland, B.A.; 1 Protestant employee; 400 congregation. 565 Dorchester cor St Charles Borromée st.

Dominion Square Methodist Church, built of stone in 1865. First ministers Revs. James Elliott, D.D., and William Briggs D.D.; present minister Rev. Samuel Protestant P. Rose; 3 employees; 600 congregation. 894 Dorchester cor Windsor st.

West End Methodist Church was built of stone in 1890, at the corner of Seigneurs and Notre Dame sts. First minister Rev. William J. Shaw, D.D. At the commencement of the year 1890 it was sold, and the present church was built of stone on the corner of Coursol and Canning sts. First and present minister Rev. Charles R. Flanders; 1 Protestant employees; 1000 congregation. Cor Coursol and Canning sts.

First French Methodist Church, built of stone in 1862, as a French Presbyterian Church, by the Rev. A.P. Duclos. First opened as a Methodist Church in 1873. First minister Rev. Louis Napoleon Beaudry; present minister Rev. Edward de Gruchy; 2 Protestant employees; 250 congregation. 431 Craig cor St Elizabeth st.

Second Methodist Church, built of stone in 1870, by the congregation formerly worshipping in Ottawa street. First minister Rev. William Hansford, D.D.; present minister Rev. J. Tallman Pitcher; 1 assistant minister; 4 Protestant employees; 1000 congregation. 119 Mountain st.

East End Methodist Church, built of stone in 1844. First minister Rev.; present minister Rev. Alfred McCann; 4 Protestant employees; 1000 congregation. 118 Lagauchetière n DeSalaberry st.

Sherbrooke Street Methodist Church, built of stone in 1853. First ministers Revs. John Borland and S. J. Hunter, D.D.; present minister Rev. T. G. Williams, D.D.; 2 Protestant employees; 550 congregation. 546 Sherbrooke cor St Charles Borromée st.

Point St Charles Methodist Church, built of brick in 1864. First minister Rev. Dr. Douglas; present minister Rev. John Scanlon; 3 Protestant employees; 1000 congregation. 592 Wellington st.

Eglise Evangélique Méthodiste, built of brick in 18 First and present minister Rev. M. Sadler; 1 Protestant employee; 200 congregation. 142½ Delisle st.

St Henry's Methodist Church, built of brick in 1880. First minister Rev. Edward Lawrence; present minister Rev. William Harris; 1 Protestant employee; 300 congregation. Cor St. Antoine st and Metcalfe av.

Cote St Antoine Methodist Church, built of brick in 1888. Present minister Rev. Frederick Tripp; 1 Protestant employee; 200 congregation. Cote St. Antoine road.

Hochelaga and Cote St Louis Methodist Church, built of brick in 1888. First and present pastors Revs. A. G. Robinson and Rev. H. Walker; 1 Protestant employee; 200 congregation. Cor Mount Royal av and Berri st.

DesRivières Street Mission, built of brick in 1861, by the congregation of St James Church; 1 Protestant employee; 100 congregation. 13 DesRivières st.

Brewery Mission, presently formed in connection with St James Methodist Church; 90 congregation. Miss M. Douglas, president; Miss Cadwell, sec. 97 College st.

BAPTIST CHURCHES.

No.	Name of Church,	Address,	Built	In	Present Clergyman.	Assistants.	Emoluments, playment	Congregation
1	First Baptist Church	2162 St Catherine.	Stone	1871	Rev. Donald Grant		2	400
2	French Bap. Ch. (L'Oratoire)	14 Mance	Stone	1882	Rev. A. M. Therrien		2	70
3	Grace Baptist Church	2321 St. Catherine		1889	Rev. J. D. Fulton	1		600
4	Olivet Baptist Church	183 Mountain	Stone	1879	Rev. A. G. Upham		2	700
5	Mission Hall	43 Centre	Brick	1888	Mr. J. B. Warnicker		1	300
6	Winstanley Hall	1423 Delisle	Brick	1888			1	260
7	Evangelistic Mission	2254 St Catherine.		1889				150
8	Gain Street Mission	Gain	Brick	1888				75

There are four BAPTIST CHURCHES, two HALLS and two MISSIONS in Montreal. January, 1891.

First Baptist Church was built of stone, on St Helen st, in 1877. It was sold, and a new one erected on Beaver Hall hill in 1858. In 1878 this church was sold to the Reformed Episcopal congregation. The present church on St Catherine street was erected in 1871. First pastor Rev. Joshua Donovan ; present pastor, Rev. Donald Grant; 2 Protestant employees ; 400 congregation. 2162 St Catherine cor City Councillors.

French Baptist Church (L'Oratoire), built of stone in 1882. First pastor Rev. Theodore Lafleur ; present pastor Rev. Alphonse L. Thérien ; 2 Protestant employees; 70 congregation. 14 Mance above St Catherine st.

Grace Baptist Church, worshipping in Queen's Hall, 2321 St. Catherine street; opened in 1889. First and present minister Rev. Justin D. Fulton, D.D. ; 1 assistant minister ; 2 lay assistants ; 600 congregation. Queen's block, 2321 St Catherine st.

Olivet Baptist Church, built of stone in 1879. First pastor Rev. John Gordon ; present pastor Rev. Albert G. Upham ; 2 Protestant employees ; 700 congregation. 183 Mountain cor Osborne st.

Mission Hall, built of brick ; opened in 1888. First pastor Rev. Charles S. J. Boone ; present pastor J. B. Warnicker ; 1 Protestant employee ; 300 congregation. 43 Centre st.

Winstanley Hall, built of brick ; opened in 1888 ; conducted by the Young Men of Olivet Baptist Church ; 1 Protestant employee. 260 congregation. 1423½ Delisle st.

Evangelistic Mission, opened in 1889 ; conducted by the Ladies of Grace Baptist Church ; 150 congregation. 2254 St Catherine st.

Gain Street Mission, built of brick ; opened in 1888 ; conducted by the Young Men of the First Baptist Church ; 75 congregation.

CONGREGATIONAL CHURCHES.

No.	Name of Church	Address	Built	In	Present Clergyman	Assist.	Congregation
1	Zion Church	Mance	Stone		Rev. W. H. Warriner	2	350
2	Calvary Church	302 Guy	Stone	1876	Rev. E. M. Hill	3	750
3	Emmanuel Church	2431 St Catherine.	Stone	1876	Rev. Wm. H. Pulsford	3	900

There are three CONGREGATIONAL CHURCHES in Montreal. January, 1891.

Zion Church was originally built of stone on Beaver Hall hill. First minister Rev. Henry Wilkes, D.D. It was sold. The Church is now on the corner of Mance and Milton streets. Rev. W. H. Warriner, B.A., B.D., is the present minister ; 2 Protestant employees ; 350 congregation. Cor Mance and Milton sts.

Calvary Church, built of stone in 1876. First minister Rev. Joseph Lawson Foster, LL.B.; present minister Rev. Edward Munson Hill, M.A.; 3 Protestant employees ; 750 congregation. 302 Guy st.

Emmanuel Church, built of stone in 1876. First minister Rev. J. Frederick Stevenson, D.D.; present minister William Hanson Pulsford, M.A. ; 3 Protestant employees ; 900 congregation. 2431 St Catherine cor Stanley st.

NEW JERUSALEM CHURCH.

1	New Jerusalem Church	25 Hanover	Brick	1862	Rev. Edwin Gould	1	50

There is one NEW JERUSALEM CHURCH in Montreal. January, 1891.

New Jerusalem Church, built of brick in 1862. First and present minister Rev. Edwin Gould; 1 Protestant employees; 50 congregation. 25 Hanover st cor Dorchester st.

GERMAN LUTHERAN CHURCH.

1	St John's G. L. Evangel. Ch.	129 St Dominique	Stone	1858	Rev. H. Rembe	1	600

There is one GERMAN LUTHERAN CHURCH in Montreal. January, 1891.

St John's German Lutheran Evangelical Church, built of stone in 1858. First pastor Rev. G. Werner ; present pastor Rev. Heinrich Rembe ; 1 Protestant employee ; 600 congregation. 129 St Dominique st.

CATHOLIC APOSTOLIC CHURCH.

1	Catholic Apostolic Church	35 Cathcart		18	Rev. Mr. Ross	1	30

There is one CATHOLIC APOSTOLIC CHURCH in Montreal. January, 1891.

Catholic Apostolic Church. First and present minister and pastor Rev. Mr. Ross ; 1 Protestant employee ; 30 congregation. 35 Cathcart st.

REFORMED EPISCOPAL CHURCH.

1	St Bartholomew's Church	18 Beaver Hall hill	Stone	1858	Rev. C. Tully	4	600

There is one REFORMED EPISCOPAL CHURCH in Montreal. January, 1891.

St Bartholomew's Church, built of stone in 1858, by the first Baptist Congregation. It was sold in 1877 to the Reformed Episcopal Church. In same year it was opened by the Right Rev. Bishop Ussher, D.D. Present minister Rev. Charles Tully, F.R.G.S., F.S.S.C., rector ; 4 Protestant employees ; 600 congregation. 18 Beaver Hall hill

PLYMOUTH BRETHREN.

Name of Church.	Address.	Built.	In	Present Clergymen	Assistants	Employees	Congregation
Plymouth Brethren	32 University			Brethren		1	200

There is one PLYMOUTH BRETHREN CONGREGATION in Montreal. January, 1891.

Plymouth Brethren, meetings conducted by Brethren; 1 Protestant employee; 200 congregation. 32 University st.

ADVENT CHRISTIANS.

| 1 Advent Chris. Congregation | 2272 St. Catherine | | | Wm. W. Robertson | | 1 | 150 |

There is one ADVENT CHRISTIAN CONGREGATION in Montreal. January, 1891.

Advent Christian Congregation. Services conducted by Wm. W. Robertson; 1 Protestant employee; 150 congregation. 2272 St. Catherine st o McGill College av.

UNSECTARIAN PLACES OF WORSHIP.

	Name	Address	Built		Present Clergymen			
1	Evangelistic Hall for Girls	2254 St. Catherine			Miss Barber		1	100
2	W. C. T. U. Shelter Mission	564 Dorchester	Brick		Mr. Ohling		2	25
3	Montreal Y. M. C. A.	749 Craig			Members		2	500
4	Y. W. C. A. Hall	101 Metcalfe			Mrs. Seymour		2	30
5	Montreal Welsh Union	749 Craig			Members		1	200
6	Scandinavian Mission	43 St. Fran. Xav.			Rev. O. J. Kloewjord		1	150
7	Gospel Book Room	8 Phillips sq.			Christian Workers		1	50
8	Christians	186 Bleury					1	25
9	Church of Christ (Scientist)	2268 St. Catherine	Brick	1889	Christian Scientist		2	50
10	Mont. Inst. of Chris. Science	2268 St. Catherine		1889	Miss C. M. Shannon			
11	Christian Science Dispensary	2268 St. Catherine		1889	Christian Scientist			

There are eleven UNSECTARIAN PLACES OF WORSHIP in Montreal. January, 1891.

Evangelistic Hall for Girls, in connection with Miss Barber's Evangelistic work amongst young girls; conducted by Miss Barber; 1 Protestant employee; 100 congregation. 2254 St. Catherine st.

Women's Christian Temperance Union Shelter Mission, built of brick; conducted by Mr. Ohling; 2 Protestant female employees; 25 congregation. 564 Dorchester st.

Montreal Young Men's Christian Association.—Services conducted by members (undenominational); 2 Protestant employees; 500 congregation. Young Men's Christian Association building, 749 Craig st facing Victoria sq.

Young Women's Christian Association Hall.—Evangelistic services; conducted by Mrs. Seymour; 2 Protestant employees; 30 congregation. 101 Metcalfe st.

Montreal Welsh Union.—Evangelistic services in the Young Men's Christian Association rooms on Sunday afternoons; conducted by members; 1 Protestant employee; 200 congregation. Young Men's Christian Association building, 749 Craig st facing Victoria sq.

Scandinavian Mission (undenominational); conducted by Rev. O. J. Kloewjord; 1 Protestant employee; 150 congregation. 43 St. François Xavier st.

Gospel Book Room, built of brick; undenominational. Gospel Meetings conducted by Christian workers; 1 Protestant employee; 50 congregation. 8 Phillips sq.

Christians, gathered together in the name of the Lord; 1 Protestant employee; 25 congregation. 186 Bleury st St. Catherine st.

Church of Christ (Scientist), built of brick, opened in 1890; conducted by a Christian Scientist; 2 employees; 50 congregation. 2268 St. Catherine st.

Montreal Institute of Christian Science, established in 1889, for the purpose of teaching Christian Science as taught by the Bible and Science, and Health. First and present principal Miss C. M. S. Shannon, C.S.S.; 2268 St. Catherine st.

Christian Science Dispensary, established in 1889, for demonstrating love and the teachings of Our Lord Jesus Christ. Superintended by a Christian Scientist. 2268 St. Catherine st.

UNITARIAN CHURCH.

| 1 Church of the Messiah | Beaver Hall Hill | Stone | 1844 | Rev. W. S. Barnes | | 3 | 300 |

There is one UNITARIAN CHURCH in Montreal. January, 1891.

Church of the Messiah was built of stone in 1844, and opened in May, 1845; it was rebuilt in April, 1848, a larger building than the first and opened for worship in September. It was partially destroyed by fire October 21, 1869; restored and occupied in June, 1870. First minister Rev. John Cordner, LL.D.; present minister Rev. William S. Barnes; 3 Protestant employees; 300 congregation. Cor Beaver Hall hill and Lagauchetière st.

JEWISH SYNAGOGUES.

	Name	Address	Built	In	Present Clergymen			
1	Spanish and Portuguese Cong.	Stanley	Stone	1890	Rabbi Rev. M. De Sola		4	225
2	German Polish Congregation	59 McG. Col. av.	Stone	1886	Rab. Rev. E. Friedlander		4	225
3	Russian Congregation	St. Constant	Brick	1883	S. Benjamin			180
4	Congregation Benai Jacob			1886	M. Margolins			195
5	Temple Emmanu-El	2462 St. Catherine		1882	Rev. M. Block			300

There are four JEWISH SYNAGOGUES and one REFORMED JEWS in Montreal. January, 1891.

Spanish and Portuguese Congregation, founded in 1768. First Synagogue near the Court House. The present Synagogue was built of stone, in 1890. First rabbi Rev. Jacob Cohen; present rabbi Rev. Meldola De Sola; 4 employees. Nationalities of inmates: 6 Jewish Polish females; 5 Jewish Polish males. 225 Sabbath attendance. Stanley & St. Catherine st.

German and Polish Congregation, founded in 1860. The first Synagogue in St. Constant st. was built in 1860 of brick, the present Synagogue was built in 1886 of stone. First rabbi Rev. E. Friedlander; 4 employees; 225 Sabbath attendance. 59 McGill College av.

Russian Congregation, founded in 1883. Synagogue built of brick. 37 St. Constant st. First minister J. Saxe; present minister S. Benjamin. 180 Sabbath attendance.

Congregation Benai Jacob, founded in 1886, M. Margolins minister. 195 Sabbath attendance.

Temple Emmanu-El, organized in 1880. First minister Reverend S. Marks; present minister Reverend M. Block; 300 attendance. 2462 St. Catherine st.

PROTESTANT HOSPITALS.

¶ There are seven PROTESTANT HOSPITALS in Montreal. January, 1891.

Montreal General Hospital, built of stone ; founded in 1821, by citizens of Montreal, for the reception and care of sick and maimed of both sexes, without regard to nationality or creed. It has 325 life governors, 3 private wards and 24 public wards, with 248 beds. There is a medical superintendent : 5 resident physicians : 2 non-resident physicians ; 7 visiting physicians : 7 visiting surgeons : 5 specialists : 2 aurists and occulists : a resident apothecary ; medical students ; a lady superintendent for the female department ; 34 female nurses ; 6 male officers ; 24 Catholic female patients ; 47 Protestant female patients ; 36 Catholic male patients ; 64 Protestant male patients ; 1 Jewish male patient ; 20 Protestant female employees ; 18 Protestant male employees. This Institution is visited by clergymen of various denominations. A citizens committee of management of 9 who superintend and direct the general affairs of the hospital with a clerk of committee. The number of out-door patients during the week ending February 22nd were 300 Catholics and 94 Protestants. The daily average of in-door patients being 356, of visitors 624 weekly. The nationalities of the inmates are : 3 Catholic females b in U. S. ; 11 Catholic Irish females ; 2 Catholic English females ; 1 Catholic Scotch female ; 3 Catholic Newfoundland females ; 7 Catholic Fr. Canadian females ; 14 Catholic English males b in C ; 9 Catholic English males ; 9 Catholic Irish males ; 1 Catholic Newfoundland male ; 1 Catholic Swedish male ; 2 Catholic Scotch males ; 21 Protestant English females ; 10 Protestant Scotch females ; 1 Protestant Irish female ; 28 Protestant English females b in C ; 1 Protestant Newfoundland female ; 2 Protestant Swedish female ; 10 Protestant Irish females ; 3 Protestant Welsh females ; 7 Protestant Scotch females b in C ; 10 Protestant Fr. Canadian males ; 28 Protestant English males b in C ; 26 Protestant English males ; 10 Protestant English Scotch males b in C ; 10 Protestant Scotch males ; 12 Irish males b in C ; 4 Protestant Irish males ; 1 Protestant Newfoundland male ; 1 Protestant Welsh male ; 2 Protestant American males ; 1 Protestant Swedish male ; 1 Protestant Danish male. 536 Dorchester st.

Western Hospital of Montreal, built of stone ; founded in 1877 by Major H. Mills, for the treatment of diseases peculiar to women, and as a lying-in hospital. It is under the supervision of the professor of midwifery in Bishop's College. It has two consulting physicians and surgeons ; 10 attending physicians and surgeons ; 1 medical assistant ; a lady matron ; a ladies' committee of 36 ; a gentlemen's committee of 6 ; and a board of management of 17 ; 2 female Catholic nurses ; 3 female Protestant nurses ; 2 female Catholic employees ; 1 Catholic male employee ; 9 Catholic patients ; 16 Protestant patients. Nationalities : 1 Fr. Canadian Catholic female ; 6 Irish Catholic females ; 3 Irish Protestant females ; 1 Irish Catholic female b in C ; 2 English Catholic females b in C ; 5 English Protestant females b in C ; 3 English Protestant females ; 3 Scotch Protestant females ; 1 German Protestant female ; 1 American Catholic female ; 1 Irish Catholic male ; 1 English Protestant male. 1251 Dorchester st n Essex av.

Montreal Maternity Hospital, built of stone ; founded in 1854, by the University of McGill College, for the reception of lying-in women. It has a house surgeon ; a lady matron ; 5 assistants ; 2 female employees ; 1 male employee ; 26 inmates. Nationalities : 1 Catholic Fr. Canadian female ; 1 Catholic English female b in C ; 4 Protestant English females ; 10 English Protestant females b in C ; 1 English Protestant male b in C. It is maintained by voluntary contributions and a small grant from the Quebec Government. 93 St Urbain st.

Strong's Private Hospital, built of brick, established by Samuel Strong, in 1879, for the reception of paying patients, to be attended by their own medical advisers. This hospital was the first of its kind opened in Montreal, and is under the management of Mrs. Strong, an experienced "Nightingale" nurse. First and present proprietor Samuel Strong ; 6 Protestant female nurses ; 3 Protestant female employees ; 6 Protestant female patients ; 2 Catholic male patients ; 3 Protestant male patients. Nationalities : 2 Protestant Fr. Canadian females ; 6 Protestant English females b in C ; 6 Protestant English females ; 2 Catholic Fr. Canadian males ; 4 Protestant English males. 15 University st.

Miss Gee's English Nursing Institution and Private Hospital, built of brick, established in 1886. First and present proprietress Miss M. C. Gee ; 12 Protestant fe-

male nurses ; 3 Protestant female employees ; 2 Protestant female patients ; 3 Protestant male patients ; 1 Catholic male patient. Nationalities : 17 Protestant English females ; 1 Protestant Scotch female ; 1 Catholic Irish male ; 1 Protestant Irish male ; 1 Protestant English male ; 1 Protestant Scotch male. 38 and 40 McGill College avenue.

Dr. Gardner's Private Hospital, built of stone ; established in 1887, for the care and treatment of private patients. First and present proprietor Dr. Wm. Gardner ; 6 female nurses ; 13 female patients ; 4 female employees ; 1 male employee. Nationalities of inmates : 19 Protestant English females b in C ; 1 Protestant English male ; 1 Protestant English male b in C. 107 Union av.

Turkish Bath Sanitarium and Private Hospital, built of brick ; established in 1869, for the reception of private patients suffering from Rheumatic complaints. Dr. J. Alexander, proprietor ; Dr. D. A. D. McBean, director ; 4 female attendants ; 5 male attendants ; 8 female patients ; 12 male patients. Nationalities of inmates : 8 Protestant English females ; 1 Protestant Scotch female ; 1 Catholic Irish female b in C ; 2 Protestant English females b in C ; 2 Catholic Irish males ; 1 Protestant Irish male ; 3 Protestant Scotch males ; 2 Catholic Fr. Canadian males ; 3 Protestant English males ; 6 Protestant English males b in C. 140 St Monique st.

Montreal General Hospital Dispensary, built of stone ; founded in 1821, by the citizens of Montreal, for the dispensing of medicines and treatment of out-door sick patients. It is under the care of a pharmaceutist and several medical attendants. During the week ending February 22nd, there was an attendance of 300 Catholic and 93 Protestant patients. This Institution is maintained by voluntary contributions and an annual grant from the Quebec Government. 95 St Dominique st.

Montreal Dispensary, organized in 1750, for the purpose of affording relief to the sick poor, without regard to nationality or religion. Last year over 13,000 applications for relief were attended to by this institution. It is maintained by private subscriptions and a government grant. 145 St Antoine st.

PROTESTANT BENEVOLENT INSTITUTIONS.

There are sixteen PROTESTANT BENEVOLENT INSTITUTIONS in Montreal. January, 1891.

Ladies Benevolent Institution, built of stone ; founded in 1832 by a committee of ladies for the destitute Protestant women and children of Montreal. First lady matron Mrs. Wyatt ; present lady matron Mrs. Louisa Glover ; 8 Protestant female employees ; 1 Protestant male employee ; 45 destitute Protestant girls ; 63 destitute Protestant boys ; 36 destitute Protestant women. 154 Protestant inmates. Nationalities ; 31 Berthelet st.

Ladies Benevolent Convalescent Home, built of stone ; founded in the Wheeler wing by the Ladies Benevolent Society in 1881, opened in 1882. First and present lady matron Mrs Louisa Glover ; 8 Protestant female employees ; 4 Protestant female convalescents. Nationalities of inmates : 7 Protestant English females b in C ; 1 Protestant German female b in C ; 1 Protestant Scotch female ; 4 Protestant English males b in C. 31 Berthelet st.

Church Home, founded in 1855, by Mrs. Francis Fulford ; incorporated in 1875, in connection with the Anglican Church, for the shelter and support of aged and infirm women of the middle class in reduced circumstances. President Right Rev. W. B. Bond, Lord Bishop of Montreal ; matron Miss Dunning ; 5 lady officers ; 24 ladies committee of management ; 17 aged women. Nationalities of inmates : 8 Protestant English females ; 5 Protestant Irish female ; 5 Protestant English females b in C ; 1 Protestant female American ; 2 Protestant Scotch females ; 7 Protestant Irish female b in C. ; 1 Irish Catholic female. 403 Guy st.

Protestant Orphan Asylum, built of stone in 1848 ; established in 1822, by Protestant ladies of Montreal, as an asylum for orphan children. It is supported by public subscriptions, endowments and a grant from the Quebec Government. First directress Mrs. Aird ; present directress Mrs. John Torrance ; superintendent C. Thomas ; 2 Protestant female employees ; 8 Protestant female orphans ; 15 Protestant male orphans. Nationalities of inmates : 1 English male ; 13 English males b in C ; 2

Irish males b in C ; 4 English females ; 3 English females b in C ; 3 English males ; 2 Negro females b in C ; 1 Negro male b in C. 293 St Catherine st.

St Margaret's Nursery for Foundlings and House of Mercy for Fallen Women; founded in 1887 by Sister St Margaret. First and present sister in charge Sister St Margaret ; Miss J Humphrey, matron ; 1 Protestant female nurse ; 10 Protestant female penitents ; 12 Protestant female foundlings. 15 Protestant male foundlings. Nationalities of inmates. 11 Protestant English females ; 13 Protestant English females b in C ; 15 Protestant English males b in C. 12 Kensington av.

Protestant Infants' Home, built of brick ; founded in 1870 by a committee of Protestant citizens as a home for destitute Protestant infants under five years of age. Incorporated in 1871. President Hon J. K. Ward ; first directress Mrs. B. T. Davis; matron Mrs. Van Allen ; 10 Protestant female nurses ; 2 Protestant female employees ; 1 Protestant male employee ; 27 Protestant infant females ; 26 Protestant infant males. Nationalities of inmates : 7 Protestant English females b in C ; 3 Protestant Irish females ; 7 English Protestant females ; 1 Protestant New-foundland female ; 2 Protestant Scotch females ; 1 Protestant American male. 506 and 508 Guy st.

St George's Home, built of stone ; founded in 1834, by the St George's Society, as a receiving home for English emigrants ; incorporated 1861. First president Hon. George Moffat ; present president J. H. Redfen ; Mrs. Kennedy matron ; 1 Protestant English female emigrant ; 3 Protestant English male emigrants ; 2 Protestant English female employees, 1 Protestant English male employee. Nationalities of inmates : 3 English Protestant females ; 4 English Protestant males. 133 St Antoine st.

St Andrew's Home, built of stone ; founded in 1856 by St Andrew's Society, as a receiving home for Scottish emigrants, and for benevolent purposes. Present superintendent Donald Campbell ; present matron Mrs. Donald Campbell ; 5 Protestant Scotch male employees. Nationalities of inmates : 3 Protestant Scotch females ; 5 Protestant Scotch males. 475 Aqueduct st is Dorchester st.

Boys' Home, built of brick ; founded in 1870, by Charles Alexander and a committee of gentlemen to provide a home for boys willing to be assisted under moral and religious influences. First superintendent John Ritchie ; present superintendent James R. Dick ; 3 Protestant female employees ; 4 Protestant male assistant ; 4 Protestant male employees ; 72 Protestant male inmates. Nationalities : 32 Protestant English males b in C ; 6 Protestant English females ; 29 Protestant English males ; 6 Protestant Irish males ; 8 Protestant Scotch males. 115, 117 and 119 Mountain st.

St Margaret's Home for the Incurable and Infirm, built of stone ; established in 1885 ; incorporated in 1890. It is under the direction of the Sisters of St. Margaret, in connection with the Anglican Church: Sister Elizabeth Margaret in charge. 5 sisters ; 1 Catholic female employee ; 2 Protestant female employees. 13 Protestant incurable and infirm patients. Nationalities of inmates : 17 Protestant females b in C ; 4 Protestant American females ; 4 Protestant English females ; 1 Protestant Scotch female ; 1 Protestant Irish female. 660 Sherbrooke st.

Hervey Institute and Home and School of Industry, built of stone ; founded in 1847, by Miss Eliza Hervey, as a home for half orphan children. First lady matron Mrs. Eliza Hervey ; present lady matron Mrs. William Miller ; 50 Protestant orphan girls ; 10 Protestant orphan boys ; 4 Protestant female employees. 215 Mountain st.

Protestant House of Industry and Refuge, built of brick ; founded in 1863 by a committee of Protestant citizens ; incorporated in 1865 as a night refuge and home for destitute Protestant poor of Montreal. It is maintained by private subscriptions and a small annual grant from the Quebec Government. First secretary and superintendent William Brown; present secretary and superintendent David MacMillan ; first matron Mrs. McDonald ; present matron Mrs. Maria McMillan ; 144 Protestant male night refuges ; 144 Protestant male inmates. Nationalities of inmates : 34 Fr. Canadians ; 58 English ; 28 Irish ; 5 Scotch ; 1 Welsh ; 4 German ; 1 Norwegian ; 2 Danes ; 1 Swiss ; 1 Jersey ; 1 Hindoo ; 1 Newfoundland ; 1 Nova Scotian ; 6 Americans. 689 to 693 Dorchester st.

Young Women's Christian Association Convalescent Home for sick servant girls, and well recommended servant girls out of place. It was founded in 1881, and is unsectarian. Present lady superintendent Mrs. Jane Flaws ; 1 Protestant female employee ; 2 Catholic convalescent servant girls ; 2 Protestant convalescent servant girls ; 2

Catholic servant girls out of place ; 8 Protestant servant girls out of place. 73 Drummond st.

Sheltering Home, built of brick ; opened in 1886 by the Women's Christian Temperance Union, for sheltering homeless women and girls and aiding them to a better life. First and present Lady Superintendent Miss Emily G. Barber ; first and present matron Miss Agnes Montgomery ; 2 Protestant female employees ; 13 Protestant female. Nationalities of inmates : 6 Irish Protestant female ; 4 Irish Catholic females ; 2 Scotch Protestant female , 4 English Protestant females. 564 Dorchester st.

Women's Protective Emigration Society; founded 1881, by a committee of ladies, as a non-sectarian receiving home for young emigrant women on their arrival. First president Miss Jane Moffat ; present president Mrs. Gillespie ; first matron Miss McKendrick ; present matron Mrs. Mahoney ; 8 Protestant English female boarders ; 1 Protestant English female employee. Nationalities of inmates : 1 Catholic English female b in C ; 6 Protestant English females b in C ; 2 Protestant Danish female. 141 Mansfield st.

Rescue Home, built of brick ; established in 1890, in connection with the social reform work of the Salvation Army. First and present superintendent Captain Louis Obert ; 3 Protestant female employees. Nationalities of inmates : 3 Protestant Scotch females ; 6 Protestant Irish females ; 11 Protestant English females ; 1 Protestant American female ; 2 Protestant English males b in C. 11 Plateau st.

COLLEGES AND UNIVERSITIES.

There are eleven PROTESTANT COLLEGES in Montreal, January, 1891.

McGill College and University; founded in 1821, by the Hon. James McGill, for the purpose of education and the advancement of learning in the Province of Lower Canada. It comprises : the Faculty of Arts, the Donalda Special Course for Women, the Faculty of Applied Science, the Faculty of Medicine, the Faculty of Comparative Medicine and Veterinary Science, and the Faculty of Law.

The statutes and regulations of the University have been framed on the most liberal principles, with a view of affording all classes of persons the greatest possible facilities for the attainment of mental culture and professional training. In its religious character the University is Protestant but not denominational, and while all possible attention is given the character and conduct of students, no interference with their peculiar views is sanctioned.

The educational work of the University is carried on in McGill College and the affiliated colleges and schools. It has 8 endowed chairs, 10 exhibitions and scholarships, and 11 endowments of medals and prizes.

The Governing Body of the University is as follows : Visitor His Excellency The Right Honorable Lord Stanley of Preston, G.C.B., P.C., Governor General of Canada, etc ; Honorable Sir Donald A. Smith, K.C.M.G., LL.D. (Hon. Cantab), president and chancellor of the University, and 13 governors ; principal Sir William Dawson, C. M. G., M.A., LL.D., F.R.S., vice-chancellor and 32 fellows. It has 6 professors emeriti ; 4 Catholic professors ; 39 Protestant professors ; 13 Protestant lecturers ; 1 Protestant lady superintendent ; 1 Protestant lady instructress in Gymnastics ; 107 Protestant female students ; 2 Catholic female student ; 652 Protestant and Catholic male students ; 14 Protestant male employees ; James W. Brakenridge, B.C.L., secretary. McGill College, 803 Sherbrooke st.

Faculty of Arts. Principal Sir William Dawson, LL.D. (ex-officio) ; dean of the faculty Alexander Johnson, LL.D. ; honorary librarian Rev. Geo. Cornish, LL.D. ; 9 professors ; 3 assistant professor ; 4 lecturers ; 216 male students.

Donalda Special Course for Women. Lady superintendent Miss Helen Gairdner. 108 lady students.

Faculty of Applied Science. Principal Sir Wm. Dawson, LL.D. (ex-officio) ; dean of the faculty Henry T. Bovey, M.A., M.Inst.C.E., 9 professors ; 3 associate lecturers ; 4 assistants ; 80 students.

Faculty of Law. Principal Sir William Dawson, LL.D. (ex-officio) ; dean N. W. Trenholme, Q. C., M. A., D.C.L., Gale professor of Roman and International law ; 10 professors ; 32 students.

Faculty of Medicine. Principal Sir William Dawson, C.M.G., LL.D., F.R.S., professor of Natural History ; dean of the Faculty Robert Craik, M.D., professor of hygiene and public health ; 3 emeritus professors ; 13 professors ; 9 demonstrators and instructors ; 263 students.

The William Molson Hall, being the west wing of McGill College buildings, in which the library is situated, was erected in 1861, through the munificent donation of the founder, whose name it bears.

The Peter Redpath Museum, built of stone ; founded in 1880 by Peter Redpath, Esq., for the use of the College.

McGill College Observatory, Lat. N. 45° 30' 17''. Long. 4h. 54m. 18s.5s. Height above the sea level 187 feet. Superintendent C. H. McLeod, Ma.E. ; assistant superintendent G. H. Chandler, M.A. ; assistant F. H. Hamilton, B.A.Sc. Meteorological observations are made every fourth hour, beginning at 3h. on Eastern standard time. Independent bi-hourly temperature observations are also made. The Anemometer and Vane are on the summit of Mount Royal, at a point about three-quarters of a mile north-west of the Observatory, 57 feet above the surface of the ground, and 810 feet above the sea level. McGill College, 803 Sherbrooke st.

Nationalities : 9 Protestant English females b in C ; 5 Protestant English females ; 2 Protestant English males ; 7 Protestant Irish males b in C ; 10 Protestant Irish males b in C ; 3 Protestant Irish females ; 2 Protestant Irish males ; 1 Protestant Scotch female b in C ; 1 Protestant Scotch female. 803 Sherbrooke st.

Faculty of Comparative Medicine and Veterinary Science (formerly Montreal Veterinary College) ; founded in 1866, for the surgical treatment of animals, by Duncan McEachran, F.R.C.V.S. It was made a faculty of McGill University in 1889. First and present principal and founder D. McEachran, F.R.C.V.S., now dean of the Faculty ; 3 professors ; 5 associate professors ; 1 demonstrator of pathology ; 6 examiners ; 1 matriculation examiner ; 56 students ; 1 Protestant female employee ; 3 Protestant male employees. Nationalities of inmates : 1 Catholic Fr. Canadian female ; 2 Catholic Irish females ; 1 Protestant English male b in C ; 1 Protestant Scotch male ; 1 Catholic Fr. Canadian male. There is a stable built of brick with 21 stalls for horses. 6 and 8 Union av.

Montreal Diocesan Theological College, built of stone ; founded in 1873, incorporated in 1873, affiliated to McGill University in 1880. It was founded for the purpose of providing young men with the best facilities of theological training under the supervision of the Lord Bishop of the diocese. First president Right Rev. Bishop Oxenden ; present president the Right Rev. Lord Bishop of the diocese. First principal Rev. J. A. Lobley, M.D., D.C.L. ; present principal Rev. Canon Henderson, D.D. ; 7 rev. lecturers ; 26 Protestant male students ; 2 Protestant female employees ; 1 Protestant male employee. Nationalities of inmates : 6 Protestant English females b in C ; 1 Protestant Irish female ; 17 Protestant English males b in C ; 3 Protestant English males ; 4 Protestant Irish males ; 1 Protestant Scotch male. 896 Dorchester st.

Presbyterian College, built of stone, founded in 1867, for the education of young men for the ministry of the Presbyterian Church. Affiliated with McGill University in 1868. First and present principal Rev. D. H. Mac-Vicar, D.D., L.L.D., Fellow of McGill University ; 4 rev. professors ; 82 rev. lecturers ; 82 Protestant male students ; 6 Protestant female employees ; 1 Protestant male employee. Nationalities of inmates : 14 Protestant Scotch females b in C ; 54 Protestant Scotch males ; 10 Protestant Irish males ; 10 Protestant English males ; 15 Protestant Fr. Canadian males. 67 and 69 McTavish st.

Methodist Theological College, built of stone, founded in 1873, by the Wesleyan Methodist Church, for the education of students for the Methodist ministry. First and present principal Rev. G. Douglas, D.D., L.L.D. ; 5 professors ; 64 Protestant male students ; 3 Protestant female employees ; 3 Protestant male employees. Nationalities of inmates : 1 Protestant Fr. Canadian male ; 24 Protestant English males b in C ; 11 Protestant English males ; 5 Protestant Irish males ; 1 Protestant West Indian male ; 2 Protestant Irish females b in C ; 1 Protestant English female b in C. 228 University st.

Congregational College of Canada, built of stone in 1884. This college was first founded in Toronto in 1839, for the education of students for the ministry of the Congregational Church. It was removed to Montreal in 1864. First principal Rev. Adam Lillie, D.D. ; present principal Rev. William M. Barbour, D.D. ; 4 rev. professors ; 2 theological students ; 4 Protestant female employees ; 20 Protestant inmates. Nationalities of inmates : 2 Protestant Irish males ; 1 Protestant Scotch males ; 2 Protestant English males ; 10 Protestant English males b in C ; 3 Protestant English females b in C ; 1 Irish female. McTavish st n Sherbrooke.

College of Homœopathic Physicians and Surgeons ; established in 18 . John Wanless, M.D., L.F.P.S., M.C.P.S., dean ; Frederick Muller, M.D., registrar ; 4 professors ; 1 Scotch male employee.

Sabrevois Mission College, in connection with the Anglican Church, built of brick ; founded at Sabrevois in 1865 for the education of French children ; removed to Montreal in 1878. First principal Rev. L. N. Tucker, M.A. ; present principal, Rev. Dolard Larivière, B.A. ; 3 Protestant female teachers ; 2 Protestant male teachers ; 31 Protestant female pupil boarders ; 7 Catholic female pupil boarders ; 7 Catholic male pupil boarders ; 32 Protestant male pupil boarders ; 4 Protestant female employees ; 1 Protestant male employee. 88 Fr. Canadian inmates. 117 Chatham st.

Montreal Veterinary Medical Association ; founded in 1875, by D. McEachran, F.R.C.V.S. Present office bearers : D. McEachran, F.R.C.V.S., hon. president ; Charles McEachran, D.V.S., president ; M.C. Baker, D.V.S., first vice-president ; Wesley Mills, M.A., M.D., D.V.S., second vice-president ; John McCrank, secretary-treasurer ; G. A. Miller, librarian ; 60 active members. Meetings are held in the College Lecture Room, 6 and 8 Union av., fortnightly, from October to April.

Faculty of Medicine University of Bishop's College, built of brick, founded in 1871, by the Corporation of the University, for the study and furtherance of medical science. First dean of the Faculty, Wm. Hingston, M.D. ; present dean of the Faculty Francis W. Campbell, M.D., M.A., L.R.C.P., London ; 15 Protestant professors ; 1 Catholic male student ; 4 Catholic female students ; 5 Protestant female students ; 24 Protestant male students. Nationalities of inmates : 2 German Protestant females b in Canada ; 1 Irish Protestant female b in C ; 2 German Protestant males b in C. 1815 Ontario st.

Montreal College of Pharmacy, built of brick ; founded in 1855 ; incorporated in 1879. First president Nathan Mercer ; present president, David Watson ; 4 professors of Pharmacy ; 62 male pupils ; 32 Catholics, 30 Protestants ; 2 Protestant male employees. 595 Lagauchetière st.

PROTESTANT SCHOOLS.

There are forty-eight PROTESTANT SCHOOLS in Montreal. January, 1891.

Bute House, built of brick ; established in 1860 as a boarding and day school for young ladies. Firs and present principal Mrs. Mary Watson ; 10 Protestant female teachers ; 65 Protestant female pupils ; 1 Jewish female pupil ; 1 Protestant boarding pupils ; 4 Protestant female employees. Nationalities of inmates : 20 Protestant English females. 166 Mansfield st.

British and Canadian School, at the cor. of Cotté and Lagauchetière sts., is believed to be the oldest existing common school in Canada. It was founded in 1822 through the exertions of Mr. Wm. Lunn, Mr. Kenneth Dowie and Mr. Daniel Fisher. The Hon. Louis J. Papineau was the first vice-president. In 1823 His Excellency Lord Dalhousie became Patron. The school was at first held in a hired house. The present building, a substantial stone edifice, was erect d about 1826 and enlarged and rearranged in 1874. In 1866 this school was under special legislative authorization transferred to the Protestant Board of School Commissioners under whose care it still remains. The first master was Mr. Hutchings. Present principal E. T. Chambers, who is assisted by 11 Protestant female teachers. 180 Protestant male pupils ; 112 Protestant female pupils ; 1 Catholic male pupil ; 1 Catholic female pupil ; 25 Jewish female pupils ; 21 Jewish male pupils. Cor Lagauchetière and Cotte st.

Elliock School, built of brick ; founded in 1887. First and present principal Rev. John Williamson ; 5 Protestant male assistant teachers ; 55 Protestant male pupils ; 1 Protestant male employee. 1143 Dorchester st.

McGill Normal School, built of stone ; founded in 1857 by the Government of the United Provinces of Upper and Lower Canada as a training school for Protestant teachers of Lower Canada. First principal Dr John Wm. Dawson ; present principal Dr S. P. Robins ; 3 Protestant female teachers ; 4 Protestant male teachers ; 86 Protestant female pupils ; 10 Protestant male pupils ; 2 Catholic female pupils ; 30 and 32 Belmont st.

Mrs. Millar's and Miss Pitt's Young Ladies Boarding and Day School, built of stone ; established in 1880. First and present principals Mrs. Millar and Miss Pitt ; 4

boarding pupils; 20 day pupils; 5 Protestant female teachers; 2 Protestant male teachers; 1 Protestant female employee. Nationalities: 44 Protestant English females; 2 Protestant males. 261 Peel st.

High School of Montreal, built of brick; founded in 1843 by citizens of Montreal as a proprietary school. First principal Rev.—Simpson; present principal H. Aspenwall Howe, M.A., LL.D.; controlled by the Protestant Board of School Commissioners; 254 pupils; 2 Catholic male pupils; 252 Protestant male pupils; 11 Protestant male teachers. Held temporarily in Fraser Institute and Berthelet st school. A new building of stone in course of erection.

St John the Evangelist School, built of stone in 1889; established in 1861, on Aylmer st, by the Rev. Edmund Wood, M.A., as a Church school for boys. First principal Rev. Edmund Wood; present principal Rev. Arthur French, M.A Oxon.; 5 assistant masters; 3 female employees; 1 male employee; 66 pupils. Nationalities of inmates: 9 female Anglican English; 31 male Anglican English.

Girls High School of Montreal; founded in 1875, built of stone in 1877, destroyed by fire in November, 1890. It is under the control and management of the Protestant Board of School Commissioners. First lady principal Mrs. Louisa Scott; present principal Mrs. J. L. Fuller; 11 Protestant female teachers; 3 Protestant male teachers; 3 Catholic female pupils; 285 Protestant female pupils; 12 Jewish female pupils. Between Metcalfe and Peel sts. Since the destruction of the building by fire the Senior classes have been held in the Victoria School, St Luke st.

Preparatory High School, built of brick in 1883, under the control of the Protestant Board of School Commissioners as a Preparatory school for boys. Head master Alex N. Shewan, M.A.; 2 assistant masters; 1 lady teacher; 290 Protestant male pupils. Burnside place cor Mc call and Peel sts.

The Misses Forneret's Seminary for Young Ladies, built of stone; opened in 1849; 2 Protestant female teachers; 30 female Protestant pupils; 6 Protestant male pupils; 1 female Protestant employee. 372 Dorchester st.

Miss Gardner's Private School, built of brick; established in 1872, as a private school for young ladies and children. First and present principals the Miss s Gardner; 1 Catholic female teacher; 5 Protestant female teachers; 2 Protestant female pupils; 28 Protestant male pupils; 1 Catholic female employee; 1 Protestant female employee. Nationalities of inmates: 4 Protestant Scotch females b in C.; 1 Catholic Irish female; 2 Protestant Scotch male b in C. 47 Victoria st.

Grace Church Day School, built of brick in 1856, under the control of Grace Church officers. First principal Miss Millen; present principal Miss M. Gordon; 2 Protestant female teachers; 30 Protestant female pupils; 90 Protestant male pupils. Nationalities: 3 English females b in C.; 1 English male b in C.; 1 Irish male. 464 Wellington st.

Model Schools of McGill Normal School, built of stone and founded in 1857. First principal Dr. J. W. Dawson (Now Sir William); present principal Sampson Paul Robins, M.A., LL.D.

Boys School, head master Thomas B. Smiley; 2 Protestant female assistant teachers; 7 Catholic male pupils; 97 Protestant male pupils.

Girls School, head mistress Jane E. Swallow; 2 Protestant female assistant teachers; 3 Catholic female pupils; 115 Protestant female pupils.

Sherbrooke Street School, built of stone in 1874, under the control of the Protestant Board of School Commissioners. First principal T. W. Mills, M.D.; present principal C. A. Humphrey; 11 Protestant female teachers; 1 Catholic female pupil; 280 Protestant female pupils; 1 Catholic male pupil; 300 Protestant male pupils; 30 Jewish female pupils; 56 Jewish male pupils; 1 Protestant male employee. Nationalities of inmates: 1 Protestant English females; 3 Protestant English males. 347 Sherbrooke, 347 St Dominique and 2 and 3 St Hypolite sts.

Royal Arthur School, built of brick in 1870, by the Protestant Board of School Commissioners. First principal F.W. Kellay, B.A.; present principal William Patterson, M.A.; 10 Protestant female teachers; 1 Protestant male assistant; 1 Catholic female pupil; 223 Protestant female pupils; 1 Catholic male pupils; 233 Protestant male pupils; 1 Protestant male employee. 63 Workman st.

Hochelaga School, built of brick, transferred from the dissentient school trustees of Hochelaga, in the annexation of the city, in 1884, to the Protestant Board of School Com-

missioners. First principal under the Board Miss Mary Harper; present principal Miss F. A. Truell; 2 Protestant female teachers; 1 Catholic female pupils; 27 Protestant female pupils; 5 Catholic male pupils; 28 Protestant male pupils; 1 Protestant female employee. Nationalities of inmates: 1 Protestant English female; 1 Protestant English male. Cor Logan and Prefont. ine sts.

Misses Smith and Freary's Private School; established in 1880. First principal Miss C. Smith; 2 Protestant female teachers; 10 Protestant female pupils; 7 Protestant male pupils. Nationalities of inmates: 4 Protestant English females b in C.; 1 Protestant English male b in C. 113 St Urbain st.

Frites College School, built of stone; established in 1887, for the higher education of boys. First and present principal Traill Oman, M.A., Math.; 1 Protestant female teacher; 1 Protestant male teacher; 10 Catholic male pupils; 38 Protestant male pupils; 6 Jewish male pupils. Nationalities of inmates: 1 Catholic Fr. Canadian female; 3 Protestant Scotch females; 3 Protestant Scotch males. 2448 St Catherine cor Drummond.

Dorchester Street School, built of brick; established in 1874, under the control of the Protestant Board of School Commissioners, as a mixed day school. First principal Mr. Barwick; present principal Miss L. Coo; 4 Protestant female teachers; 2 Catholic female pupils; 80 Protestant female pupils; 60 Protestant male pupils; 6 Jewish female pupils; 5 Jewish male pupils. Nationalities of inmates: 1 Protestant English females. 483 Dorchester st.

St Urbain Street School, built of brick in 1888; under the control of the Protestant Board of School Commissioners. First and present principal Miss Maggie Campbell; 3 Protestant female teachers; 17 Protestant female pupils; 2 Catholic male pupils; 135 Protestant male pupils; 1 Protestant male employee. Nationalities of inmates: 3 Protestant Fr. Canadian females; 1 Protestant Fr. Canadian male. 803 St Urbain.

Type Writing School, established in 1887. First and present principal Mrs. J. Balk k; 18 Protestant female pupils; 2 Protestant male pupils; 1 Protestant female employee. Mechanics Hall building. 204 James st.

Britannia School, built of brick; established 1877, as a mixed day school, under the control of the Protestant Board of School Commissioners. First principal Miss Whinfield; present principal Miss J. A. Maver; 3 Protestant female teachers; 1 Protestant female employee; 58 Protestant female pupils; 1 Catholic male pupil; 72 Protestant male pupils. Nationalities of inmates: 3 Protestant French females b in C. 9 Britannia st, Point St Charles.

Seminary for Young Ladies, built of stone; founded in 1872. First and present principal Miss Bolger; 3 Protestant female teachers; 18 Protestant female pupils; 12 Protestant male pupils. Nationalities of inmates: 2 Protestant English females b in C. 734 Sherbrooke st.

Berthelet Street School, built of brick; founded in 1865; under the control of the Protestant Board of School Commissioners. First and present principal Seneca Page Rowell; 10 Protestant female assistant teachers; 1 Catholic male pupil; 328 Protestant female pupils; 329 Protestant male pupils; 1 Protestant male employee. Nationality of inmates: 3 Protestant English females; 3 Protestant English males. 31 Berthelet st.

Victoria School, built of brick in 1888; under the control of the Protestant Board of School Commissioners, as a mixed day school. First and present principal S. H. Parsons, B.A.; 1 Protestant male assistant; 11 Protestant female teachers; 333 Protestant female pupils; 308 Protestant male pupils; 1 Protestant male employee. Nationalities of inmates: 2 Protestant English females; 2 Protestant English males. 30 St Luke off ry.

Senior School of Montreal, built of brick in 1884; founded in 1843 by the Protestant Board of School Commissioners. First principal F. S. Haight, M.A.; present principal J. McKercher, B.A., LL.B.; maintained by Government grant, City taxes, and by pupils' tuition fees. 131 pupils; 1 Catholic female pupil; 10 Protestant male pupils; 2 Jewish male pupils; 67 Protestant female pupils; 3 Protestant female employees; 2 Protestant male employees; inmates. Nationalit cc. 31 Berthelet st.

Grammar School, established in 1885, as a boarding and day school for boys. First and present principal William W. Mowat; 1 Protestant female teacher; 4 Protestant male teachers; 2 Catholic male pupils; 61 Protestant male pupils; 1 Protestant female employee. Nationalities of inmates: 1 Protestant Scotch females; 2 Protestant Irish female; 6 Protestant Scotch males; 2 Protestant Irish male b in C. 2498 St. Catherine st.

Primary School, head mistress, Lucy H. Derick; 1 Protestant female assistant teacher; 52 Protestant female pupils; 65 Protestant male pupils; 1 Catholic male pupils 30 Belmont st nr Beaver Hall hill.

Institut Méthodiste Français, built of brick in 1879 by the Missionary Society of the Methodist Church of Canada, as a French Protestant mission boarding school. First and present principal Rev. Wm. Hall, M.A., 2 Protestant female teachers; 3 Protestant male teachers; 6 Catholic female pupils; 26 Protestant female pupils; 7 Catholic male pupils; 28 Protestant male pupils; 4 Protestant female employees; 1 Protestant male employee. Nationalities: 6 Catholic Fr. Canadian females; 7 Catholic Fr. Canadian males; 11 Protestant Fr. Canadian females; 20 Protestant Fr. Canadian males; 17 Protestant English females b in C.; 11 Protestant English males b in C.; 4 Protestant Iroquois females; 2 Protestant Iroquois males; 78 inmates. Green av n St Antoine st.

City School, built of brick; founded in 1850 by the Protestant Board of School Commissioners. First superintendent Henry Arnold; present superintendent A. W. Kneeland, M.A., Ph.D.; 11 Protestant female teachers; 1 Protestant male teacher; 223 Protestant female pupils; 212 Protestant male pupils; 1 Protestant female employee; 1 Protestant male employee; 10 Jewish female pupils; 7 Jew male pupils. Nationalities of inmates: 2 Protestant English females b in C.; 1 Protestant English female; 1 Protestant English male. 73 Panet and 36 De Salaberry sts.

St Gabriel School, built of brick; in 1879 by the Protestant Board of School Commissioners, as a mixed day school. First principal A. W. Kneeland, B.C.L.; present principal A. C. Galbraith; 7 Protestant female teachers; 1 Protestant English male employee; 154 Protestant female pupils; 168 Protestant male pupils. Nationality: 1 English male inmate b in C. 64 Ryde st, Point St Charles.

Mission Française de St Jean Baptiste, in connection with the Presbyterian Board of Missions, built of brick and founded in 1838, as a day and evening school. Supported by the Presbyterian Board of Missions. First and present principal Mr. Guillaume Charles; 1 Protestant female teacher; 1 Protestant male teacher; 20 Catholic female pupils; 17 Catholic male pupils; 3 Protestant female pupils. 144 Dufferin st.

First French Methodist Day School, built of brick; opened in 1890 as a day mission school for young children. First and present directress Miss Maynard; 30 pupils; 300 Dorchester st, bet Jacques Cartier and Wolfe sts.

Montreal Commercial School, built of brick; established in 1857 as a day and evening school. First and present principal Wm. J. N. Turner; 8 Protestant female pupils; 6 Catholic male pupils; 31 Protestant male pupils. 276 St Urbain st nr Ontario st.

College of Business, founded in 1888, by George W. Thompson. First and present principal George W. Thompson; 58 pupils; 2 Catholic female pupils; 8 Protestant female pupils; 48 Protestant male pupils; 1 Catholic female employee; 1 Protestant female employee. 239 St. James st.

Riverside School, built of brick in 1876 by the Protestant Board of School Commissioners, a mixed school. First principal A. Duncan; present principal W. A. Kneeland, B.C.L.; 11 Protestant female teachers; 280 Protestant female pupils; 275 Protestant male pupils; 1 Protestant male employee. Nationalities: 3 English Protestant females; 2 English Protestant males. 52 Favard st., Point St Charles.

Educational Classes, opened in 1886 as evening classes for working girls; conducted by voluntary teachers; supported by voluntary contributions. Nonsectarian. Held in the Evangelist hall, 2254 St Catherine st n Victoria st.

Mr. Thompson's Evening School, founded in 1888, by G. W. Thompson. First and present principal G. W. Thompson; 26 pupils; 6 Protestant female pupils; 20 Protestant male pupils; 1 Protestant female employee. 239 St James st.

Mrs. C. H. Thompson's Young Ladies Day School, built of stone; established in 1883. First and present principal Mrs C. H. Thompson; 2 Protestant female teacher; 15 Protestant female pupils; 10 Protestant male pupils; 1 Protestant female employee. Nationalities of inmates: 2 Protestant English females; 1 Protestant English male. 22 St Monique st.

Montreal Business College, founded in 1864 by Bryant & Stratton, first principals; present principals and proprietors Davis & Buie; 7 teachers; 375 pupils; 3 Catholic

male teachers; 2 Protestant female teachers; 2 Protestant male teachers; 200 Catholic femalepupils; 50 Catholic male pupils; 75 Protestant female pupils; 41 Protestant male pupils. 5 Place d'Armes.

Miss Delisle's Private School, built of brick; founded in 1889. First and present principal Miss Delisle; 1 Catholic female teacher; 80 Catholic female pupils; 100 Catholic male pupils. Nationalities of inmates: 1 Catholic Fr. Canadian female. 5 School House st.

School of Language, established in 1889. First and present principal A. Gehrei; 2 Protestant male teachers; 50 pupils. Nationalities: 1 Catholic French female; 1 Catholic Irish female; 1 Protestant English female b in C.; 1 Protestant Swiss male. 8 McGill College av.

Mr. and Mrs. Thompson's Evening Classes; established in 1883. First and present principal Mr. C. H. Thompson; 1 female teacher; 14 Protestant female pupils; 8 Protestant male pupils. 22 St Monique st.

Ann Street School; founded in 1860, as a mixed day school for boys and girls, under the control of the Protestant Board of School Commissioners. First principal S. P. Rowle; present principal H. M. Cockfield, B.A.; 11 Protestant female teachers; 3 Catholic female pupils; 203 Protestant female pupils; 181 Protestant male pupils. Nationalities of inmates: 1 Protestant English female; 4 Protestant English males b in C. 171 and 173 Ann st.

Trafalgar Institute, built of brick; founded in 1887, by the trustees of the late Donald Ross; for the higher education of women. First and present principal Miss Grace Fairley; 6 Protestant female assistant tutors; 1 Protestant male tutor; 1 Catholic male tutor; 60 Protestant female pupils; 1 Catholic female pupil. 83 Simpson st.

Kindergarten, built of stone; established in 1885, for the training of young children on the Froebel system. First and present principals Misses McIntosh; 3 Protestant female teachers; 37 Protestant female pupils; 1 Catholic male pupil; 23 Protestant male pupils; 1 Catholic female employee. Nationalities of inmates: 1 Catholic Irish female b in C. 4 Protestant females b in C. 27 Victoria st.

Kindergarten, built of brick; established in 1890. First and present principal Miss Mary Irene Bazin. 1 Protestant female pupil; 4 Protestant male pupils. 467 St Urbain.

A. Roy Macdonald's Junior School for Dancing, Deportment and Physical Culture; established in 1882. First and present principal A. Roy Macdonald; 350 female pupils; 352 male pupils; 3 Protestant female employees; 1 Protestant male employee. 2221 St Catherine st.

Professor Durkee's School of Dancing and Deportment; established in 1882. First and present principal Professor C. W. Durkee; 298 female pupils; 219 male pupils; 2 Protestant female employees; 2 Protestant male employees. 2269 St Catherine st.

Baron de Hirsch Institute, built of stone; founded in 1890, by the Montreal Young Men's Hebrew Society, as a free day school for Jewish children. First and present principal William H. Baker; 2 Protestant female teachers; 1 Hebrew male teacher; 1 Hebrew female employee; 1 Hebrew male employee; 55 Hebrew female pupils; 80 Hebrew male pupils; 7 Jewish inmates. Nationalities of inmates: 2 Hebrew females; 1 Hebrew males. 7 St Elizabeth st.

Montreal School of Cookery, built of brick; founded in 1889, by Mrs. F. Wolferstan Thomas. First principal Miss Violet Goodacre; present principal Miss Amy Gertrude Richard; 2 Protestant female assistants; 56 pupils; 3 Protestant female employees. Nationalities of inmates: 2 Protestant English females; 2 Protestant English females b in C. 735 Sherbrooke st.

Montreal Riding School; established in 1872; built of brick. First director Clement Halloway; present director Samuel Osborne. It has a stable built of brick with stalls for 35 horses and shed accommodation for carriages; 50 female pupils; 80 male pupils; 8 Protestant male employees. Nationalities of inmates: 2 Protestant English females; 2 Protestant English females b in C.; 2 Protestant English males. 77 and 79 Burnside place.

Jewish Free School, under the management of the Spanish and Portuguese Synagogue; founded in 1874. First principal Rev. A. DeSola, LL.D.; present principal Rev. Meldola De Sola; 1 Jewish male teacher; 1 Protestant male teacher; 40 Jewish female pupils; 30 Jewish male pupils. Basement of Synagogue Stanley st.

CATHOLIC RELIGIOUS AND TEMPER-ANCE SOCIETIES.

There are twenty-four CATHOLIC RELIGIOUS and TEMPERANCE SOCIETIES in Montreal.

Société Bienveillante de Notre Dame de Bonsecours; founded in 1853, for the mutual insurance of its members and for the benefit of their widows and orphans. First president Hubert Paré; present president Jean Bte. Larue; 1 Catholic male employee; 21 members; 15 widows. 68 St James st.

St Patrick's Total Abstinence and Benefit Society; founded by Rev. P. Phelan, P.S.S., first director and president, (afterward Bishop of Kingston, Ont.), in the old Recollet Church, on 23rd of February, 1840; present director and president Rev. J. A. McCallen, P.S.S.; first vice-president Hon. Edward Murphy; 175 members. St Patrick's Parish hall, 92 St Alexander st.

St Patrick's Society; founded in 1852, by Rev. Patrick Dowd, P.S.S., to assist Irish emigrants landing in Montreal. First director Rev. P. Dowd; present director Rev. James Callaghan; first president Sir Francis Hincks; present president H. J. Cloran; members. Cor McGill and Notre Dame sts.

Irish Catholic Benefit Society; founded in 1850. First and present director Rev. P. Dowd, P.S.S.; first president Joseph J. Kennedy; present president Arthur Jones; 100 members. Cor McGill and Notre Dame sts.

Les Precurseurs de la Temperance; founded in 1877, by Rev. Father L. Lauzon, O.M.I. Present director Rev. Father J. Jodoin, O.M.I.; 10 officers; 100 members. Basement of Eglise St Pierre. 109 Visitation st.

Société de Tempérance de l'Eglise St Pierre; founded in 1877, by Rev. Father Lauzon, O.M.I.; director Rev. Father S. Brault, O.M.I.; president Mathias Boivin; 25 members of committee; 500 members. 109 Visitation st.

Maison de Refuge Française; founded in 1886, as a night refuge for French from France by the Union Nationale Française, without regard to creed; Victor Ollivon, president; 1 Catholic female employees; 1 Catholic male employees; 3 Catholic French female; 9 Catholic French male refugees. Nationalities of inmates: 4 Catholic French females; 10 Catholic French male. 34 St Constant st.

Union Nationale Française; founded in 1886, as a benevolent society for Frenchmen from France. Victor Ollivon, president; R. de Mesle, secretary; 300 members. 34 St Constant st.

Union des Bons Livres; founded in 1844; Rev. M. Hamon, P.S.S., director. Library consists of about 11,000 volumes. 1717 Notre Dame st.

L'Union des Commis Marchands de Montréal; founded in 18 ; L. E. Cloutier, president; E. R. Beaudry, corresponding secretary; 220 members. 64 St Denis.

Congrégation de St Anne, for married women; founded in 1850. First director Rev. Father Leonard, O.M.I.; present director Rev. Father J. Lefebvre, O.M.I.; 40 officers; 2900 members. St Peter's Church, 109 Visitation st.

Congrégation de la Ste Vierge Marie; for young men; founded in 1864 by Rev. Father Leonard, O.M.I.; Director Rev. Father H. Legault, O.M.I.; 900 members. Basement of St Peter's Church, 109 Visitation st.

Congregation des Filles de l'Immaculée Conception (Eglise St Pierre); founded in 1855, for girls. First director Rev. Father Leonard, O.M.I.; present director Rev. Father Guillet, O.M.I.; 44 officers; 752 members. Chapelle de la Maitrise St Pierre, 109 Visitation st.

Society of the Holy Name, in connection with St. Mary's Church of Our Lady of Good Counsel; founded in 1883 for men. Director Rev. P. F. O'Donnell; 5 officers; 130 members. St Mary's Church cor Craig and Panet sts.

Society of St Vincent de Paul; founded in 1887 for men. First and present president James Morley; 4 officers; 80 members. St Mary's Church, cor Craig and Panet sts.

Sacred Heart Society; founded in 1879, for boys. First director Rev. Simon Lonergan; present director Rev. Brother Medrick; 4 officers; 100 members. St Mary's Church cor Craig and Panet sts.

Sodality of the Holy Rosary; founded in 1858 for married women. Directress Mrs. Street; 4 officers; 150 members. St Mary's Church cor Craig and Panet sts.

Pious Union of Our Lady of Good Counsel, with authority to affiliate other associations to the shrine of Our Lady of Good Counsel of Genazzano, Italy; directed by

the Clergy of St Mary's Church; 700 members. St Mary's Church cor Craig and Panet sts.

Catholic Order of Foresters, St Mary's Branch; established in 1890. Chief Ranger John Dillon; Chaplain Rev. P. F. O'Donnell; 10 officers; 50 members. 30 Panet st.

Children of Mary; founded in 1879, for young ladies. First directress Miss L. Croslin; present directress Reverend Sister St Olive of the Congregation of Notre Dame; 4 officers; 740 members. St Mary's Church cor Craig and Panet sts.

Société de Colonisation du District de Montréal, Section de Notre Dame et St Jacques; founded in 1886 by Rev. Abbé Rousselot. First president Rev. Victor Rousselot, O.M.I.; present president François Froideveaux; 15 members; 1 Catholic male employee. 63 St Gabriel st.

Société de Colonisation du Diocèse de Montréal; established in 1879. Monseigneur E. C. Fabre, Archbishop of Montreal, president; Rev. J. M. Emard, secretary; 11 members of the board; and the Catholic families of each parish. Office cor Lagauchetière and Cathedral sts.

Congregation du Saint Coeur de Marie, for men; founded in 1852. Director Rev. Father J. Lefebvre, O.M.I.; 50 officers; 900 members. 109 Visitation st.

Société de Bienfaisance Française; founded in 1886. President M. Victor Ollivon; R. de Mesle, secretary; 300 members. 34 St Constant st.

CATHOLIC SOCIETIES.

There are seven CATHOLIC SOCIETIES in Montreal. January, 1891.

French Canadian Philharmonic Society of Montreal. Honorary president Hon. Honoré Mercier, premier, M.P.P.; H. St Pierre, president; 7 officers; 6 committee men; 51 lady members; 55 gentleman members.

Société Historique; founded in 1857 by Jacques Viger, for the study of Canadian history. Abbé H. A. Verreau, president; R. Bellemare, secretary; 10 members; 1 Catholic male employee. Jacques Cartier Normal School, Sherbrooke st head of Visitation st.

Société de Médecine Pratique de Montréal; founded in 1888. First and present president Wm. H. Hingston, M.D.; A. A. Foucher, M.D. secretary; 100 members. 36 St Denis st.

Scholasticate of the Jesuit Fathers, built of wood; founded in 1885 by the Rev. Henri Hudon. Object—philosophy and theology. Maintained by the Company of Jesus. First superior Rev. Father Vignon; present superior Rev. Father Beaudevin. Cor Papineau road and Rachel st.

Catholic Young Men's Society, founded in 1865, by Rev. Patrick Dowd, P.S.S., first director, to encourage and cultivate a love for Catholic literature; present director Rev. Jas. Callaghan, P.S.S.; first president P. J. Coyle; present president J. J. Ryan. St Patrick's Parish Hall, 92 St Alexander st.

Young Irishmen's Literary and Benefit Association; founded in 1874; incorporated in 1875, for the literary and mutual improvement of its members. It comprises dramatic and debating clubs and gymnasiums. President, Joseph O'Brien; 12 officers; 36 committee men; 250 members. Nationalities of inmates: 1 Irish Catholic females; 1 Irish Catholic male. 19 and 21 Dupré lane.

St Ann's Young Men's Society, built of brick in 1884 as a meeting place for Catholic young men's recreation and benevolent societies in connection with St Ann's Parish Church. First and present president Rev. Father Strubbe, C.S.S.R.; 300 male Catholic members; 1 Catholic male employee. 1 Catholic Newfoundland female; 1 Catholic Newfoundland male; 2 inmates. 157 Ottawa st n Young st.

PROTESTANT SOCIETIES.

There are twenty-one PROTESTANT SOCIETIES in Montreal. January, 1891.

Colonial and Continental Church and School Society, incorporated in 1854, to assist clergymen, catechists and schoolmasters in the Colonies of Great Britain. President Right Rev. Lord Bishop of Montreal; Venerable Archdeacon Evans, M.A., superintendent; 21 members. Meetings held in the Synod Hall, 75 University st.

Montreal Auxiliary of the British and Foreign Bible Society; organized in 1820, for the sale and dissemination of the Holy Scriptures in all languages, under the patronage of His Excellency the Right Hon. Earl of Dalhousie, Governor-in-Chief of the United Provinces of Upper and Lower Canada. First president T. Porteous; present president Sir J. W. Dawson, L.L.D., F.R.S., K.C. M.G.; 6 Protestant female employees; 8 Protestant male employees; members. Nationalities of inmates; 1 Protestant English female; 1 Protestant Irish female; 1 Protestant English male. 2175 St Catherine st.

Montreal Auxiliary to the Ladies Bible Association; founded in 1860, in connection with the British and Foreign Bible Society. President Lady Dawson; 6 Protestant female employees. 2175 St Catherine st.

Montreal Religious Tract Society; organized in 1860, in connection with the London Religious Tract Society, for the distribution of tracts. President J. A. Matheson; 1 Protestant male employee. 2175 St Catherine st.

Sunday School Union, founded in 1836, as an organization of citizens interested in Sunday School work. President F. W. Kelley, Ph.D.; 1 Protestant male employee; 2175 St Catherine st.

Philosophical and Literary Society of the Presbyterian College; founded for the cultivation of the reasoning faculty, literary taste and rhetorical powers of its members by means of discussion, readings, the delivery of essays, etc. President, A. McGregor, B.A.; 6 officers; 3 councillors; members. 67 McTavish st.

Students' Missionary Society of the Presbyterian College, founded in 18—; president C. H. Vessot; 5 officers; 5 members of executive committee; 7 members of news committee; members, the students of the College. Presbyterian Theological College, 67 McTavish st.

Students' Missionary Society, in connection with the Diocesan Theological College; founded in 1873. First president Rev. J. A. Lobley, M.A., D.C.L.; present president Rev. Canon Henderson, D.D.; members, students of the College. 246 Dorchester st.

Alumni Association of the Presbyterian College; founded in 18—, for the promotion of a college spirit and the advancement of the work of the Institution. President Rev. J. R. Gamble, B.A.; 4 officers; 5 members of the executive committee; students of the college. 67 McTavish st.

Alumni Association of the Diocesan Theological College; founded in 1888; its object being to bring together the students and graduates for mutual help and edification, to provide them with means of concerted action, and to furnish some organ for the expression of their views and feelings, in connection with the College. First and present president Rev. Principal Henderson, D.D.; members all students and graduates whose names are on the College calendar. 896 Dorchester st.

Royal Arcanum in Council; established 1883, as a great fraternity, teaching by its ceremonials and work the purest lessons in virtue, mercy and charity, which are its principal points of doctrine. First regent J. E. Ferns; present regent J. E. S. Cass; 10 officers; 45 members. Odd-fellows Hall, Craig st.

Young Women's Christian Association Industrial School and Day Nursery; established in 1886, by the ladies committee of the Young Women's Christian Association, to educate and provide the children of working women a temporary home and Christian training. First president Mrs. C. V. Dewitt; present president Mrs. Wm. McDonough; 1 Protestant female teacher; 2 Protestant female employees; 15 children in home. Nationalities of inmates: 11 Protestant English females; 8 Protestant English females b in C. 174 Mountain st.

St George's Young Men's Christian Association; founded in 1865. Very Rev. Dean Carmichael, president; W. H. Walkley, secretary; 50 members. St George's School room, 13 Stanley st.

Montreal Branch of the Domestic and Foreign Missionary Society of the Church of England in Canada, organized in 1883. First and present president the Right Rev. Lord Bishop of Montreal. It is under a board of management composed of all the Bishops of the ecclesiastical provinces; 6 clergymen and 2 laymen from each Canadian Diocese; 55 members of board of management. Synod Hall, 75 University st.

English Workingmen's Benefit Society of Montreal, established 1861, incorporated 1869. Patron The Right Reverend William Bennett Bond, D.D., Lord Bishop of Montreal; first president Stanley Bagg; present president

R. Hall; chaplain Reverend Edmund Wood, M.A.; 24 officers; 323 members. Oddfellows' Hall, 662½ Craig st.

Girls' Friendly Society, in connection with the Church of England; founded in 1835. Objects; Mutual edification and moral benefit of Young Girls belonging to the Church of England. Patron the Right Rev. Lord Bishop of Montreal. First lady president Mrs. Henshaw; present president Mrs. Leslie Skelton; 4 officers; 100 members. Synod Hall, 75 University st.

Women's Auxiliary Missionary Society of the Diocese of Montreal; founded in 1887. First and present president Right Reverend William Bennett Bond, LL.D.; 927 members. Synod Hall, 75 University st.

Gospel Book Room (unsectarian), founded in 1889 for the distribution of Tracts and Christian Literature; 2 Protestant female employees. 8 Phillips sq.

Society for the Prevention of Cruelty to Women and Children; established in 1882, by a committee of Protestant citizens. First president Henry Lyman; present president Samuel Carsley; 1 Protestant male employee; Geo. W. Marshall, secretary. Office in Protestant House of Industry. 693 Dorchester st.

Canadian Society for the Prevention of Cruelty to Animals; established in 1869; incorporated in 1870. First president William Workman; present president Charles Alexander; 137 members; 3 Protestant male employees. 176 St James st.

Synod of the Diocese of Montreal; founded in 1850. First president the Most Reverend Francis Fulford, D.D., Metropolitan of Canada; present president Right Rev. William Bennett Bond, D.D., Lord Bishop of Montreal; 344 members. 75 University st and 12 Burnside place.

NATIONAL SOCIETIES

St George's Society; founded in 1834, incorporated in 1861, as a society of Englishmen for patriotic and benevolent purposes, and to help and assist English immigrants; honorary patron His Excellency the Governor General of Canada; patron the Lord Bishop of Montreal; first president Hon. George Moffatt; present president C. P. Sclater; 2 Protestant employees; 40 officers; 350 members. St George's Home, 13 St Antoine st.

St Patrick's Society; founded in 1856; incorporated in 1863. First president Benjamin Holmes; present president H. J. Cloran; T. F. McGrail, secretary; 150 members. Temple Block, McGill st.

St Andrew's Society, founded in 1835, by a committee of Scottish citizens, to help distressed Scottish poor in the city and emigrants on their arrival. First president Hon. Peter McGill; present president Sir Donald A. Smith, K.C.M.G., M.P.; 400 members; 1 Protestant male employee; 1 Protestant female employee. 403 Aqueduct st.

Caledonian Society of Montreal; established in 1850 for the practice and encouragement of Scottish games, and the cultivation of a taste for Scottish history and poetry and to unite more closely Scotchmen and those of Scottish descent. First president Lieut. Col. Fletcher; present president S. C. Stevenson, B.As; 6 officers; 12 committee men, 900 members. Annual subscription $1.00. St Andrew's Home, 403 Aqueduct st.

German Society; established 1835 as a benevolent society for German citizens of Montreal. First president Hon. Louis Gugy; present president William C. Munderloh; 6 officers; 70 members. Ed. Sandemeier, secretary. 61 St Sulpice st.

St Jean Baptiste Society, founded in 1834; incorporated in 1849, as a society of French Canadians, for patriotic and benevolent purposes, and to help and assist fellow-countrymen; L. O. David, president; Judge L. O. Loranger, first vice-president; principal Archambault, second vice-president.

Irish Protestant Benevolent Society; founded in 1856, by Protestant citizens of Montreal, for the purposes of assisting Irish Protestant emigrants arriving in Montreal, and relieving destitute Irish Protestants during the winter season. First president Benjamin Workman, M.D.; present president Richard White; 8 officers; 15 members of council; 3 reverend chaplains; 5 physicians; 3 auditors and 3 sub committees; 250 members. Protestant House of Industry. 693 Dorchester st.

Italian Society, founded in 1886; incorporated in 1889, by Italian citizens of Montreal, as a benevolent society for Italian emigrants arriving in Canada. First president Alexis Finoglio; present president Albert Dino; 9 officers; 150 members. 1625 Notre Dame st.

Scandinavian Society; founded in 1870, by Scandinavian citizens of Montreal, as a National benevolent society for Danish, Norwegian and Swedish emigrants arriving in Montreal President and chaplain Rev. O, Klevjord; 8 officers; 150 members. 41 St François Xavier st.

Montreal Welsh Union, founded in 1887, by the Welsh citizens of Montreal; Thomas Harries, president. 42 Victoria sq.

Swiss Society; founded in 1874, by Swiss citizens of Montreal, as a benevolent society for Swiss emigrants. First president A. Bacher; present president Paul Gental; 7 officers; 25 members. 34 St Constant st.

Sons of England Benevolent Society; Victoria Jubilee Lodge No 41; founded in 1874, for the mutual benefit of its members. President F. Brownhill; J. Edwards, secretary 15,200 members in this province. 4 College st.

BANKS IN MONTREAL.

There are Eleven CHARTERED BANKS and SIX BRANCH BANKS in Montreal, with a total Capital of $43,583,600, having a Reserve Fund of $17,369,300. The 17 Banks and Branches employ 324 persons.

Banks—Chartered and Chartered Branches.

Bank of Montreal—Capital $12,000,000; Reserve fund $6,000,000 ; 72 employees ; 3 sleeping in Bank building. Nationalities of inmates: 2 English Protestant males ; 2 English Protestant males b in C ; 1 Scotch Protestant male b in C. 107 St James st.

Canadian Bank of Commerce—Capital $6,000,000; Reserve fund $1,000,000; 19 employees in Bank ; 14 Protestant male employees. 157 St James st.

Merchants Bank of Canada—Capital $5,797,200; Reserve fund $2,335,000 ; 44 employees in Bank; 17 sleeping in Bank building. 205 St James st.

Bank of British North America—Capital £1,000,000 sterling ; Reserve fund £233,000 ; 30 employees in Bank ; 3 Catholic male employees ; 22 Protestant male employees ; 13 Sleeping in Bank building. Nationalities : 2 English female, 2 Irish female b in C, 1 English male ; 5 English males b in C ; 1 Scotch male; 1 Scotch male b in C ; 1 Irish male. 240 St James st.

Quebec Bank—$2,500,000 Capital; Reserve fund $500,000 ; 10 employees in Bank ; 10 Protestant male employees; 2 sleeping in Bank building ; 1 Catholic female employee ; 1 Catholic male employee ; Nationalities : 2 Catholic Fr. Canadians. 1790 Notre Dame st.

The Molsons Bank—Capital $2,000,000 ; Reserve fund $1,075,000 ; 30 employees in Bank ; 21 atholic male employees ; 18 Protestant male employees ; 5 sleeping in Bank building ; 1 Catholic female employee ; 5 Protestant male employees ; 2 Protestant female employees. 200 St James st.

Bank of Toronto—Capital $2,000,000 ; Reserve fund $1,200,000 ; 23 Catholic male employees. 166 St James st.

Ontario Bank—Capital $1,500,000; 10 employees in Bank ; 2 Catholic male employees ; 8 Protestant male employees ; 2 sleeping in Bank building ; 1 Catholic Irish male. 8 Place d'Armes.

Merchants' Bank of Halifax, authorized Capital $1,500,000; Paid-up Capital $1,100,000 ; Reserve Fund $375,000 ; 11 Protestant male employees ; 1 sleeping in Bank building ; 3 Protestant English females ; 7 Protestant English males. 1700 Notre Dame st.

Banque du Peuple—Capital $1,200,000 ; Reserve fund $400,000 ; 17 employees in Bank ; 17 Catholic male employees ; 3 sleeping in Bank building ; 2 Catholic females; 1 Catholic male; Nationalities: 3 Catholic Fr. Canadians b in C. 95 St James st.

Union Bank of Canada—Capital $1,200,000 ; Reserve fund $200,000 ; 9 employees in Bank ; 2 Catholic male employees ; 7 Protestant male employees ; 6 sleeping in Bank building ; 4 Catholic female ; 4 Protestant females ; 3 Protestant males. 1703 Notre Dame st.

Bank of Nova Scotia—Capital $114,300; Reserve Fund $200,000 ; 5 employees in Bank ; 1 Catholic male ; 4 Protestant males. 230 St James st.

Banque d'Hochelaga—Capital $310,100; Reserve fund $125,000 ; 17 employees in Bank ; 15 Catholic male employees. 107 St James st.

Banque Jacques-Cartier—Capital $500,000; Reserve fund $140,000 ; 16 employees in Bank ; 1 Catholic female employee ; 15 Catholic male employees ; 4 sleeping in Bank building ; 1 Catholic Fr. Canadian male ; 3 Catholic Fr. Canadian females. 7 Place d'Armes.

Banque Ville-Marie—Capital $500,000 ; Reserve fund $90,000 ; 11 employees in Bank ; 11 Catholic male employees ; 6 sleeping in Bank building ; 4 Catholic females ; 2 Catholic males ; Nationalities : 6 Catholic Fr. Canadians b in C. 153 St James st.

Banque Nationale—Capital $1,200,000 ; Reserve fund $100,000 ; 10 Catholic male employees. 6 Sleeping in Bank building ; 2 Catholic female employees ; 4 Catholic male employees. Nationalities : 6 Catholic Fr. Canadians. St James st, cor Place d'Armes.

SAVINGS BANKS.

There are Five SAVINGS BANKS in Montreal, employing 39 persons.

Montreal City and District Savings Bank ; 17 Catholic male employees. 176 St James st.

Savings Bank Department Bank of Montreal ; 2 employees in Bank. St James st facing Place d'Armes.

Savings Bank Department Merchants Bank of Canada ; 2 employees in Bank. 205 St James st.

Savings Bank Department The Molsons Bank ; 2 employees in Bank. 200 St James st.

Post Office Savings Bank, Montreal, with two branches. Hormisdas Alexis Bejrer, manager ; 6 Catholic male employees ; 1 Protestant male employee. St James cor St François Xavier sts.

CLUBS.

St James Club, built of stone, established in 1857 governed by a committee of 9 gentlemen, as a literary and social club, where neither politics or religion are discussed. Chairman John Cassels ; secretary and manager George E. Small ; 6 Protestant female employees ; 28 Protestant male employees ; 360 members. Nationalities of inmates :

Metropolitan Club, established in 1874 as a literary and social club First president Robert Archer ; present president Sir Joseph Hickson ; C. R. Christie, hon. secretary-treasurer ; 6 Catholic female employees ; 2 Catholic male employees ; 6 Protestant male employees. Nationalities of inmates : 4 Catholic Irish females ; 1 Catholic English female ; 1 Catholic English female b in C ; 4 Catholic Irish males ; 1 Catholic Irish male b in C ; 2 Catholic English males ; 2 Protestant English males ; 1 Protestant Scotch male ; 1 Protestant Scotch male b in C. 57 Beaver Hall hill.

Club Canadien de Montreal ; established in 1875 as a literary and social club for gentlemen. First president J. D. Pelletier ; present president A. B. Desmarteau ; 181 life members ; 47 subscribers ; 2 female employees ; 10 male employees. Nationalities of inmates : 6 Catholic Fr. Canadian females ; 9 Catholic Fr. Canadian males. 330 Lagauchetière st.

City Club, founded in 1883, as a literary and social club for gentlemen. First and present president R. J. White; 350 members ; 3 Protestant female employees ; 20 Protestant male employees. Nationalities of inmates : 3 Protestant English females ; 20 Protestant English males. St James cor St François Xavier st.

Montreal Press Club; founded in 1882. First president R. S. White, M.P ; present president J. Lessard, M.P.P. ; 6 officers ; 8 members of council ; 100 members. 48 St James st.

TEMPERANCE SOCIETIES.

Church of England Temperance Society (Montreal Branch); founded in 1889. First and present president Right Reverend Wm. Bennett Bond, LL.D., Lord Bishop of Montreal ; 6 vice-presidents ; 4 officers ; 21 councillors ; branches in the various parishes. Rev John Ker, secretary. Meetings held in Synod Hall, 75 University st.

Royal Templars of Temperance, Dominion Council instituted in 1884.

1st Dominion Councillor Rev. A. M. Phillips, Toronto.
1st Dominion Secretary J. H. Land, Hamilton.
Present Dominion Councillor A. M. Featherston, Montreal.

Present Dominion Secretary J. H. Land, Hamilton.
Grand Council of Quebec, instituted in Dec., 1887.
1st Grand Councillor A. M. Featherston, Montreal.
1st Grand Secretary W. E. Manson, Montreal.
Present Grand Councillor Rev. W. F. Perley, Knowlton.
Present Grand Secretary S. J. Symons, Montreal.
1st Council instituted in Province of Quebec, Pioneer Council No. 1, Martinville, 1883.

Membership.	Royal.	Select.
Ontario	9,600	3,400
New Brunswick	650	39
Quebec	2,078	179
British Columbia	104	94
Manitoba	1,600	149
P. E. Island	46	
Newfoundland	120	

Total membership in the Dominion 14,198, of these 3,841 have taken the second select degree, and about 400 have taken the knight templars degree.

Subordinate Councils.—Metrop lis No. 5 : Friday, in: R. T. Hall, 118 Mansfield st ; St Lawrence No. 6 : Friday, in Baptist Mission room, Point St Charles ; Dunnett No. 7 : Tuesday, in St Mark's Hall, Dalhousie st ; R e/iance No. 12 Monday, in Sher ooke Street Methodist Church : Advance No. 17 : Friday, in West End Hall, 134 Chatham st ; Orient No. 19 : Tuesday, in Sons of England Hall, 6 Craig st : Sceptre No. 17 : Monday, in R. T. Hall, 118 Mansfield st ; Rescue No. 28 : Thursday, in the basement of Methodist Church, Coteau St Louis ; Victoria No. 43 : Thursday, in the Hall, 1944 St Catherine st.

Independent Order of Good Templars, founded in 1851. It is the largest temperance organization in the world, with lodges meeting weekly in every part of the globe, and a membership roll of over 900,000. Grand chief templar for the Province of Quebec Rev. James Lawson ; grand secretary D. H. Howard. There are 8 lodges in Montreal with about 1,000 members, comprising the following :— *Good Samaritan*, meets at Centre st. Mission Hall ; *Star of the East*, meets at 1240 Notre Dame st ; *Gordon*, meets at St Mar.'s Hall, Hochelaga ; *Balmoral*, meets at Methodist Church, Melcalfe av ; *Richelieu* and *Terra Nova*, meets at 246 St James st ; *Perseverance*, meets at 90 Suzanne st ; *J. b. Gough* meets at 466 St Urbain st. District chief templar Alex. G. Ellis ; secretary A. Wardley.

Independent Order of Temperance Volunteers, founded in 1889 ; organized especially for young people of both sexes, under 21 years of age ; 150 members. Commander Alex. Geo. Ellis ; president A. Wand ; secretary Fred. Munn. Meets at 40 Emily st (temporarily), on Tuesday evenings at 8 o'clock.

Citizens League of Montreal, for suppressing the illicit sale of intoxicating liquors, the protection of women and children, and the morality of the city. First president Hon. G. H. Drummond ; present president J B. Rolland ; 4 officers ; 11 members of the executive committee ; 150 members ; 1 Protestant male employee. 181 St James st.

MILITARY.

Montreal Drill Hall, built of stone in 1885 by the Government of Canada, for the use of the active militia. It comprise s a large drill shed and the armories and offices of the city regiments and the brigade offices of the 5th and 6th military districts. Guardian Capt J.B. Emond ; 6 armory caretakers ; 1 furnace man. Nationalities of inmates : 1 Catholic Fr. Canadian female ; 1 Catholic Fr. Canadian male, Craig st between German and St. Constant sts.

Military District No. 5.—Lieut.-Col. C. F. Houghton, D. A.G.; Lieut.-Col. G. Mattice, brigade-major ; Lieut.-Col. F. M. Pope.

Military District No. 6.—Lieut.-Col. Gustave d'Odet D'orsonnens, D.A.G ; Major Alexander Roy, brigade-major; acting district paymaster Lieut.-Col. D'Orsonnens; acting-superintendent of stores Lieut.-Col. John Fletcher.

CITY REGIMENTS.

No. 1 Troop Duke of Connaught's Canadian Hussars. Commanding officer Major Colin MacArthur ; 3 officers ; 5 troopers.

Montreal Field Battery of Artillery. Commanding officer Lieut.-Col. A. A. Stevenson : 6 officers ; 74 non-commissioned officers and privates.

Montreal Brigade of Garrison Artillery, 6 batteries. Commanding officer Lieut.-Col. S. G. Turnbull; 26 officers ; 252 non-commissioned officers and privates.

Montreal Engineers, 1 company. Commanding officer Lieut.-Col. Wm. Kennedy ; 3 officers ; 84 non-commissioned officers and privates.

1st Prince of Wales Regiment of Rifles, 6 companies. Commanding officer Lieut.-Col. T. P. Butler ; 26 officers ; 252 non-commissioned officers and privates.

3rd Victoria Rifles of Canada, 6 companies. Commanding officer Lieut.-Col. F. C. Henshaw ; 26 officers ; 252 non-commissioned officers and privates.

5th Royal Scots of Canada, 6 companies. Commanding officer Lieut.-Col. John Hood ; 26 officers ; 250 non-commissioned officers and privates.

6th Fusiliers, 6 companies. Commanding officer Lieut.-Col. F. Massey ; 26 officers ; 252 non-commissioned officers and privates.

65th Battalion (Mount Royal Rifles), 8 companies. Commanding officer Lieut.-Col. C. A. Dugas ; 32 officers ; 336 non-commissioned officers and privates.

65th Battalion of Infantry, 6 companies. Commanding officer Lieut.-Col. J. Brosseau ; 26 officers ; 252 non-commissioned officers and privates.

Victoria Rifles Armory Association, built of brick in 1887, for the exclusive use of the 3rd Battalion Victoria Rifles of Canada. First and present president Col. Fred. Henshaw ; 300 shareholders ; 8 male employees. Nationalities of inmates : 1 Protestant English female ; 1 Protestant English male. 37 to 43 Cathcart st.

Headquarters of the Montreal Division of the Salvation Army, built of brick in 1887. First officer in charge Adjutant F. Van Allan ; present officer in charge Staff Captain Stephen Marshall ; 32 Protestant female officers ; 10 Protestant male officers ; 2 Protestant male employees. Nationalities of inmates : 1 Protestant English female b in C ; 1 Protestant Scotch female ; 1 Protestant English male b in C ; 1 Protestant English male. 26 St Alexander st.

RAILWAYS.

Grand Trunk Railway of Canada, established in 1852, first opened in 1852. First president Benjamin Holmes; present president L. J. Seargeant ; vice-president Wm. Wainwright ; Assistant general manager Chas. Percy ; general freight agent John Burton ; treasurer Robert Wright ; general passenger agent William Edgar. It has in the office, stores, etc., in Montreal 200 female employees and 618 male employees ; in the mechanical department in Montreal 1967 male employees, being a total of 2785 employees in this city. During the month of January, 1891, the average of cars arriving in the city was : 17 sleeping and parlor cars ; 107 passenger cars, and 621 freight cars per day, or 278 sleeping and parlor cars ; 2810 passenger cars, and 19,269 freight cars during the month. Offices and Works, St Etienne st, Point St Charles. Depot Bonaventure Station, St James st.

Canadian Pacific Railway Company, first established in 18 , line first opened in 18 . This line has 3000 continuous miles of steel rails, and also a continuous line of telegraphic communication in Canadian territory, stretching from Halifax, N.S., on the Atlantic seaboard to Vancouver, B.C., on the Pacific coast. First president Sir George Stephen, Bart.; present president Wm. C. Van Horne; vice-president Thomas G. Shaughnessy ; traffic manager Geo. Olds ; secretary Charles Drinkwater ; city passenger agent A. B. Chaffee, jr.; genera passenger agent D. McNicoll. It has in the depots, offices, stores, etc., in Montreal 27 female employees and 882 male employees ; in the mechanical department in Montreal 2349 male employees ; being a total of 2628 employees in Montreal. During the month of January, 1891, the average of cars arriving in the city was : 11 sleeping and parlor cars, 62 passenger cars, and 200 freight cars daily, or 321 sleeping and parlor cars, 1922 passenger cars, 6200 freight cars per month. Head office and Depot, Windsor st, Montreal.

Canada Atlantic Railway, during the month of January, had an average of 27 sleepers and parlor cars, and 54 passenger cars, arriving in Montreal at Bonaventure Station.

Central Vermont Railway, during the month of January, had an average of 155 sleepers and parlor cars, and 320 passenger cars, arriving in Montreal, at Bonaventure Station.

Delaware and Hudson Railway, during the month of January, had an average of 60 sleepers and parlor cars, and 124 passenger cars, arriving in Montreal at Bonaventure Station.

Montreal Street Railway Co have in use 1150 horses; 125 street cars; 105 sleighs; 65 busses, 950 male employees; 23½ miles of track. Office 17 Place d'Armes hill.

TELEGRAPHS.

Great North-Western Telegraph Co.; established in 1847. First president O. S. Wood; present president Erastus Wiman; H. P. Dwight, vice-president and general manager. This company operates the lines of the Montreal, Dominion and Canada Mutual Telegraph Company. It has 35 female operators; 225 male operators, clerks and linemen in Montreal. 50 St François Xavier st.

Canadian Pacific Railway Company's Telegraph; established in 1886. President William C. Van Horne; Charles R. Hosmer, manager of Telegraphs; James Kent, superintendent, Montreal. This company has 5,500 miles of direct communication stretching from Canso, N. S., on the Atlantic Ocean to Los Angeles, Lower California, on the Pacific Ocean, comprising a total wire mileage of 25,000 miles. It has 6 female employees and 60 male employees in the city. All the wire from the railway tracks are conveyed to the head office by cable. Head office, 4 Hospital st.

TELEPHONES.

Bell Telephone Company of Canada (Montreal Branch), established in 1880. Paid up Capital $1,500,000. First president Andrew Robertson; present president C. F. Sise; 100 female operators; 23 male clerks; 25 inspectors; 65 linemen; 101 factory men. 30 St John st.

Federal Telephone Co., established in 1888. First and present president Wm. Cassels; 23 linesmen; 34 operators; 18 factory men. Office 11 St Sacrament st; factory, 30 College st.

POST OFFICE.

Montreal Post Office, built of stone, in 1876. Postmaster, A. Dansereau; 1 assistant postmaster; 1 accountant and secretary; 7 first class clerks; 18 second class clerks; 65 third class clerks; 2 probationary; 70 letter carriers 4 not classified; 22 temporaries; 12 porters; 2 females at stamp counter.

Post Office Inspector's office, E. F. King, inspector; 2 assistant post office inspectors; 2 second class clerks; 2 third class clerks; 1 temporary; 1 messenger. Railway mail service; 1 chief railway mail clerk; 47 railway mail clerks; 2 temporary clerks; 3 mail transfer agents. 127 St James st.

GAS COMPANY.

Montreal Gas Company; established 1847. First president Thomas Molson; present president Jesse Joseph; 24 male employees in offices, 310 male employees in works; 2 gas houses. Offices 11 St James st, works on Ottawa and Harbor sts.

ELECTRIC LIGHT.

Royal Electric Company; established in 1884. First president W. R. Elmenhorst; present president Hon. J. R. Thibaudeau; Charles W. Hagar, manager; 151 male and 22 female employees in factory; 14 male employees in office; 15 linemen; 26 patrolmen and trimmers; 45 other male employees. Office and works 54 and 55 Wellington st.

HOTELS.

Windsor Hotel, built of stone; established in 1877. This hotel is one of the finest and most palatial on the American continent, and covers a site of over 250 x 350 feet. It has 400 apartments, and a dining room 111 feet in length and 55 feet in breadth, with accommodation for over 800 guests. It is situated in one of the most pleasant sites

in the city, and is in close proximity to the new Roman Catholic Cathedral, St George's Anglican Church, the Methodist and Presbyterian churches, and the Grand Trunk and Canadian Pacific Railway stations. The rates are from $3 50 to $5.00 per day, according to location. First and present proprietors The Windsor Hotel Company; first manager R. H. Southgate, present manager George W. Swett; 101 guests; 80 female employees; 137 male employees. Dominion sq cor Dorchester st.

St Lawrence Hall, built of stone; established in 1851. First and present proprietor Henry Hogan. This hotel has over 300 well lighted and airy rooms, and a dining room 100 feet long by 50 feet broad, capable of accommodating over 400 guests; rates from $2.50 to $3.50 per day. It has 40 guests, 50 female employees; 60 male employees. 139 to 143 St James st.

Balmoral Hotel, built of stone; established 1886. First proprietor E. W. Dunham; present proprietor James Smith. This hotel has 400 apartments, and a dining room affording accommodation for 400 guests; rates from $2 to $3 per day. It has 18 female and 32 male employees. 1894 to 1910 Notre Dame st.

Albion Hotel, built of stone; established in 1841. This hotel occupies one of the most central positions in the city, being in close proximity to the wharves, railway stations, City Hall, Post Office and principal thoroughfares. It has a large dining room and 160 apartments, capable of accommodating 200 guests. Rates from $1.50 to $2.00 per day. Kinne & Peavey, proprietors; 35 female employees; 15 male employees. 143 McGill st.

ASSOCIATIONS.

Montreal Wholesale Dry Goods Association, established in 1879, to promote the advancement of the Dry Goods Trade. First president Andrew Robertson; present president James Slessor; 29 members; 1 male employee. 39 St Sacrament st.

Wholesale Grocers' Association of Montreal, established January, 1884, for the purpose of promoting the prosperity of the grocery interests; to enforce the principles of justice and equity in all business transactions; to regulate terms of credit and discounts of the trade; and to take such action in commercial matters as may be considered necessary to protect the grocery trade. First president George Childs, who has acted in that capacity from the first. The Association is now a branch of the Board of Trade. 39 St Sacrament st.

Canadian Fire Underwriters' Association, founded in 1883 for the maintenance of fire insurance rates and promoting the interests of fire insurance in Canada. First president G. F. C. Smith; present president S. C. Duncan Clarke; 35 members, comprising all insurances companies licensed to do business in Canada; 3 male employees. 47 St John st.

Montreal Board of Trade; established in 1842. First president T. J. Brancoust; present president J. R. Cleghorn; Geo. Hadrill, secretary; 1300 members; 3 Protestant male employees. 10 St John and 39 St Sacrament sts.

Montreal Corn Exchange Association; established and incorporated in 1863. President R. M Esdaile; Geo. Hadrill, secretary; 155 members; 3 Protestant male employees. 10 St John and 39 St Sacrament sts.

Montreal Marine Underwriters' Association; established in 1890, to secure beneficial interchange of views upon matters appertaining to marine insurance. First and present president John Popham; 11 members. 30 St Sacrament st.

Montreal Stock Exchange, incorporated in 1874. James Burnett, chairman; H. C. Scott, secretary; 40 members; 1 male employee. 11 St Sacrament st.

Art Association of Montreal, built of stone; founded and incorporated in 1860, for the encouragement and furtherance of fine arts. First president Right Rev. Francis Fulford, D.D., Lord Bishop of Montreal and Metropolitan of Canada; present president Hon. Sir Donald A. Smith, K.C.M.G., M.P.; 10 governors; 63 life members; 388 annual members; 2 Protestant female employees; 3 Protestant male employees. 17 Phillips sq.

Montreal Society of Decorative Art; incorporated 1879; organized by a committee of ladies, for the encouragement of Fine Art work. First president Mrs. John Molson; present president Mrs. George W. Stephens; 3 lady vice-presidents; 10 ladies of the executive committee; 23 ladies of the general committee; 9 gentlemen of the advisory council; 101 lady members; Miss Hill, secretary-treasurer ; 1 Protestant female employees. 2288 St Catherine st.

Art Class; established in 1883, under the direction of W. Brindley, R.C.A ; 30 female students ; 2 male students ; 1 male employee. 17 Phillips sq.

Dominion Commercial Travellers Association; established in 1875, as a mutual benefit society for commercial travellers. First president Andrew Robertson ; present president Frederick Hughes ; 2000 members ; 1560 resident members in Montreal ; 1 Protestant male employee. H. W. Wadsworth, secretary. 260 St James st.

Dominion Commercial Travellers Mutual Benefit Society. Object : a life insurance for commercial travellers on the assessment plan. First president Fred. Birks ; present president Dr. Chas. Ault ; 900 members ; 1 male employee. Henry Wadsworth, secretary-treasurer. 260 St James st.

Montreal Horticultural Society and Fruit Growers Association of the Province of Quebec; founded in 1849 as the Montreal Agricultural and Horticultural Society, reorganized in 1878 as above. First president J. D. Gibb ; present president Prof. D. P. Penhallow ; 500 members. Library, Fraser Institute. 811 Dorchester st.

Montreal Diocesan Lay Helpers Association; founded in 1889. First and present president the Lord Bishop of the Diocese ; 3officers ; 20 members. J. W. Marling, secretary. Synod Hall, 75 University st.

Firemen's Benevolent Association; founded in 1846. President Chief Z. Benoit ; secretary Captain J. Beckingham ; hon treasurer ex-Chief Patton ; 126 members. The object of the Association is to assist and provide for members and firemen disabled in the discharge of their duty, and to assist the widows of deceased members ; there are now eight widows on the books, each receiving the sum of $100 per annum. Central Fire Station, Craig st.

Press Association of the Province of Quebec; founded in 1876. First president L. C. Belanger ; present president Joseph Lessard, M.P.P. ; 75 members ; Robt. E. Samuel, secretary. Gazette Office. 137 St François Xavier st.

CUSTOMS

Custom House, built of stone about 1853 by the Royal Insurance Company, purchased by the Government for custom house purposes about 1869. M. P. Ryan, collector of customs; John Lewis, surveyor and warehousekeeper. Collector's Office ; 3 male employees ; Long Room ; 16 male employees ; Record Office ; 4 male employees ; Shipping Office ; 2 male employees ; Statistical Office ; 2 male employees. Surveyor and Warehouse Keeper's Office ; 6 male employees ; Daily Register Office ; 2 male employees ; Locker's Office ; 2 male employees ; Tide Surveyor's Office ; 2 male employees ; Landing Waiter's Office ; 10 male employees; Gauger and Weigher's Office ; 4 male employees ; Housekeeper and Messenger ; 1 male employee ; Examining Warehouse ; 34 male employees. Corner Commissioners and Common sts.

Inland Revenue Offices, formerly the Custom House, built of stone in 1837. District inspector Raphael Bellemare ; 1 collector ; 1 deputy collector ; 1 deputy ; 1 accountant ; 1 assistant accountant ; 1 cashier ; 1 public analyst ; 1 food inspection officer ; 37 excise officers ; 1 messenger and house keeper. Custom House sq.

Provincial Revenue, District of Montreal. W. B. Lambe, collector of provincial revenue ; Philorom Lamontagne, deputy collector. 63 St Gabriel st.

Marine and Fisheries Department. H. St Osmond agent. 183 Commissioners st.

Immigration Offices. J. Daly, Dominion agent, 527 St James st.; E. Masquette, Provincial Government agent ; Rev. Robert Acton, chaplain 281; Craig st.

SUGAR REFINERIES.

Canada Sugar Refinery, built of brick ; established in 1854, by John Redpath & Son. It became a joint stock company in 1879. First president John Redpath ; present president Hon. Geo. A. Drummond ; W. W. Watson, secretary ; 300 male employees. Office 39 St François Xavier st. Refinery and works 191 St Patrick st.

The St Lawrence Sugar Refining Company, Limited; established 1879. President W. R. Elmenhorst ; vice-president A. Baumgarten ; secretary-treasurer Theo. Lubbet. This company has 1 female employee and 270 male employees, besides giving employment to a great many supernumerary hands outside the refinery. Refinery Notre Dame st., offices 39 St Sacrament st.

BAGS, CORDAGE, TWINES.

Canada Jute Company (Limited); established in 1882 for the manufacture of jute and cotton bags, twines, etc.; capital $100,000. First and present president Hon. Geo. A. Drummond ; 28 female employees ; 20 male employees. Manufacturing capacity 30,000 bags per day ; John Morrison, manager. 17 to 21 St Martin st.

Consumers Cordage Company, Limited; established in 1890, for the manufacture of ropes, bags, cordage, etc. First and present president J.F. Stairs, M.P. ; the Montreal branch factory has 70 female and 150 male employees. Office New York Life Building ; factory St Patrick st.

ENGINEERS.

Canadian Society of Civil Engineers, founded in 1887, to facilitate the acquirements and interchange of professional knowledge among its members and to encourage original investigation. First president Thomas C. Keefer, C.E. ; present president Colonel Sir Casimir Gzowski, C.E., A.D.C. K.C.M.G. ; Henry T. Bovey (dean of the Faculty of Applied Science, McGill University), secretary ; 1 Catholic female employee ; 1 Protestant male employee ; 650 members. Bank of Montreal building, 112 Mansfield st.

Brotherhood of Locomotive Engineers, established in 1863, for the mutual benefit of its members, and in cases of sickness, accident or death, to render aid and assistance to their families. (*Point St. Charles G. T. R. Branch No.* 89). Present chief engineer F. P. Lyle ; 10 officers ; 50 members. St Charles Club Room, Pt St Charles. (*Lalumière C. P. R. Branch No.* 388). First and present chief engineer Frank Houlahan ; 10 officers ; 25 members. 111 Moreau st, Hochelaga.

Brotherhood of Locomotive Firemen, first organized in 1873, as a benevolent association, to provide means for the support of those of its membership who through sickness or accident are in need of aid, and in case of death support for the widow and child, mother or sister. (*St Adolphus C. P. R. Branch* 333). First master A. Pring ; present master Patrick McFall ; 10 officers ; 35 members. 111 Moreau st, Hochelaga. (*St Lawrence Branch No.* 15). Thomas Wilson, master ; 12 officers ; 48 members. St Charles Club Room, Pt St Charles.

ARTS AND MANUFACTURES.

Council of Arts and Manufactures of the Province of Quebec, founded in 1873, by the Legislature of Quebec for the encouragement of Arts and Manufactures and the promotion of Industrial and Technical Education, etc. Honorable F. Langelier, president ; S. C. Stevenson, B.A., secretary ; 17 members ; 1 Protestant male employee ; 1 Catholic male employee ; 31 classes ; 30 teachers ; 841 pupils. 76 St Gabriel st.

Fine Art Institute, built of stone, and founded in 1879 by Madame Mederic Lanctot, the first and present principal ; 1 Catholic female teachers ; 77 Catholic female pupils ; 7 Catholic male pupils. 229 St Denis st.

INSTITUTES.

Mechanics' Institute, built of stone ; founded in 1828, by a committee of gentlemen, as a reading room and library for the mechanics of Montreal. First president Hon. L. Gugy ; present president William Rutherford ; 800 members; 6 male employees. Nationalities of inmates : 6 Protestan Scorch females ; 1 Protestant Scotch male. 204 St James st.

Fraser Institute, built of brick ; established in 1878, by Trustees of the estate of the late Hugh Fraser, as a free public library. First and present president Hon. J. J. C. Abbott, Q.C., senator ; 4 governors ; 12 executive committee ; 1 librarian ; 1 lady assistants ; 9 male employees. Nationalities of inmates : 3 Protestant English females ; 1 Protestant English males. 809 and 811 Dorchester and 9 University sts.

L'Institut Canadien; founded in 1844, by L. Racine, as a public library ; it was incorporated in 1882 with the Fraser Institute. First president A. C. Nelson ; present president Hon. J. J. C. Abbott ; secretary E. F. Malconronne ; 4 governors ; 11 executive committee ; 1 lady assistant librarians ; 10,000 volumes. Fraser Institute, 81 Dorchester st.

GENERAL.

Faculty of Medicine and Law of Laval University; founded in 1887, by Laval University, Quebec. First rector Rev. Jans. E. Hamel; present rector Rev. J. Pte. Froulx; 11 Catholic professors of medicine; 10 Catholic professors of law; 100 Catholic medical students; 30 Catholic law students; 2 Catholic male employees. Nationalities of inmates; 4 Catholic Fr. Canadian females; 5 Catholic Fr. Canadian males. 45 Jacques Cartier sq. and 1324 Notre Dame st.

Board of Health of the Province of Quebec (Conseil d'Hygiène de la Province de Quebec; established in 1887, for the sanitary investigation into diseases and deaths, and for the protection of public health. First and present president Dr. E. P. Lachapelle; 7 members; 2 Catholic male employees. Provincial Government building, 76 St Gabriel st.

Society for Historical Studies; founded in 1885, for the investigation and study of Canadian History. First president Thomas McDougall; present president W. J. White, M.A., B.C.L. J. P. Edwards, hon. secretary; 30 members. Natural History Room, 2 University st.

Montreal Natural History Society, built of brick; established in 1827, incorporated in 1832, for the promotion of the study of Natural History in Canada. Honorary president Sir Wm. Dawson; present president B. J. Harrington, B.A., Ph.D.; 300 members. 1 Protestant English male employee. 32 University and 35 Cathcart sts.

Dominion Alliance (Quebec Provincial Branch), founded in 1879, for the suppression of the Liquor Traffic. First president Hon. James Ferrier; present president John R. Dougall; 32 vice-presidents; 60 general committeemen; 2000 members; 2 Protestant male employees. 42 Victoria sq.

Medico Chirurgical Society, for the advancement of medical science and discussion of matters relating to the medical profession. President P. J. Shepherd, M.D.; 1 Protestant male employee; 90 members. 14 Phillips sq.

Odontological Society, founded in 1879, for the advancement and study of dental science. First president E.R. Ibbotson, L.D.S.; present president A. S. Brosseau, L.D.S.; 40 members. 14 Phillips sq.

Mendelssohn Choir; founded in 1863 by Joseph Gould. The Choir has been in successful operation for twenty-seven years under the superintendence and management of Mr Gould. It is composed of 135 members, comprising 80 lady members and 55 gentlemen members. Crescent St School room. 3 Crescent st.

Montreal Philharmonic Society, organized in 1875, by Arthur M. Perkins; incorporated in 1882, for the performance of standard choral works. First president Gilbert Scott; present president Hector Mackenzie; chorus of 240 voices; orchestra of 40 pieces. Office of Secretary-Treasurer Room 8, 1774 Notre Dame st.

The Barnjum Gymnasium, established in 1865 and conducted until 1888 by F. S. Barnjum, for the physical training and culture of young men, ladies and young children of both sexes; continued since 1888 by the present principal Helen O. Barnjum, for the physical culture of ladies and children only; 300 female pupils; 50 male pupils; 1 Protestant female employee; 1 Protestant male employee. 13 University st.

Grand Trunk Railway Literary and Scientific Institute, founded in 1857, for the literary, scientific and mutual improvement of the employees of the Grand Trunk Railway Company of Canada. First president H. E. Trevithick; present president Sir Joseph Hickson; 34 officers; 800 members; 1 Protestant male employee. The library contains about 5,500 volumes. Sebastopol st, Point St Charles.

Victoria Skating Rink, built of brick in 1864; established by the Board of Directors. First president F. Torrance; present president Li. Col. Henshaw; first superintendent F. Gillett; present superintendent Isaac Lea. members; 7 male employees. 4) Drummond n Dorchester st.

Academy of Music, built of stone; established 1874. First proprietor E. A. McDowell; present proprietor and manager H. Thomas; 3 female employees; 23 male employees; seating capacity 1800. 1310-19 Victoria st.

Theatre Royal, built of stone, opened in June, 1852. It has seating capacity for 1740 persons, and a stage 40 feet in length by 60 feet in breadth. First proprietor J. W. Buckland; present proprietors Sparrow & Jacobs; Lew Rohdt, manager; 5 female employees; 33 male employees. 19 and 21 Cotté st.

Montreal Rolling Mills Company. Andrew Allen, president; Wm. McMaster, manager; 25 female employees; 600 male employees in works; 17 male employees in offices. 3096 Notre Dame st.

Montreal Jail, built of stone in 1834. First governor and warden Charles Wand; present governor and warden Louis Payette; 12 prison guards; 1 sergeant; 10 warders; 1 gate keeper; 1 engineer; 1 steward; 209 Catholic male prisoners; 55 Protestant male prisoners; 1 Jewish male prisoner; 147 Catholic female prisoners; 14 Protestant female prisoners; 372 inmates. Nationalities; 90 Catholic Irish females b in C; 78 Catholic Fr. Canadian females; 10 Protestant English females; 4 Protestant Scotch females; 103 Catholic Irish males b in C; 75 Catholic Fr. males; 9 Catholic English males b in C; 10 Protestant English males b in C; 10 Protestant Scotch males b in C; 5 Protestant English males; 1 Jewish male. *Warden's residence;* 4 Catholic Fr. Canadian females; 2 Catholic Fr. Canadian males. 871 Notre Dame.

The Mercantile Agency; Dun, Wiman & Co., established in 1842. W. W. Johnson, manager. 4 female employees; 17 male employees. 1072 St James st.

The Bradstreet Mercantile Agency; established in 1849. John A. Fulton, superintendent; 1 female employee; 15 male employees. 1724 Notre Dame st.

L'Agence Commerciale; established in 1896; 2 female employees; 12 male employees. 10 Place d'Armes.

REGISTRY OFFICES.

Registry Office—Montreal West. Warwick H. Ryland Court house, 1577 Notre Dame st.

Registry Office—Montreal East. J. C. Auger. 63 St Gabriel st.

Registry Office—Jacques Cartier and Hochelaga. N. M. Lecavalier and F. Filiatreault. 63 St Gabriel st.

CEMETERIES.

Notre Dame des Neiges—Catholic; established 1854. Evariste Dupré, superintendent; 3 employees. Situated at Notre Dame des Neiges.

Mount Royal—Protestant; established in 1852. The dead of the Church of England, of the Presbyterians, the Methodist, the Congregational, the Baptist and the Unitarian Churches are buried in the grounds on Mount Royal.

Jewish Burying Places; established in 18 . Managed by a committee of Jews, and is situated outside Mount Royal Cemetery.

INSTITUTIONS OUTSIDE CITY LIMITS.

THEY ARE NOT ENUMERATED IN MONTREAL CENSUS.

Villa Maria Convent Mother House of the Congregation of Notre Dame, built of stone at Notre Dame de Grace, in 1880. Founded by the Venerable Mother Marguerite Bourgeoys, in 1657, for the education of young girls. First lady superioress Venerable Mother Marguerite Bourgeoys; present lady superioress Reverend Mother St Jean de la Croix; 132 nuns; 134 novices; 5 Catholic female employees; 18 Catholic Male employees. Parish of Notre Dame de Grace.

Convent Villa Maria (Congregation of Notre Dame), built of stone in 1846. Founded by the Religious of the Congregation of Notre Dame as a boarding school for young ladies. First lady superioress Reverend Mother St Nativity; present lady superioress Reverend Mother St Providence; 30 sister teachers; 23 Catholic female employees; 18 Catholic male employees; 250 Catholic female pupils. Notre Dame de Grace.

Chapelle du St Rosaire et de la Réparation, built of stone in 1884. 540 congregation. Parish of Notre Dame de Grace.

Mackay Institution, built of stone; founded in 1878, by the late Joseph Mackay, for the education and industrial training of deaf, dumb and blind children. It is supported by an annual grant from the Quebec Government, pupils' fees, and annual subscriptions. First superintendent Thomas Widd; present superintendents Mr. and Mrs. J. Iurie Ashcroft; 4 Protestant female teachers; 2 Protestant male teachers; 4 Protestant female employees; 2 Protestant male employees; 1 Protestant female blind child; 4 Protestant male blind children; 18 Protestant female deaf children; 22 Protestant male deaf children. Sunday services are held in one of the large class rooms from 3 to 4 p. m. It is situated at Cote St Antoine, consequently is not counted in the Census of Montreal.

Asile des Aliénés de St Jean de Dieu, built of brick in 1873; destroyed by fire 6th May, 1890, loss $1,000,000; rebuilt temporarily in 1890, of wood, covered outside with galvanized iron, painted red in imitation of brick. It comprises 14 different pavilions of two stories each, connected by covered corridors, 7 on each side of the avenue,— the women being on one side and the men on the opposite side. The Asylum was founded, in 1875, by the Reverend Sisters of the House of Providence, under whose care and direction it remains, for the care and protection of insane persons and idiots of both sexes. It has 3 resident physicians; 2 visiting physicians; 2 resident chaplains, Revs. F. X. Leclaire and H. R. Laberge. First and present lady superioress Reverend Sister Thérèse de Jésus; 150 nuns as nurses and helpers; 64 Catholic male attendants; 6 Catholic female night attendants; 4 male night attendants; 6 Catholic female employees; 40 Catholic male employees, such as engineers, firemen, cooks, bakers, shoemakers, tailors, farmers, etc., gardeners, stablemen, etc.; 577 female patients and 605 male patients, towards whose support an annual grant of $100 per head is made by the Quebec Government; 112 private patient boarders. The grounds belonging to the Institution comprise about 600 acres; a new 6 storey reservoir, built of brick, is on the brow of the river, on a line with the Asylum. It gives an abundant water supply to the 14 pavilions, the stables, cow houses, etc , and supplies water for heating the entire buildings and for the several laundries. This wonderful Institution is under the able management of the Reverend lady superioress Sister St. Thérèse de Jésus. It issituated at Longue Pointe, 6 miles from Montreal, consequently it is not enumerated in Lovell's Historic Report of the Census of Montreal.

PROTESTANT INSANE HOSPITAL.

At River St Pierre. January, 1891.

Protestant Hospital for the Insane, built in 1889 of stone, founded in 1890, by public subscription, for the reception of Protestant lunatics, under the supervision of a medical specialist. It has 1 visiting physician; a committee of management; 7 Protestant female nurses; 8 Protestant male attendants; 7 Protestant female employees; 7 Protestant male employees; 116 inmates. As the number of patients increases, 1 nurse will be added to every 10 patients, as received. The Institution is maintained by fees of boarding patients and a Government grant of $116 per head for public patients. It is situated at Verdun, consequently is not connected in this Census of Montreal.

CENSUS OF MONTREAL.

As I have not succeeded, after a persistent canvass, to secure a sufficient number of subscribers to warrant the publication of my projected CENSUS OF MONTREAL. I have asked those who desire the issue to become 500 LINE CONTRIBUTORS, by giving their NAME, PROFESSION, or BUSINESS, and ADDRESS for publication in this Historic Record of Montreal. I have great pleasure in acknowledging a cheerful and telling response, which enables me to risk publication without a serious loss.

MONTREAL, 31st January, 1891.   JOHN LOVELL, *Compiler.*

MONTREAL LINE CONTRIBUTORS.

LEGAL PROFESSION.

There are 23 Judges, 1 Recorder, 2 Police Magistrates and Judges of Sessions, 233 Magistrates, 300 Advocates, 1 Sheriff, 1 Prothonotary, 1 Clerk of Appeals, and 119 Notaries in Montreal, among whom are:

HON. SIR ANTOINE A. DORION, Chief Justice, Court of Queen's Bench, 2153 Notre Dame st.
HON. SIR FRANCIS GODSCHALL JOHNSON, Chief Justice, Superior Court, 81 Union av.
HON. C. J. TESSIER, Puisné Judge Court of Queen's Bench.
HON. ALEXANDER CROSS, Puisné Judge Court of Queen's Bench, 151 Cote des Neiges road.
HON. F. GEORGE BABY, Puisné Judge, Court of Queen's Bench, 77 Mansfield st.
HON. L. R. CHURCH, Puisné Judge Court of Queen's Bench, 643 Sherbrooke st.
HON. J. G. BOSSÉ, Puisné Judge Court of Queen's Bench.
HON. MARCUS DOHERTY, Judge Superior Court, 24 St Famille st.
HON. LOUIS A. JETTÉ, Judge Superior Court, 75 Dubord st.
HON. CHARLES I. GILL, Judge Superior Court, 642 St Denis st.
HON. MICHEL MATHIEU, Judge Superior Court, resides in St Lawrence Hall, 139 St James st.
HON. LOUIS O. LORANGER, Judge Superior Court, 34 St Denis st.
HON. H. T. TASCHEREAU, Judge Superior Court, 68 St Hubert.
HON. J. A. OUIMET, Judge Superior Court, 575 Sherbrooke st.
HON. C. C. DELORIMIER, Judge Superior Court, 395 St Denis st.
HON. JONATHAN S. C. WURTELE, Judge Superior Court, 78 Union av.
HON. M. M. TAIT, Judge Superior Court, 994 Sherbrooke st.
HON. CHARLES PEERS DAVIDSON, Judge Superior Court, 74 McGill College av.
HON. SIMEON PAGNUELO, Judge Superior Court, 383 Sherbrooke st.
DENNIS BARRY, Judge Magistrates' Court, 790 Lagauchetiere st.
B. A. T. DEMONTIGNY, Recorder, 154 St Denis st.
MATHIAS C. DESNOYERS, Police Magistrate and Judge of Sessions, 25 Berri st.
C. AIMÉ DUGAS, Police Magistrate and Judge of Sessions, 408½ St Denis st.
CHARLES CHAMPAGNE, Judge Magistrates Court, 1538 Notre Dame.
HON. J. R. THIBAUDEAU, Sheriff, 17 Laval av.
J. A. FRANCHÈRE, Deputy Sheriff, 26 Berri st.
HON. ARTHUR TURCOTTE, Prothonotary.
GEORGE N. KERNICK, 1st Deputy Prothonotary, 467 St Denis st.
L. W. MARCHAND, Q.C., Clerk of Appeals, 20 Berri st.
L. OUIMET, Deputy Clerk of Appeals, 78 St Denis st.
J. E. CHAMPOUX, Clerk of Tutelle and Deputy Prothonotary, 103 Cadieux st.
L. H. COLLARD, Deputy Clerk Court of Review, 109 German st.
L. W. SICOTTE, Clerk of the Crown and Peace, 202 St Hubert st.
C. R. DOUCET, Deputy Clerk of the Crown and Peace, 48 Berri st.
A. CHERRIER, Clerk of Circuit Court, 1538 Notre Dame st.
C. BONACINA, Deputy Clerk Circuit Court, 149 Laval av.
J. B. TRUDEL, Clerk of Magistrates Court, 113 St Hubert st.
C. J. HIMSWORTH, Deputy Clerk Magistrates Court, 1538 Notre Dame st.
L. FORGET, Clerk Recorder's Court, 2 Mitchison av.
A. BISSONETTE, High Constable, 68 Berri st.
JAMES DOUGLAS, Deputy High Constable, 346 Craig st.
W. H. RYLAND, Registrar Montreal West, 321 Dorchester st.
J. C. AUGER AND C. L. CHAMPAGNE, Joint Registrars Montreal East.
LECAVALIER & FILIATRAULT, Registrars Hochelaga and Jacques Cartier.
E. O. CHAMPAGNE, Inspector of Steam Boilers, 143 St Lawrence st, Mile End.
LOUIS PAYETTE, Jailer, 871 Notre Dame st.
C. A. VALLÉE, Deputy Jailer, 871 Notre Dame st.
A. C. LALONDE, Law Stamp Office, 135 St Christophe st.
JACQUES A. PLINGUET, Law Stamp Office Circuit Court, 183a Drolet st.
A. DELISLE, Librarian, 82 St Denis st.
C. LECLAIR, Chief Crier Court of Queen's Bench, St Rose.
P. C. WATTIER, Chief Crier Superior Court, Plessis st.
A. CLERMONT, Guardian of Court House, 1517 Notre Dame st.

ADVOCATES.

There are 300 Advocates in Montreal, among whom are:

ADAM, DUHAMEL & PLOURDE, Avocats, 1618 rue Notre Dame.

J. L. ARCHAMBAULT, Q.C., Advocate, 15 St James st.

ARCHIBALD & FOSTER, Advocates, Commissioners, etc., 181 St James st.

BARNARD & BARNARD, Advocates, 180 St James st.

J. & W. A. BATES, Advocates, Barristers, etc., 66 St James st.

E. BAUSET, Advocate, New York Life Building, Place d'Armes

O. BEAUDET, B.C.L., Advocate, 138 St James st, house 2533 Notre Dame st.

LOUIS BELANGER, B.C.L., Advocate, 57 St Gabriel st.

BERARD & BRODEUR, Advocates, 42 St Vincent st. Bell Telephone 2223.

BERGEVIN & PAPINEAU, Advocates, 58 St James st.

BURROUGHS & BURROUGHS, Advocates, 12 Place d'Armes sq.

CHAPLEAU, HALL, NICOLLS & BROWN (Hon. J. A. Chapleau, Q.C., M.P., John S. Hall, Jun., Q.C., M.P.P., Armine D. Nicolls, Albert J. Brown), Advocates, Barristers, Commissioners, etc., Temple Building, 185 St James st.

A. G. B. CLAXTON, Advocate, 180 St James st.

CRESSE & DESCARRIES, Avocats, etc., 79 rue St Jacques. Boite Postale 329. Bell Tel. 1085.

SELKIRK CROSS, Advocate, Solicitor, etc., Standard Building, 157 St James st.

DAVIDSON & RITCHIE, Advocates, 190 St James st.

T. C. & R. G. DE LORIMIER, Advocates, 61 St Gabriel st.

R. DES RIVIÈRES, B.C.L., Advocate, 10 Hospital st.

DOHERTY & DOHERTY, Advocates, Barristers, etc., 180 St James st.

J. M FERGUSON, B.C.L., Advocate and Commissioner; money to loan on mortgage, Temple Building, 185 St. James st.

GEOFFRION, DORION & ALLAN, Advocates, Solicitors, etc, Imperial Building, 107 St James st., facing Place d'Armes.

MARTIN HONAN, Advocate, Room 45 Imperial Building, 107 St James st, facing Place d'Armes.

A. HOULE, Advocate, 1601 Notre Dame st.

L. J. R. HUBERT, Advocate, Room 2, Flat 4, 180 St James st.

J. O. JOSEPH, Q.C., Advocate, 82 St François Xavier st.

J. C. LACOSTE, Advocate, 1601 Notre Dame st.

LACOSTE, BISAILLON, BROSSEAU & LAJOIE, Advocates, 11 and 17 Place d'Armes hill.

LAFLAMME, MADORE, CROSS & LAROCHELLE, Advocates, New York Life Bdg.

HUSMER LANCTOT, Advocate, 1598 Notre Dame st.

LAVALLEE & LAVALLEE, Advocates, 61 St Gabriel st.

M. J. C. LARIVIERE, Advocate and Commissioner for Manitoba, 41 St Vincent st. Bell Tel. 2211.

JOSEPH STANISLAS LEROUX, Advocate, 1572 Notre Dame st.

LIGHTHALL & MACDONALD, Advocates, 180 St James st.

MARCEAU & LANCTOT, Barristers, 1608 Notre Dame st.

G. E. MATHIEU, L. L. L., Advocate, New York Life Bdg, Place d'Armes.

J. H. MIGNERON, Advocate, 74 St James st.

G. MIREAULT, Advocate, 1601 Notre Dame st.

ALFRED MONK, Advocate, 180 St James st.

OUIMET & EMARD, Advocates, 180 St James st.

M. J. F. QUINN, Q.C., Rooms 98 and 100 Temple Building, 185 St James st.

RAINVILLE, ARCHAMBAULT & GERVAIS, Advocates, New York Life Bdg, Place d'Armes.

CHARLES RAYNES, B.A., B.C.L., Advocate, Barrister, etc., Commissioner for Ontario and Manitoba, Savings Bank Chambers, 180 St James st. Tel. 2426.

ROBERTSON, FLEET & FALCONER, Advocates, Barristers and Solicitors, 157 St James st.

ROBIDOUX, PREFONTAINE, ST JEAN & GOUIN, Advocates, 1709 Notre Dame st.

J. A. ST JULIEN, B.C.L., L.L.L., Advocate, 1598 Notre Dame st.

TAYLOR & BUCHAN, Advocates, Temple Building, 185 St James st.

F. W. TERRILL, Advocate, 121 Lansdown Avenue, Cote St Antoine.

PHILIPPE VANDAL, B.C.L., Advocate, 10 Exchange Court.

W. S. WALKER, Barrister, 1737 Notre Dame st.

ACCOUNT BOOK MANUFACTURERS.

There are 12 Account Book Manufacturers in Montreal, among whom are:

CHARLES F. DAWSON, Mercantile Stationer and Account Book Manufacturer; Engraving, Lithographing and Printing, 233 St James st.

JOHN LOVELL & SON, Blank Account Book Manufacturers, 23 and 25 St Nicholas st.

ACCOUNTANTS

There are 68 Accountants in Montreal, among whom are :

BILODEAU & RENAUD, Accountants and Commissioners ; Specialty, Settlement of Insolvent Estates, 15 St James st.

CHAS. R. BLACK, Accountant, 30 St John st.

CALDWELL, TAIT & WILKS, Accountants, Auditors, Commissioners, 207 St James st.

P. E. EMILE DE LORIMIER, Accountant, 107 St James st.

CHAS. DESMARTEAU, Accountant, 1598 Notre Dame st.

GEORGE DURNFORD, Chartered Accountant, 196 St James st.

JOHN McD. HAINS, Accountant, Trustee Receiver, etc., Fraser Building, 43 St Sacrament

J. B. HUTCHESON, Accountant, Auditor and Financial Agent, 204 St James st.

LACHLAN MACKAY, Accountant, Auditor, Real Estate and Financial Agent, Temple Building, 185 St James st.

JOHN McDONALD, Accountant and Auditor, Imperial Building, 107 St James st.

RIDDELL & COMMON, Chartered Accountants and Auditors, Commissioners for the Canadian Provinces and the State of New York, Western Chambers, 22 St John st.

P. S. ROSS & SONS. Chartered Accountants and Commissioners, 18 St Alexis st.

AERATED WATERS.

There are 8 Aerated Water Manufacturers in Montreal, one of whom is :

J. CHRISTIN & Co., Aerated Water Manufacturers. Their Champagne Cider is a Specialty, ask for it, 149 Sanguinet st.

AGENTS.

There are 1022 Agents in Montreal, among whom are :

ECREMENT & Co., L'Agence Générale de Propriétés Fonciers, Directeur de la Société Canadienne Belge, la Transoceania, 77 rue St Jacques

FURNIVAL & Co., Lithographing and Printing Machinery ; J. Movins & Son, Aniline Dyes ; Stoer Bros. & Cales, Lithographing Inks, etc., 32 St Sulpice st.

J. F. GIBSONE, Agent in Glass, Metals, Chemicals, Oils, 10 St Sacrament st.

H. T. LEVY, Collecting, House, Land and General Agent, 5 St Thérèse st.

H. McLAREN & Co., General Agents in Canada for Magnolia Artificial Metal Co. of London and New York, 30 St François Xavier st.

J. T. SCANLAN, representing P. & C. L. Drouat, France, 26 St. Sacrament st.

AGRICULTURAL IMPLEMENTS.

There are 11 Agricultural Implement Makers in Montreal, among whom are :

THE A. HARRIS, SON & Co. Agricultural Implements, 72 College st.

R. J. LATIMER, all kinds of Carriages and Farm Implements, 66 College st.

THE MASSEY MNFG. Co., 66 McGill st.

J. O. WISNER, SON & Co., Agricultural Implements, D. F. Réaume, Manager, 86 and 88 McGill st.

ANALYTICAL LABORATORY.

TO FARMERS AND LAND OWNERS :

S. E. Wheeler, Twenty Years' Experience as an Analyst (Late Assistant to Dr. J. Baker Edwards, Public Analyst for Montreal), is open to make Analysis of Ores, Minerals, Spring and Mineral Waters on Moderate Terms. Persons opening up New Grounds should take the opportunity of having any Mineral, etc., found in quantities or any Mineral Spring discovered on their premises examined as they may thereby be put in possession of valuable information. S. E. Wheeler also examines Drugs, Foods and Preparations of all kinds. For information and particulars of fees, etc., address (temporary office) S. E. Wheeler, care of James Innes, 643 Craig st., Montreal. Free Consultation by appointment.

ARBITRATORS.

There are 8 Arbitrators in Montreal, one of whom is :

FELIX BOISMENU, Arbitrator Valuator, 17 Place d'Armes hill. Tel. 2277. Private residence 264 St Hubert st.

ARCHITECTS.

There are 73 Architects in Montreal, among whom are :

J. A. U. BEAUDRY, Architect, 107 St James st.

ALCIDE J. CHAUSSE Architect, 77 St James st and 1541 St Catherine st. Tel. connection.

CHRISTOPHER CLIFT, Room 8, 180 St James st.

J. B. DOUGLAS, Architect and Valuator, Standard Building, 157 St James st.

A. F. DUNLOP, Architect and Valuer, Temple Building, 185 St James st.

FOWLER & BOWE, Architects, 198 St James st

88   *Montreal Line Contributors.*

Archits.—Continued.

J. RAWSON GARDINER, Architect, Room 97 Temple Building, 185 St James st.

J. W. & E. C. HOPKINS, Architects and Valuers, 145 St James st.

ALEX. C. HUTCHISON, Architect, Valuator of Real Estate, Buildings, etc., 181 St James st.

A. H. LAPIERRE, Architect and Measurer, 3 Place d'Armes hill.

SIMEON LESAGE, Architect and Valuator, 17 Place d'Armes hill.

P. LORTIE & FILS, Architectes et Mesureurs, 1933 rue Notre Dame. Bell Tel. 1836, Federal Tel. 2207.

O. MAILLOUX, Architect and Valuator, 160½ St Antoine st.

ERIC MANN, Architect, Valuator, etc., Waddell Building, 30 St John st. Bell Tel. 2566.

JOS. A. MERCIER, Architecte, 25 rue St Jacques.

L. R. MONTBRIAND, Architecte et Mesureur, 1583 St Catherine st. Telephone 6703.

H. CHAS. NELSON, Architect, 1724 Notre Dame st.

JAMES NELSON, Architect and Valuator, 1724 Notre Dame st.

H. M. PERRAULT, Architect and Valuator, 17 Place d'Armes hill.

PERRAULT & MESNARD, Architects, 11 and 17 Place d'Armes hill. Bell Telephone 696, Federal Telephone 838.

J. B. RESTHER & FILS, Architects, Rooms 60 and 66 Imperial Building, 107 St James st. Bell Tel. 1800.

V. ROY & L. F. GAUTHIER, Architectes et Evaluateurs, 180 rue St Jacques. Bell Tel 2758.

CASIMIR ST JEAN, Architecte, Evaluateur, &c., 180 rue St Jacques.

W. T. THOMAS, Architect, 204 St James st.

WRIGHT & SON, Architects and Valuators, etc., Mechanics Institute Building, 204 St James st.

ARTIFICIAL FLOWERS.

P. N. BRETON, Artificial Flowers of all kinds kept constantly on hand; also, Special Line of Artificial Wreaths, Crosses, Pillows, etc., for Funeral Purposes, 1664 St Catherine st.

ARTISTS.

There are 13 Artists in Montreal, one of whom is:

EUGENE L'AFRICAIN, 1608 Notre Dame st.

ASBESTOS.

There are 5 Asbestos Dealers in Montreal:

THE ANGLO CANADIAN ASBESTOS COMPANY (LTD.). Irwin, Hopper & Co., Managing Directors, 30 St François Xavier st.

BROWN & CO., Asbestos, Phosphate and Scrap Iron Merchants, 8 Custom House sq.

FENWICK ARNOLD & Co., Asbestos, Cotton Waste, etc., 57 St François Xavier st.

IRWIN, HOPPER & Co, Asbestos and Phosphate Miners and Shippers, Managing Directors of The Anglo-Canadian Asbestos Co. (Ltd.), The English Portland Cement Co. (Ltd.), 30 St François Xavier st.

WILLIAM SCLATER & Co., Asbestos Manufacturers, 42, 44 and 46 Foundling st.

AUCTIONEERS.

There are 30 Auctioneers in Montreal, among whom are:

BENNING & BARSALOU, Trade Auctioneers and Commission Merchants, 86 St Peter st.

D. H. & W. H. FRASER, General Auctioneers, Valuators and Real Estate Agents, 320, 322, 324 St James st.

M. HICKS & Co. (M. Hicks, E. O'Brien), Auctioneers and Commission Merchants, 1821 and 1823 Notre Dame st. Advances Made on Consignments. Charges Moderate and Returns Prompt. Specialties: Turkish Rugs, Art Objects: Fine Pictures by Old and Modern Masters, &c., always on hand.

RAE & DONNELLY, General Auctioneers, Valuators and Commission Merchants. Largest Auction Rooms in Canada; Liberal Cash Advances made on all Kinds of Merchandise. Fire Losses Adjusted and Valuations made. Charges Moderate and Prompt Returns, 241 and 243 St James st.

JAMES STEWART & Co., General Auctioneers, 16 St Sacrament st.

D. TIGH & Co., Auctioneers and Commission Agents, 305 St James st.

AUDITORS.

There are 18 Auditors in Montreal, one of whom is:

HENRY WARD & Co., Auditors, Real Estate and Financial Agents, 260 St James st. Bell Tel. 1882.

AWNING MANUFACTURERS.

There are 4 Awning Manufacturers in Montreal, one of whom is:

DEMERS & Co., Awning Manufactory, 1658 Notre Dame st.

BABY CARRIAGE MANUFACTURERS.

There are 8 Baby Carriage Manufacturers in Montreal, among whom are:

GENDRON MANUFACTURING CO., Manufacturers of Baby Cabs. Tricycles, Bicycles, Velocipedes and Children's Waggons, L. Charlebois, Manager, 1910 Notre Dame st.

BAILIFFS.

There are 59 Bailiffs in Montreal, among whom are:

OLIVIER C. COUTLEE, Bailiff for the Court of Queen's Bench and Superior Court, and Special Constable, 20 St James st., house 827 Sanguinet st. Bell Telephone No. 7.

BAKERS.

There are 93 Bakers in Montreal, among whom are:

JAMES M. AIRD, New Bread and Cake Bakery, office and store 99 and 103 St Urbain st. Bell Tel. 1340B, Fed. Tel. 803

ALEX. ARCHIBALD, Baker. 260 St Charles Borromée st.

JAMES H. McKEOWN, Baker and Confectioner, 370 St Antoine st. Bell Telephone 8114. Daily delivery to all parts of the city.

JOHN NOBLE, Plain and Fancy Bread, 137 St Urbain st.

WILLIAM REID, Baker; Fancy Bread a specialty, 154 St Urbain st.

JAMES STRACHAN, Plain and Fancy Breads of all kinds, delivered daily, city and country, 142 German st.

ALFRED C. TRUTEAU, Baker, 275 Dorchester st.

BAKING POWDER.

There are 6 Baking Powder Manufacturers in Montreal, among whom are:

W. D. McLAREN, Manufacturer of the Cook's Friend Baking Powder, 55 and 57 College st.

NATIONAL BAKING POWDER AND SPICE MILLS, Manufacturers, Agency and other Specialties, H. B. Potter, Montreal.

BAMBOO GOODS.

There is one Manufacturer of Bamboo Goods in Montreal:

R. OGAWA & CO., Manufacturers of Fine Bamboo Goods, 21 Beaver Hall hill.

BAND INSTRUMENTS.

There are 6 Band Instrument Dealers in Montreal, among whom are:

ED. HARDY, Band Instruments, Vocal and Instrumental Music, 1615 Notre Dame st.

G. VIOLETTI, Importer Harps and Manufacturer of Band Instruments; Repairing a Specialty, 1635 Notre Dame st.

BANKS.

There are 16 Banks in Montreal, among which are:

BANQUE DU PEUPLE,

Established in 1835; incorporated in 1837; Capital $1,200,000; Reserve Fund $330,000.

J. S. BOUSQUET, *Cashier.*

37 St. James st.

This office has 17 employees.

BANK OF TORONTO,

Established in 1856; incorporated by Act of Parliament in 1856; Capital $2,000,000; Reserve Fund $1,500,000. Head Office in Toronto.

J. MURRAY SMITH, *Manager.*

168 St. James cor St. John st.

This office has 13 employees.

BANQUE VILLE MARIE,

Established in 1872; incorporated in 1872; Capital $500,000; Reserve Fund $20,000.

WILLIAM WEIR, *President.*
W. STRACHAN, *Vice President.*
U. GARAND, *Cashier.*

153 St. James st.

This office has   employees.

CANADIAN BANK OF COMMERCE,

Established in 1867; incorporated in 1867; Capital $6,000,000; Reserve Fund $800,000. Head office in Toronto.

DIRECTORS:

GEORGE A. COX, *President.*
JOHN I. DAVIDSON, *Vice-President.*

GEORGE TAYLOR,	W. B. HAMILTON,
JAMES CRATHERN,	M. LEGGAT,
J. HOSKIN, Q.C., LL.D.,	ROBERT KILGOUR.

B. E. WALKER, *General Manager.*
J. H. PLUMMER, *Asst. Gen. Manager.*
A. M. CROMBIE, *Manager at Montreal.*

157 St. James st.

This office has 19 employees.

BANKERS.

There are 7 Private Bankers in Montreal, among whom are:

J. B. PICKEN & Co., Banking and Exchange, 124 St James st.

BASKET MAKERS.

There are 3 Basket Makers in Montreal, among whom are:

F. PELOSSE, Basket Maker—all kinds—808 Craig st.

BEDDING MANUFACTURERS.

There are 12 Bedding Manufacturers in Montreal, among whom are:

JAMES STEEL, Practical Manufacturer and Expert on Mattresses and Bedding Materials, 1826 Notre Dame st.

J. E. TOWNSHEND, Bedding Patented for its Purity; Feather Dressers; Woven Wire Bed Manufacturers, 2306 St Catherine st.

BILLIARD ROOMS.

There are 4 Billiard Rooms in Montreal, among which are:

BALMORAL HOTEL, Billiard Room, Refitted, Now Open, John Donahue, proprietor.

BILLIARD TABLE MANUFACTURERS.

There are 2 Billiard Table Manufacturers in Montreal, among whom are:

D. NIGHTINGALE, Mnfr. Pool and Billiard Tables and Balls; Tables Altered, etc., 1742 Notre Dame

BISCUIT AND CRACKER BAKERS.

There are 8 Biscuit and Cracker Bakers in Montreal, among whom are:

THE MONTREAL BISCUIT Co., Manufacturers of all kinds of Biscuits and Crackers, 82 and 84 McGill st.

BLACKSMITHS.

There are 164 Blacksmiths in Montreal, among whom are:

J. K. MACDONALD, Blacksmith, Bellhanger and Locksmith, 762 Craig st.

BOILER COVERINGS.

There are 4 Boiler Covering Manufacturers in Montreal, among whom are:

WILLIAM SCLATER & Co., Boiler Coverings, 42, 44 and 46 Foundling st.

BOILER MAKERS.

There are 16 Boiler Makers in Montreal, among whom are:

WARDEN KING & SON, Manufacturers of Spence's Patent Sectional, Champion and Daisy Hot Water Boilers, Steamfittings of all Sizes, Plumbers' Wares, Soil Pipes and Fittings, Stable Fittings and General House Castings, etc., Sole Manufacturers of New York Safety Dumb Waiters, 637 Craig st.

J. B. VINCENT, Builder of Steam Boilers, Bridges, and all kinds of Boiler Plate Work, 228 Richmond st.

W. C. WHITE, Builder of Steam Boilers, Boats, Bridges, Tanks, etc., Nazareth, Brennan and Dalhousie sts.

BOOKSELLERS.

There are 72 Booksellers in Montreal, among whom are:

C. O. BEAUCHEMIN & FILS, Booksellers and Printers, Account Book Manufacturers, 256 St Paul st.

CADIEUX & DEROME, Booksellers and Stationers, 1603 Notre Dame st.

W. DRYSDALE & Co., Publishers, Booksellers and Stationers, Wholesale and Retail; Books in all Departments, 232 St James st, Branch 2365 St Catherine st.

G. A. & W. DUMONT, Libraires, 1826 rue Ste Catherine

F. E. GRAFTON & SON, Importers of Books, Stationery and Magazines; Educational and Sunday School Supplies of all kinds, 252 St James st.

P. KELLY, Bookseller and Music Dealer, Publisher Montreal Songster, 154 St Antoine st.

JAMES MILLOY, Stationery, &c., 2117 St Catherine st.

THE MONTREAL NEWS Co., ltd., Wholesale News Dealers, Booksellers and Stationers, General Agents for all the leading English and American periodicals. Catalogues furnished on application, 386 and 388 St James st.

E. PICKEN, Bookseller, 33 Beaver Hall hill.

D. & J. SADLIER & Co., Catholic Publishers, Booksellers and Stationers, Church Ornaments, Vestments, Statuary and Religious Articles, 123 Church st, Toronto, 1669 Notre Dame st, Montreal.

MRS. H. T. SAIT, Stationery, &c., 2099 St Catherine st.

BOOTS AND SHOES.

There are 197 Wholesale and Retail Boot and Shoe Dealers in Montreal, among whom are:

A. BASTIEN, Boot and Shoe Dealer; Best and Most Complete Assortment, 1987 Notre Dame st cor St David lane.

J. & T. BELL, Manufacturers Fine Boots and Shoes, 1665 and 1667 Notre Dame st.

L. CHEVALIER, Marchand de Chaussures, 1600 rue Notre Dame.

JAMES CORCORAN, Boots and Shoes, 2076 Notre Dame st.

FOGARTY & BRO., cor St Lawrence and St Catherine sts.

ARTHUR HÉTU, Fine Boots and Shoes Retail, 209 St Lawrence st.

MALLETTE & MARTIN, Boots and Shoes, 116 McGill st.

ZOTIQUE PILON, 1389 and 1391 Notre Dame st.

RONAYNE BROS., Boots and Shoes, Wholesale and Retail, 17 Chaboillez sq.

C. SCHOLFIELD & Co., Manufacturers of Boots and Shoes, 1646 Notre Dame st.

J. SLOAN & SON, Fine Boots and Shoes ; Custom Work and Repairing a Specialty, 199 St Antoine st. Bell Tel. 2307.

W. R. THOMPSON, Boots and Shoes, Wholesale and Retail, 100 McGill st, opp St Ann's Market

B. VAILLANCOURT, Boots and Shoes, 173 Jacques Cartier st.

JAMES WHITHAM & Co., Fine Boots and Shoes, 43, 45 and 47 St Maurice st.

BOOT AND SHOE MANUFACTURERS.

There are 53 Boot and Shoe Manufacturers in Montreal, among whom are :

ARCHIBALD & TURNER, Fine Boots and Shoes, 758 Notre Dame st.

G. BOIVIN, Specialties : Patent G. B. one piece Boot and C. P. R. Bals, Patented 1890. The best for Comfort, Durability, Cheapness ; they will not get out of shape, 286 and 288 St Paul st.

P. HEMOND & SON, Wholesale Manufacturers of Boots and Shoes. Specialties : Hand Made Slippers and Cacks (turned), Office and Warehouse 220 St Paul, Factory 13 to 21 St Therese st.

Z. LAPIERRE, Wholesale Boot and Shoe Manufacturer, 294 and 296 St Paul st.

JAMES LINTON & Co., Wholesale Manufacturers and Dealers in Boots and Shoes, 35 to 43 Victoria sq.

JAS. McCREADY & Co., Wholesale Boot and Shoe Manufacturers, office corner St Peter and Youville sts.

J. I. PELLERIN & FILS, Wholesale Manufacturers of Shoes ; Cheap Slippers a Specialty, 985 Notre Dame st.

GEO. T. SLATER & SONS, Manufacturers Fine Shoes, corner St Alexander and Jurors sts.

THOMPSON & Co., Fine Boots and Shoes, 172½ Craig st.

BOTTLE IMPORTERS.

There are 3 Bottle Importers in Montreal, among whom are :

BLACKLOCK BROS., Importers of Ale, Wine and Spirit Bottles, 17 Common st

BOX MAKERS.

There are 22 Box Makers in Montreal, among whom are :

G. & J. ESPLIN, Box Manufacturers, cor Duke and Ottawa sts.

BRASS FOUNDERS.

There are 14 Brass Founders in Montreal, among whom are :

CUTHBERT & SON, Brass Founders and Finishers, 23 and 25 College st.

ROBERT MITCHELL & Co., Manufacturers of Gas and Electric Light Fixtures, Gas Meters, Engineers,' Plumbers,' Gas and Steam Fitters' Supplies, factory St Cunegonde, office cor Craig and St Peter sts.

BREWERS.

There are 10 Brewers in Montreal, among whom are :

DAWES & Co., 521 St James st.

BROKERS.

There are 101 Brokers in Montreal, among whom are :

R. MOAT & Co., Stock Brokers, 12 Hospital st.

F. NASH, Member Montreal Stock Exchange, 30 Hospital st.

H. McLAREN & Co., Metal and General Brokers, 30 St François Xavier st.

BRUSH MANUFACTURERS.

There are 8 Brush Manufacturers in Montreal, among whom are :

MEAKINS & Co., Manufacturers of Brushes of all Kinds, Painters' and Artists' Fine Brushes a Specialty ; Special Attention Given to Mill and Machinery Brushes. Send for Catalogue, 313 St Paul st.

K. OLSEN, Norwegian Brush Factory ; all Machine Brushes made to order ; Special attention to Mills and Factories, 84 St Maurice st.

BUILDERS.

There are 39 Builders in Montreal, among whom are :

LAPHAM BROS., Builders and Turning, &c., 1 St Philip st.

BUILDERS—*Continued.*

WILLIAM LAVERS, Bricklayer and Builder, 70 St Hypolite st, above Sherbrooke st. Bell Tel. 6212.

MARTEL & BLACKLOCK, Builders, 9 Aylmer st. Bell Telephone 4049.

R. G. SALLOWAY, Carpenter and Builder, 41 Mance st.

BUTCHERS.

There are 770 Butchers in Montreal, among whom are:

ANDRE LEROUX & Co., Butchers and Dealers in Beef, Mutton, Veal, Lamb and Salt Meats, 153 Wellington st.

BUTTER DEALERS.

There are 32 Butter Dealers in Montreal, among whom are:

JAMES DALRYMPLE, Wholesale Dealer in Butter. The trade supplied from the best Eastern Townships and Morrisburg Dairies, 96 and 98 Foundling st.

J. E. MACLEAV, Dealer in Butter, Eggs, Milk and Cream, 47 University st. Bell Tel. 4477.

CABINETMAKERS.

There are 52 Cabinetmakers in Montreal, among whom are:

JOHN TRESIDDER & Co., Cabinetmakers, 1280 Dorchester st.

CALCIUM LIGHT.

There is one Calcium Light Company in Montreal:

MONTREAL CALCIUM LIGHT CO., Oxygen and Hydrogen Gas, 27 St Antoine st.

CAN WORKS.

There is one Can Works in Montreal.

ACME CAN WORKS, Liquid Paint Tins, Irons, Round and Square, Cans, etc., Wm. Walker, 177 St Antoine st.

CARPENTERS AND BUILDERS.

There are 102 Carpenters and Builders in Montreal, among whom are:

T. CHARPENTIER, JUN., Carpenter and Builder, 818 Mignonne st.

COUVRETTE & FILS, Entrepreneurs Menuisiers, 114 rue St Jacques.

WM. SWAN, Carpenter and Builder, 117½ St Antoine st.

CARPET CLEANING.

There are 5 Carpet Cleaners in Montreal, among whom are:

CARPET BEATING AND RENOVATING CO., H. N. Tabb, Manager, 11 Hermine st.

MONTREAL CARPET BEATING CO., 623 Lagauchetière st. Bell Telephone 716, Federal Telephone 810.

THE RENOVO PROCESS, 185 St James st. Bell Tel. 2147.

CARRIAGE LEATHERS.

There is one Carriage Leather Factory in Montreal:

MONTREAL CARRIAGE LEATHER CO., J. Alex. Stevenson, Proprietor; Manufacturers of the " Stag " Brand Patent, Enamel, Top, Winker, Dash, Landau, Buffings and Colored Trimming Leathers, etc., Office 20 Lemoine st. Works, Town of St Henry.

CARRIAGES AND SLEIGHS.

There are 84 Carriage and Sleigh Makers in Montreal, among whom are:

BERARD & MAJOR, Light and Heavy Carriages and Sleighs of all descriptions, 1945 St Catherine st.

N. & A. C. LARIVIÈRE, Builders of Carriages, Sleighs and Street Cars. The only firm in Canada to which has been awarded 5 Gold, 5 Silver and 2 Bronze Medals, 74 St Antoine st.

R. J. LATIMER, Carriages and Sleighs of all kinds, " Nice," " Good," " Cheap," 92 McGill st.

B. LEDOUX is the only Builder in Canada who has won Medals and Diplomas at the Centennial Exhibition of Philadelphia, U. S., 1876, and N. S. W., 1877, in competition with the world, 131 St. Antoine st.

THE MASSEY MNFG. CO., 66 McGill st.

CARTAGE.

There are 8 Cartage Agents in Montreal, among whom are:

MELDRUM BROS., General Carters and Coal Dealers, office 32 Wellington st.

CATERERS AND CONFECTIONERS.

There are 9 Caterers and Confectioners in Montreal, among whom are:

WELSH & ROUGH, Caterers, who supply everything necessary for First-Class entertainments, with use of China, Glass, Silverware, Cutlery, Linen, Napkins, Tables, Flowers, Waiters, &c., &c., either outside or in their beautiful upper Dining Hall, the Finest in the City to display Elocution, Oratory or Song, with use of lower Hall if desired. Full Dinner from 11.30 a.m. to 3 p.m. and to Order from 7 a.m. to 8.30 p.m. 1796 Notre Dame near St Peter st.

CEMENT.

There are 13 Cement Dealers in Montreal, among whom are:

THE ENGLISH PORTLAND CEMENT Co. (LTD.), Irwin, Hopper & Co., Managing Directors, 30 St François Xavier st.

CHEMICALS.

There are 3 Chemical Dealers in Montreal, among whom are:

WILSON, PATERSON & CO., Importers of Chemicals, Oils, etc. and Naval Stores, 5 Custom House sq.

CHEMISTS AND DRUGGISTS.

There are 124 Chemists and Druggists in Montreal, among whom are:

C. J. COVERNTON & CO., Dispensing and Family Chemists, cor Bleury and Dorchester sts., branch 469 St Lawrence st.

ED. F. G. DANIEL, Chemist and Druggist, formerly first assistant at Laviolette & Nelson's, 1564 Notre Dame st., opp Court House. Bell Tel. 2269.

DR. GUSTAVE DEMERS, druggist, 2193 Notre Dame st.

ADALBERT GAUVREAU, Dispensing Chemist; Agent for the Lightning Wizard Oil, 513 St James st near G. T. R. Depot.

S. LACHANCE, Proprietor of Father Matthew Remedy, Dr. Sey's Remedy, Persian Lotion, Indigenous Bitters and Audette's Hair Promoter, 1538 St Catherine st.

LAVIOLETTE & NELSON, Chemists, Proprietors of Dr. Chevalier's Spruce Gum Paste, Dr. Nelson's Prescription and Goudron de Norwège, and Agents for French Patent Medicines, 1605 Notre Dame st.

DR. J. LEDUC & CO., Dispensing Chemists, cor Notre Dame st and Chaboillez sq.

B. E. McGALE, Pharmaceutical and Dispensing Chemist, 2123 Notre Dame st.

R. McNICHOLS, Chemist; Prescriptions Carefully Compounded; Toilet Articles, Perfumeries and Patent Medicines, 1497 St Catherine st.

DR. F. L. PALARDY, Chemist and Druggist; Diseases of the Skin a Specialty, 396 St James st. Bell Tel. 1085, Federal Tel. 2263.

PHARMACIE DECARY, Produits Chimiques et Pharmaceutiques; Articles de Toilette et Parfumerie. Service de Nuit et du Dimanche, coin des rues St Denis et Ste Catherine.

PICAULT & CONTANT, Wholesale and Retail Druggists; Prescriptions a Specialty, 1475 Notre Dame st.

CHESTER'S CURE.

USE CHESTER'S CURE for Asthma, Bronchitis, Catarrh, Coughs, Colds, etc. For sale by all Druggists.

CHINA, GLASS AND EARTHENWARE.

There are 11 Wholesale China, Glass and Earthenware Merchants in Montreal, among whom are:

J. L. CASSIDY & Co., Importers of China, Glass, Earthenware, Plated Goods, Lamps, Gasaliers, etc., 339 and 341 St Paul st.

A. F. WILEY & CO., China, Glassware and Lamp Goods, 1803 Notre Dame st.

CIGAR MANUFACTURERS AND IMPORTERS.

There are 28 Cigar Manufacturers and Importers in Montreal, among whom are:

FISH & CO., Wholesale Importers of Havana Cigars, 33 St Nicholas st.

J. M. FORTIER, Cigar Manufacturer, 153 St Maurice st.

ADAM GERKIE, Importer and Dealer in Genuine Havana Cigars. Carries a large Assortment of all the leading brands of Cigars suitable for the Trade, 147 McGill st.

B. GOLDSTEIN & CO., Wholesale Importers of Fine Havana Cigars, 43 Recollet st.

L. O. GROTHE & CO., Cigar Manufacturers, 15 and 17 St Peter st.

I. HARRIS & SON, Othello Cigar Factory, 47 and 49 College st.

HAVANA CIGAR CO., Manufacturers of the Finest Brands of Cigars, 773 Craig st.

PENNINGTON & CO., Montero Cigar Factory, Manufacturers of the Celebrated "Montero," "Mercier" and "Kennel" Brands; Superior Hand-Made Havana Cigars a Specialty, 631 Lagauchetière st.

SMITH, FISCHEL & CO., Cigar Manufacturers, 46, 48 and 50 College st.

T. J. WINSHIP & CO., Luntin Cigar Factory, Manufacturers of Cigars and Dealers in Leaf Tobacco, 476 St Paul st.

CIVIL ENGINEERS.

There are 49 Civil Engineers in Montreal, among whom are:

J. A. U. BEAUDRY, Civil Engineer, 107 St James st.

J. P. B. CASGRAIN, Civil Engineer, Dominion and Provincial Land Surveyor, Solicitor of Patents, etc., 181 St James st.

CIVIL ENGINEERS—*Continued.*

CHAS. E. GOAD, C. E., Temple Building, Montreal ; Quebec Bank Chambers, Toronto and 33 New Broad st, E. C., London, Eng.

SIMEON LESAGE, Civil and Hydraulic Engineer, 17 Place d'Armes hill.

J. EMILE VANIER, Civil and Hydraulic Engineer, Provincial Land Surveyor, Patent Solicitor, Rooms 60, 65 and 66 Imperial Building, 107 St James st., h 418 Rachel st. Bell Tel. 1800

L. R. VOLIGNY, Civil Engineer and Draughtsman, Solicitor of Patents, Room 79 Imperial Building, 107 St James st. facing Place d'Armes.

CLOTHING MANUFACTURERS.

There are 17 Clothing Manufacturers in Montreal, among whom are :

G. F. BURNETT & Co., Clothing Manufacturers, 752 Craig st.

J. COHEN & Co., Manufacturers and Wholesale Clothiers, 441 St Paul st.

J. W. MACKEDIE & Co., Manufacturers of Clothing, Wholesale, 31 and 33 Victoria sq.

COAL OIL.

There are 12 Coal Oil Dealers in Montreal, among whom are :

FRS. MARTINEAU, Coal Oil, 1381 and 1383 St Catherine st.

C. PEVERLEY, American and Canadian Refined Oils ; Dominion Agent for Pratt's Astral Oil, 65 St Peter st.

COAL AND WOOD MERCHANTS.

See also Wood Dealers.

There are 78 Coal and Wood Merchants in Montreal, among whom are :

ANDREW BAILE, Wholesale and Retail Dealer in all Kinds of Coal, 69 McGill st.

H. BRADY, Coal and Wood Merchant ; Kindling Wood a Specialty, 287 St Antoine cor Guy st.

L. COHEN & SON, Coal and Wood, 154 William st.

JOHN COSTIGAN & Co., 2430 Notre Dame st and 196 St James st.

J. O. LABRECQUE, COUSINEAU & CIE., Coal and Wood Merchants, 83 Wolfe st.

MASSON & ASSELIN, Importers and Dealers in all kinds of Coal, 21 Youville, in rear 29 McGill st. Telephone 2271.

MELDRUM BROS., Coal Dealers and General Carters, office 32 Wellington st.

SYDNEY AND LOUISBURG COAL AND RY. CO., Ltd., " Reserve " Mines, Consulate of the Argentine Republic, Vice-Consulate of the Republic of Uruguay, Cable Address " Henshaw," Watkin's Cove, F. C. Henshaw, Agent, 8 Custom House sq. Bell Telephone 638.

B. L. & I. VIPOND, Wood and Coal, 113 Craig and 590 St Lawrence sts.

WILSON BROS., Coal and Wood, 605 Notre Dame st.

COIN DEALERS.

There is one Coin Dealers in Montreal.

P. N. BRETON Buys and Sells Canadian Coins and Medals, also Publisher of Breton's Illustrated Canadian Coin Collector, 313 Illustrations, Price 50 Cents. 1664 St Catherine st.

COFFEE AND SPICE MILLS.

There are 11 Coffee and Spice Mills in Montreal, among whom are :

BOURGEAU & HERRON, Trade Coffee and Spice Mills, 51 College st.

CHASE & SANBORN, Coffee Merchants, 435 St Paul st.

COLLECTORS.

There are 63 Collectors in Montreal, among whom are :

N. CHEVALIER, Collector, 80 St James st.

COMMISSION MERCHANTS.

There are 155 Commission Merchants in Montreal, among whom are :

BLAIKLOCK BROS., Commission Merchants, 17 Common st.

DUCKETT, HODGE & Co., Exporters of Butter and Cheese, and General Produce Commission Merchants, cor William and Grey Nun sts.

HOWE, McINTYRE & Co., Millers' Specialties and Produce, 299 Commissioners st.

A. L. HURTUBISE & Co., Commission Merchants, 42 Jacques Cartier sq.

KINGMAN, BROWN & Co., Shipping and Commission Merchants, Selling Agents International Coal Company, Managing Agents Black Diamond Steamship Co. of Montreal, 14 Custom House sq.

STEWART MUNN & Co, Commission Merchants, 22 St John st.

C. N. D. OSGOOD, General Commission Merchant and Manufacturers' Agent, 69 St Peter st.

D. SMITH, JUN., & Co., General and Commission Merchants, Paper, Paper Stock and Scrap Metals, 43 and 45 William st.

STEEL & CAMPBELL, Commission Merchants, Wholesale Flour, Feed, Grain, Pork, Lard, &c., Office and Storerooms 331 Commissioners st.

C. G. WATT & Co., Produce and Commission Merchants, 281 and 283 Commissioners st.

COMPANIES.

There are 263 Companies in Montreal, among whom are :

GAS CONSUMERS' BENEFIT CO.,Geo. W. Gaden, Manager. Sole Agents in the Dominion for the celebrated Jackson Automatic Gas Burners, Improved Gas Stoves and Gas Devices of all kinds, Hill's Odorless and Steamless Cookers. Office and Sample Room 2110 St Catherine st.

THE DOMINION LEATHER BROAD CO., Leather Boards and Stiffeners, Asbestos Mill Board, Friction Board Roofing, Carpet and Lining Felts, 5 St Peter st.

CONFECTIONERS.

There are 190 Confectioners in Montreal, among whom are :

JAMES M. AIRD, Confectioner,Cake Baker, also Lunch Rooms ; Lunches at any hour of the day, 1877 Notre Dame st. Bell Tel. 1340 A.

MRS. W. G. BLINKO, Choice Confectionery ; Cakes and Candies fresh every day. 49 St Antoine st.

KELLOGG & Co., Wholesale Manufacturers of Confectionery ; Specialty : French and American Hand-Made Creams, Fine English Chocolates and Medicated Work, 411 St James st.

A. H. McDONALD, Confectioner, 2503 Notre Dame st.

N. LACHANCE,Confectioner, 1041 St Lawrence.

J. W. SUTHERLAND, Confectioner, Cakes and Pastry of all kinds ; Maker of the original "Sutherland" Fruit Pies, 93 and 95 Wellington st.

JAS. W. TESTER & Co., Steam Confectionery works. Every description of Staple and High Class Confectionery ; Maple Sugar in bulk a specialty, 68 and 70 McGill st.

J. TOMLINSON, Choice Confectionery. Melton-Mowbray, Mutton, Veal, Ham and other Pies, 119 St. Antoine st.

CONTRACTORS.

There are 283 Contractors in Montreal, among whom are :

WILLIAM BYRD, Contractor : Estimates given for Constructions and Alterations, 681 and 683 Lagauchetière st. Bell Telephone 390.

ERZEAR BENOIT, General Contractor, 9 Hudon st, Hochelaga.

L. COUSINEAU, Contractor, 410 Richmond st. ell Tel. 8032, house 96 St Matthew st.

THE SHEDDEN Co., Limited, Contractors, Warehousemen, General Forwarders and Carriers, and Cartage Agents for the Grand Trunk Railway Co., the Chicago and Grand Trunk Railway Co., the Northern Pacific and Manitoba Co., etc., 188 St James st.

CORDS, TASSELS AND FRINGES.

There is one Manufacturers of Cords, &c., in Montreal, among whom are :

MOULTON & Co., Manufacturers of Cords, Tassels and Fringes, 10 St Peter st.

COTTON BELTING.

There is one Cotton Belting Manufacturers in Montreal :

F. REDDAWAY & Co., A. G. Fenwick, Agent, Cotton Belting and Hose, 57 St François Xavier st.

CUSTOMS AND FORWARDING AGENTS.

There are 11 Customs and Forwarding Agents in Montreal, among whom are :

BLAIKLOCK BROS., Customs and Forwarding Agents, 17 Common st.

BOYD & Co., Custom House and Forwarding Agents and Warehousemen, 13 Common st.

T. M. BRYSON & Co., Custom House Brokers and Warehousemen, 413 to 417 St Paul st.

WM. REED & Co., Custom and Forwarding Agents, 209 Commissioners st.

CUTLERS.

There are two Cutlers in Montreal.

JAMES FOWLER, 639 Craig st, Manufacturer and Importer of Fine Cutlery, Agent for the celebrated Heinisch' Tailor and Barber Shears.

JOHN H. PARKER, Banjo Expert, Manufacturer of the "Perfection" Banjos, 2083 St Catherine st.

DANCING.

There are 4 Professors of Dancing in Montreal, among whom are :

PROF. C. W. DURKEE, Teacher of Dancing, Hall & Scott's Building, 2269 St Catherine st.

DENTISTS.

There are 42 Dentists in Montreal, among whom are :

DR. A. BROSSEAU, Spécialité pour Extraction de Dents sans Douleur. Dentiers les plus perfectionnés, 7 rue St Laurent. Bell Tel. 6201.

DR. J. G. GENDREAU, Chirurgien-Dentirte, 20 rue St Laurent. Extraction de Dents sans Douleur, par l'Electricité. Dentiers faits d'après les Procédés les plus Nouveaux. Bell Tel. 2818.

DENTISTS—*Continued.*

HORACE PEPIN, Dentiste, Extractions, Obturations, Dentiers Garantis, 1698 Notre Dame st.

DR. F. X. SEERS, Dentist, 387 Craig st. Bell Tel. 6906.

DRS. TRESTLER & GLOBENSKY, Dentists, 1892 Notre Dame st. Tel. 1592.

W. H. DION YOUNG, D.D.S., L.D.S., Surgeon Dentist, 1694 Notre Dame st.

DIE SINKERS.

There are 4 Die Sinkers in Montreal, among whom are:

JAMES CLELAND, Die Manufacturer, 16 St George st. Federal Tel. 632.

G. W. DAWSON, Die Sinker and Engraver, 765 Craig st.

KEIFFER & QUESNEL, Die Makers, 27 College.

DIVING APPARATUS.

There is one Diving Apparatus Manufacturer in Montreal:

JOHN DATE, Manufacturer of Diving Apparatus, 654 Craig st. Bell Tel. 431, Fed. Tel. 681.

DOOR AND SASH FACTORIES.

There are 17 Door and Sash Factories in Montreal, among whom are:

JOS. PAQUETTE, Manufacturer of Doors, Sashes, etc., 286 Craig st.

F. TREMBLAY, Door and Sash Factory, 92 and 94 Prince st.

DRAIN PIPES.

There are 8 Drain Pipe Dealers in Montreal, among whom are:

ALEXANDER BREMNER, Drain Pipes, Portland, Roman and Canada Cements, &c., 50 Bleury. Bell Telephone 356, Federal Telephone 683.

W. & F. P. CURRIE & CO.,
    Wholesale General Merchants,
    Importers of Drain Pipes, Vent Linings,
Fire Bricks, Fire Clay, Flue Covers,
    Whiting, China Clay, Water Lime,
Portland Cement, Plaster of Paris, Borax, &c.,
    100 Grey Nun st.

FRS. MARTINEAU, Drain Pipes, 1381 and 1383 St Catherine st.

W. McNALLY & CO., Drain Pipes, Cements, Builders' and Contractors' Supplies. 52 McGill cor Wellington st.

DRESSMAKERS.

There are 347 Dressmakers in Montreal, among whom are:

MADAME J. FORTIN, Modiste, Dress and Mantle Maker, 1937 Notre Dame st. opp Dupré lane.

DRUGGISTS—WHOLESALE.

There are 9 Druggists, Wholesale, in Montreal, among whom are:

KENNETH CAMPBELL & Co., Wholesale Druggists, 603 Craig st.

DR. J. LEDUC & Co., Wholesale Druggists, cor Notre Dame st and Chaboillez sq.

LYMAN SONS & Co., Drugs, Chemicals and Apparatus, Surgical Instruments, Perfumery, 380 St Paul st.

DRUGGISTS' SUNDRIES.

There are 17 Dealers in Druggists' Sundries in Montreal, among whom are:

ALPHA RUBBER Co., LTD., Manufacturers of Druggists' and Stationers' Rubber Goods, 48 and 50 Nazareth st.

DRY GOODS—RETAIL.

There are 173 Retail Dry Goods Dealers in Montreal, among whom are:

ARCAND FRÈRES, Etablis en 1881. Marchands de Nouveautés, 111 rue St Laurent coin de la rue Lagauchetière, Montreal.

L. E. BEAUCHAMP & CIE., Dry Goods, " Red Ball," 1477 rue Notre Dame

BOISSEAU BROS., Fancy and Staple Dry Goods, 235 and 237 St Lawrence st.

GAGNON FRÈRES, Fancy and Staple Dry Goods, 175 St Lawrence st.

HENRY HAMILTON, Fancy and Staple Dry Goods, corner St James st and Victoria square.

JULES HUOT, Fancy and Staple Dry Goods, 151 St Lawrence st. Bell Telephone 2188.

P. LAFRANCE & CIE., Fancy and Staple Dry Goods, 227 St Lawrence st.

JOSEPH LALONDE, Fancy and Staple Dry Goods, 1111 St Lawrence st.

DRY GOODS—WHOLESALE.

There are 56 Wholesale Dry Goods Merchants in Montreal, among whom are:

L. H. BOISSEAU & Co., Wholesale and Fancy Dry Goods, 39, 41 and 43 St Sulpice st.

BOURGOUIN, DUCHESNEAU & Co., Wholesale Importers Staple and Fancy Dry Goods, etc., 301 St Paul st and 19 St Jean Baptiste st.

JAMES BROWN & SON, Wholesale Dry Goods; Cottons a Specialty. 775 Craig st.

ERNEST DELAUNAY, Importer of Dry Goods, 25 St Helen st.

JOHN T. DONNELLY & Co., Successors to James Donnelly & Son, Importers of British and Foreign Dry Goods and Manufacturers' Agents, 3 Lemoine st.

GAULT BROS., & Co. Wholesale Fancy and Staple Dry Goods and Manufacturers of Canadian Woolens, 21 St Helen st. cor Recollet st.

S. GREENSHIELDS, SON & Co., Wholesale Dry Goods, 17, 19 and 21 Victoria sq. and 730, 732, 734 and 736 Craig st.

JACQUES GRENIER & Co., Wholesale Dry Goods Merchants, 292 St Paul st. and 133 Commissioners st

JAMES JOHNSTON & Co., Wholesale Dry Goods Importers and Dealers in Canadian and American Manufactures, 26 St Helen st.

W. LESPERANCE & Co., Successeurs de P. M. Galarneau & Cie., Importateurs de Marchandises Sèches, 350 St Paul st.

LONSDALE, REID & Co., Wholesale Dry Goods Importers and Dealers in Canadian Staple Goods, 18 St Helen st.

J. G. MACKENZIE & Co., Wholesale Dry Goods, 381 and 383 St Paul st.

THOMAS MAY & Co., Wholesale Fancy Dry Goods and Millinery, Victoria sq.

HENRY MORGAN & Co., Importers of Dry Goods, Carpets, etc., Phillips sq.

ROBERTSON, LINTON & Co., Wholesale Dry Goods Importers and Dealers in Canadian Woolens cor Lemoine and St Helen sts.

ROSS, FORSTER & Co., Wholesale Dry Goods, 9 & 11 Recollet st.

JOHN STIRLING & Co., Importers of British and Foreign Dry Goods, Wholesale, 373 St Paul st.

ISIDORE THIBAUDEAU & Co., Wholesale Dry Goods, 317 St Paul st.

THIBAUDEAU BROS., & Co., Wholesale Dry Goods Importers, 332 St Paul st. and 163 Commissioners st.

DYE WORKS.

There are 11 Dye Works in Montreal, among whom are:

ROYAL DYE WORKS, 706 Craig st. Montreal. Established 1870. John L. Jensen, Proprietor.

ELECTRIC LIGHT COMPANIES.

There are 2 Electric Light Companies in Montreal, among which are:

THE ROYAL ELECTRIC Co., Manufacturers for the Dominion of Canada of the Thomson and Thomson-Houston Arc and Incandescent Light Systems; also, Incandescent Light from Arc Circuits, Office, Factory and Lighting Station 54, 56, 58 and 60 Wellington st.

ELECTRICAL SUPPLIES.

There are 6 Electrical Supply Dealers in Montreal, among whom are:

T. W. NESS, The Leading Electrical Supply House in Canada, 644 Craig st.

ELECTRICIANS.

There are 4 Electricians in Montreal, among whom are:

MOUNT BROS., Bells, Annunciators and Electrical Supplies, Telephones, Watchmen's Clocks, etc., 766 Craig st.

ELECTROPLATERS.

There are 7 Electroplaters in Montreal, among whom are:

BAILLY & McLEE, Electro Platers; all kinds of Household Ware and Brass Goods Plated at lowest cost, 120 St Antoine st.

ELECTRO PLATED WARE.

There are 8 Electro Plated Ware Dealers in Montreal, among whom are:

SIMPSON, HALL, MILLER & Co., Manufacturers of Fine Electro Plated Ware, Gold, Silver and Nickel Plating, A. J. Whimbey, Manager, 18 De Bresoles st and 145 Le Royer st.

ENGINEERS.

There are 14 Engineers in Montreal, among whom are:

ROBERGE & SHEPHERD, Engineers, Machinists, Blacksmiths, Steam Fitters and Tool Makers, White's Lane.

J. & R. WEIR, Engineers, Boiler Makers and Machinists, Nazareth and Brennan sts.

ANDREW YOUNG, Engineer and Machinist, Shafting, Hangers and Pulleys, 768 Craig st.

ENGRAVERS.

There are 34 Engravers in Montreal, among whom are:

G. W. DAWSON, Engraver and Die Sinker, 765 Craig st.

FANCY GOODS.

There are 35 Fancy Goods Dealers in Montreal, among whom are:

THE F. CARSTENS MANUFACTURING Co., Fancy Goods, 2 Bleury st cor Craig st.

B. MARCUSE, Wholesale Importer of Fancy Goods and Art Novelties, 823 Craig st, Montreal.

THE UNIVERSAL, G. W. Clarke, Fancy Goods, Stationery, etc., 238 and 240 St James st.

FEATHER MANUFACTURERS AND DYERS.

There are 7 Feather Manufacturers and Dyers in Montreal, among whom are:

WILLIAM SNOW, Manufacturer of Ostrich Feathers; Feathers Dyed a Brilliant Black; Feathers Cleaned, Curled and Dyed every Color, 1913½ Notre Dame st.

FIRE WORKS.

There is one Fire Work Manufactory in Montreal:

FIRE WORKS MANUFACTORY, 1658 Notre Dame st.

FINANCIAL AGENTS.

There are 42 Financial Agents in Montreal, among whom are:

L. A. HART, Notary, Investment Securities. Imperial Bldg., 107 St James st.

FISH, POULTRY AND GAME.

There are 30 Dealers in Fish, &c., in Montreal, among whom are:

NICHOLSON & CO., Importers and Dealers in Fish, Oysters, Game and Poultry, 46 Victoria sq.

STEWART MUNN & CO., Fish Merchants, 22 St John st.

FLAVORING EXTRACTS.

There are 2 Flavoring Extract Dealers in Montreal, among whom are:

HENRI JONAS & CO., Flavoring Extracts, French Mustards, Olive Oils, Grocers', Confectioners', Druggists' and Brewers' Supplies, Sardines, French Peas, Truffles, Mushrooms and Gelatine, 10 DeBresoles st.

FLORISTS,

There are 7 Florists in Montreal, among whom are:

WILSHIRE BROS., Florists, cor Mount Royal av. and Outremont road.

FLOUR AND FEED.

There are 99 Flour and Feed Dealers in Montreal, among whom are:

BRODIE & HARVIE, Flour Merchants, Manufacturers of Brodie & Harvie's Self-Raising Flour, Oatmeal, Graham Flour, Cracked Wheat, Rye Flour, Hominy, Cornmeal, Bran, Feed Stuffs; Families Supplied, 10 and 12 Bleury st.

BRUNEAU, CURRIE & CO., Flour, Feed and Produce Merchants, Office 8 and 10 Foundling st.

COUTU & JACQUES, Flour and Feed Merchants, Agency of the Manitoba Milling and Brewing Co., 203 Commissioners st.

J. E. HUNSICKER, Flour and General Produce Commission Merchant, 22 Foundling st.

W. F. JOHNSTON, Flour, Hay, Grain, Mill Feed and Country Produce, Wholesale, 10, 12 and 14 Port st.

STEWART MUNN & CO., Flour Merchants, 22 St John st.

J. L. SMITH & SON, Flour Merchants and Millers' Agents, 225 Commissioners and 1 Custom House sq.

W. HOWE SMITH & CO., Flour and Grain, 16 St Sacrament st.

FLOUR MILLS.

There are 7 Flour Mills in Montreal, among whom are:

W. W. OGILVIE, Proprietor of the Royal, Glenora, Goderich, Seaforth and Winnipeg Flour Mills, St Gabriel Locks, 191 and 193 Seigneurs st and 21 Mill st, Office 38 and 40 Foundling st.

FORWARDERS.

There are 21 Forwarders in Montreal, among whom are:

G. E. JAQUES & CO., 110 Common st, Agents Merchants Line of Steamers. Freight Contracts made to all Ports in Ontario and Western States.

FOUNDERS.

There are 37 Founders in Montreal, among whom are:

CENTRAL FOUNDRY, Heavy and Light Castings to order, at shortest notice, Thomas Scanlan, proprietor, 27 and 33 Queen st. Bell Tel 2222.

CLENDINNING'S FOUNDRY, every description of Castings, Light or Heavy, made from the best Scotch and American Pig Iron, on Shortest Notice. Pattern sent for. Wm. Clendinning & Son, 145 to 179 William st. Bell Tel. 280, Federal Tel. 1188.

T. CREVIER & FILS, Stove Founders and Tinsmiths, 541 Craig st.

EAGLE FOUNDRY, GEO. BRUSH, Proprietor, Engine and Boiler Works, Castings and Forgings and General Machine Work, 14 to 34 King st.

PARKER'S FOUNDRY, Every Description of Castings, Light or Heavy, made from the Best Quality of Iron. Moses Parker, Dalhousie st. Bell and Fed. Tel.

FRUIT DEALERS.

There are **110 Fruit Dealers** in Montreal, among **whom are**:

BOWES & McWILLIAMS, Commission Merchants and Dealers in Fruit and Produce, 1836 Notre Dame st.

FRANK J. HART, Fruit and Commission Merchant—Established in 1855—159, 161 and 163 McGill st. cor Lemoine st.

McBRIDE, HARRIS & Co., Fruits, Nuts and Canned Goods, 134 McGill, 1 to 21 College and 1 Longueuil lane.

FUNERAL DIRECTORS.

The are **17 Funeral Directors** in **Montreal**, among **whom are**:

G. ARMSTRONG & Co., Undertakers and Practical Embalmers—always open—32 Victoria sq.

C. A. DUMAINE, Funeral Director, 1353 Notre Dame st.

HALPIN & VINCENT, Funeral Directors, 1375 Notre Dame st.

R. SEALE & Son, Funeral Directors, 41a and 43 St Antoine st.

TEES & Co., Manufacturers of Funeral Furniture and Funeral Directors, 300 St James st.

FURNITURE.

There are **62 Furniture Manufacturers in Montreal, among whom are**:

GEO. H. LABBE & CO'S, Show Rooms and Store Houses, 453 and 455 St James and 131 to 135 Inspector sts, have a floor capacity of $8,000 square feet, by far the largest in Canada. There you find no less than 60,000 Chairs of every description at 28c up; 1200 Complete Bed Room Suites at $10.50 up; 220 Parlor Suites at $20.00 up; hundreds of Tables, Sideboards, Bedsteads, Washstands, Cupboards, Chiffonniers, Wardrobes, Mattresses, Pillows, Spring Beds, &c., in fact all articles of usefulness at prices which it is hard to compete against. A visit to this mammoth establishment will more than repay the visitor. This firm export their goods to almost every corner of the Globe.

S. R. PARSONS, Furniture, Upholstery and Bedding, 1813 and 1815 Notre Dame st.

RENAUD, KING & PATTERSON (late Wm. King & Co.), Furniture and Bedding Manufacturers, Wholesale and Retail, Warerooms 652 Craig st., Factory and Storehouse 62 and 64 College st.

ROLLAND & BRO'S is the best house for Cabinet Hardware and Upholstery Goods; also all kinds of Furniture, Spring Beds, Mattresses; English Iron and Brass Bedsteads imported direct. Will take note " on regular terms " from a trustworthy person, 442 and 444 St James st.

JAMES STEEL, Leading Furniture Dealer in the Dominion of Canada, 1820 Notre Dame st.

R. X. TOMBYLL, Manufacturer of Parlor Sets, Easy Chairs and Lounges; Wire Back Chairs, a Specialty. 566 and 568 Craig st. cor Place d'Armes Hill

FURRIERS, WHOLESALE.

There are **20 Wholesale Furriers** in **Montreal, among whom are**:

JAS. CORISTINE & Co., Fur Merchants and Felt Hat Manufacturers, 471 to 477 St Paul st.

L. GNAEDINGER, SON & Co, (E. W. Gnaedinger, Jos. Boudeau), Wholesale Hatters and Furriers, 92 and 94 St Peter st, Montreal.

GREENE & SONS Co., Hats, Furs, etc., 513 to 525 St Paul st.

J. L. MARCOU & Co., Established 1862, Furriers, 1744 Notre Dame st.

SILVERMAN, BOULTER & Co., Furs, Hats, Caps, etc., 495 St Paul st and 51, 53 and 55 St Peter st.

E. STUART, Fur Manufacturer, 1919 Notre Dame st.

FUR DRESSERS.

There are **6 Fur Dressers** in **Montreal, among whom are**:

MONTREAL FUR DRESSING AND DYEING WORKS, 68 Prince st.

GENTS' FURNISHINGS—WHOLESALE.

There are **6 Wholesale Gents' Furnishing Dealers in Montreal, among whom are**:

BLANCHET & MOQUIN, Gents' Furnishings; Shirts of all Kinds Made to Order, 2121 Notre Dame st. Bell Tel. 1363.

MACFARLANE & PATTERSON, Wholesale Gents' Furnishings, 8 St Helen st.

GINGER ALE MANUFACTURERS.

There are **11 Ginger Ale Manufacturers in Montreal, among whom are**:

CHAS. GURD & Co. Order Gurd's Ginger Ale, —superior to all others—43 Jurors st.

ROBERT MILLAR, Manufacturer Ginger Ale, Royal Edinburgh Ginger Beer, Cream Soda, Cider, etc., 69 St Antoine st.

C. ROBILLARD & Co., Ginger Ale, Cider, Ginger Beer, Cream Soda, etc., 27 St André st. Bell Tel. 6102.

GLOVE MANUFACTURERS.

There are 4 Glove Manufacturers in Montreal, among whom are:

J. Z. Desormeau & Cie., Mfrs. de Gants et Mitaines, 236 rue St Paul.

M. Malone, Glove Manufacturer, 2600 and 2602 Notre Dame st.

GRAIN DEALERS.

There are 99 Grain Dealers in Montreal, among whom are:

James Kerr, Dealer in Cattle Supplies, Grain and No. 1 Baled Hay, 239 Wellington st. Bell Tel. 561, Federal Tel. 1720.

O. McDonnell, Grain and Feed Merchant, 130 Wellington st.

Louis Roch, Grain Dealer, 12 Maisonneuve st.

GRANITE WORKS.

There are 5 Granite Works in Montreal, among which are:

R. Forsyth, Granite Works, 130 Bleury st.

C. A. MacDonell, Granite and Marble Works, 59 St Alexander cor Lagauchetière st.

GROCERS—WHOLESALE.

There are 41 Grocers, Wholesale, in Montreal, among whom are:

L. Chaput, Fils & Cie., Importers of Teas, Groceries and Liquors, 2 and 4 De Bresoles st., 17 St Dizier st, and 123 to 131 Le Royer st.

George Childs & Co., Wholesale Grocers, 20 1/2 22 St François Xavier st.

A. Cusson & Fils, Importers of Teas, Groceries, Wines, etc., 210 St Paul st and 61 Commissioners st.

Gaucher & Telmosse, Etablie en 1867. Importateurs de Vins, Liqueurs, Epiceries, Provisions, etc., 242, 244 et 246 rue St Paul, 87, 89, 91 et 93 rue des Commissaires.

Pegon, Hubert & Cie., Importateurs et Epiciers en Gros, 304 et 306 rue St Paul et 143 et 145 rue des Commissaires.

Hudon & Orsali, Wholesale Importers Groceries and Provisions, 278 St Paul st and 121 and 123 Commissioners st.

Charles Lacaille & Co., Importers of Wines, Liquors, Teas and Groceries, 329 St Paul st and 12 to 14 St Dizier st.

Lockerey Bros., Importers and Jobbers and Wholesale Grocers, 77 and 79 St Peter st and 51 and 53 St Sacrament st.

J. A. Mathewson & Co., Importers and Wholesale Grocers, 202 McGill st.

N. Quintal & Fils, Importateurs de Vins, Liqueurs, Cigares, Epiceries, etc., 274 rue St Paul et 113 et 115 rue des Commissaires

Regan, White & Co., Importers and Wholesale Grocers, cor St Helen and Lemoine sts.

John H. Semple, Wholesale Grocer, Nun's Building, 35 St Peter st. and 48 Foundling st.

Turner, Rose & Co., Importers and Wholesale Grocers, 309, 311 and 313 Commissioners st.

J. O. Villeneuve & Co., Wholesale Dealers in Wines, Groceries, Provisions, 1258 and 1260 St Lawrence st. Fed. Tel. 1514, Bell Tel. 103.

GROCERS, WHOLESALE AND RETAIL.

There are 985 Grocers, Wholesale and Retail, in Montreal, among whom are:

Décary & Laurier, Groceries and Provisions, 1393 Ontario st.

Thomas Lamb, Established 1872, Wholesale and Retail Grocer, 19 Chaboillez sq. corner Chaboillez st, near new G. T. R. and C.P.R. Depots. Bell Tel. 190, Federal Tel. 2205.

R. McShane, Wholesale and Retail Grocer and Provision Merchant, cor McGill and Commissioners sts. opposite St Ann's Market.

Maison St Denis, Groceries et Liqueurs de Premier Choix, E. Houle & Cie., coin des rues St Denis et Ontario. Bell Tel. 6746.

J. E. Manning, Dealer in Choice Family Groceries, Wines, etc., 1, 3 and 5 St Antoine st.

V. Raby, Wholesale and Retail Grocer, Choice Wines, Liquors and Provisions, etc.; Eastern Townships' Butter a Specialty, 2401 Notre Dame st. cor Guy st. Bell Tel. 8242.

Severe Thibault, 1333 Notre Dame st.

GUARANTEE COMPANIES.

There is one Guarantee Company in Montreal:

The Guarantee Company of North America, Bonds of Securityship, Edward Rawlings, Vice-President and Managing Director, 157 St James st.

GYMNASIUMS.

There are 2 Gymnasiums in Montreal, among which are:

Barnjum's Gymnasium, 19 University street. Classes for Ladies and Children conducted by Miss Barnjum. Further information can be had from the Principal between the hours of 9 and 10 o'clock every morning except Saturday.

HARDWARE.

There are 71 Hardware Merchants in Montreal, among whom are:

EDWARD CAVANAGH, Hardware, Oils, Paints, Coal, 2547 to 2553 Notre Dame st.

CAVERHILL, LEARMONT & Co., Wholesale Shelf Hardware Merchants, Warerooms, Sample Rooms and Offices Caverhill's Buildings, St Peter st.

T. C. COLLINS, Hardware Agent, 6 St John st.

CRATHERN & CAVERHILL, 89 St Peter st.

L. H. HEBERT, Hardware and Iron Ware, Wholesale only, 297 and 299 St Paul st and 21 St Jean Baptiste st.

GRAVEL & BOULARD, House Builders' Hardware, Ranges, Cooking and Hall Stoves, Cutlery, Cooking Utensils, etc. : Tools a specialty ; Paints, Oils, Varnishes, Glass, Putty, Brushes, etc., 293 St Lawrence st.

R. & W. KERR, Hardware, Stoves, etc., 1895 Notre Dame st.

DAVID MADORE, Wholesale Importer Hardware, Paints, etc., 281 to 285 St Paul st. and 5 to 11 St Gabriel st.

FRS. MARTINEAU, Hardware, Shelf and Heavy, 1381 and 1383 St Catherine st.

PARKES, REEKIE & Co., Hardware Agents, 692 Craig st.

A. PRUD'HOMME & FRÈRE, Importers of Hardware, Paints and Oils, 1940 Notre Dame st West, Montreal.

L. J. A. SURVEYER, Established 1866. Hardware, 6 St Lawrence st.

JAS. WALKER & Co., Importers of Hardware, 234 St James st. and 543 Craig st.

J. H. WILSON, Wholesale and Retail Hardware, Paints, Oils and Varnishes, all kinds of Carriage Goods ; Coal of all kinds, 1874 Notre Dame st.

HATTERS AND FURRIERS.

There are 46 Hatters and Furriers in Montreal, among whom are:

I. BOILEAU, Hatter and Furrier, 1584 Notre Dame st.

J. R. BOURDEAU, Hat Manufacturer and Practical Furrier, 97 St Lawrence st., house 97½ do. Bell Tel. 2312

M. DROUIN, Chapelier et Manchonnier de Pratique, Médaille de Bronze et Diplome d'Honneur de Londres de 1886, Exposition Colonial et Indienne, 172 St Lawrence st.

L. GNAEDINGER, SON & Co. (E. W. Gnaedinger, J. Bourdeau), Wholesale Hatters and Furriers, cor St Peter and Recollet sts.

JOHN HENDERSON & Co., Hatters and Furriers, 229 St James st—their new warehouse.

H. F. HOERNER, Hatter and Furrier, 449 St Lawrence. Fur Garments made to order, repaired, dyed and remade.

J. A. LANTHIER & Co., Hats and Furs, 2141 Notre Dame st.

LORGE & Co., First Premium Practical Hatters, 21 St Lawrence st.

J. L. MARCOU, Established 1862, Hatter and Furrier, 1744 Notre Dame st.

ALEX. NELSON & Co., Direct Importers and Manufacturers of Furs, 107 and 107½ Bleury st.

C. ROBERT, Hat Manufacturer and Practical Furrier, 79 St Lawrence st, house 53 German st.

O. A. WILLIE, Hatter and Furrier ; always on hand a large Assortment of Hats in the latest styles, and Ladies' and Gentlemen's Fine Furs Manufactured on the premises, 1790 Notre Dame cor St Peter st.

HAY, STRAW, &c.

There are 46 Hay and Straw Dealers in Montreal, among whom are:

MARSAN & BROSSEAU, Wholesale Merchants of Hay, Straw, Grain and Feed, Offices, Warehouses and Stables 65 Common cor Queen, opp. Black's Bridge

JAMES SCOTT & Co., Dealers in Hay, Straw, Oats, Bran, Moulé, Potatoes, Chicken Feed, etc., 132 St Antoine st.

WILSON BROS., Hay, Grain, etc., 605 Notre Dame st.

HERBORIST.

There are — Herborists in Montreal, among whom are:

A. LEFEBVRE, Herboiste, Canadien Specialiste, 2243 Notre Dame st.

HIDES AND SKINS.

There are 9 Hide and Skin Dealers in Montreal, among whom are:

CALIXTE GALIBERT & SON, Hides and Wool and Leather, 929 St Catherine st.

JOHN PRICE, Dealer in Hides, Calfskins and Pelts, 79 College st.

HOTELS.

There are 167 Hotels in Montreal, among which are:

HOTEL BALMORAL, Located in the Heart of the City, near Depots and Steamboat Landings, now under entirely new Management. Unrivalled by any Hotel in Canada in its Cuisine and Service. James Smith, Proprietor. 1892 Notre Dame st.

LALONDE HOTEL, Augustin Lalonde, Proprietor, 57 to 65 Chaboillez sq.

T. VALADE, LONDON HOUSE, $1.00 per day, 67 Chaboillez sq., opp G. T. R. Station.

T. H. WADDELL, Kingston Hotel, 689, 691 and 693 Craig st.

HOUSE FURNISHINGS.

There are 17 Dealers in House Furnishings in Montreal, among whom are.

ROY FRÈRES, House Furnishings and Shelf Hardware, Paints, Oils, Glass, etc., 167 St Lawrence st. Bell Telephone 1593.

WARMINTON'S, 2208 St Catherine st, J. S. Cowan, Manager.

HOUSEHOLD GOODS.

There are 27 Dealers in Household Goods in Montreal, among whom are :

CHARLAND & LAHAISE, Full Line of Household Goods ; most liberal terms, 33 and 35 St Lawrence st. Tel 1240

ICE DEALERS.

There are 7 Ice Dealers in Montreal, among whom are :

O. L. HENAULT, Wholesale and Retail Ice Dealer. Orders Specially and Promptly attended to. Order by either Telephone. Always the best Stock of Ice on hand. 1310 Notre Dame st.

JOSEPH QUINN, Central Ice Office, 104 William st.

ST LAWRENCE ICE Co., J. Christin & Co., Proprietors. Always the Best Stock on hand and right in the centre of the City, 149 Sanguinet st.

IMPORTERS.

There are 21 Importers in Montreal, among whom are :

J. DORKEN, Agent and Importer, 43 St Sacrament st.

H. DUVERGER, Wholesale Importer ; Specialty: Rubber Goods, Gloves, Hosiery, 1886 Notre Dame

HENDERY & WILLIAMSON, Importers of Teas, Dried Fruit and Spices, 1 Custom House square

J. HOOLAHAN, Wholesale Importer and Manufacturers' Agent, 2186 Notre Dame st.

E. LEFORT & CIE., General Importers, Agents for the Products of Roure-Bertrand Fils, Grasse, France, and Gelle Frères Paris, France, 338 St Paul st. Bell Tel. 451.

TELLIER, ROTHWELL & Co., Importers of French, English and German specialties and Manufacturers of Laundry Blues and Stove Polishes, 8 DeBresoles st.

THIBAUDEAU BROS. & Co., Importers of English, French, American and German Goods, 332 St Paul st.

WULFF & Co., Importers of Mirror Glass, Dextrine, Glycerine, French and German Glues, Aniline Dyes, Coll. Papers, etc., 32 Sulpice st.

INDIAN CURIOSITIES.

There are 3 Dealers in Indian Curiosities in Montreal, among whom are :

DEMERS & Co., Montreal Indian Store, 1658 Notre Dame st.

INSURANCE AGENTS.

There are 86 Insurance Agents in Montreal, among whom are :

EDWARD L. BOND, British and Foreign Marine Insurance Co., Reliance Marine Ins. Co., London Assurance Co.(Fire), Lloyds Plate Glass Ins. Co., 30 St François Xavier st.

C. E. GAULT, Insurance Agent and Stock Broker, 17 St John st.

ROBERT HAMPSON, Insurance Offices. 18 Corn Exchange, 39 St Sacrament st.

INSURANCE OFFICES.

There are 93 Insurance Offices in Montreal, among which are :

AGRICULTURAL INSURANCE CO. OF WATERTOWN, N. Y.; Assets over $2,000,000 ; C. R. G. Johnson, General Agent, 42 St John st.

ATLAS ASSURANCE Co., Head Office London, England ; Founded A.D. 1808 ; Capital £200,000 sterling : Canadian Branch, Louis H. Boult, Branch Manager, 79 St François Xavier st.

THE ACCIDENT INSURANCE Co. of North America Insures against All Classes of Personal Accident, Edward Rawlings, Vice-President and Managing Director, Head Office, 157 St James st.

THE CANADA LIFE ASSURANCE Co., Head Office Hamilton, Ont. Capital and Assets $12,000,000. President, A. G. Ramsay ; Manager for Province of Quebec, J. W. Marling. The Oldest Canadian Life Co., 186 St James st.

CITIZENS INSURANCE Co. of Canada, Fire and Accident, Hon. J. J. C. Abbott, Q.C., President ; E. P. Heaton, General Manager ; Wm. Smith, Secretary, 181 St James st.

THE COMMERCIAL UNION ASSURANCE Co., LTD., of London, England. Fire, Life, Marine. Capital and Assets over $25,000,000. Evans & McGregor, Managers Canadian Branch, Head Office, 731 Notre Dame st.

EASTERN ASSURANCE Co. OF CANADA, Capital $1,000,000 ; C. R. G. Johnson, General Agent, 42 St John st.

LANCASHIRE FIRE INSURANCE Co., Capital $15,000,000, Belleau & Bomford, Agents, 43 and 45 St John st.

LIVERPOOL AND LONDON AND GLOBE INSURANCE COMPANY, Fire and Life, G. F. C. Smith, Chief Agent and Resident Secretary, Company's building, 16 Place d'Armes corner St James st.

LONDON AND LANCASHIRE LIFE ASSURANCE Co. ; Sir Donald A. Smith, K.C.M.G., Chairman ; B. Hal. Brown, Manager for Canada.

Head Office for Canada : Cor St James st and Place d'Armes sq, Montreal.

THE LONDON ASSURANCE. Incorporated 1720. Total Assets $18,000,000. Liability of Shareholders unlimited. Fire Risks accepted. E. A. Lilly, Manager for Canada. 1762 Notre Dame st.

THE MANUFACTURERS LIFE AND ACCIDENT INSURANCE COMPANY, Rt. Hon. Sir John A. Macdonald, P.C., G.C.B. Combined Capital $3,000,000. Selby, Rolland & Lyman, Provincial Managers, 162 St James st

NATIONAL ASSURANCE CO. OF IRELAND. Head Office, Dublin ; Established in 1822 ; Capital £1,900,000 sterling ; Canadian Branch, Louis H. Boult, Chief Agent, 79 St François Xavier st.

NEW YORK LIFE INSURANCE COMPANY, Head Office for Canada, Company's Building, Place d'Armes sq., David Burke, General Manager for Canada.

NORTHERN ASSURANCE COMPANY OF LONDON, ENGLAND, Income and Funds 1888 :

Capital and Accumulated Funds $32,905,000
Annual Revenue from Fire and Life
Premiums and from Interest upon
invested Funds....................... 4,835,000
Deposited with the Dominion Government for security of Canadian
Policy-Holders 200,000
Branch office for Canada, 1724 Notre Dame st, Montreal, Robert W. Tyre, Manager for Canada.

PHŒNIX FIRE INSURANCE Co. of Hartford, —Established 1854 — Cash Capital $2,000,000, Total Cash Assets $5,305,004.23, Gerald E. Hart, General Manager ; Laurin & Smith, Montreal Agents, 114 St James st., opposite Post Office

QUEEN INSURANCE Co., of Liverpool and London, Fire and Life, H. J. Mudge, Chief Agent, 1759 Notre Dame st. Total Funds in hand over $7,000,000. Claims Paid over $35,000,000. Special City Agents : J. Cradock Simpson, Edmond Turgeon, R. G. Brown, G. R. Robertson, Capt. J. J. Riley, N. R. Mudge.

THE STANDARD LIFE ASSURANCE Co.
OF EDINBURGH, Scotland,
Established in 1825.
Head Office in Canada, Montreal,
W. M. RAMSAY, Manager, Standard Building, 157 St James st.

ROYAL INSURANCE CO. OF ENGLAND, Wm. Tatley, Chief Agent and Resident Manager ; Special Agents French Department, E. Hurtubise and A. St Cyr ; Special Agents English Department, Jas. Allin, David Denne and W. S. Robertson of G. R. Robertson & Sons, 1707 Notre Dame st.

SUN LIFE ASSURANCE Co. OF CANADA, R. MACAULAY, President and Managing Director ; T. B. MACAULAY, Secretary and Actuary. The only Company in Canada Issuing Unconditional Life Policies, 164 St James st.

UNION ASSURANCE SOCIETY (FIRE), A.D. 1714, of London, G. B. Assets about Two and Quarter Millions Sterling. T. L. Morrisey, Resident Manager.

UNION MUTUAL LIFE INSURANCE Co., incorporated 1848, Walter I. Joseph, Manager. Only Company Governed by the Maine Non-Forfeiture Law, which Protects Policies from Forfeiture through default of Payment of Premiums until the Reserve is exhausted. Asset a$6,205,018.84. Deposit with Canadian Government, 30 St François Xavier st.

UNITED FIRE RE-INSURANCE Co., of Manchester, England, Chief Office for the United States and Canada, Montreal Life Building, New York, William Wood, Manager Canadian Branch, Temple Building, 185 St James st., Montreal, Percy F. Lane, Superintendent. Fire Re-Insurance only.

THE UNITED STATES LIFE INS. Co., of New York, E. A. Conway, Manager, 180 St James st, Montreal.

INVALID CHAIRS.

There are 2 Invalid Chair Makers in Montreal, among whom are :

J. CARLISLE, Invalid Chair Depot, 1666 Notre Dame st.

IRON AND STEEL.

There are 28 Iron and Steel Merchants in Montreal, among whom are :

BENNY, MACPHERSON & Co., Wholesale Iron, Steel and Metal Merchants, 388, 390 and 392 St Paul st., Iron and Steel Stores, De Bresoles.

DRUMMOND, MCCALL & Co., Iron, Steel and Metal Merchants and Manufacturers, New York Life Building, Place d'Armes

SESSENWEIN BROS., Dealers in Scrap Iron and Metals, 126 William st.

WINN & HOLLAND, Importers and Manufacturers' Agents, Iron, Steel, Chemicals, &c., 49 St François Xavier st.

JEWELLERS.

There are 164 Jewellers in Montreal, among whom are :

J. T. BOLT, Manufacturing Jeweller, 657 Craig.

RICHARD HEMSLEY, Importer and Manufacturer Fine Watches and Jewellery, 255 and 257 St James st.

WILLIAM McGILTON, Manufacturing Jeweller; Diamond Setting a Specialty, 673 Craig st.

J. J. SOLY, Jeweller and Engraver ; Chronometer, Repeater and Fine Watch Work a Specialty, 100½ St Antoine st.

J. U. THIBAUDEAU, Manufacturing Jeweller, 33 St John st.

KID GLOVE MANUFACTURERS.

There are 4 Kid Glove Manufacturers in Montreal, among whom are :

J. B. A. LANCTOT, Mnfr. of Summer and Winter Kid Gloves and Mitts, Wholesale and Retail, 99 St Lawrence st.

THOURET, FITZGIBBON & CO., Kid Gloves a Specialty, 140 McGill st.

· LADY DOCTRESSES.

There are 19 Lady Doctresses in Montreal, among whom are :

MRS. CUMMINGS, Ladies' Doctress, 55 St Antoine st.

MRS. E. HUNT, Ladies' Doctress, 65½ St Antoine st.

LAND SURVEYORS.

There are 10 Land Surveyors in Montreal, among whom are :

J. A. U. BEAUDRY, Dominion and Provincial Land Surveyor, 107 St James st.

H. M. PERRAULT, Land Surveyor, 17 Place d'Armes hill.

LARD MANUFACTURERS.

N. K. FAIRBANK & CO., Lard Manufacturers, 185 Wellington st.

LAUNDRY BLUE.

There are 2 Laundry Blue Manufacturers in Montreal, among whom are :

TELLIER, ROTHWELL & CO., Manufacturers of Laundry Blues and Stove Polishes, and Importers of Glues, Glycerine, Aniline Dyes, Metallic Capsules, Tinfoil and Essential Oils, 8 DeBresoles.

LAUNDRIES.

There are 40 Laundries in Montreal, among whom are :

TROY STEAM LAUNDRY, for fine laundry work only. The most thoroughly equipped Laundry on Troy principles in Canada, 140 St Peter st. cor Craig

MONTREAL STEAM LAUNDRY CO. (Ltd), 21 and 23 St Antoine st. The Largest and Most Complete Laundry in the Dominion.

ENGLISH LAUNDRY, Head-Quarters 35 University st, Mrs. Gilmour and Mrs. Scott, Managers. Bell Telephone 4981.

LEATHER DEALERS.

There are 43 Leather Dealers in Montreal, among whom are :

ANGUS, MOONEY & CO., Leather Dealers, 9 St Helen st.

M. C. GALARNEAU, Marchand de Cuir et Fournitures à Cordonniers et Importateurs d'Empeignes Anglaises, 279 rue St Paul

H. LAMONTAGNE, Sole and Harness Leather, Shoe Findings, Manufacturers of Fitted Uppers, 480 St Paul st. and 297 Commissioners st.

LECLERC & CO., Wholesale Dealers in Leather, Hides, Skins, etc., 26 Lemoine st.

McINDOE & VAUGHAN, Leather Dealers, 7 Lemoine st.

DAVID REA & CO., Importers of Fine Leather and General Merchandise, Bookbinders' Leather and Cloth in every Color, Morocco for Upholsterers, German Slipper Patterns in every quality, Jacquand's French Blacking, 30 Hospital st.

E. A. WHITEHEAD & CO., Leather Commission Merchants, Agents for " Sturtevant " Peg Wood, Evans' Artificial Leather Co., Importers of Elastics, Linings, Prunellas and Calfskins, English Oak Tanned and Foreign Leathers, 35 Lemoine st.

J. G. M. WHITNEY & CO., Importers of Leather and Shoe Goods, Agents for G. A. Mooney & Co.'s Dongola Kid, Calf and Sheep Skins, 14 Lemoine st.

LEATHER BELTING.

There are 6 Leather Belting Manufacturers in Montreal, among whom are :

JAMES LESLIE, Manufacturer of Leather Belting, Card Clothing, Loom Reeds and Harness, Cotton and Woolen Mill Supplies, Junction of Craig and St Antoine sts.

LIME BURNERS.

There are 6 Lime Burners in Montreal, among whom are:

CYRILLE A. GERVAIS, Lime Burner ; constantly on hand a large quantity of Lime of first quality, delivered to order, 440 to 450 Cadieux st.

OLIVIER LIMOGES, Lime Burner ; constantly on Hand a Large Quantity of Lime of First Quality Delivered to Order, 477 and 479 Papineau road.

LIME MANUFACTURERS.

There are 6 Lime Manufacturers in Montreal, among whom are:

HENRY GAUTHIER, Lime Manufacturer, 86 Fullum st.

LITHOGRAPHERS.

There are 13 Lithographers in Montreal, among whom are:

THE BURLAND LITHOGRAPHIC Co.,
Engravers
and Fine Color Printers,
Maps and Chart Makers,
9 Bleury st,
Montreal.

LIVERY STABLES.

There are 30 Livery Stables in Montreal, among which is:

STARR & KINSELLA, Dominion Boarding and Livery Stables, 70 Mansfield st, n Dorchester st.

LOTTERY.

THE PROVINCE OF QUEBEC LOTTERY, Authorized by the Legislature ; Monthly Drawings for year 1891 : January 14, February 11, March 11, April 8, May 13, June 10, July 8, August 12, September 9, October 14. November 11, December 9.

Prizes value, $52,740.00. Capital Prize, One Real Estate worth $15,000.00.

Ticket $1 ; 11 Tickets for $10.

Drawings take place on the second Wednesday of every month, at 10½ o'clock A. M., at Head Office, 81 St James st., Montreal, Canada.

For Tickets, Circulars, Agencies, or further information, address S. E. LEFEBVRE, 81 St James st., Montreal, Canada. Telephone 2876

LUMBER MERCHANTS.

There are 50 Lumber Merchants in Montreal, among whom are:

DOBELL, BECKETT & Co. of Quebec, Lumber Merchants; Montreal Office 14 Custom House square.

O. DUFRESNE, JUN., & FRERE, Lumber Dealers and Manufacturers, 2388 Notre Dame st. ; saw mills at Windsor Mills, P.Q.

LALONDE & GIRARD, Lumber Merchants; also Planing and Saw Mills, Doors, Sashes, Blinds and Moulding, Office and Factory 1000 St Lawrence. Bell Tel. 2551.

LARIVIÈRE & DUBÉ, Lumber, Architraves, Skirtings, Mouldings, Turning and Scroll Sawing, 74 St Antoine st.

DAMASE PARIZEAU, Lumber Merchant, Head Office, cor Craig and Bonsecours sts ; Yards cor Craig and Bonsecours sts, 514 Lagauchetière and Notre Dame st, Hochelaga, opp C. P. R. Station, res at Boucherville.

RIOPEL & BOURDON (Successors to E. Malo), Lumber Merchants, 53 Vitré st. Bell Tell. 6214.

JOS. ROBERT & FILS, 107 Papineau av., Manufacturers of Sashes Doors, etc. LUMBER DEALERS. Have the Largest and Most Complete Kiln Dry House in America.

THIBODEAU & BOURDON, Wholesale and Retail Lumber Merchants, 1203 St Catherine st cor Papineau road.

LUNCH ROOMS.

There are 21 Lunch Rooms in Montreal, among which is:

MERCHANTS' LUNCH ROOMS. F. Upton, Proprietor, 24 and 26 Hospital st.

MACHINISTS.

There are 35 Machinists in Montreal, among whom are:

ASPINALL & BROWN. Blacksmiths, Machinists, Manufacturers of Fire Escapes, Portable Forges, Railway and Warehouse Trucks, &c., 191 Fortification lane.

CANADA MACHINERY AGENCY, W. H. Nolan, Manager, 185 St James st.

DARLING BROTHERS, Manufacturers of Machinery Power and Hydraulic Hoists ; Sole Makers of the Nordberg Expansion Governor, Webster Heater. Claussen Friction Pulley and the Fox Low Water Alarm, Reliance Works, 112 Queen st, Montreal.

I. FRECHETTE & Co., General Machinists, New and Second-Hand Machinery Brought and Sold, Machine shop attached, 688 Craig st.

ROBERT GARDNER & SON, Manufacturers of Lathes, Tools and Machinery, Shaftings, Hangers and Pulleys, Steam Engines, Boilers, etc., Nazareth, Brennan & Dalhousie sts.

MACHINISTS—*Continued.*

MILLER BROS. & TOMS (successors to MILLER BROS. & MITCHELL), established 1869, Machinists, Millwrights and Engineers, Manufacturers of Safety Elevators (Hand and Steam, Hydraulic and Electric) and general Machine Work, 110 to 122 King st., Montreal. Toronto Office 74 York st.

MANTELS, GRATES AND TILES.

There are 3 Mantel, Grate and Tile Manufacturers in Montreal, among whom are:

EDWARD EARL & Co., Mantels, Grates and Tiles, Marble and Granite Works, 69 Bleury st.

PARKES, REEKIE & Co., 692 Craig st.

MANUFACTURERS' AGENTS.

There are 134 Manufacturers' Agents in Montreal, among whom are:

BACON BROS., Manufacturers' Agents, Steel, Iron, etc., 377 St Paul st.

R. C. BRUCE, Manufacturers' Agent'and Commission Merchant; Gents' White Shirts and Underwear a Specialty, 14 Lemoine st.

T. C. DOYLE, Manufacturers' Agent, 2 Gain st. Federal Tel. 1348.

MILLICHAMP, COYLE & Co., Agents Cotton and Woolen Manufacturers, Montreal and Toronto, 423 St Paul st.

J. T. SCANLAN, General European Agencies, 26 St Sacrament st.

SCHEAK & SCHEAK, Manufacturers' Agents, Temple Building, 185 St James st.

JOHN S. SHEARER & Co., Manufacturers' Agents, 7 St Helen st.

THOMAS WILSON & Co., Manufacturers' Agents and Dealers in Fancy Goods, Room 28 Balmoral block.

MARBLE WORKS.

There are 8 Marble Works in Montreal, among which are:

A. R. CINTRAT undertakes all kinds of Marble Works, 36 Windsor st.

R. FORSYTH, Marble Works, 130 Bleury st.

J. W. McNEIL, Marble and Granite Works, 205 Mountain st.

MARRIAGE LICENSE ISSUERS.

There are 10 Marriage License Issuers in Montreal, among whom are:

HUGH BRODIE, New York Life Bdg.

T. P. BUTLER, Q.C., Marriage Licenses Issued, 156 St James st. Bell Telephone 1795.

CUSHING & DUNTON, 110 St James st.

JOHN H. ISAACSON, 46 St François Xavier st.

LIGHTHALL & LIGHTHALL, Room 303 New York Life Building.

MEAT PACKERS.

There are 3 Meat Packers in Montreal, among whom are:

THE CANADA MEAT PACKING Co., cor Wellington and Murray sts.

MEDICINE COMPANY.

There is one Medicine Co. in Montreal.

THE DAWSON MEDICINE Co., Specialties: Dawson's Chocolate Creams, the Great Worm Remedy; Dawson's Stop-it, for Toothache; Dyspepsine, the Great American Remedy for Dyspepsia, 169 St Lawrence st.

MERCHANT.

JAMES INGLIS, Merchant, 8 Custom House sq.

MERCHANT TAILORS.

There are 118 Merchant Tailors in Montreal, among whom are:

M. J. ADLER, Merchant Tailor, 47 Beaver Hall hill.

M. BACHMANN, Artistic Merchant Tailor, 409 St James st.

J. H. BLUMENTHAL & SONS, The Mammoth Clothiers and Gents' Outfitters; Custom Tailoring a specialty, 1445 to 1451 St Catherine st.

L. C. DE TONNANCOUR, Merchant Tailor, 8 St Lambert st.

J. L. DUHAMEL, Marchand Tailleur, 1680 rue Ste Catherine, 3me porte de la rue St Denis, Montréal.

U. DUBREUIL, Merchant Tailor, 66 St Lawrence st.

GIBB & Co., Merchant Tailors and Gents' Furnishings, 148 St James st.

G. A. LAMONTAGNE & CIE, Marchands Tailleurs, 1536 rue Ste Catherine.

E. LEMIEUX, Merchant Tailor and Gents' Furnishings; fine assortment always in stock; 3 St. Lawrence st. Bell Tel. 2647.

D. McENTYRE, SON & Co., Fine Custom Tailors, 53 Beaver Hall hill.

E. McENTYRE, Merchant Tailor, 116 St James st.

J. J. MILLOY, Ladies' and Gentlemen's Tailor, 259 St James st.

HUGH ROSS, Merchant Tailor, 206 St James st.

M. RYAN & Co., Merchant Tailors, 92 St James st.

G. B. SADLER, Merchant Tailor, 2138 Notre Dame st.

Z. TURGEON, Merchant Tailor, 77 St Lawrence st. Bell Telephone 6611.

METAL WORKS.

There are 5 Metal Workers in Montreal, among whom are:

DOMINION METAL WORKS, GARTH & CO., Hot Water and Steam Engineers, Manufacturers and Furnishers of Cast Iron, Steam, Water & Soil Pipe Fittings, Malleable Iron Fittings, Bushings, Plugs, etc., Iron and Brass, Steam & Water Stop Cocks, Iron & Brass Globes, Water Valves, etc., Steam Whistles, Steam Pumps, Injectors, Coils, Radiators, Hot Water Furnaces, Sanitary Earthenware and Baths, etc., Van Duzen's Steam Jet Pumps, Loose Pulley Oilers, 536 to 542 Craig st.

MONTREAL SMELTING AND REFINING WORKS, Gauge Glasses and Metals, G. Langwell & Son, Proprietors, 10 Dorchester st.

MILLERS.

There are 7 Millers in Montreal, one of whom is:

IRA GOULD & SONS, City Flour Mills, Millers of Choice Roller Flour, office cor Grey Nun and William sts.

MILLINERY—WHOLESALE.

There are 6 Wholesale Millinery Dealers in Montreal, among whom are:

JOHN A. PATERSON & CO, Importers of Millinery and Fancy Dry Goods, 12 and 14 St Helen st.

MILLINERS.

There are 52 Milliners in Montreal, among whom are:

MRS. FLORANT, Fashionable Millinery, 1068 Ontario st.

MRS. J. F. FOSBRE,—all the latest Novelties in Millinery and Fancy Goods, 2072 Notre Dame st. cor Colborne st.

MRS. LAFORTUNE & CO, Dressmakers and Choice Millinery, 1777 St Catherine st.

MRS. J. McGINTY, Choice Millinery, 1749 St Catherine st.

MISS A. G. O'NEIL, Choice Millinery, 2096 Notre Dame st.

MRS. H. POITRAS, Millinery and Fancy Goods; Mourning Goods a Specialty, 1989 Notre Dame st.

MRS. O. ST. PIERRE, Choice Millinery, 1743 St Catherine st.

MILLWRIGHTS.

There are 6 Millwrights in Montreal, one of whom is:

ALEX. JEFFREY, Millwright, Contractor and Manufacturer, 57 Canning st.

MIRROR MANUFACTURERS.

There are 10 Mirror Manufacturers in Montreal, among whom are:

CANADA GLASS SILVERING AND BEVELLING Co., Manufacturers of Mirrors, Bevelled Panels for Doors, etc.; Old Mirrors Resilvered, 623 Lagauchetière st. Bell Telephone 1390.

MONGENAIS, BOIVIN & CO., Mirror Plates, 338 St Paul st.

MOULDINGS AND MIRRORS.

There are 10 Moulding and Mirror Plate Manufacturers in Montreal, among whom are:

CORRAN MANUFACTURING CO., Manufacturers of Mirrors, Mouldings, Frames and Looking Glasses and Fine Art Goods, 146 McGill st.

MUCILAGE MANUFACTURERS.

There is one Mucilage Manufacturer in Montreal:

E. AULD, Mucilage and Lithogram Composition, Manufacturer of Inks, etc., 759 Craig st.

NAVIGATION COMPANIES.

There are 2 Navigation Companies in Montreal, among whom are:

OTTAWA RIVER NAVIGATION CO., R. W. Shepherd, president; R. W. Shepherd, jun., manager and secretary-treasurer, 87 and 88 Common st.

NESTLE'S FOOD.

THOS. LEEMING & CO., Nestle's Food and Condensed Milk, 25 St. Peter st.

NEWSPAPERS AND PERIODICALS

IN MONTREAL.

DAILIES.

There are 6 French and 4 English Daily Newspapers in Montreal, as follows:

DAILY STAR, annual subscription $3; Weekly $1; Graham & Co., Proprietors and Publishers, 163 and 165 St James st.

Employs 52 females; 93 males.

GAZETTE (THE), annual subscription to Daily $6, to Weekly $1, *in advance;* The Gazette Printing Co., Proprietors and Printers; Richard White, Managing Director, cor Craig and St François Xavier sts.

Employs 8 females; 147 males.

LA MINERVE, annual subscription to Daily, *in advance* $6; Country, *in advance* $5; Weekly $1; T. Berthiaume, Publisher, 1610 Notre Dame st.

Employs 12 males

NEWSPAPERS—*Continued.*

LA PATRIE (Liberal), annual subscription to Daily $3, *in advance*; H. Beaugrand, Publisher and Printer. 31, 33 and 35 St Gabriel st.

Employs 3 females; 27 males.

LA PRESSE (Independent), annual subscription to Daily $3; to Weekly $1.00, *in advance*; T. Berthiaume, Publisher, 69 St James st.

Employs 2 females; 54 males.

LE MONDE, annual subscription to Daily $3, *in advance*; to Weekly $1; La Compagnie d'Imprimerie et de Publication du Canada, Publishers and Printers, 1650 Notre Dame st.

Employs 4 females; 44 males.

L'ÉTENDARD, Morning, Noon and Evening; L. A. Caron, manager, 37 St James st.

L'INDÉPENDANT, Daily; Rémi Tremblay, Editor and Proprietor, 32 St Gabriel st.

Employs 1 female; 66 males.

MONTREAL HERALD, annual subscription to Daily $6; to Weekly $1, *in advance*; The Herald Co., Limited, Proprietors and Printers, 6 Beaver Hall hill.

Employs 17 females; 82 males.

MONTREAL WITNESS, annual subscription to Daily in City $4; in Country $3, postpaid; Weekly $1, Weekly to Ministers, 50 cents, postpaid; John Dougall & Son, Proprietors and Printers, 321 and 323 St James st.

Employs 62 females; 104 males.

WEEKLIES.

There are 8 French and 14 English Weeklies in Montreal, among which are:

CHURCH GUARDIAN, Weekly; annual subscription $1.50, 190 St James st.

DOMINION ILLUSTRATED, weekly; annual subscription $4; Sabiston Lithographic and Publishing Co., Printers and Publishers, Gazette Building, cor St François Xavier and Craig sts.

Employs 53 females; 92 males.

FAMILY HERALD (Family Herald and Weekly Star) $1 per annum, *in advance*; Graham & Co., Proprietors and Printers, 163 St James st.

Printed at the Star Office.

JOURNAL OF COMMERCE, FINANCE AND INSURANCE REVIEW, Weekly; annual subscription, City $3, Country $2; M. S. Foley, Editor, Proprietor and Printer, 171 and 173 St James st.

Employs 20 females; 26 males.

LA SEMAINE RELIGIEUSE DE MONTRÉAL, Revue Hebdomadaire, Publiée tous les Samedis; abonnement $1 par an. Revs. J. M. Emard and P. N. Bruchesi, Éditeurs, Imprimée au No. 193 rue St Urbain.

Employs 1 female; 4 males.

LE MONDE ILLUSTRÉ, Berthiaume & Sabourin, 40 Place Jacques Cartier.

Employs 16 females; 24 males.

LE MONITEUR DU COMMERCE, Weekly; annual subscription $2.50; F. D. Shallow, Proprietor and Publisher, 43 St Gabriel st.

Employs 1 female; 6 males.

LE PRIX COURANT, Commercial Weekly; annual subscription: City $2.00; Country $1.50, *in advance*; J. Monier, Editor; La Société de Publication Commerciale, Publishers, 32 St Gabriel st.

Employs 1 female; 4 males.

LE PRIX COURANT, *Quebec Edition*; M. J. Bouchette, Manager, Quebec Office, 98 St Peter st, Lower Town, Quebec.

THE SHAREHOLDER, a Weekly Financial Paper, $2.00 per annum; Circulates Throughout the Dominion, Great Britain and the United States, 774 Craig st.

Employs 1 female; 5 males.

THE TRADE BULLETIN, the Financial, Commercial and General Produce Review, Shipping List and Live Stock Reporter; Henry Mason, Proprietor, 6 Beaver Hall hill.

Printed at the Herald Office.

THE TRADE REVIEW, a Weekly Commercial, Financial and Insurance Paper, 40 pages. The Leading Trade Journal; $2.00 per annum; Henry Harvey, Editor and Publisher, 47 St John st.

Printed by John Wilson.

TRUE WITNESS, Weekly; annual subscription *in advance* $1; J. P. Whelan, Proprietor, 761 Craig st.

Employs 2 females; 23 males.

FORTNIGHTLIES.

There is 1 French and 2 English Fortnightlies in Montreal:

INSURANCE AND FINANCE CHRONICLE, a Semi-Monthly Publication, devoted to the interests of Insurance and Finance; annual subscription $2.00, *in advance*; published by R. Wilson Smith, British Empire building, 1724 Notre Dame st.

Printed by John Lovell & Son.

CANADA ARTISTIQUE, fortnightly, annual subscription $2; A. Filiatreault, Publisher, 312 Craig.

Printed by John Lovell & Son.

MONTHLIES.

There are 7 French and 11 English Monthlies in Montreal, among which are:

CANADIAN JOURNAL OF FABRICS, Monthly, subscription $1 per annum, *in advance*; E. B. Figgar, Publisher, 43 St Sacrament st.

Printed by John Lovell & Son.

CANADIAN MAGAZINE OF SCIENCE AND INDUSTRIAL ARTS, AND PATENT OFFICE RECORD, semi-official Monthly; Illustrated; annual subscription $2.50; The Burland Lithographic Co. (Limited), Proprietors and Publishers, 5, 7 and 9 Bleury st.

Printed by Burland Lithographic Co.

EDUCATIONAL RECORD, Monthly; annual subscription $1; Canadian Subscription and Publishing Co., Publishers, 821 Craig st.

Printed at the Gazette Office.

HOME FASCINATOR, Monthly; annual subscription $1.00; Home Fascinator Publishing Co., Publishers, 214 St James st.

Printed by John Lovell & Son.

ILLUSTRATED JOURNAL OF AGRICULTURE, Monthly; annual subscription $1; Eusèbe Sénécal & Fils, Printers and Publishers. 20 St Vincent.

INDEX OF CURRENT EVENTS, Monthly; annual subscription $6; Henry Dalby, Publisher and Proprietor, 1833 Ontario st.

Printed by John Lovell & Son.

JOURNAL D'HYGIÈNE POPULAIRE, a Monthly Publication, Treating of Sanitary Matters. and Intended for Home Reading; annual subscription $1.50;

Dr. J. I. DESROCHES, Editor-Proprietor;

Dr. J. A. BEAUDRY, Manager,

P. O. Box 2027, Montreal.

JOURNAL DE L'INSTRUCTION PUBLIQUE, Monthly; annual subscription $1; C. O. Beauchemin & Fils, Printers and Publishers, 256 St Paul st.

LE JOURNAL D'AGRICULTURE ILLUSTRE, Monthly; annual subscription $1; Printed and Published by Eusèbe Sénécal & Fils 20 St Vincent st.

LA REVUE CANADIENNE, Monthly; annual subscription $2.00; P. O. Box 1525, 35 St James st.

LOWER CANADA JURIST, Monthly; annual subscription $4; John Lovell & Son, Proprietors and Printers, 23 and 25 St Nicholas st.

L'UNION MÉDICALE DU CANADA, Monthly; annual subscription $3; Students $2: Dr. A. Lamarche, Proprietor, 30 St Gabriel st.

MONTREAL PHARMACEUTICAL JOURNAL, Jas. D. Paterson, Manager.

PRESBYTERIAN COLLEGE JOURNAL, an Eight Page Magazine. Collegiate, Religious and Literary; Published Monthly during the Session. under the Auspices of the Philosophical and Literary Society of the Presbyterian College. Subscription $1.00.

PRESBYTERIAN RECORD, Monthly; annual subscription 50c in parcels to one address, 25c per copy. Issued by authority of the General Assembly of the Presbyterian Church in Canada. James Croil, editor; Gazette Printing Co., printers. Office 198 St James st.

QUARTERLIES.

There are 2 Quarterlies in Montreal, among which are:

CANADIAN ANTIQUARIAN AND NUMISMATIC JOURNAL, Published Quarterly; annual subscription $2.00; Remittances to Roswell C. Lyman, Treasurer, P. O. Box 1310.

CANADIAN RECORD OF SCIENCE, Quarterly, Price $3; Editor's address, 32 University st.

ANNUALS.

There are 2 English Annuals in Montreal, as follows:

CANADIAN TEXTILE DIRECTORY, Published Annually, by E. B. Biggar, 45 St Sacrament st.

Printed by John Lovell & Son.

LOVELL'S MONTREAL DIRECTORY, Published Annually, Price $3, payable on delivery, John Lovell & Son, Proprietors and Printers, 23 and 25 St Nicholas st.

NITROUS OXIDE.

MONTREAL NITROUS OXIDE CO., Pure Oxygen for Medical Purposes, 25 St Antoine st.

NOTARIES PUBLIC.

There are 119 Notaries in Montreal, among whom are:

ARCHAMBAULT & LECLERC, Notaries and Commissioners, 1608 Notre Dame cor St Gabriel. Bell Telephone 511.

A. BOUCHARD, LL.B., Notary. 25 St James

HUGH BRODIE, Notary Public, Commissioner for Ontario and Quebec, Issuer of Marriage Licenses, New York Life Building, Place d'Armes

AMEDEE CHAURET. B.C.L., Notary Public, Commissioner of Superior Court, 114 St James st.

RONZO H. CLERK, B.A., B.C.L., Notary, Commissioner for Ontario and Quebec. Room 40. Second Floor, Temple Building, 185 St James st. Tel. 2945

O. CREPEAU. LL.B., Notary; Money Loaned, 180 St James st. Bell Tel. 2695. Residence cor Centre and Shearer sts.

COUTLÉE & LAMARCHE, Notaries. Commissioners, etc.; Money to lend on Real Estate, 22 St James st. Bell Telephone 605.

CUSHING & DUNTON, Notaries, Commissioners and Issuers of Marriage Licenses, 110 St James st.

DECARY & BRUNET, Notaries and Depositaries of the Papers of the late E. McIntosh, 1933 Notre Dame st.

THEO DOUCET. Notary Public and Commissioner for Quebec and Manitoba, 190 St James st.

JOHN FAIR, Notary. Commissioner for taking Affidavits, Temple Building, 185 St James st.

NOTARIES PUBLIC—*Continued.*

E. C. P. GUY, B.C.L., Notary Public, Commissioner authorized to take Affidavits for the Provinces of Quebec and Ontario, etc., Manager for the Estate of the late C. E. Schiller, Office 82 St François Xavier st.

L. A. HART, Notary, Mortgage and Debenture Investment, Imperial Building, 107 St James st.

JOHN H. ISAACSON, Notary Public, Commissioner for Receiving Affidavits for Ontario, New Brunswick and Manitoba, Issuer of Marriage Licenses, 49 St François Xavier st.

ODILON LABADIE, B.C.L., Notary Public, Commissioner Superior Court, Justice of the Peace, 15 St Lambert st.

C. A. LEVEILLE, Notary Public, Commissioner for Quebec, 35 St James st.

Jos. LEVY, B.C.L., Notary and Commissioner; Estates managed; 36 St Vincent st.

LIGHTHALL & LIGHTHALL, Notaries; Marriage Licenses Issued, Room 303 New York Life Building, Place d'Armes.

A. C. LYMAN, M.A., B.C.L., Notary Public, Commissioner for Ontario and Quebec, Office Standard Building, 157 St James st.

MARLER, McLENNAN & FRY, Notaries, Standard Building, 157 St James st.

JOSEPH MELANÇON, Notary, 48 St James st.

PAPINEAU, MARIN, MACKAY & MORIN, Notaries, Commissioners, etc.; Notaries of the Corporation of the City of Montreal; Money to lend on Mortgages, General Notarial Business; Settlement of Estates and Successions a Specialty, 56 St James st.

PERODEAU & DE SALABERRY, Notaries Public, Commissioners, Financial and Real Estate Agents. New York Life Building, Place d'Armes.

E. W. H. PHILLIPS, Notary, 11 Hospital st.

NURSERYMEN.

There are 8 Nurserymen in Montreal, among whom are:

STONE & WELLINGTON, Nurserymen. Largest Nurseries in Canada; over 500 acres. Branch Office 242 St James st., Montreal, Jas. W. Beall, manager, Central Office. Toronto Nurseries, Fonthill, Ont.

OFFICE FURNITURE.

There are 6 Office Furniture Manufacturers in Montreal, among whom are:

H. NIGHTINGALE, Manufacturer of and Dealer in Office, Store and School Furniture; Fine Desks a Specialty, 9 St John st.

TEES & CO., Desk Makers and Manufacturers of Revolving Bookcases, Parquet Flooring and Funeral Supplies, 300 St James st.

OIL MANUFACTURERS.

There are 13 Oil Manufacturers in Montreal, one of whom is:

VACUUM OIL CO., Manufacturers of Fine Engine, Cylinder, Machine and General Lubricating Oils, 617 New York Life Bldg. Tel. 1061.

OIL CLOTH MANUFACTURERS.

There is one Oil Cloth Factory in Montreal:

THE DOMINION OIL CLOTH CO., Andrew Allan, President; John Baillie, Manager, Factory and Office cor St Catherine and Parthenais sts.

OLD CURIOSITY SHOP.

There is one Old Curiosity Shop in Montreal.

J. HARRIS & Co., there is one Olde Curiositie and Boke Shoppe, 2116 St. Catherine st.

OPTICIANS.

There are 11 Opticians in Montreal, one of whom is:

H. SANDERS, Optician, 202 St James st.

ORGAN BUILDERS.

There are 11 Organ Builders in Montreal, one of whom is:

L. MITCHELL, Organ Builder, 30 Donegana st.

PAINT MERCHANTS.

There are 87 Paint Merchants in Montreal, among whom are:

J. A. DENIS, Marchand de Peinture, Ferronneries et Tapisseries en gros et en détail, Peintre de Maison et d'Enseignes; seule Agent pour l'Escabeau de Baily & Lambert, 206½ rue St Laurent.

R. G. GAUCHER, Fire and Water-Proof Paint, Hardware Importer, 219 and 221 St Paul st.

FRS. MARTINEAU, Paints, Oils and Colors, 1381 and 1383 St Catherine st.

PAPER BOX MANUFACTURERS.

There are 5 Paper Box Manufacturers in Montreal, among whom are:

THE MAJOR MANUFACTURING CO., LTD., Paper Box Makers, Wire Cloth of all description. Redilles for Mining Purposes. Agents for Mill Felts and Machine Cloth, 23 and 25 Cotté st.

MILLER BROS. & CO., Manufacturers of Paper Boxes, Paper Collars, Egg Cases, etc., etc., 30 to 38 Dowd st.

THE SIMS PAPER BOX CO., Manufacturers of Paper Boxes, Egg Cases, Sample Cards, etc., 54 Latour st.

OCEAN STEAMSHIPS.

There are 8 Lines of Ocean Steamship Office in Montreal, among which are:

ALLAN LINE ROYAL MAIL STEAMSHIPS.

Sailing regularly between Montreal, Quebec, Londonderry and Liverpool.

Shortest Passage, only FIVE DAYS from Land to Land.

Passenger accommodation unsurpassed.

H. & A. ALLAN,
General Agents,
Montreal.

BEAVER LINE OF STEAMSHIPS,

Owned by the Canada Shipping Co., Ltd., sailing between Montreal and Liverpool during the summer months and between New York and Liverpool during the winter months, H. E. MURRAY, general manager, 1 Custom House sq.

DONALDSON LINE OF STEAMSHIPS,

Sailing between Montreal and Glasgow.

CONSIGNED TO ROBERT REFORD & CO.

Office 23 and 25 St. Sacrament street.

Alcides,	3500 Tons.	Captain	ROLLO.
Amarynthia,	4000 "	"	CRIGHTON.
Concordia,	2600 "	"	TAYLOR.
Circe,	2400 "	"	JENNINGS.
Colina,	2000 "	"	BROWNE.
Warwick,	2000 "	"	COUTTS.

Agents in Glasgow, DONALDSON BROS.

THOMSON LINE OF STEAMSHIPS,

Sailing between Montreal and London, Newcastle-on-Tyne, Dundee, Leith, Aberdeen and Mediterranean Ports.

CONSIGNED TO ROBERT REFORD & CO.

Office 23 and 25 St. Sacrament street.

Gerona,	3500 Tons,	Captain	ANDERSON.
Fremona,	3500 "	"	TAIT.
Escalona,	2000 "	"	CUMMINGS.
Dracona,	2000 "	"	HOWICK.
Barcelona,	2000 "	"	BOYLE.
Avlona,	2000 "	"	YULE.

Agents and owners, WM. THOMSON & SONS, Dundee, Scotland.

ROSS LINE OF STEAMSHIPS,

Sailing between Montreal and London.

CONSIGNED TO ROBERT REFORD & CO.

Office 23 and 25 St. Sacrament street.

Storm King,	3500 Tons,	Captain	CROSBY.
Ocean King,	2500 "	"	O'TOOLE.
Norse King,	3500 "	"	JOHNSTON.
Erl King,	2200 "	"	JAMES.

Agents in London, WM. ROSS & CO., 3 East India avenue.

HANSA STEAMSHIP COMPANY,

OF HAMBURG.

Service by the following Steamers:

Pickuben,	(new)	4200	Tons.
Stubbenhuk,	(new)	4200	"
Grimm,	(new)	3600	"
Steinhoft,	(new)	3500	"
Kehrwieder,		3000	"
Braumwall,	(new)	4000	"
Wandrahm,	(new)	3600	"
Cremon,		3000	"
Grassbrook,		3000	"

Between Hamburg and Antwerp and Montreal.

Agents:

AUGUST BOLTEN, Hamburg.

GRISAR & MARSILY, Antwerp.

STEINMANN & CO., Antwerp.

MUNDERLOH & CO., General Agents.

Montreal Office 61 St Sulpice st.

WHITE STAR STEAMSHIP COMPANY.

B. J. Coghlin, Agent. 364 St Paul st.

PAINTERS AND DECORATORS.

There are 87 Painters and Decorators in Montreal, among whom are:

D. A. BEAULIEU, Painter and Decorator, 1986 St. Catherine st.

C. T. CHARLEBOIS, Painter and Decorator, 1810 and 1812 St Catherine st.

L. N. DENIS, Painter, Decorator, Paper Hanger, &c., 299½ St Lawrence st.

FAVREAU & CIE., Peintres, Décorateurs, Poliseurs, Imitateurs, &c., 1114 Ontario st.

A. FRAPPIER & CIE., Peintures et Couleurs, 537b Craig st.

T. A. GAUTHIER, Peintre de Maisons, d'Enseigne, Décorateur, Imitateur, Tapissier et Blanchisseur, 13 rue St Urbain.

G. GLENNY, Paint Store, House, Sign and Carriage Painter, 100 Centre st.

O. M. LAVOIE, Peintre Décorateur, 1631 rue Notre Dame

H. A. MILLER, Painter and Decorator, 1996 St Catherine st.

JOHN B. OWENS, Painter and Decorator, 114 Bleury st. Estimates Given for New Work. Bell Tel. 2237, Federal Tel. 634.

PAUZE & LAMOUCHE, Painters and Decorators, 1788 St Catherine st.

T. POLITO, Glass Bending Works, and Painting in all its Branches, 39 University st.

J. ALPH. ROBY, Painting and Gilding in all its Branches; Fine Work a Specialty, 119 St Dominique st.

ROBERT H. TAYLOR, Painter, Paper Hanger and Gilder; Pictures Framed on Short Notice, office 1539 St Catherine st.

PAPER MAKERS.

There are 14 Paper Makers in Montreal, among whom are:

ALEX. BUNTIN & SON, Paper Manufacturers and Wholesale Stationers, 345 St Paul st., mills at Valleyfield, Que.

CANADA PAPER Co., Limited, Paper Makers and Wholesale Stationers, 578 to 582 Craig st., Montreal ; and Front st. West, Toronto

DOMINION PAPER COMPANY,
Manufacturers of
Fine News, Book, Printing,
Blank Wall Hanging, Tints, Colors,
Bleached Manilla, Unbleached Manilla,
White Manilla, Leather Colored Manilla,
Impression Manilla,
Special Sizes and Weights made to Order.
Mills at Kingsey Falls, P.Q.
Office 100 Grey Nun st,
Montreal.

ALEX. McARTHUR & Co., Paper Makers, Office and Warerooms 389 St Paul st., Factory Harbor and Logan sts., Paper Mills, Joliette, Que.

ROLLAND PAPER Co.; Mills at St Jerome; office at Montreal, J. B. Rolland & Fils, 6 to 14 St Vincent st.

PAPER STOCK, &c.

There are 7 Paper Stock Dealers in Montreal, one of whom is:

J. R. WALKER, Importer and Dealer in Paper Stock, Woolen Rags, Pig and Scrap Metals, Raw Hair, Old Rubber, etc., 15 Common st.

PATENT SOLICITORS.

There are 8 Patent Solicitors in Montreal, among whom are:

F. H. REYNOLDS, Solicitor of Patents, Temple Building, 185 St James st.

PAWNBROKERS.

There are 7 Pawnbrokers in Montreal, among whom are:

L. ARONSON, Pawnbroker; Money Advanced on all Kinds of Security, 517 Craig n St Lawrence st.

PHOTOGRAPHERS.

There are 32 Photographers in Montreal, among whom are:

G. C. ARLESS & Co, Photographers. We Make a Specialty of Children's Pictures and Enlarging and Copying Old Pictures, 261 St James st.

CUMMING & BREWIS, Art Studio ; Landscape and Instantaneous Photography a specialty, 117 and 119 Mansfield st.

EMILE LACAS & Co., Photographers, 10½ Phillips sq. E. Lacas, ex-Manager of Mulnier House, Paris, France.

N. C. LALONDE & SON, Photographers, 2092 St Catherine st.

WM. NOTMAN & SON, Portraits, Views, Amateur Outfits and General Photo Stock, 17 Bleury st.

J. G. PARKS, Photographer, 2264 St Catherine st.

ALFRED G. WALFORD (late of Summerhayes & Walford), Photographer, cor St Catherine and Victoria sts.

PHYSICIANS AND SURGEONS.

There are 249 Physicians and Surgeons in Montreal, among whom are:

L. E. FORTIER, M.D., 1208 Mignonne st.

DR. F. MÜLLER, Homeopathic Physician, 113 Stanley st.

PIANOS AND ORGANS.

There are 20 Piano and Organ Dealers in Montreal, among whom are:

J. H. CARSON, Provincial Agent for the celebrated Karn Piano and Organ. Highest awards received for Excellence of Tone and Elegance of Workmanship. Illustrated Catalogues on application, 42 Victoria sq.

FOISY FRERES, Sewing Machines, Pianos and Organs, Sole Proprietors of the Raymond Sewing Machine for the Province of Quebec, 10 St Lawrence st. cor Vitré st. Bel Tel. 1644.

LAURENT, LAFORCE & BOURDEAU, American and Canadian Pianos and Organs, 1637 Notre Dame st.

C. W. LINDSAY, Piano and Organ Dealer, 2270 St Catherine st.

NEW YORK PIANO Co., Agents for the following High-Class Pianos : A. Weber, New York, Decker & Son, New York, J. P. Hale, New York, Vose & Sons, Boston, Herr Piano Co., Montreal, N. Y. Piano Co., Montreal ; Organs : Thomas & Co.; Tuning and Repairing Pianos and Organs a Specialty, 228 and 230 St James st.

POIRIER & ARCAND, 317 St James st.

L. E. N. PRATTE, American, European and Canadian Pianos, Organs and Harps, 1676 Notre Dame st.

PLASTERER CONTRACTORS.

There are 15 Plasterer Contractors in Montreal, among whom are:

W. J. COOK, Plain and Ornamental Plasterer, 11 Concord st.

JEAN BTE. MAILHIOT & SON, Plasterers and Contractors, 4 Visitation st.

PLATE GLASS.

There are 2 Plate Glass Importers in Montreal, one of whom is :

MONGENAIS, BOIVIN & Co., Importers of Plate Glass, 338 St Paul st.

PLUMBERS, GAS AND STEAM FITTERS.

There are 117 Plumbers in Montreal, among whom are :

BAIRD & Co., Plumbers, Gas and Steam Fitters, Tinsmiths. etc., 100 Wellington st.

JOHN BURNS & Co., Plumbers, Gas and Steam Fitters, Manufacturers of Steel Cooking Ranges; Hotel Furnishings, all kinds, 675 Craig st.

CARROLL BROS., Practical Sanitarians, Plumbing, Heating and Ventilating, 795 Craig st. Bell Tel. 1834, Fed. Tel. 1605.

T. CHRISTY, Sanitary Plumber, Steam and Gas Fitter, 135 Bleury st.

JOHN DATE, Plumber, Gas and Steam Fitter, 654 and 656 Craig st. Bell Tel. 431, Fed. Tel. 681.

F. DUCLOS, Plumber, Roofer. Tinsmith, Gas and Steam Fitter ; Sky Lights a Specialty (late at 463 St James st.), 786 Inspector st.

F. F. FROIDEVAUX, Plumber, Gas and Steam Fitter and Range Maker, 264 St Lawrence st. and 195 St Charles Borromée st.

GORDON & EGAN, Plumbers. Gas and Steam Fitters, 120 Mansfield st.

THOMAS LINKLATER, Plumber, Gas and Steam Fitter, Copper and Sheet Metal Worker, 245 Commissioners st.

ALEXANDER MACKAY, Practical Plumber, Gas, Steam and Hot Water Fitter, 8 Beaver Hall hill and 40 St Elizabeth st.

McCRAE & WATSON, Plumbers, Gas and Steam Fitters, 796 Dorchester st. Tel. 4188

JOHN MARTIN & SON, Plumbers, Gas and Steam Fitters, 25 and 27 St Antoine st.

E. C. MOUNT & Co., Plumbers, Gas and Steam Fitters, Roofers, etc., 766 Craig st.

PELLETIER & BROSSEAU, Plumbers, Gas and Steam Fitters, Roofers, Skylight and Cornice Makers and Bellhangers, 106 St Louis st. Fed. Tel. 193, Bell Tel 1827.

J. THIBEAULT, Sanitary Plumber, Roofer, Tinsmith, Gas and Steam Fitter. etc.. 33 College st.

PLUMBERS' SUPPLIES.

There are 12 Dealers in Plumbers' Supplies in Montreal, one of whom is :

FRS. MARTINEAU, Plumbers' Supplies, 1381 and 1383 St. Catherine st.

PORK PACKERS.

There are 8 Pork Packers in Montreal, among whom are :

M. LAING & SONS, Packers and Lard Refiners, Office 151 and 153 Guy st. Packing House 95 to 101 Parthenais st.

M. T. McGRAIL & SON, Pork Packers, Curers of Provisions and Commission Merchants, 21 to 29 Wellington st. n McGill st.

POULTRY, GAME, &c.

There are 19 Dealers in Poultry, Game, &c., in Montreal, among whom are :

E. GAUTHIER, Dealer in Meat, Poultry, Fruits, etc., 99 St Antoine st.

PRINTERS—BOOK AND JOB.

There are 64 Book and Job Printers in Montreal, among whom are :

D. BENTLEY & Co., Fine Job Printers; Commercial Printing a Specialty, 1746 Notre Dame near St John st.

. EMILE DEMERS, Libraire, Imprimeur, 1590 rue Notre Dame

W. H. EATON & SON, Commercial Printers, 570 Craig st.

N. F. & V. GUERTIN, Printers and Blank Book Manufacturers, 79 St James st.

A. T. LEPINE & Co., Job Printers, 32 St Gabriel st.

JOHN LOVELL & SON, Book and Job Printers and Blank Book Manufacturers, 23 and 25 St Nicholas st.

WATERS BROS. & Co, Printers and Publishers, The Leading Job Printing House in Montreal, 751 Craig st.

JOHN WILSON, Book and Job Printer ; established in 1852. 47 St John st.

PRODUCE DEALERS.

There are 105 Produce Dealers in Montreal, among whom are ;

J. HAMILTON & Co, Wholesale Dealers in Country Produce, 22 St Peter st.

HISLOP, MELDRUM & Co., Wholesale Dealers in Butter, Eggs, Cheese and Country Produce, 235, 237 and 239 Commissioners st.

McLEAN & CAMPBELL, Wholesale Dealers in Eggs, Butter, Cheese and Country Produce. 20 Foundling st.

STEWART MUNN & Co., Produce Merchants, 22 St John st.

PROVISIONS.

There are 36 Provision Dealers in Montreal, among whom are:

AUBIN & THIBAULT, Marchands de Provisions, Beurre, Fromage, Œufs, etc., 335 rue des Commissaires

BELL, SIMPSON & Co., Wholesale Provision and Commission Merchants, 472 St Paul st. and 287 and 289 Commissioners st.

T. S. VIPOND & SON, Provisions, Importers of Teas, Molasses, etc., Dealers in Flour, Pork, Lard, Fish, Grain, etc., 32 and 34 Foundling st. Telephone 370.

PUBLIC WEIGHERS.

The are 4 Public Weighers in Montreal, among whom are:

MARSAN & BROSSEAU (successors to J. A. Cushing), licensed Public Weighers, Head Office, 65 Common cor Queen st.

PUBLISHERS.

There are 32 Publishers in Montreal, among whom are:

G. F. GODDARD, Subscription Books, Chas. Scribners' Sons' Publications, Agents for Stanley's "In Darkest Africa," 750 Craig st.

JOHN LOVELL & SON, Publishers of English Copyright Series of Novels and General Publishers, 23 and 25 St Nicholas st.

LE SUD PUBLISHING Co., Ltd., T. A. Evans, Secretary-Treasurer, 84 B Temple Building, 185 St James st.

RADIATORS.

H. McLAREN & Co., Eastern Agents for Toronto Radiator Manufacturing Co., "Safford" Radiators, 30 St François Xavier st.

RAILWAY SUPPLIES.

There are 27 Railway Supply Dealers in Montreal, among whom are:

JOHN McINTOSH & SON, Manufacturers of Railroad and Contractors' Supplies; Shipping Repairs a specialty, Vulcan Iron Works, cor Brennan and Nazareth sts.

CHAS. E. SPRAGGE, Railway Supplies and Commission Agent, Agent for Burrell & Co., London; Randolph & Clowes, Waterbury; N. K. Fairbank & Co., Chicago; Litofuge Mfg. Co., New York; Ferro Coppertin Anti-Friction Metals, etc., 8 Custom House sq.

J. & H. TAYLOR, Railway Equipment and Engineering Appliances, Steel Rails, Steel Tires, Tubes, U. S. Metallic Engine Packing, Gauges, Pop Valves, Scotch Gauge Glasses, Steam and Hydraulic Pipe, Iron Clad Track Washers, Traversing, Locomotive and Track Jacks, Car Replacers, etc., 16 St John st.

WALTER TOWNSHEND, Railway Supplies, Steel Rails, etc., Standard Building, 157 St James st.

REAL ESTATE AGENTS.

There are 69 Real Estate Agents in Montreal, among whom are:

GEO. H. L. BLAND, Trustee, Real Estate, Financial and General Agent, Room 65 Temple Bdg., 185 St James st.

RICHEMONT L. DE MARTIGNY, Real Estate Agent, 85 St James st.

J. G. GUIMOND & Co., Real Estate Agents, 82 St François Xavier st.

CHARLES HOLLAND, Real Estate, 249 St James st.

B. HUTCHINS & Co., Real Estate, Rental and Financial Agents; Stocks, Bonds, Mortgages and Cash Loans Negotiated, New York Life Building, Place d'Armes sq., Montreal. Tel. 2486

H. JOSEPH & Co., Real Estate and General Agents; Special attention given to Management of Estates, Canada Chambers, 16 St Sacrament st.

E. A. W. KITTSON, Real Estate and Financial Agent, Room 73 Temple Bdg., 185 St James st.

ALPHONSE LABADIE, Real Estate and Insurance Agent, 15 St Lambert st. Bell Tel. 1504, Fed. 885.

McCUAIG & MAINWARING, Real Estate and Investment Brokers, 147 St James st. and 18 Victoria st.

JOHN MORRIS, Real Estate and Financial Agent; Rents Collected and Property Managed, 126 St James st.

JAMES MUIR, Real Estate Agent, Room 5, Mechanics' Institute, 204 St James st.

J. CRADOCK SIMPSON, Real Estate, Insurance, Mortgage Loans; Real Estate Bought and Sold on Commission; Insurance Risks Placed; Loans Negotiated; Estates Managed; Rents Collected. Office and Real Estate Auction Sales Room in Citizens' Insurance Bdg., Ground Floor, 181 St James st; Federal and Bell Telephone connection.

R. K. THOMAS, Real Estate, Insurance and Investment Agent, Waddell Building, 30 St John st. cor Notre Dame st. Bell Telephone 699, Federal Telephone 271.

J. S. THOMSON & Co., Real Estate Agents and Auctioneers, 184 St James st.

ERNEST D. WINTLE, Real Estate, Insurance and Mortgage Agent, Offices in North British Chambers, 11 Hospital st. Bell Tel. 2603.

RESTAURANTS.

There are 310 Restaurants in Montreal, among which are :

J. B. ARCAND, St James Restaurant, 84 St James st.

W. M. KEARNS, Restaurant, 1747 Notre Dame st.

JOSEPH REBER (Successeur de M. Castongnay), Maison St Gabriel, coin des rues St Jacques et St Gabriel

REVERE HOUSE, P. Rivard & Co., Proprietors, 33 and 35 Cathedral st.

JOHN J. WALKER, Chateau de Ramezay (Restaurant), cor Jacques Cartier square and Notre Dame street (opposite City Hall), built A.D. 1720. The oldest historical building in Montreal.

ROLLING MILLS.

There are 3 Rolling Mills in Montreal, among which are :

ABBOTT & Co, Metropolitan Rolling Mills, Nail, Spike and Horseshoe Works, Office 55 St Sulpice ; Rolling Mill and Factory, DeLorimier av.

MONTREAL ROLLING MILLS Co., Manufacturers Cut Nails, Wire Nails, Horse Nails, Horse Shoes, Wrought Iron Pipe, Shot, White Lead, Tacks, Brads, etc., 204 St James st.

ROOFERS.

There are 49 Roofers in Montreal, among whom are :

BRODEUR & LESSARD, Roofers, Skylight and Galvanized Iron Cornice Makers and Plumbers ; Gas and Steam Fitting a Specialty, 421½ Craig st. Bell Tel. 2194

CANADA GALVANIZING AND STEEL ROOFING Co., Manufacturers of Corrugated Iron and Metal Roofing, all descriptions, 22 Latour st.

MONTREAL ROOFING Co., cor Latour st and Busby lane.

TOWLE & MICHAUD, Manufacturers and Roofers, 1334 St Catherine st.

ROOFING MATERIAL.

There are 9 Roofing Material Manufacturers in Montreal, one of whom is :

GEO. W. REED, Roofing and Roofing Materials, Asphalt Floorings, Galvanized Iron Skylights and Cornices, Refrigerators, &c., 783 and 785 Craig.

RUBBER GOODS.

There are 6 Rubber Goods Manufacturers in Montreal, one of whom is :

THE CANADIAN RUBBER Co. OF MONTREAL, Office 333 St Paul st., Montreal, and cor Yonge and Front sts., Toronto

SADDLERY MANUFACTURERS.

There are 42 Saddlery Manufacturers in Montreal, among whom are :

E. N. HENEY & Co., Manufacturers of and Dealers in Saddlery, Hardware and Carriage Findings, 337 St Paul st.

ROBERT IRWIN, Saddler and Harness Maker, 165 McGill st. Established 1835.

J. W. ROBERTS, London Saddlery, 336 St James st.

SAFE MANUFACTURERS.

There are 6 Safe Manufacturers in Montreal, among whom are :

ALFRED BENN, Manager GOLDIE & McCULLOCH, for Quebec and Maritime Provinces, Safes, Vaults and Machinery, also Amberg Cabinet Letter Files, 298 St James st.

G. CHAPLEAU, Dominion Safe and Steel Range Works, 320 St Lawrence st. Bell Tel. 133, Fed. Tel. 828

SAFETY EXPLOSIVES.

WILLIAM SCLATER & Co., Safety Explosives, 42, 44 and 46 Foundling st.

SALES STABLES.

There are 20 Sales Stables in Montreal, one of whom is :

WM. JACOB, Carriage, Saddle and General Purpose Horses ; always on hand good variety, 21 Hermine st.

SANITARIANS.

There are 40 Sanitarians in Montreal, one of whom is :

HUGHES & STEPHENSON, Practical Sanitarians, Plumbing, Heating, Ventilating, 747 Craig st.

SAW AND PLANING MILLS.

There are 20 Saw and Planing Mills in Montreal, one of whom is :

R. MACFARLANE, Steam Saw and Planing Mills, Manufacturer of Sashes, Doors, Blinds, Mouldings, etc., 409 to 421 Richmond st.

SCALE MANUFACTURERS.

There are 5 Scale Manufacturers in Montreal, among whom are:

JAMES FYFE, Manufacturer of Superior Quality Scales, cor St Paul and St Peter sts.

ALEX. GORDON, Manufacturer of Superior Quality Scales, 73 College st.

E. & C. GURNEY & Co., Wholesale Manufacturers Stoves, Grates, Scales, Steamfittings, Plumbers' Supplies, Locks, Lock Furniture, Registers, Hardware, etc., 385 & 387 St Paul st.

O. P. PATTEN, Fairbanks' Scale Warehouse, 419 & 421 St Paul st.

THE WARREN SCALE CO., Manufacturers of all Classes of Scales and Trucks; Repair Work of heavy Scales a Specialty, 454 and 456 St Paul st.

SCHOOLS.

There are 118 Schools in Montreal, among which are:

ELIOCK SCHOOL, Rev. John Williamson, Principal, 1143 Dorchester st.

THE GRAMMAR SCHOOL; Boarding and Day School for Boys of all Ages. Preparation for McGill College, the Military College, Kingston; and for Commercial pursuits. PROSPECTUSES on application to the Head Master, W. W. MOWAT, Glasgow University, 2498 St Catherine st cor Crescent st.

FITTES COLLEGE SCHOOL—COURSES OF STUDY: Classical, Mathematical and Commercial Classes resumed January 6th. 1891.
TRAILL OMAN, M.A.
Corner Drummond and St Catherine sts, Montreal.

KINDERGARTEN, Froebel's System, and Preparatory School, Misses McIntosh, 27 Victoria st.

SCULPTORS.

There are 33 Sculptors in Montreal, among whom are:

C. MARIOTTI, Sculptor in Marble, 17 Beaver Hall hill.

SECOND-HAND STORES.

There are 41 Second-Hand Stores in Montreal, among which are:

H. ALBERT, Dealer in New and Second-Hand Clothing, Trunks, Boots and Shoes, Furniture, Tools, etc., 493 Craig st.

LIVINSON & FRANKLIN, Stoves, Carpets, Furniture, etc., Dealers in New and Second-Hand Clothes, 265 Craig st.

I. LIVINSON, Dealer in New and Second Hand Clothes, Carpets, Furniture, Stoves, etc., 419½ Craig st.

SEED MERCHANTS.

There are 4 Seed Merchants in Montreal, among whom are:

DUPUY & CIE., Graines de Légumes, Graines de Semence, Grains de Fleurs, Pots a Fleurs, etc., 38 Place Jacques Cartier.

WILLIAM EVANS, Seedsman to the Council of Agriculture for the Province of Quebec. Importer and Grower of Field, Garden and Flower Seeds, Agricultural Implements, Guano, Superphosphate and other Fertilizers; Warehouses : 89, 91 and 93 McGill st, 104, 106 and 108 Foundling st and 42 Normand st, Montreal; Nurseries and Seed Farm, Broadlands, Cote St Paul. Fruit and Ornamental Trees, Shrubs, Roses, Green-house and Bedding Plants, Vegetable Plants, Small Fruits, &c. English and French Catalogues mailed free on application.

WM. EWING & Co., Seed Merchants, Importers of Garden, Farm and Flower Seeds; Special Quotations for Clover and Timothy, Catalogues Sent Free, 142 McGill st.

SEWING COTTON.

There are 2 Agents for Sewing Cotton in Montreal.

JOHN DEWHURST & SONS (LTD.), Cotton Spinners and Manufacturers of Sewing Cotton, Skipton, Eng., 73 St James. Representative, John Royan. Bell Tel. 1704. P. O. Box 449.

ROBERT HENDERSON & Co., Agents Chadwick's Spool Cotton, 492 St Paul st.

SEWING MACHINE MANUFACTURERS.

There are 3 Sewing Machine Manufacturers in Montreal, one of whom is:

THE WILLIAMS MANUFACTORY CO. (Ltd.), Sewing Machines, 1733 Notre Dame st.

SHIP CHANDLERS.

There are 6 Ship Chandlers in Montreal, one of whom is:

WILLIAM SCLATER & Co., Ship Chandlers, 42, 44 and 46 Foundling st.

SHIP LINERS.

There are 2 Ship Liners in Montreal, one of whom is:

JOHN LEE & Co., Ship Liners, Carpenters, Caulkers and Spar Makers. Atlantic Chambers, 207 Commissioners st.

SHIRT MANUFACTURERS.

There are 11 Shirt Manufacturers in Montreal, among whom are:

J. D. ANDERSON, JUN., Manufacturer of Shirts, and Overalls; Communion Veils a Specialty. All kinds of Machine Braiding, 18 Lemoine st.

J. F. HAWKE, The Shirt Maker, 1 Bleury cor Craig st.

SOAP AND OIL MANUFACTURERS.

There are 13 **Soap and Oil Manufacturers** in Montreal, among whom are:

DARLING & BRADY, Soap and Candle Manufacturers, 96 St Charles Borromée st.

W. STRACHAN & Co., Soap and Oil Manufacturers, 36, 38 and 40 Jacques Cartier st.

SOLICITORS.

There are 8 **Solicitors** in Montreal, one of whom is:

W. J. WHITE, Solicitor and Commissioner, 204 St James st.

SPORTING GOODS.

There are 11 **Dealers in Sporting Goods** in Montreal, one of whom is:

WARMINTON'S, 2208 St Catherine st, J. S. Cowan, Manager: Tents, Camp Furniture, Fishing Tackle, &c.

SPRING MANUFACTURERS.

There are 9 **Spring Manufacturers** in Montreal, among whom are:

K. W. BLACKWELL, Manufacturer of Springs of all kinds: also Steel Castings, cor Canal and Condé sts, Point St Charles.

B. J. COGHLIN, Manufacturer Railway and Carriage Springs and Axles, Hardware Merchant, Railway Supplies, Electro Plated and B. P. Ware, 364 St Paul st.

W. & F. P. CURRIE & CO.,
Manufacturers of
Bessemer Steel
Sofa, Chair and Bed Springs,
100 Grey Nun st.

STAMPED AND JAPANNED WARE.

There are 8 **Stamped and Japanned Ware Manufacturers** in Montreal, one of whom is:

THOMAS DAVIDSON & Co., Stamped and Japanned Ware, etc., 474 St Paul st., Montreal; 11 Front st., Toronto.

STATIONERS—WHOLESALE.

There are 12 **Wholesale Stationers** in Montreal, among whom are:

THE BARBER AND ELLIS CO., 823 Craig st. Envelope and Paper Makers and Manufacturing Stationers, Dealers in Bookbinders', Paper Box Maker's and Printers' Supplies.

W. V. DAWSON, Wholesale Stationer, Agent for Cowan & Sons, Paper Makers, and Dawson Bros' publications, 20 DeBresoles st.

JOSEPH FORTIER, Manufacturing Stationer, Printer, Ruler, Stamper, Binder and Blank Book Maker, 258 St James st. Bell Tel. 245, P. O. Box 626

ROBERT MILLER, SON & Co., Wholesale Stationers, School Book Publishers, Bookbinders and Blank Book Manufacturers, 1872 Notre Dame st., west of McGill st.

J. B. ROLLAND & FILS, Wholesale Stationers, Booksellers and Importers, 6 to 14 St Vincent st.

STEEL CASTINGS.

There are 9 **Manufacturers of Steel Castings** in Montreal, one of whom is:

K. W. BLACKWELL, Steel Castings by the Crucible Process and Springs of all kinds, cor Canal and Condé sts, Point St Charles.

STEEL STAMP MANUFACTURERS.

There are 4 **Steel Stamp Manufacturers** in Montreal, one of whom is:

G. W. DAWSON, Steel Stamps, Letters and Figures, 765 Craig st.

STENCIL MANUFACTURERS.

There are 4 **Stencil Manufacturers** in Montreal, one of whom is:

G. W. Dawson, Stencils and Rubber Stamps, 765 Craig st.

STENOGRAPHERS.

There are 18 **Stenographers** in Montreal, among whom are:

HOLLAND BROS. & URQUHART, Stenographers, 1742 Notre Dame st.

STOVE MANUFACTURERS.

There are 35 **Stove Manufacturers** in Montreal, among whom are:

G. CHAPLEAU, Dominion Safe and Steel Range Works, 320 St. Lawrence. Bell Tel. 133, Fed. Tel. 828.

E. & C. GURNEY & Co., Wholesale Manufacturers Stoves, Grates, Scales, Steamfittings, Plumbers' Supplies, Locks, Lock Furniture, Registers, Hardware, etc., 385 and 387 St Paul st.

H. R. IVES & Co. (Established 1859), Manufacturers of Hardware, Stoves, Architectural Iron Work, etc., Queen st.

McCLARY MANUFACTURING CO., Manufacturers Stoves, Ranges, Furnaces for Wood and Coal, Oil Stoves, Zinc and Crystalized Stone Boards, all kinds of Japanned, Pressed and Pieced Tinware, Refrigerators, etc., 375 St Paul st.

GEORGE R. PROWSE, Wrought Steel Ranges, Dealer in House Furnishing Hardware, Combination and Hot Air Furnaces, 224 St James st.

STRAW GOODS.

There are 2 Straw Goods Manufacturers in Montreal, one of whom is:

DOMINION STRAW GOODS CO., 21 Gosford st.

TEAS AND COFFEES—WHOLESALE.

There are 29 Tea and Coffee Merchants in Montreal, among whom are:

W. D. STROUD & SONS, Tea and Coffee Importers, Wholesale only, 33 St Sacrament st.

WELSH & ROUGH, Celebrated "Bharata Teas," Wholesale and Retail, 1796 Notre Dame st.

TELEPHONE MANUFACTURERS.

There are 2 Telephone Manufacturers in Montreal, one of whom is:

T. W. NESS, Manufacturer of Warehouse and Main Line Instruments, 644 Craig st.

TENT, AWNING AND TARPAULIN MANUFACTURERS.

There are 4 Tent, Awning and Tarpaulin Manufacturers in Montreal, among whom are:

MONTREAL TENT, AWNING AND TARPAULIN CO., W. H. Griffin, Manager, 44 Foundling st.

THOMAS SONNE, Tents, Awnings, Flags, Tarpaulins, etc., 187 Commissioners st.

THREADS.

There are 3 Wholesale Thread Dealers in Montreal, one of whom is:

THOMAS SAMUEL & SON, Agents for Barbour's Linen Thread, 8 St Helen st.

TILES FOR HALLS, HEARTHS, &c.

There are 8 Tile Manufacturers in Montreal, one of whom is:

PARKES, REEKIE & CO., 692 Craig st.

TINWARE—WHOLESALE.

There are 8 Wholesale Tinware Merchants in Montreal, one of whom is:

L. H. HEBERT, Importateur de Ferronneries, Quincailleries, Strictement en Gros, 297 et 299 rue St Paul et 21 rue St Jean Baptiste

TINSMITHS.

There are 84 Tinsmiths in Montreal, one of whom is:

G. YON, Tinsmith, Plumber and Roofer, 1888 St Catherine st.

TOBACCONISTS.

There are 28 Tobacconists in Montreal, among whom are:

A. DUBORD & CIE., Importateurs et Manufacturiers de Tabacs en Poudre, etc., en Gros et en Détail, 227 et 229 rue St Paul

EMPIRE TOBACCO CO., Manufacturers of Fine Tobacco, 758 Notre Dame st.

M. HIRSCH, General Tobacconist, Head Quarters Hirsch's Perique Mixture, 122 St James opp Post Office. Bell Telephone 2083

LUCKEY & REYNOLDS, Havana and Domestic Cigars, Billiard and Pool Room, 361 St James st.

J. RATTRAY & CO., Wholesale Tobacconists, Warehouse 75 St James st., Factory 80 St Charles Borromée st.

GEORGE STREMENSKI, Wholesale and Retail Tobacconist, 1735 St Catherine st.

TRUSS MANUFACTURERS.

There are 5 Truss Manufacturers in Montreal, among whom are:

F. GROSS, Canada Truss Factory, Established 1856, 712 Craig st.

J. HUDSON, Trusses, Artificial Legs, Crutches, Ear Trumpets, etc., 687 Craig st.

TRUST AND LOAN COMPANY.

THE TRUST AND LOAN CO. OF CANADA, Money Loaned on Farm and City Properties, R. J. Evans, Commissioner, 26 St James st.

TURKISH BATH.

TURKISH BATH INSTITUTE, St Monique st, near Windsor Hotel.

TYPEWRITERS.

There are 2 Agencies of Typewriters in Montreal, among whom are:

SMITH PREMIER TYPE WRITER, Holland Bros, Agents for Quebec and Eastern Ontario, 71 Temple Building, 185 St James st.

SPACKMAN & CO., Remington Type Writer, 248 St James st.

UMBRELLA MANUFACTURERS

There are 6 Umbrella Manufacturers in Montreal, one of whom is:

THE DOMINION UMBRELLA FACTORY, F. W. Gross, Umbrellas on hand, re-covered and repaired, 714 Craig st.

UPHOLSTERERS.

There are 73 Upholsterers in Montreal, among whom are:

ROY & CO., Upholsterers and Cabinetmakers, 1717 St Catherine st.

JAMES STEEL, Manufacturer, Dealer and Importer of Cheap, Medium and Fine Upholstery Goods and Furniture of every description, 1826 Notre Dame st.

VALUATORS.

There are 39 Valuators in Montreal, among whom are:

JOS. A. MERCIER, Mesureur et Evaluateur, 25 rue St Jacques.

JAMES STEEL, Expert Valuator, Auctioneer and Commission Merchant, Superior Storage, and Cash Advanced on all Goods, 1826 Notre Dame st.

VERMICELLI MANUFACTURERS.

There are 2 Vermicelli Manufacturers in Montreal, one of whom is:

THE DOMINION VERMICELLI AND MACARONI Co., Coutu & Jacques, proprietors, 1415 Notre D ame st.

VETERINARY SURGEONS.

There are 21 Veterinary Surgeons in Montreal, among whom are:

O. BRUNEAU, Veterinary Surgeon, Principal of the Montreal Veterinary School in connection with the Victoria Medical and Chirurgical School, Office 9 Hermine st, Infirmary 7 Hermine st. Bell Telephone 547, Federal Telephone 600, h 20 Park av.

McEACHRAN BAKER & McEACHRAN, Veterinary Surgeons, 6 Union av.

VOICE CULTURE.

W. BOHRER, Voice Culture, 2436 St Catherine st. Tel. 4374.

CHARLES GEDDES, Voice Culture, Queen's Hall, 2221 St Catherine st.

MADAME DE ANGELIS WATERS — Singing — 709 Sherbrooke st.

WAGON MAKERS.

There are 5 Wagon Makers in Montreal, among whom are:

R. J. & N. KENDAL, Wagon Makers and Painters, 244 and 246 Richmond st.

WALL PAPER MANUFACTURERS.

There are 2 Wall Paper Manufacturers in Montreal:

COLIN MCARTHUR & CO., Manufacturers of Wall Paper of all grades from the commonest Brown Blank to the finest Borders and Decorations, 15 Voltigeurs st. cor Notre Dame st.

FRS. MARTINEAU, Wall Paper, 1381 and 1383 St Catherine st.

WAREHOUSEMEN.

There are 13 Warehousemen in Montreal, among whom are:

ED. BEAUVAIS & CO., General Warehouse, Bond 76 V. R., Custom House Brokers, Money Loaned on Merchandise, 5 and 7 De Bresoles st. Bell Telephone 706, Federal 213.

J. W. HILL, Warehouseman, 48 William st.

MONTREAL WAREHOUSING CO., George E. Hanna, Manager and Secretary, Office 234 Wellington; stores cor Wellington and Colborne sts. and 122 Mill st.

WAX THREAD HARNESS MACHINES.

J. O'FLAHERTY, Pearson's Wax Thread Harness Machines, 248 St James st.

WEEKLY PAYMENT STORES.

There are 5 Weekly Payment Stores in Montreal, one of which is:

FOUCHER FILS & CIE., Weekly Payment Store, 1798 St Catherine st.

WHITE LEAD.

There are 9 White Lead Manufacturers in Montreal, one of whom is:

MCARTHUR, CORNEILLE & CO. (successors to John A. McArthur & Son), Manufacturers and Importers of White Lead, Colored Glass, Varnishes, Oils, Chemicals and Dye Stuffs, 310 to 316 St Paul st and 147 to 151 Commissioners st.

WINDOW GLASS.

There are 7 Dealers in Window Glass in Montreal, one of whom is:

FRS. MARTINEAU, Window Glass, 1381 and 1383 St Catherine st.

WINE MERCHANTS.

There are 22 Wine Merchants in Montreal, among whom are:

WILLIAM FARRELL, Wine Merchant, 420 St Paul st.

FRED. KINGSTON, General Wine and Spirit Merchant, 25 Hospital st. Ask for " Specialty Sherry."

MATHIEU FRERES, Wine Merchants, Special Agents for the Grand Mark " Specification Charentaise, " and for the Celebrated Wines and Spirits of W. & A. Gilbey, London, England, 87 St James st.

MONGENAIS, BOIVIN & Co, Wines and Liquors, 338 St Paul st.

WIRE MANUFACTURERS.

There are 5 Wire Manufacturers in Montreal, among whom are

DOMINION WIRE MANUFACTURING Co., Limited, Manufacturers of Barb and Plain Fencing Wire of all kinds, Wire Nails and Wood Screws, Factory at Lachute, Que., offices 27 Front st. East, Toronto. 185 St James st., Montreal.

J. ROSS, SON & Co., Montreal Insulated Wire Works, Manufacturers of Insulated Wires and Wires for Annunciators, Offices, Magnets and Dynamos, Factory 39 and 41 William st.

WOOD DEALERS.

There are 78 Wood Dealers in Montreal, among whom are:

ED. DUCHESNEAU, 635 Dorchester st. opp Dufferin sq.

A. HURTEAU & FRERE, Marchands de Bois de Sciage, 92 rue Sanguinet.

WOOLENS.

There are 17 Wholesale Woolen Dealers in Montreal, one of whom is:

THOURET, FITZGIBBON & Co., Wholesale Woolens and Tailors' Trimmings, 140 McGill st.

WOOD AND PHOTO ENGRAVING.

There are 3 Wood and Photo Engravers in Montreal, one of whom is:

MONTREAL WOOD & PHOTO ENGRAVING Co., James L. Wiseman, Manager, 186 St James st.

YEAST MANUFACTURERS.

FLEISCHMANN'S VEGETABLE COMPRESSED YEAST MANUFACTURERS. Our Yeast has no equal. Factory Depot. 70 St Antoine st.

LOVELL'S GAZETTEER AND HISTORY OF CANADA.

MY first attempt to obtain subscriptions, to enable me to issue this great work, failed for want of sufficient means to pursue a canvass throughout the Dominion.

An attempt is now being made to form a Joint Stock Company, with a capital of $200,000, in shares of $100 each, to be called THE CANADIAN PUBLISHING COMPANY, LIMITED.

For Prospectus and details, see pages 2, 3 and 4 of the Cover of this HISTORIC REPORT OF CENSUS OF MONTREAL; and, especially, read MR. BIXBY'S Letter, and some of the OPINIONS OF THE ONTARIO PRESS.

JOHN LOVELL, *Publisher.*

MONTREAL, March, 1891.

SUBSCRIBERS TO LOVELL'S CENSUS OF MONTREAL.

Académie d'Hochelaga... 1	Beauchamp Louis......... 1	Bonacina Chas........... 1	Caldwell John........... 1
Académie du Sacré Cœur. 1	Beauchamp W............ 1	Bond E. L.............. 4	Caldwell Mrs. J......... 1
Académie St. Antoine... 1	Beauchemin C. O., & Fils. 1	Bouchard A............. 1	Caldwell, Tait & Wilks.. 1
Adam, Drümel & Picard. 1	Beaudoin S. W.......... 1	Bouchard J. B., M.D.... 1	Caldwell Wm............ 1
Adam F. T............. 1	Beaudry J. A. U........ 1	Boucher A. J........... 1	Callahan & Co.......... 1
Adam J. B............. 1	Beaudry J. E........... 1	Boucher J. O........... 1	Cameron, Currie & Co... 1
Adler M. J............ 1	Beaudry Mrs. Victor.... 1	Boucher P. H........... 1	Cameron G. A........... 1
Aird James M.......... 3	Beaudry N............. 1	Boudreau J............. 1	Cameron Geo. W......... 1
Aitken John, & Co...... 1	Beaupré Ulric.......... 1	Boudreau J. M......... 1	Cameron K............. 1
Alain Theo............ 1	Beausoleil Eugène...... 1	Boudreau W........... 1	Campbell F. W......... 1
Albert Harris......... 1	Beauvais Arthur........ 1	Boughton Wm.......... 1	Campbell David, & Son.. 1
Alexander Chas........ 1	Beauvais Ed., & Cie.... 1	Boulit Louis H........ 3	Campbell Kenneth, & Co. 3
Allan J. H. B......... 1	Beckett R. A.......... 1	Bourassa G., père..... 1	Campbell Robt......... 1
Allan John........... 1	Beckett R. A., & Co... 3	Bourassa H., & Co..... 1	Canada Bank Note Co... 1
Allard Henry......... 1	Beckham James......... 1	Bourdeau J. R........ 1	Canada Cordage Co..... 5
Allard J............. 1	Beckham Robt.......... 1	Bourdon J............ 1	Canada Galvanizing and
Alley Fred. R........ 1	Beckham & Scott....... 1	Bourdou Louis........ 1	Steel Roofing Co.... 1
Ames, Holden & Co.... 4	Bédard L. A........... 1	Bourgeau & Herron..... 1	Canada Glass Silvering &
Anderson J. D........ 1	Bédard L., N. P....... 1	Bourgeois U.......... 1	Bevelling Co....... 1
Anderson J. T........ 1	Bédard N. F.......... 1	Bourgouin & Cailleux.. 1	Canada Jute Co........ 1
Anderson John, & Son.. 1	Bédard P............. 1	Bourgouin H.......... 1	Canada L. fe Insurance. 1
Axwell D. A.......... 1	Beemer H. J.......... 1	Bourgouin fils....... 1	Canada Meat Packing Co. 1
Arcand & Frères...... 1	Beers & Parrin....... 1	Bourdon J. H........ 1	Canada Paper Co...... 1
Arcand J. B.......... 1	Béguin L............ 1	Bourque H........... 1	Canada Shipping Co... 1
Archambault & Frères.. 1	Bélque & Co......... 1	Bourret H. A........ 1	Canada Switch Mfg. Co. 1
Archambault G. A., M. D. 1	Béland H. D......... 1	Bouthillier The...... 1	Canadian Rubber Co... 1
Archambault H. A..... 1	Bélanger J.......... 1	Bouthillier & Trudel.. 1	Canuff B. F......... 1
Archambault Jos...... 1	Belec Jos., O....... 1	Bowie D. E......... 1	Canuff P. N......... 1
Archambault J. L..... 1	Bell J. & T......... 1	Boyd J. & Co....... 1	Cantlie James A., & Co. 1
Archambault J. N..... 1	Bellemare A......... 1	Boyd Ryrie & Campbell. 1	Carbray, Routh & Co... 1
Archambault L. H..... 1	Bellhouse, Dillon & Co. 1	Boyd W. E.......... 1	Carle T............ 1
Archambault & Leclerc. 1	Bellotti A.......... 1	Brakenridge J. W.... 1	Carlisle John....... 1
Archambault U. E..... 1	Belve D............ 1	Bradford Ed........ 1	Carmichael Rev. Dean.. 1
Archibald Alex....... 1	Benjamin V. R....... 1	Brady H........... 1	Caron F. S......... 1
Archibald J. S., Q. C...10	Benn Alfred........ 1	Brabash A......... 1	Caton L. A......... 1
Arless G. C., & Co.... 1	Bennett J. D....... 1	Bramley W......... 1	Carrières J. H..... 1
Armstrong C. N....... 1	Bennett R. D....... 1	Brault & McGoldrick.. 1	Carroll Bros....... 2
Armstrong J. O....... 1	Benning & Barsalou.. 1	Brault Pierre...... 1	Carroll & Co....... 1
Armstrong & Radford.. 1	Benny Robert....... 1	Brazeau Alphonse... 1	Carter F........... 1
Arnold Brother....... 2	Benoit A. B........ 1	Brazeau & Leduc.... 1	Carsley S.......... 1
Arnott J. A.......... 1	Benoit F. X........ 1	Bremner A......... 1	Carson J. H........ 1
Arnott John R........ 1	Benoit O. D........ 1	Brennan J......... 1	Carson John........ 1
Aronson L............ 1	Benson A. A........ 1	Breton P. M....... 1	Carstens Fred...... 1
Ashford C............ 1	Bentley D.......... 1	Brien 1	Casgrain F. T., M.D.. 1
Asile de la Providence.. 1	Bérard & Major..... 1	Briggs Wm. M...... 2	Casselman & Co..... 1
Asile Nazareth....... 1	Bergeron T......... 1	Brisebois F........ 1	Casseday John L., & Co. 1
Askew Edw........... 1	Bergevin D......... 1	Brodeur Dr. A..... 1	Castle & Son....... 1
Atwater Henry W..... 1	Bernard S. W....... 1	Brodie & Harvey.... 1	Cauchon O......... 1
Aubin & Thibault..... 1	Bernier O.......... 1	Brogan A.......... 1	Cavanagh Edward.... 1
Aubry Alp........... 1	Bernier, Frère & Cie. 1	Brophy, Cains & Co.. 1	Caverhill J. L..... 1
Anger J. C........... 1	Bernier Oct........ 1	Brossard, Chaput & Co. 1	Caverhill, Kissock & Bin-
Auld John............ 1	Bernstein & Wolsey.. 1	Brossard Dr....... 1	more.......... 1
Auld R. S., & Co..... 1	Berry M. S......... 1	Brosseau Dr. A.... 1	Central Agency, The.. 1
Auld W. C............ 1	Berthiaume J....... 1	Brosseau A. T., M. D. 1	Chaffee A. B., jun... 2
Aumond R............ 1	Berthiaume & Sabourin. 1	Brosseau H. H..... 1	Charat J. O....... 1
Baby H.............. 1	Berthiaume Fils.... 1	Brouillette Charles. 1	Chamberland O..... 1
Bachmann Max........ 1	Bertrand O. J..... 1	Brown Bros........ 1	Chaplean G....... 1
Bacon Brothers....... 1	Bhemet D. S....... 1	Brown Geo., & Son.. 1	Chapman Alex...... 1
Bagall, White & Co.... 1	Bidard L. A....... 1	Brown James, & Son. 1	Chapman Wm. H..... 1
Bailey John.......... 1	Billotti A......... 1	Brown Joseph...... 1	Chaput & Frères... 1
Baker Malcolm C...... 1	Bilodeau F. X..... 1	Brown P.......... 1	Chaput, L., Fils & Cie. 1
Bank of British North	Binette Alfred.... 1	Brown W. F....... 1	Charette A....... 1
America..........20	Birks Henry....... 1	Bruneau Jos...... 1	Charland & Lahaise. 1
Bank of Montreal......6	Birks Richard..... 1	Bruneau O........ 1	Charlebois C. T... 1
Bank of Toronto...... 1	Bissonnett A...... 1	Brunet Francis... 1	Charlebois J. E... 1
Barber, Ellis & Co.... 1	Black J. F........ 1	Brunet J. A...... 1	Charlebois R..... 1
Barber Mfrs.......... 1	Blackader Edward H.. 1	Brunet J. B...... 1	Charpentier & Porcheron. 1
Barclay J. R., & Co... 1	Blackwell K. W.... 1	Brunet J. U...... 1	Charters Edw..... 1
Baridon J. R......... 1	Blaiklock & Bros... 1	Brunneau J....... 1	Chartrand Geo.... 1
Baril G. S........... 1	Blain Joel........ 1	Bryden W. S...... 1	Chausse Charles... 1
Barker Wm........... 1	Blais Alfred...... 1	Bryson K. H...... 1	Chauvé F........ 1
Barré J. L........... 1	Blanchet L........ 1	Bryson T. M., & Co. 1	Chausse J. Alcide.. 1
Barrette & Frère..... 1	Bland G. H. E..... 1	Bulman J. A. Proudfoot. 1	Cheesborough Mfg. Co. 1
Barrière H........... 1	Blinko Mrs. W. G.. 1	Bulmer B., jun., & Brothers 1	Cheney G........ 1
Barry R. C........... 1	Blomm, Desforges & Latou-	Bumbray L....... 1	Chester W. E.... 1
Barry Thomas........ 1	relle........... 1	Bunin A., & Co... 1	Chevalier G. A... 2
Barsalou J., & Co.... 1	Blumenthal J. H., & Son. 1	Bureau La....... 1	Chevalier J., M.D. 1
Barthé J. Arthur..... 1	Blumenthal V. C... 1	Burke David..... 1	Chevalier Louis.. 1
Bastien W. L......... 1	Board of Trade.... 1	Burke M......... 1	Chevalier J..... 1
Bastien A............ 1	Boas Feeder...... 1	Burland Lithographic Co.,	Childs Geo., & Co.. 1
Bastien O............ 1	Boas Feeder, & Co.. 2	The.......... 1	Chisholm Alex... 1
Bates J. & W. A...... 1	Bock O. E......... 1	Burnett G. F.... 1	Cholette & Gauthier. 1
Battersby D.......... 1	Bode H........... 1	Burns John, & Co.. 1	Choquet F. X.... 1
Baxter M. S., W. Box &	Bohrer W......... 1	Burrell W. G.... 1	Chouinard A..... 1
Co............... 2	Boilean A......... 1	Burroughs & Burroughs. 1	Chouinard P. Z.. 1
Baylis Jos. & Co..... 1	Boileau I......... 1	Bushnell Co., The, Ltd... 1	Christin F. A... 1
Beau C.............. 1	Boisseau Frère.... 1	Byrd Wm......... 1	Christin J., & Co.. 1
Beattie Henry........ 1	Boivin G.......... 1	Byrne Miss M. F.. 1	Christy T....... 1
Beauchamp A. A...... 1	Booker I.......... 1	Cadieux & Derome.. 1	Church John.... 1
Beauchamp Jos....... 1	Bolt Joseph T..... 1	Cadieux L. A.... 1	Circe N........ 1
Beauchamp L. E., & Cie. 1	Bonbic Louis...... 1	Colcott J. V.... 1	Cinzens Ins. Co.. 1

City & District Savings Bank 2	Cutler P. A.......... 1	Dixon Henry G. S......... 1	Ekers H. A.......... 1
Claggett C. C 1	Cyr J. Aif 1	Dixon J. P.......... 1	Ellegood J.......... 1
Clark George.......... 1	Dagan Alphonse.......... 1	Dixon Rev. J. H.......... 1	Elliott E.......... 1
Clark Jas. T.......... 1	Dagenais H 1	Dixon John E. T.......... 1	Elliott T.C.......... 1
Clarke G. W 1	Dagenais Jes.......... 1	Dobbia C. H.......... 1	Emo Wm., jun.......... 1
Clarke W. C.......... 1	Daigneau J.......... 1	Dods P. D., & Co.......... 1	End George.......... 1
Claude Pierre.......... 1	Dalton P. J 1	Dodwell & Hogg.......... 2	Empire Tobacco Co.......... 4
Cleland G. R.......... 1	Damdurand O.......... 1	Doin Armand.......... 1	English J., & Co.......... 1
Clement A. E 1	Dandurand Raoul.......... 1	Dominion Blanket Co.......... 1	Ennis J. H 1
Clement A. J.......... 1	Daniels T. H 1	Dominion Commercial Travellers Association. 1	Esplin G, & J 1
Clement V. A.......... 1	Dansereau F. X 1		Equitable Life Insurance Co.......... 4
Clerk Alex 1	Dansereau P.......... 1	Dominion Leather Board Co.......... 1	
Cloran M. M 1	Daoust A. S 1	Dominion Type Founding Co.......... 1	Esdaile J. & R.......... 4
Cloutier H.......... 1	Daoust & Frère.......... 1		Estate Boyer.......... 1
Coblan Manufacturing Co. 1	Daoust P.......... 1	Dominion Wire Mnfg. Co., Ltd.......... 1	Ethier B., jun.......... 1
Cohen J., & Co.......... 1	Dastous W 1		Ethier E. L.......... 1
Cohen L., & Son.......... 1	Davidson Thos , & Co..... 1	Donnelly John T., & Co.... 1	Evans Bros.......... 1
Cole Geo.......... 1	Davidson W. B., & Sons.. 2	Donaghue P. L.......... 1	Evans Jas. S., & Co 1
Cole H. F. M.......... 1	Davidson Wm. C.......... 1	Donahue John.......... 1	Evans & McGregor.......... 1
Cole Mrs. Agnes.......... 9	Davis C. J. W 1	Dorais T. H.......... 1	Evans & Sons.......... 1
Coleman William.......... 1	Davis M.......... 1	Doré E.......... 1	Evans W. C.......... 1
College Ste. Marie.......... 1	Dawes & Co.......... 1	Doré H. O.......... 1	Everett J.C.......... 1
Colleret E. D 1	Dawes Robt., jun.......... 1	Doré R. O.......... 1	Ewing S. H. & A. S 2
Collin N., & Cie.......... 1	Dawson Geo. W 1	Dorval Joseph.......... 1	Express Co., Can., G. Brice
Collins D.......... 1	Dawson W.......... 1	Dougall John, & Son...... 2	Fabre & Gravel.......... 1
Colson Chas.E.......... 1	Dawson W. V 1	Dougherty W. F.......... 1	Fafard J. Q.......... 1
Connaughton James.......... 1	Day & Deblois.......... 1	Douglas Corsan, M. D.... 1	Fair John.......... 1
Conroy J. M., & Co.......... 1	Decary & Frères.......... 1	Douglas J. H.......... 1	Fairbanks N. K., & Co... 1
Conseil Prov. d'Hygiène.. 1	Decary G. B.......... 1	Douglas J. M., & Co...... 1	Fartell W 1
Consumers Cordage Co.. 5	DeCow Douglas.......... 1	Dow Wm., & Co.......... 1	Farquharson Wm.......... 1
Conway J.......... 1	Deguire Rev. P.......... 1	Dowd Rev. P.......... 2	Faucher & Fils.......... 1
Coogan Richard.......... 1	De Lahaie C 1	Dowker, McIntosh & Co... 1	Fauteux Louis.......... 1
Cook A.......... 1	Delaney W. J.......... 1	Doyle & Anderson.......... 1	Featherston A. M.......... 1
Cooke George.......... 1	Delorme A.......... 1	Doyle J. E., & Co 1	Fee & Martin.......... 1
Cooper F.......... 1	Delorme Bros.......... 2	Drake W.......... 1	Fenwick Arnold, & Co..... 1
Corbeil A 1	Delorme E.......... 1	Dreyfus H. J.......... 1	Fenwick G. F., M. D..... 1
Corbeil Jos.......... 1	Delorme L. N.......... 1	Drouin P. E.......... 1	Ferneyhough S. A., & Co.. 1
Corbeil Wilfred.......... 1	Delorme Simeon.......... 1	Drummond, McCall & Co... 1	Ferns J. H.......... 1
Corcoran Jas.......... 1	DeLorimier P. E. Emile.. 1	Drysdale D., & Co.......... 2	Feron M., & Son.......... 1
Coristine James, & Co.... 1	DeLorimier S. A.......... 1	Drysdale David.......... 2	Ferrari C.......... 1
Corriveau David.......... 1	Delourey Mrs.......... 1	Drysdale W., & Co....... 20	Filiatrault Aristide.......... 1
Corriveau Joseph.......... 1	Delvecchio A. P., M. D.. 1	Dubord A.......... 1	Filiatrault J.......... 1
Costen T., & Co.......... 1	DeMartigny R. L.......... 1	Dubord A., & Co.......... 1	Filiatrault & Lesage.......... 1
Costigan W. T., & Co ... 1	Demers & Co.......... 1	Duchesneau Ed.......... 1	Filion P.......... 1
Cote A. R 1	Demers Albert.......... 1	Duchesneau Jos.......... 1	Findlay W. E 1
Coté Geo.......... 1	Demers Dr. G.......... 1	Duckett, Hodge & Co..... 1	Finlay —, jun.......... 1
Coté H. D.......... 1	Demers Emile.......... 1	Duclos F.......... 1	Finlay Robert.......... 1
Coté Henry.......... 1	Demers George.......... 1	Duclos Joseph, & Co..... 1	Finley F. G.......... 1
Coté J. H 1	Demers L. E.......... 1	Dufort & Desrochers..... 1	Finnie John T., M. D 1
Coté I. A 1	Demers P.......... 1	Dufour Pierre.......... 1	Fischer G. F.......... 1
Coté M.......... 1	Demers F. J., M. D....... 1	Dufour T.......... 1	Fisher Alexander.......... 1
Cotté Alex 1	De Montigny O. P....... 1	Dufresne L. P.......... 1	Fisk Newell.......... 1
Cottingham W. H 1	Demuy, Louis.......... 1	Dufresne O., jun., & Frère. 1	Flanaghan S 1
Coupal Gedeon.......... 1	Deniers Emile.......... 1	Dufresne R.......... 1	Fleischmann & Co.......... 1
Courtemanche O.......... 1	Denis Joseph.......... 1	Duhamel A.......... 1	Fleury & Bouthillier.......... 1
Courville P. N.......... 1	Denis R. J 1	Duhamel Jos. N.......... 1	Florant E. N.......... 1
Coutlee & Lamarche.......... 1	Denis T. J.......... 1	Dumaresq E.......... 1	Fogarty & Bro.......... 1
Coutlee O. C 1	Deom & Co.......... 1	Dumond G. A.......... 1	Foisy A 1
Covernton C. J.......... 1	Depatie A.......... 1	Damouchel A. T.......... 1	Foisy Frères.......... 1
Covernton C. J., & Co ... 1	Depatie W.......... 1	Dumouchel L. N 1	Foisy Thos. F. G.......... 1
Cowan John.......... 1	DeSalaberry C.......... 1	Dumuy La 1	Foley J. Leslie, M. D..... 1
Cowan William.......... 1	Desaulniers C. E. S...... 1	Duncan G. B.......... 1	Foley Mrs. M.......... 1
Cowper P 1	Desaulniers Frères.......... 1	Duncan John, & Co 1	Forde & Casey.......... 1
Craig Alex.......... 1	Desaulniers L.L.L., M. D, 1	Duncan R., & Co.......... 1	Forget L. J.......... 1
Crane & Baird.......... 1	Desautels A 1	Dunlop A. F.......... 1	Forman John.......... 1
Crathern & Caverhill.......... 1	Deschamps Z.......... 1	Dunlop, Lyman & Macpherson.......... 1	Forte C.......... 1
Crepeau O.......... 1	Desjardins Augustin.......... 1		Fortier Arch.......... 1
Crepeau J. G., N. P..... 1	Desjardins Chas.......... 1	Dunlop W. W 1	Fortier H 1
Crepeau J. N. C.......... 1	Desjardins D.......... 1	Dunton R. A.......... 3	Fortier J. M.......... 1
Cresse & Descarries.......... 1	Desjardins J. E.......... 1	Dupré Frères.......... 1	Fortier Jos.......... 2
Crevier T., & Fils.......... 1	Desjardins L. E.......... 1	Dupuis Frères.......... 1	Fortin O.......... 1
Cross Selkirk.......... 1	Desjardins Nap.......... 1	Dupois, Lanoix & Co..... 1	Fosbre Mrs. J. F.......... 1
Crossby P. A.......... 6	Deslauriers J.......... 1	Dupuy A., & Co.......... 1	Foster John.......... 1
Croteau George.......... 1	Desmarais A. L.......... 1	Dupuy Alex.......... 1	Foster Mrs.......... 1
Cumming Mrs 1	Desmarais G. A.......... 1	Durand A.......... 1	Fournier L.......... 1
Cumming W. T.......... 1	Desmarais M.......... 1	Durand Henri.......... 1	Francis F. W.......... 1
Cunningham Bros.......... 1	Desmarteau Chs.......... 1	Durand N.......... 1	Francis W. & B.......... 1
Cunningham & LeMessurier 1	Desormeau J. Z., & Co .. 1	Durand P. L.......... 1	Franchère L. O.......... 1
	Despocas W. H.......... 1	Durnford Geo.......... 1	Francœur & St. Marie 1
Cunningham & Robertson. 1	Destroches J. J.......... 1	Durocher Isaac.......... 1	Frappier A., & Co.......... 1
Curran & Grenier 1	Destrosiers J. H. E.......... 1	Durocher Isidore B.......... 1	Fraser D. H.......... 1
Currie J 1	DesRosiers J.A 1	Durocher J. E.......... 1	Fraser Donald.......... 1
Currie J. T 1	Devault G. C., & Co 1	Dusseault Miss 1	Fraser Institute.......... 1
Currie W., & F. P., & Co.. 1	Devins R. J 1	Daverger W 1	Fraser, Viger & Co.......... 1
Currie Wm 1	Diocesan Theological College 1	Dyer John.......... 1	Frechette E., & Cie.......... 1
Currier C. H.......... 1		Dyer W. A., & Co....... 1	Freeman A., & Co.......... 1
Curtis H. H.......... 1	Dion A.......... 1	Eadie S.......... 1	Freeman K.......... 1
Cushing C.......... 1	Dion H.......... 1	Earl Ed., & Co.......... 1	Frigon J.......... 1
Casson & Forest.......... 1	Dion L. E.......... 1	Earl Edward.......... 1	Frothingham & Workman. 1
Cuthbert Robt.......... 1	Dionne A.......... 1	Eaton W. H.......... 1	Fulton J. M. A.......... 1
	Dionne A., & Co 1	Ecroyd Thomas.......... 1	Fyfe Chas.......... 1

Fyfe James ... 1
Goden G. W ... 1
Gagnon C. E., & Co ... 1
Gagnon & Meunier ... 1
Gagnon Mrs ... 1
Gagnon N ... 1
Gagnon P ... 1
Gagnon & Tousignant ... 1
Gairdner R. H ... 1
Galarneau Henry ... 1
Galarneau M. C ... 1
Galibert C., & Fils ... 1
Gallagher Hugh ... 1
Gallery Bros ... 1
Gallery Bros ... 1
Gallery P ... 1
Garand M ... 1
Gardner Robt., & Son ... 1
Gareau Alphonse ... 1
Gareau E. R ... 1
Gareau, Marchand & Co ... 1
Gariepy H., & Co ... 1
Gariepy J. P ... 1
Garth & Co ... 5
Gaucher R. G ... 1
Gaudin Rev ... 1
Gaudry J. C ... 1
Gault A. F., & Co ... 5
Gauthier A ... 1
Gauthier Albert ... 1
Gauthier Edmond ... 1
Gauthier G ... 1
Gauthier Henry ... 1
Gauthier Thos ... 1
Gauvreau A ... 1
Gauvreau Ed ... 1
Gazette Printing Co ... 1
Gelinas E ... 1
Genéreux E. A ... 1
Gendron Mfg. Co ... 1
Geoffrion, Dorion & Allan ... 1
Gerhardt & Co ...
Germain D. N., & Co ... 1
German Club ... 1
Gerth A. A ... 1
Gervais & Frère ... 1
Gervais Cyrille A ... 3
Gervais J. E ... 1
Gibb & Co ... 1
Giguère J ... 1
Giguère J. H ... 1
Gilbert & Pelletier ... 1
Gillespie James F ... 1
Girard P. M ... 1
Girard A., jun ... 1
Girard Leopold ... 1
Girard Ls ... 1
Girouard M ... 1
Giroux O ... 1
Glen David ... 1
Glenny C ... 1
Gnaedinger L., Son & Co ... 2
Globe Spice Mills Co ... 2
Goad C. E ... 1
Goddard G. F ... 1
Gohier R ... 1
Goodrick H ... 1
Gordon Bros ... 1
Gorman M ... 1
Goudin Rev ... 1
Gouette M., & Co ... 1
Gould C. H ... 1
Goulet A. H ... 1
Goulet Frères ... 1
Goulet L. H ... 1
Grace Wm ... 3
Grafton F. E., & Sons ... 1
Graham Geo ... 1
Graham Hugh ... 50
Graham T ... 1
Graham Wm ... 1
Grandbery O. E ... 1
Grant Angus ... 1
Grant C ... 1
Granton C ... 1
Gravel & Bouchard ... 1
Gravel, Daquette & Duhamel ... 1
Gravel Frères ... 1
Gravel Ledger ... 1
Gravel & Paré ... 1

Gravel Raphael ... 1
Gravel Wm. H ... 1
Gray H. R ... 1
Greenberg M ... 1
Greene & Sons ... 1
Greenshields S., Son & Co ...
Greeves H. L ... 1
Grenier C. J ... 1
Grenier J ... 1
Grenier Vital ... 1
Griffin J ... 1
Grimson G. & J. E ... 1
Grondin A ... 1
Grothé D. O ... 1
Grothé F. A ... 1
Grothé L. O., & Co ... 1
Grundler A ... 1
Guerin C. L ... 1
Guerin Dr ... 1
Guerin F. X ... 1
Guérin Theophile ... 1
Guenin N. F. & V ... 1
Guimond J. G ... 1
Gurd Charles, & Co ... 1
Gurd D. F., M. D ... 1
Gurney E. C., & Co ... 1
Guy E. C. P ... 2
Hadrill Alf. W ... 1
Hagar Charles W ... 1
Haines & Co ... 1
Haldimand W. L., & Son ... 1
Hall W., M. A ... 1
Halpin & Gauthier ... 1
Hamelin & Cadieux ... 1
Hamilton Henry ... 1
Hamilton N. E ... 1
Hanley Thos ... 1
Harman J. J ... 1
Hannan M., & Co ... 1
Hanson Brothers ... 1
Hanson J. H ... 1
Hanson William ... 1
Harkness P ... 1
Harrington John ... 1
Harris Henry ... 1
Harrison Th ... 1
Harrower G. H ... 1
Hart C. T ... 1
Hart D ... 1
Hart Gerald E ... 2
Hart J. G ... 1
Hart L. T ... 1
Hart Wm ... 1
Harte Henry S ... 1
Hartt W ... 1
Haskell John F ... 1
Hastie H ... 1
Hatton & McLennan ... 1
Havana Cigar Co ... 1
Hawke J. L ... 1
Hay M ... 1
Haycock & Dodgson ... 1
Hearle J. G ... 1
Heara & Harrison ... 1
Heasley Geo. R ... 1
Hebert L. H ... 1
Helduard Frere ... 1
Henderson Bros ... 1
Henderson J. T ... 1
Henderson & Jetter ... 1
Henderson John, & Co ... 1
Henderson L. G ... 1
Henderson R., & Co ... 1
Hendery & Williamson ... 1
Henry E. N., & Co ... 1
Henry Philip ... 1
Henry W ... 1
Henshaw F. C ... 1
Hérard L. J ... 1
Herbert William ... 1
Heroux & Tremblay ... 1
Hetier Gustave ... 1
Hétu Jos. E ... 1
Hétu L. O ... 1
Heuser E., & Co ... 1
Heward S. B ... 1
Hicks M., & Co ... 1
Hill & Forbes ... 1
Hill J. W ... 1
Hilton J. F ... 1
Hirsch Michael ... 1

Hirtz Jules ... 1
Hislop, Meldram & Co ... 2
Hodgson J ... 1
Hodgson, Sumner & Co ... 1
Hodson W. H ... 1
Horner H. F ... 1
Hogan H ... 2
Holden A ... 1
Holland Charles ... 1
Holland G. A., & Son ... 1
Holland R, Henry, & Co ... 1
Hood Hugh W ... 1
Hood Wm. & Son ... 1
Hoolahan J., & Co ... 1
Homier Jos ... 1
Hope W ... 1
Hope W. P ... 1
Hopkins J. W ... 1
Hopper G. W ... 1
Horne Geo ... 1
Houde Charles ... 1
Houde Ls. A., jun ... 1
Houghton John ... 1
Houle A ... 1
Houle Pierre ... 1
Howard G. S ... 1
Howard J. H ... 1
Howell Miss ... 1
Hubb, B & Brown ... 1
Hubert E ... 1
Hudon, Hebert & Cie ... 2
Hudon & Orsali ... 1
Hudson's Bay Knitting Co ... 1
Hudson Fred. W ... 1
Hudson J ... 1
Huet J. Ed., M. D ... 1
Hulek A ... 1
Humphrey J ... 1
Hunsicker J. F ... 1
Hunt, Barnes & Co ... 1
Huot J ... 1
Huot Lucien ... 1
Hurteau A., & Frères ... 1
Hurtubise A. L ... 1
Hurtubise D. R ... 1
Hutchins B ... 1
Hutchison J. B ... 1
Hutton James, & Co ... 1
Hyman S ... 1
Imbleau A ... 1
Innes James ... 1
Irish D. T ... 2
Irwin, Hopper & Co ... 1
Irwin E., & Co ... 1
Irwin Robert ... 1
Ives H. R. & Co ... 1
Jackson H. F ... 1
Jacob Wm ... 1
Jacobs M., & Co ... 1
Jacotel F., & Co ... 1
Jamieson R., C., & Co ... 1
Jeannotte H., M. D ... 1
Jeannotte J ... 1
Jenning A ... 1
Jensen John L ... 1
Johnson C. R. G ... 1
Johnson Jos ... 1
Johnston H. J ... 1
Johnston John ... 1
Johnston John & Co ... 1
Johnston W. F ... 1
Jolicoeur Z. C ... 1
Jolicoeur Z. E ... 1
Joly P. P ... 1
Jonas Henri, & Co ... 1
Jordan Thos ... 1
Joyce A ... 1
Jubinville Gregoire ... 1
Judge Edgar ... 1
Kearns W. M., & Co ... 1
Keller F ... 1
Kelly James ... 1
Kelsen A ... 1
Kendall G. H., & Co ... 1
Kendall R. J. & N ... 1
Kenehan Jos ... 1
Kennedy John ... 1
Kennedy John (Harbor Comm's office) ... 1
Kerr Chas. E ... 1
Kerr James ... 1

Kerr R ... 1
Kerr R, & W ... 1
Kerry, Watson & Co ... 1
Kernick G. W ... 1
Kilkery M ... 1
King George ... 1
King John E ... 1
Kingman, Brown & Co ... 1
Kingston F ... 1
Kinlock, Lindsay & Co ... 2
Kirkup R. L. & J. W ... 1
Kittson & Reddy ... 1
Knapp Hon. Chas. L ... 1
Kneer Thomas ... 1
Knight William H ... 1
Kornmaier R ... 1
Krause & Barbeau ... 1
Kyte S. C ... 1
Labadie & Labadie ... 1
Labadie Odilon ... 1
La Banque Jacques Cartier ...
La Banque Nationale ... 1
La Banque Ville Marie ... 10
Labbé Geo. H., & Co ... 1
Labelle C. O ... 1
Labelle & Co ... 1
Labelle F ... 1
Labelle F., & Fils ... 1
Labelle Frank ... 1
Labelle H ... 1
Labelle H. P ... 1
Labine Gust ... 1
Labine Jules ... 1
Labonté D ... 1
Labossière Calixte ... 1
Labrecque A. A ... 1
Labrecque J. O., Comineau & Co ...
Lacaille Charles, & Co ... 1
La Canadienne Life ... 1
Lachance Nap ... 1
Lachance S ... 1
La Chambre de Commerce ... 1
Lachapelle Dr ... 1
Lacoste, Bisaillon, Brosseau & Lajoie ...
Lacroix A. D ... 1
Lacy E. D ... 2
Laflamme & Co ... 1
Lafleur E ... 1
Lafleur J. B ... 1
Lafontaine J ... 1
LaFontaine R ... 1
Lsfrance P ... 1
Lafrance P. H ... 1
Laquerrier J. A., & Co ... 1
Laing M., & Sons ... 1
Laird Paton & Co ... 6
Lake of the Woods Milling Co ... 1
Lallemand A ... 1
Lalonde A ... 1
Lalonde D ... 1
Lalonde Chas ... 1
Lamalice & Frères ... 1
Lamarche Azaric ... 1
Lamarche J ... 1
Lamarche J. B ... 1
Lamarche Z. N ... 1
Lamb James ... 1
Lamb McD ... 1
Lamb R ... 1
Lamb Thos ... 1
Lamère J. E ... 1
Lamontagne H. A., & Co ... 1
Lamontagne G. A., & Cie ... 1
Lamontagne Hector ... 1
Lamontagne L ... 1
Lamontagne Louis J ... 1
Lamothe Gull ... 1
Lamoureux Joseph ... 1
Lamoureux Sinai ... 1
Lanctot J. B. A ... 1
Lanctot Theotime ... 1
Langevin & Monday ... 1
Langhoff & Co ... 2
Langhoff Joseph ... 1
Langlois Chas., & Co ... 1
Languedoc G. de G ... 1
Langwell George ... 1
Lantel S ... 1

Lanigan A. R 1
Lanoix J. U 1
Lasskau W. G. C 1
Lanthier A 1
Lanthier & Archambault. 1
Lanthier & Co 1
Lanthier J. A., & Co 1
Lapalme Alex 1
Lapart Auguste 1
Lapierre Z 1
Laplante Z 1
Lapointe Frédéric 1
Lapointe Victor 1
Lapointe W 1
Laporte A 1
Laporte H 1
Laramée D 1
Laramée J. A 1
l'Archevêque O 1
Larin Louis 1
Larivière N. & A. C 1
La Roche H. A 1
Laroche Z., M. D 1
Larose & Paquin 1
Larose Hubert 1
Larose H 1
Larose Louis F 1
Larue L., jun 1
Larue Mag 1
Latimer R. J 1
Latour A. H 1
Latreille N 1
Laughman & O'Flaherty. 1
Laurance B., & Co 1
Laurent, Laforce & Bour-
deau 1
Laurie J., & Bro 1
Laurier M 1
Laurin G 1
Laurin G., & Fils 1
Laurin J. B 1
Laurin Louis 1
Lavallée C 1
Laverdure A 1
Lavers Wm 1
Lavert Joseph 1
Lavigne & Lajoie 1
Lavigne Emery 1
Lavigne Emile 1
Lavigne G 1
Lavigne J 1
Lavolette & Nelson 1
Lavoie L. P 1
Lavoie O. M 1
Law, Young & Co 1
Lawler & Co 1
Lawler J. E 1
Lawson John 1
Lawton Thos 1
Lazarus D 1
LeBeau S 1
LeBlanc Alexandre 1
LeBlanc B. H., M D ... 1
Leblanc J 1
Leblanc J. A., M.D 1
Leblanc L 1
Leboeuf J 1
Lebœuf Samuel J 1
Lebrun L 1
Lecavalier F. X 1
Lecavalier & Cie 1
Leclaire F. & J., & Co... 1
Leclaire Mrs. S. A 1
Leclerc & Co 1
Leclerc F., & Co 1
Leclerc J. U 1
Leclerc P. E 1
Leclerc, Pelletier & Bros-
seau 1
Lecompte A 1
Lecompte Jos 1
Ledoux H 1
Ledoux D 1
Leduc Dr., & Co 1
Leduc L. C 1
Lee John, & Co 1
Leeming Thos., & Co .. 1
Lefebvre A 1
Lefebvre B 1
Lefebvre Nap 1

Lefraincois Emile 1
Lefort E., & Co 1
Lefort Jos 1
Legault Frs 1
Lemay E. H 1
Lemieux Antoine 1
Lemieux E 1
Lemieux J. H 1
Lemieux P 1
Lemire E 1
"Le Monde" 1
Leo J. S 1
Leonard J 1
Leonard Bros 1
Leonard E 1
Lepage G 1
Lepage Z 1
Lepine George 1
Lepine L 1
Lepine P 1
Lesage Simon 1
Leslie James 1
Lespérance A 1
Les Sœurs Grises 1
Le Sud Publishing Co .. 1
Letendre & Arsenault .. 1
Letang, Letang & Co ... 1
LeTourneux, Fils et Cie. 1
Leveillé C. A 1
Leveillé O 1
Levesque & Pichette ... 1
Levin B., & Co 2
Levy H. T 1
Levy Jos 1
Levy J., & Co 1
Lewis J 1
Lichtenstein E 1
Ligget T 1
Ligitstone M., & Co ... 1
Limoges Z 1
Linton James, & Co ... 1
Lippe C 1
Little A. H., & Co 1
Little W. A 1
Liverpool & London &
Globe 2
Livinson & Franklin ... 1
Loan & Mortgage Co .. 1
Locke P., & Sons 1
Lockwood W 1
Logan J. R 1
Lonergan James 1
London & Lancashire Life
Insur. Co 5
Long John 1
Longtin M., N. P 1
Lonsdale, Reid & Co .. 1
Lord & Frère 1
Lortie A 1
Loterie de la Province de
Quebec 1
Loterie Nationale 1
Lowden J. R 1
Loynachan & Bros 1
Luman H. T 1
Lusher E 1
Lyman A. C 1
Lyman H H 1
Lyman Sons & Co 5
Lyman Theo 2
Lyman W. E 1
Lymburner & Mathews . 1
Lynch Patrick 1
Lynch Thos., A 1
Lyons John T 1
MacBean D. B. A., M. D 1
MacCallum D. C 1
MacDonald A. Roy ... 1
MacDonald J. A 1
Macdonald J. K 1
Macdonald M 1
Macdonald T. V 1
Macdougall Mrs. Geo .. 1
MacFarlane R 1
MacFarlane, Patterson &
Co 1
Machilda E. A 1
Macintosh & Hyde ... 1
Mackay Bros 1
Mackedie J. W., & Co. 2
Mackenzie J. G., & Co. 1

Mackie J. F 1
Mackinnon J. B 1
MacLaren & Co 1
Maclean James 1
Maclay J. E ....
acpherson A 1
Madore Alphonse 1
Madore David 1
Magenn Jos 1
Magor Frank, & Co ... 1
Mailet Arthur 1
Mailloux O 1
Mailloux P. P 1
Mainwaring R. A 0
Major P 1
Malingre H 1
Mallette Alphonse 1
Mallette M 1
Mallette & Martin 1
Ma'lette N 1
Maltby H. L 1
Manning J. R 1
Mantha J. B. & Co ... 1
Marchand F. X 1
Marchand J. C 1
Marchand L. W 1
Marchildon F. A 1
Marcotte M 1
Marcus Alex 1
Marcuse B 1
Maréchal L. A., V.C... 1
Marien J 1
Marin J. P 1
Marlatt, Armstrong & Co. 1
Marler, McLennan & Fry. 1
Marling J. W 1
Marquette E 1
Martel & Blacklock ... 1
Martel C 1
Martel F. X 1
Martel J. P 1
Martin A 1
Martin F 1
Martin Geo 1
Martin J. B. A 1
Martin John, & Co ... 1
Martin Moïse 1
Martin Nap. P 1
Martin P. P., & Co ... 1
Martin & Rabeau 1
Martin Walter 1
Martineau Frs 1
Martineau G. E 1
Mason A 1
Mason H 1
Mason James 1
Mason Joseph 1
Massey T 1
Massey Manufacturing Co. 1
Masson A. H 1
Masson & Asselin 1
Masson Mrs. Louis ... 1
Massy Nap 1
Mathewson J. A., & Co . 1
Mathieu Dr 1
Mathieu Frères 1
Mathieu & Tremblay .. 1
Matthews Chas. E 1
Matthews Geo. H 1
Maurice J 1
Maurilius Frère 1
May Thomas, & Co .. 1
Mayrand J. H 1
Mazarel & Fils 1
McAran — 1
McAran J 1
McArthur Alex., & Co.. 1
McArthur Colin, & Co.. 1
McArthur, Corneille & Co. 1
McBean A. G 1
McBean D. G 1
McBean George 1
McBride W. D 1
McCalhiro R., N 1
McClary Manufacturing
Coy 1
McConnell J. B., M. D.. 1
McCord David R 1
McCormack Duncan .. 1
McCrory P 1
McCrudden Jas 1

McDonald A. H 1
McDonald D 1
McDonald W 1
McEachran D 1
McEntyre D., & Son .. 1
McFarlane, Austin & Ro-
bertson 1
McGale R. E 1
McGarry Geo 1
McGoun Arch 1
McGown J. G. W 1
McGregor J. H 1
McIndoe & Vaughan .. 1
McIntosh J., & Son ... 1
McKay D. C 1
McKenzie M., & Co .. 1
McKeown Jas 1
McKeown Mrs 1
McLachlan Bros., & Co.. 1
McLaren J. R., jun ... 1
McLaren, The J. C., Belt-
ing Co 1
McLaren W., & Co ... 1
McLaren W. D 1
McLaughlin M. & M F. 1
McLaurin Bros 1
McLea J. & R 1
McLean & Campbell .. 1
McLeod & Shotton ... 1
McMartin J 1
McMillan D. D 1
McNally R. J., & Co.. 1
McNally W., & Co ... 1
McNamara Dr 1
McNichols R 1
McPherson D. A 1
McQueen & Cornell .. 1
McShane James 1
McShane R 1
McVey James 1
Meagher Bros., & Co .. 1
Meakins & Co 1
Meany C 1
Mechanics Institute .. 1
Meldrum Bros 1
Meloche J. Ed 1
Melvin D. A 1
Menard M 1
Mendel E 1
Merchants Bk. of Canada. 20
Mercier L 1
Mercier N 1
Merineau A 1
Metayer J. A 1
Meunier A 1
Meunier C 1
Meunier E 1
Michaud F 1
Michaud Thos 1
Mignault Dr 1
Milette H 1
Milette P. Z 1
Millar Robt 1
Millard H. R 1
Millen John 1
Miller Bros., & Co .. 1
Miller H. R 1
Miller R 1
Millichamp, Coyle & Co.. 1
Miller R., Son & Co .. 1
Milloy J. J 1
Mills & McDougall .. 2
Mimm J. M 1
Mireau E 1
Mireault G 1
Mitchell J 1
Mitchell Robert, & Co.. 1
Moffat Packing Co ... 1
Moïsan A. L 1
Molson W. A 1
Molson's Bank 6
Monarque L 1
Moncel J. F 1
Monette Joseph 1
Monette Moïse 1
Mongeau A 1
Mongeon T. D 1
Monier J 1
Monk F. D 1
Mont Ste Marie ... 1
Montreal Gas Co ... 1

Montreal Loan & Mortgage Co.
Montreal News Co.
Montreal Rolling Mills Co.
Montreal Roofing Co.
Montreal Steam Laundry
Montreal Tent, Awning and Torpaulin Co.
Montreal Warehousing Co.
Moodie, Graham & Co.
Moore J. W. (John Crowe & Co.)
Morgan Isidore
Morgan F. E.
Morgan H., & Co.
Moris & Co.
Morin & Jallen
Morin L., E., jun., & Co.
Morin P. & N.
Morisseau E.
Morrice D., Sons & Co.
Morrier P.
Morris John
Morrison A. J., & Co.
Morton Abraham
Morton, Phillips & Co.
Mount E. C., & Co.
Mousseity J. N.
Mowat W., W.
Muir E.
Muir James
Mouriers D. A.
Mulcair Bros.
Muller F., M. D.
Mulin J. L.
Murphy A. A.
Murphy Daniel
Murphy Frank H.
Murphy L., & Co.
Murphy M. F.
Murphy Philip
Murphy S.
Murray C. M.
Murray J. C.
Massen W. W.
Myers A. E.
Myles K. J.
Nault J. S.
Naveet Joseph
Nelles J. Warner, & Bro.
Nelson Alex., & Co.
Nelson Jas.
Ness T. W.
New York Piano Co.
Nicholson Geo.
Nicholson R.
Nicolle J. A.
Nightingale H.
Nightingale S.
Noel Edmund
Normandin J.
Normandin J. & A.
Normandin Zephirin
North British & Mercantile Insurance Co.
Northen Assurance
Notman Wm., & Sons
Nouris & Peut
Nugent J. P.
O'Brien Jas., & Co.
O'Brien Mrs. E.
O'Brien P., & Co.
O'Connor Chas., M. D.
O'Connor J. D.
O'Flaherty John
O'Grady Daniel
O'Hara Thos.
O'Hara W.
O'Leary P., M. D.
O'Meara W., P. P.
O'Neil J. J.
O'Neil A. J.
O'Neill Thos. J.
Ogilvie A. W., & Co.
Ogilvy Jas. A., & Sons
Osling John
Oliver D. G.
Oliver James, & Co.
Olivier D. T.
Olivon V.
Olsen K.

Oman T.
Orphelinat St. François Xavier
Osborne Samuel
Ottawa River Navigation Co.
Ouimet Alex.
Ouimet L. H. J., Jage.
Overen J. C.
Owen H.
Owens J. B.
Packard L. H., & Co.
Pagé C.
Pagé Jos.
Pagé W. J.
Pamdica d R. E.
Palmer J., & Sons
Pandiron Ed.
Panneton J.
Panneton H.
Panneton Ls.
Papineau, Marin & Co.
Paquette Alex.
Paquette J. P.
Paquette Jos.
Paquette M.
Pardis F.
Parc A.
Parc Jos.
Parent Bros.
Paren Edmond
Parent Narcisse
Parizeau J.
Parker J. H.
Parker Moss.
Parks S. H.
Parks J. G.
Parratt John
Parsons J. E.
Parsons S. R.
Paremodie Alexis
Paremodie J. E.
Paquenade Miss V.
Paterson J. M., & Co.
Paterson John A.
Paterson W.
Paton Hugh
Patter Thos. L.
Patters n G. H.
Patterson James
Patton Jas.
Paul Walter
Pauzé & Lamouche
Payne M. C.
Payer A.
Paxton R.
Paxton Wm.
Payette A. E.
Payette A., & Fils
Payette O.
Pearson V.
Peavey C. E.
Peavey T. P.
Peddy —
Pelletier & Guy
Pelisse P.
Peltier Arthur
Peltier J.
Peltier Louis H.
Penman & Co.
Pepin Edmond
Pepin P. & Co.
Percival Jos. W.
Perland A.
Perras J. A.
Perras J. O.
Perras Ls.
Perrault J. X.
Perrault V.
Perrault V., M. D.
Perrigo Jas., M. D.
Petel Regis
Phaneuf F.
Phelan Daniel
Phelan F. E.
Phelps Geo. F.
Philip Henry
Picard P.
Picault & Contant
Piché A., M. D.
Piché, Tisdale & Pain

chand
Picken J. E.
Pigeon A. P., & Co.
Pingel J. C.
Plena Mrs. Elizabeth
Plimsoll A. H.
Poirier & Arcand
Poirier, Boxette & Neville
Poirier Jos.
Poirier J.
Poiterin A. B.
Pottras Miss H.
Pominville Alfred
Pontiot Jos.
Porter, Kemp & Tookey
Potter H. B.
Pott r W. E.
Poulin F.
Poulot Moise
Poupart Alexis
Prett A. T.
Prenoveau C. M. R.
Prevost Fils
Prevost F.
Prevost V.
Price Henry
Price James
Primeau Chs.
Primeau L. A.
Proctor C. D.
Prothonotary, S. C., Pro. Court House
Proudfoot A., M. D.
Proulx B.
Proulx J. B., ptre.
Provencher J. G. A.
Providence, Makers Mère
Provident Loan & Savings Co.
Prevost A.
Provost J. A.
Prevost F.
Prud'homme S., N. P.
Purced J. B.
Quebec Insurance Co.
Quesuel A.
Queeneville Nap.
Quirty Frères
Quint J.
Quigg Jos. E. R.
Quirk Thos. J.
Racicot A.
Raby J. B., & Co.
Raby J.
Racicot A.
Raccard L., N. J.
Railway W. J.
Ragan, Waite & Co.
Ralston M. S., & Co.
Ramsay A., & Son
Ramsay W. M.
Rangger V. E.
Rankin James L.
Raphael John F.
Raphael Wm.
Rattray Jos. C.
Rea David, & Co.
Reade John
Ready E.
Redening D. F.
Reeves George
Recroft W. H.
Reddaway E., & Co.
Reed G. V.
Reed Walter
Reed Wm., & Co.
Reeves Joseph
Reid C. V.
Reid & Dr. man
Reid Jas.
Reid Robert
Reinhardt G., & Son
Reinhardt Mnfg. Co.
Renaud Emily
Renaud, King & Patterson
Renaud Jos.
Renaud P. U.
Renaud Wm.
Renaud X.
Renauf E. M.

Reuther J. B., & Son
Reuther, Reuther & Vanier
Rey D. L.
Reynolds F. H.
Reynolds Wm.
Rheaume N., & Frère
Richard Henri
Richardson J.
Richer N.
Rickly J. B. & Co.
Riddell & Common
Ridgeway T. R.
Rilsit Horace R.
Riehe Joseph
Rienhom Jos.
Riopert & Co.
Rivest Joseph, & Cie.
Roberge A.
Robert & Turnbull
Roberts Geo.
Roberts J. W.
Roberts James
Robertson Jas.
Robertson A. S.
Robertson David, & Co.
Robertson, Fleet & Falconer
Robertson James
Robertson, Linton & Co.
Robertson Robert
Robertson W. F.
Robin & Sadler
Robins S. P.
Robinson G. G., & Co.
Robinson J. Thos.
Robitaille J.
Robitaille Alph.
Robitaille Stanislas
Rochon Pierre
Roddick J. G., M. D.
Roder J. A., M. D.
Rodier L. L.
Rodrigue Alfred
Rodrigue Max.
Rohr & Co.
Rolland A.
Rolland & Fils
Rolland J. B., & Fils
Rollin O., & Cie.
Rollin Ls.
Romayns Bros.
Rose Frères
Rose L. P.
Ross Bros. & Co.
Ross, Forster & Co.
Ross Geo. D., & Co.
Ross, Hall & Co.
Ross J., Son & Co.
Ross P. S.
Ross Wm.
Rough Alex.
Rousseau F. X.
Rousseau S.
Row John
Rowan Mrs. J. J.
Roy & Bigndon
Roy & Co.
Roy E.
Roy F. X.
Roy Frères
Roy G.
Roy & Roy
Roy T., & Co.
Royal F., M. D.
Ruel D.
Russell H.
Russell Hugh
Rutherford W., & Son.
Ryan M., & Co.
Ryan Thos.
Ryland W., registrar.
Sabourin A. C.
Sadler D. & J., & Co.
Saber W. R.
Salvas O.
Samuel Thos., & Son
Sauvageau F.
Sauvageau T., & Co.
Sauvé J., & Co.
Savage A., & Son.
Scanlan J. T.

Scanlan John 1
Scarff C. E 1
Scheragne J. N. 1
Schmidt Avg., M.D ... 1
Schneider Peter, Sons & Co 1
Schneider T 1
Schneider T. H.......... 1
Scholfield C., & Co 1
School Commissioners... 1
Sch itze Ed 1
Schwob & Bros 1
Schater Wm., & Co 1
Scott Chas. J 1
Scott D 1
Scott J., & Co 1
Scriver J F 1
Scroggie M. N.......... 1
Seale R., & Son. 1
Seuth Robert, & Sons .. 1
Selki k Cross 1
Semmens, Ward & Evel... 1
Séécal E., & Fils 1
Shallow F. D 1
Shareholder, The 1
Sharpe's City Express Co. 1
Sharpley R., & Sons 1
Shaw Bros. & Cassi's ... 1
Shaw W. I., LL. D 1
Shea John 1
Shearer & Brown 5
Shearer John S 1
Shorey H., & Co 1
Sibley Geo 1
Silverman, Boulter & Co.. 1
Simard E. G 1
Simard J 1
Simpson J, Cradock, & Co.20
Simpson, Hall, Miller & Co 1
Simpson Mrs. J. 1
Sims A. H., & C 1
Singer Mfg. Co., The. ... 1
Singleton Harry 1
Skelly John 1
Skelton Bros. & Co..... 1
Slack R 1
Slattery J 1
Sleeth D., jun 1
Sly John 1
Smardon W. F 1
Smart Charles A 1
Smith Alex 1
Smith A. E 1
Smith & Co... 1
Smith Charles F 1
Smith Fischel & Co 1
Smith J. L 1
Smith J. L., & Sons.... 1
Smith John W.......... 1
Smith R. Wilson 10
Smith Sir Donald A ...0
Smyth Jos. M 1
Snow W 1
Snow Wm 2
Soeurs de Ste. Croix.... 1
Soly J. I 1
Soly I. N 1
Sonne Thos. 1
Southam & Carey.......... 1
Sparrow & Jacobs 1
Spawn Miss J.......... 1
Spence J. C., & Sons.... 1
St. Amour A. C 1
St. Amour J. A. C 1
St. Amour J. B. C.... 1
St André A 1
St. Arnaud A. M 1
St. Arnaud G. W.......... 1
St. Cyr Frs 1
St. Germain F 1
St. James' Club.... 1
St James Theo 1
St. Jean I 1
St Julien J. A 1

St. Patrick's Academy.... 1
Stacey Ed.......... 1
Stanley Dry Plate Co ... 1
Staton E. D 1
Stearns S. P.......... 4
Stolen B. F 1
Steel James.......... 1
Stephenson G 1
Stephenson W. A 1
Sterling J., & Co.......... 1
Stevenson, Blackader & Co.......... 1
Stevenson J. A. W.......... 1
Stevenson S. C 1
Stewart A. Bishop.......... 1
Stewart J 1
Stewart James.......... 1
Stewart James, & Co.... 1
Stewart S. I.......... 2
Stewart S. T.......... 1
Stinson Chas., & Co 1
S irling J. W 1
Stone & Wellington...... 2
Stonegrave A. C 1
Stroud G. F 1
Stroud W. D., & Sons .. 2
Summerhayes & Walford.. 1
Sun Life Assurance Co ... 1
Sun Publishing Co.......... 1
Surprenant Z 1
Surveyer L. J. A 1
Sutherland J. W 1
Sutton Thomas.......... 1
Swan Wm 1
Sweeney T. J. 1
Swift Wm 1
Symons S. J 1
Syred E. Mrs 1
Tabb H.......... 3
Taillon L. O.......... 1
Tardiff M 1
Tassé, Wood & Co 1
Tate W. & T. S. 1
Tasley J 1
Taylor A. E 1
Taylor Brothers 5
Taylor & Buchan.......... 2
Taylor Captain D.......... 1
Taylor, Howe & McIntyre. 1
Taylor J. A 1
Taylor James D 1
Taylor J. M 2
Tector Wm 1
Tees & Co 1
Tees, Wilson & Co 1
Telfer W. I., M. D 1
Tellier E. H 1
Tellier, Rothwell & Co.... 1
Terrault P 1
Terry John B.......... 1
Tessier F. X.......... 1
Tessier J., & Co 1
Tessier N.......... 1
Tester Jas. W., & Co.... 1
Tetrault N., jun 1
The Beaver Oil Co 1
The Canada Sugar Refining Co.......... 1
The Dominion Transport Co.......... 1
The Geo. Bishop Engraving and Printing Co.,.... 1
The Johnston Fluid Beef Co. 1
The Major Manufacturing Co.......... 1
The Montreal Brewing Co. 1
The Montreal News Co .. 3
The Renova Co.......... 1
The Shedden Co. (Limited) 2
The St. Lawrence Sugar Refining Co.......... 1
The Williams Mfg. Co.... 1

Theo Frère 1
Theriault, Victor 1
Therien T. H.......... 1
Therrien A 1
Therrien Z.......... 1
Thibaudeau Brothers & Co 1
Thibaudeau J., & Co 1
Thibault Jos.......... 1
Thibodeau & Bourdon. ... 1
Thivierge Michel.......... 1
Thomas C 1
Thompson G. W 1
Thompson J. W.......... 1
Thompson W. R 1
Thomson J 1
Thomson J. A 1
Thomson J., & Co 2
Thorpe A 1
Thouin J. F.......... 1
Thouin & Debien.......... 1
Thouin L. G.......... 1
Thouret, Fitzgibbon & Co.. 1
Thurber A. 1
Tigh James, & Co 1
Tilton M 1
Tison C.......... 1
Tombyll R. N 1
Tomlinson J 1
Tooke R. J 1
Torrance D 1
Tough John.......... 1
Tougas L 1
Townshend J. E 1
Tremblay A 1
Tremblay J. E.......... 1
Tremblay T.......... 1
Tresidder John B.......... 1
Trigon Joseph.......... 1
Trotter Bros.......... 1
Trudeau J. M 1
Trudel A. E 1
Trudel Bouthillier.......... 1
Trudel Henry 1
Trust & Loan Co.......... 2
Turcot Isidore.......... 1
Turnbull Robt.......... 1
Turner, Rose & Co 1
Turner, St. Pierre & Co... 1
Turner W 1
Tyler B., Sons & Co 1
Tyler R., jun.......... 1
Union Bank of Canada.... 4
Usherwood J.......... 1
Vacuum Oil Co 1
Vadboncœur L. D. 1
Vaillancourt B., & Frère.. 1
Vaillancourt G.......... 7
Valade Télesphore.......... 1
Valiquette & Valiquette . 1
Vallée C., & Frère.......... 1
Vallières O 1
Valois Jos. M.......... 1
Valois Dr. M. F.E.......... 1
Vanier Emile.......... 1
Vanier J 1
Vanier Jos 1
Vanier & Lesage.......... 1
Vanier P 1
Vantier L. P.......... 1
Varey E. C 1
Varner H 1
Vermette L., M.D 1
Varner H.......... 1
Verner Dr. L.......... 1
Verret, Stewart & Co.... 1
Verromeau J. L 1
Viau & Frère.......... 1
Victoria Bottling Co., The 1
Villeneuve J. O., & Co... 3
Villeneuve J 1
Vincent Geo. T 1
Vincent J. B.......... 1
Vincent J. L 1

Violletti George.......... 1
Vipond T. S., & Son 1
Vosburgh J. B.......... 1
Voyer Benjamin.......... 1
Voyer S. J 1
Waddell Robert 1
Waddell T. H.......... 1
Walker Bros. 1
Walker D. S.......... 1
Walker Geo. A.......... 1
Walker J. H 1
Walker J. J 1
Walker James, & Co.... 1
Walker R 1
Walker Wm 1
Walsh Henry.......... 1
Walsh R 1
Wanless John 1
Ward, Carter & Co 1
Warden & Hick 1
Warrington J. T. & F.H. 1
Warren H 1
Warren Scale Co., The.... 1
Warren W. H 1
Waters Bros. & Co.......... 1
Watkins R. L 1
Watson John.......... 1
Watson John C 1
Watson W 1
Watt Alex 1
Webster G 1
Weir R., & Son 1
Weir Robert S.......... 1
Weldon Geo 1
Walsh D. H 1
Welsh J H. M 1
Welsh & Rough.......... 1
West R. T.......... 1
Whelan John P., & Co .. 1
Whisfield W.A., & Co... 1
White R., & Co.......... 1
White T 1
White W. C 2
White W. J 1
Whitham James, & Co... 1
Whitney J. E. M., & Co . 1
Whyte J. J., M. D 1
Wightman Sporting Goods Co., The 1
Wilder H. A., & Co..... 1
Wiley A. T., & Co 1
Wilkinson & Boyle.......... 1
William John.......... 1
Williams Mrs. Miles.... 1
Williamson Jas.......... 1
Wilson Alex.......... 1
Wilson Chas. Edward.... 1
Wilson F 1
Wilson J. B.......... 1
Wilson J. H 1
Wilson James, jun.......... 1
Wilson John.......... 1
Wilson Thomas, & Co.... 1
Windsor Hotel 20
Windsor J. W 1
Wirtle Ernest D 1
Wiseman James L.......... 1
Wood & Evans 1
Wood Hugh W.... .. 1
Wood P. W.......... 1
Wray J. C 1
Wright C. C 1
Wright James.......... 1
Wright & Son 1
Wylie Mrs.......... 1
Von J. G 1
Young Andrew.......... 1
Young John.......... 1
Young Men's Christian As. 1
Young W. D 1
Young W. H. Dixon.......... 1
Young W. de I 1

SUPPLEMENTARY LIST OF SUBSCRIBERS

TO

LOVELL'S HISTORIC REPORT OF CENSUS OF MONTREAL.

Abel I.............. 1
Acton George 1
Allan Robert 1
Anderson J. W. 1
André Brother 1
Archambault Israel. 1
Archambault & Leveillé ..
Archambault Ovila 1
Armour W. 1
Armstrong G., & Co 1
Arpin Zephirin 1
Ashton W. 1
Aubin Olivier........... 1
Auger Joseph 1
Aumond Mad 1
Austin Henry W 1
Babington Ed. W. 1
Bachmann M. 1
Baillie Johnston 1
Ballantyne C. C......... 1
Barbeau J. A. L........ 1
Barlow John R 1
Barnjum Helen P..... 1
Barrett E. 1
Barsalou D 1
Barton F. R. 1
Beau C.............. 1
Beaucaire Joseph 1
Beauchamp David 1
Beauchamp William.... 1
Beaudoin P. A 1
Beaudry Louis 1
Beaulieu D. A. 1
Beaupré Dolinda 1
Beaupré Olivier........ 1
Beaupré Virginie....... 1
Beauvais A 1
Beauvais L. V.......... 1
Beck Wm., & Co....... 1
Bedard Eugène 1
Beer Luke 1
Belair Albert........... 1
Belanger Alex.......... 1
Belanger E 1
Belanger Louis 1
Bellemare L 1
Benard Hildège....... 1
Benoit Elzear 1
Benoit P 1
Beraud & Brodeur..... 1
Bergeron J. H 1
Bernier Madame 1
Berry M 1
Berthelet Emelien..... 1
Berthelette H 1
Bertrand Miss Delima.... 1
Bérubé Lazare 1
Bérubé Thos.......... 1
Beveridge H. R....... 1
Bibaud S 1
Bills Jas 1
Bilodeau B. 1
Birmingham J 1
Bishop Captain........ 1
Bishop John.......... 1
Bissonnette Ant....... 1
Black Mrs. J......... 1
Blain Philias 1
Blondin Napoleon..... 1
Blumenthal J. H., & Sons. 1
Bohrer Wm........... 1
Boismenu F 1
Boisseau L. H........ 1
Boissy A 1
Bolduc M. T.......... 1
Bonin L. S........... 1
Bonner James......... 1
Boulet J. B 1
Boult Louis H........ 3
Bourdeau Aug........ 1
Bourdeau Jos. H..... 1
Bourdon Arthur...... 1
Bourdon Henri 1

Bourdon L. P. C...... 1
Bourgie H 1
Bourgeau, Howard & Co.. 1
Bourgeois I. P....... 1
Bouthillier Michel. 1
Bowes & McWilliams .. 1
Boyd Robert 1
Brabant Zéphirin..... 1
Bragg H 1
Brakenridge J. W. 5
Briggs C. A........... 1
Bronsdon J. B 1
Broomhall P 1
Brown G. A., M. D..... 1
Brown H. H 1
Brown James........ 1
Brunet Mad. Marie..... 1
Brunet Rev. H 1
Burns M. 1
Burns Mrs. A........ 1
Burroughs Miss 1
Bush J.............. 1
Bush Jos. Walter..... 1
Cable Mrs. A. D...... 1
Cadieux L. A 1
Cairns William........ 1
Caldwell Wm......... 1
Campbell D 1
Campbell C 1
Campbell J. C........ 1
Campbell Mrs........ 1
Campbell W 1
Canniff John 1
Caplan H 1
Caron O 1
Cartell John 1
Carsley Bros 1
Carter C. E 1
Carter Mrs. G....... 1
Carver C............ 1
Caven W. W 1
Chafe Mrs........... 1
Chagnon C. P....... 1
Chanteloup E 1
Charles G 1
Chapleau E. J 1
Charpentier Jos 1
Charpentier T., jun ... 1
Chartrand Alphonse.... 1
Chatrand Antoine 1
Chartrand D 1
Chatel D 1
Cherrier A 1
Chive Th 1
Cholette L. E. A...... 1
Christin H 1
Clare W. H 1
Clark D 1
Clavette Chs........ 1
Cochrane Peter 1
Cocker Thos 1
Coderre Louis 1
Connolly James..... 1
Constantineau G..... 1
Conway Mrs. R 1
Coogan Richard 1
Corneille C. C....... 1
Cornu F., M. D...... 1
Costen T. W 1
Courville Mrs. Alice .. 1
Cousineau L........ 1
Cousineau T., & Cie... 1
Coutlee & Cie 1
Coulee J. P......... 1
Couto Louis........ 1
Couture Prof 1
Convent Ste Marguerite ... 1
Couvent des SS Noms de
   Jesus et Marie 1
Couverte & Fils 1
Couvrette Miss P. F ... 1
Cox Annie.......... 1
Cox Edwin 1

Crathern John C...... 1
Creagh Miss.......... 1
Crighton Daniel 1
Currie James......... 1
Curry Francis........ 1
Cusson E. N......... 1
Cusson Zotique...... 1
Dagenais Jos 1
Daley John J........ 1
Dallas Robert........ 1
Danziger H 1
Darling & Brady 1
Darling Wm., & Co ... 1
Davian D 1
David L. A 1
David F............. 1
Davidson T.......... 2
Davison W. F....... 1
Dawson Benj 1
Dawson Sir J. W..... 1
Day John J.......... 1
Dazé M 1
Dean H. J 1
Decary Arthur, cor St
   Denis and St Catherine . 1
Decary Arthur....... 1
DeChantal Olivier ... 1
Deganne J. B........ 1
Delavigne M. A 1
De Lorimier T. C. & R. G. 1
Delouin N. L........ 1
Delorme L. N., M.D... 1
Delorme Louis 1
Delorme Mrs. V...... 1
Delorme O 1
Demers Alphonse.... 1
Demers P 1
De Mesle R 1
Dean's J. A 1
Denis T 1
Depocas A. S....... 1
Desautels X......... 1
Desforges Jos....... 1
Desjardins Dr. T. H.. 1
Desjardins Rosario .. 1
Deslauriers George .. 1
Desormeau J. Z., & Co .. 1
Desvoyaux J. N..... 1
Desy D. J 1
Devine H. B........ 1
Dixon W. H., & Co... 1
Dion C. H 1
Dion Sarah 1
Dionne A. C........ 1
Dionne & Co 1
Dockrill E.......... 1
D'Olier Robt. W.... 1
Donaghy Chs. H 1
Donaghy John...... 1
Donnelly P......... 1
Doré Mdme........ 1
Dorion Mde. Davila ... 1
Doucet Ls. A 1
Douglas Alex....... 1
Dowling James..... 1
Doyle Mrs. P. C ... 1
Drake R 1
Drapeau & Champagne .. 1
Driscoll J 1
Drolet Benj........ 1
Drolet T 1
Dronin P. F....... 1
Dubé Louis....... 1
DuBerger A. E..... 1
Dubord A., & Cie.. 1
Dubois Captain 1
Dubois J. O....... 1
Ducharme George ... 1
Ducharme Mad. Jos.. 1
Duchesne Elie 1
Dufour E. D....... 1
Dufour L. N....... 1
Dufresne A........ 1

Duhamel J. L 1
Dumaine C. A........ 1
Duncan Mrs. W. T.... 1
Dupré L. P 1
Durkee Prof 1
Daquet Dr. E. E., Longue
   Pointe............ 1
Dussault L. H 1
Duseault J 1
Eaman John 1
Eaton A. J 1
Edwards John 1
Egan R 1
Egger John........ 1
Elder A 1
Elie Z 1
Elliot W. H 1
Elliott Mrs. A...... 1
Elliott R 1
Elsdon Edgar 1
Emblem T. C...... 1
Ethier J. U........ 1
Ethier P.......... 1
Evans & McGregor... 1
Ewan Alex........ 1
Farand C 1
Fanbert Michel 1
Faust A 1
Favreau Avila 1
Favreau Ed........ 1
Feely J. H 2
Ferland L......... 1
Ferrier James..... 1
Figsby Francis A ... 1
Filiatrault T....... 1
Findlay G. H 1
Findlay J 1
Finkelstein T...... 1
Fiset L. S........ 1
Fisher H 1
Fisher M., Sons & Co.... 1
Florant Mad. A. A.... 1
Forbes H. E 1
Ford James, jun.... 1
Forest Alphonse ... 1
Forget dit Dépatie Frs. X. 1
Forrester David 1
Fortier C 1
Fortin Dame Virginie.. 1
Fortin Joseph..... 1
Fortin O., V. S.... 1
Foster Charles.... 1
Foureau Napoleon .. 1
Fournier J........ 1
Fournier J. B..... 1
Franchère L. O.... 1
Frappier Jos...... 1
Fraser Alexander.. 1
French Mrs 1
Friedman Nathan .. 1
Froidevau F. F.... 1
Fulton Gilbert..... 1
Fyfe Mrs. Chs 1
Gadbois Pierre.... 1
Gaden Wm 1
Gagnon Albina ... 1
Gagnon H 1
Gagnon L........ 1
Gagnon R....... 1
Galarneau Mrs. G... 1
Galarneau Ovide .. 1
Gales T. W...... 1
Gale — 1
Gall Mrs. Janet... 1
Gallaher Mrs. Helen . 1
Gardiner Thos.... 1
Gardiner Thos. S.. 1
Gardner Alex. W., M.D... 1
Gardner Miss 1
Gariepy H., & Co... 1
Gariepy Joseph ... 1
Gariepy Ludger... 1
Gascoigne Mrs.... 1

Gascon J. B.
Gauthier Alexis
Gauthier T. A.
Gauvreau Geo
Geddes Chs. G.
Gehret E
Geherty J
Gendreau Dr
Geodron A
Généreux J. O.
Genois Eugénie
Gervais Dr
Gervais Nap
Gethings Chas
Giguère Odilon
Gilbert Noel
Gibby Thomas
Girouard Alfred
Glackmeyer C., jun
Glassford Bros. & Pollock
Gollifer E. J
Goodrick H
Gordon D
Gordon William
Gore Charles
Gosselin Z
Goulet Alex
Goulet L. H.
Goyette Mad. Antoine
Grace M., sen
Granger C
Granger G
Grant C
Grant Mrs. L
Gravel Mrs. Jos.
Green H. A.
Greenshields Mrs
Grenier George
Griffin A
Guérin F. X.
Guertin Remi
Goslbault Julie
Goulbault O
Guillet Mad. Pierre
Guillet Hubert
Guillet L. A.
Gurd D. F., M.D.
Guthrie David
Haas J. G.
Hagar Mrs.
Hall M. Grant
Halley C
Hamel Thomas
Hammon Mrs. E.
Hanson C. D.
Hanson Mrs. F.
Harper James
Harris A
Harris S.
Hartt Wm
Hastie Wm.
Haviland E. C
Hayes L
Hemond J C
Henault O. L., & Co.
Hennult Oscar
Heney E. N., & Co.
Hewter F
Hewin William
Hiam Thos
Hicks M., et Co.
Higgins Mrs
Higginson Mrs
Hilton E. A
Hinton J. W
Hodgson Bros
Holden —
Holland N
Holloway John
Homier J. E.
Horan Mrs
Horen John
Horwell Mrs
Houle A
Howard E.
Howden, Starke et Co.
Howe H. Aspinwall
Hubbard Chs.
Hughes Chs.
Hunter James C.
Huot Elzéar
Hurigon Arthur

Hyde Alex., & Co.
Inglis A
Jackson James
Jacquel J. L
Jean Joseph
Jeanmotte A
Jetté L
Jobin Mad. Odilon
Johnson John A
Johnson T
Johnson W. C.
Joly Paul
Jones Jas.
Joseph J. O.
Joseph Walter I
Kearney Miss
Kellogg & Co.
Kelley Fred. W
Kelly Mrs
Kemp Mrs. James
Kennedy William
Kent James
Kerr James
Kerry, Watson & Co.
Kilner R. S.
King H. M.
Kinloch Mrs.
Labadie E., M.D.
L'Abbé Joseph
Labelle J. B.
Labelle J. O.
Labelle Joseph
Lakelle L. P
Laberge Jos
Labrecque Alfred
Labrecque E
Labre que J. O., Cousineau & Co.
Lacaille Chs., & Cie.
Lachapelle F. N.
Lacoste & Co.
Lacroix Chs. F.
Lasseur Mad. Pierre
Lafortune Mad. T., & Co.
Lafrenière J. O.
Lafrenière Susanne
Lafrician N
Lajoie F. G.
L'Allemand Ed.
Lalonde & Girard
Lalonde Joseph
Lalonde N. C., et Son
Lamarche Joseph
Lamarre P. M.
Lamb James
Lamb McDuff.
Lamb Thos.
Lamothe G
Lanctot George
Landreville Joseph
Lane Percy F.
Langevin Cleophas
Langlois Chs., & Co.
Langlois Sylvestre
Langlois Wilfred
Lapierre A H
Laplante Jean
Laplante J
Lakamie L. H.
Larivee Chas. E
Larivière M. J.
Larose & Paquin
Latour Dr. A. A.
Latour O.
Laurier J. L.
Laurier N
Lauzon A. I.
Lauzon Chs.
Lavallée & Lavallée
Lavallée Nazaire.
Lavers William
Lavigne A.
Lavigne Emery
Laviolette G
Lavoie O
Lawless W. C
Lawrence Ant.
Lawrence J. W.
Leather Robert
LeBlanc A
Leblanc Joseph

Lebuis A
Lecavalier & Cie.
Leclair J. H
Leclerc Jos.
Lecomte H
Lecours Joseph
L'Ecuyer Dr.
Leddy P
Lefebvre Michel, & Cie.
Legault O
Léger Jules
Leger O.
Leitch P. J.
Lemieux E.
Lennox R
Leroux F. X.
Lesiege Mrs. Dieudonné
Lesser Mona
Le Tourano Rev. I. N.
LeTourneux C
Levesque Paul C
Limoges Olivier
Lizée O
Lockerby W. W.
Logie R
Loiseau U
Loiselle Miss
Loiselle Wm
Lomas Mrs. H. S.
Lorge & Co.
Lulham George.
Lupien F. P.
Lyall Peter
Lynch Mrs. Geo
Lyons Mrs. McA.
Macdonald de E., & Co.
Macdonell C. A.
Macfarlane J. Duncan
Mackay Alex.
Mackay Lachlan
MacVicar D. H.
McAfee George
McAndrew M. J.
McBrien Mrs
McCaffrey M
McCaughan J
McCool F
McCutcheon Mrs.
McDiarmid J., & Co.
McDougall J. S.
McFarlane D.
McGreevy Mrs
McGinty Mrs John
McGlaughlin —
McGean George
McKeown Dr.
McGown J. F.
McGregor C. E.
McGuirk Mrs.
McIntosh Miss
McIntosh Mrs.
McIntosh Wm
McKercher J
McLaurin Mrs. Alex
McLean Alex
McMillan D.
McNaughton A. M.
McNeil J. W.
McQueen James
McRobie J. F.
Madley H.
Madore David
Mailhiot J. B., & Fils.
Maillet Jos
Major E. J.
Major W E
Mallard P
Mantha J. B., & Cie.
Marcil J. N.
Marien F., M. D
Marlatt & Armstrong
Marquette Mrs
Marmette Samuel
Marson Mde.
Martin E.
Martin F.
Martin & Rivet.
Martin Thos
Martin Thos
Martin W. G.
Martineau Narcisse.

Masse J. Bte.
Mattinson James
Mathurin Joseph
Matthews G. H
Marurette A. P.
Marurette L. Nap
Meakins Thos.
Meighen R
Melançon Jos
Meldrum R
Meldrum Wm
Meloche B.
Mercier Jos
Merrill Mrs.
Meunier Louis
Meurier T. L.
Michon Louis
Miller D
Miller F. C.
Millette Napoleon
Milloy James
Mills A
Millward J. E.
Minogue James
Mock Charles
Moir John A.
Moisan Philippe.
Molson James
Molson Mrs
Monette Louis.
Mongenais, Poivin & Co.
Monthriaut L. R.
Montgomery John.
Montpetit Joseph
Montpetit Marie.
Moore Alex. B. J.
Moore W.W
Moreau Ant.
Moreau Mrs.
Morin Joseph
Morin Mde.
Morin Thos
Morrice D., Sons & Co. 10
Morrier N.
Morrisey T. I.
Morrison J
Morrison W. A.
Morrow John.
Mount Dr
Mullin Daniel
Munderloh & Co.
Murphy Alex. McA.
Noad Alex
Nelson Mrs. D. R.
Nightingale S.
Noble John.
Noel G.
Nolan Mrs. M. F.
Normandin H.
Norris J
North British and Mercantile Ins. Co.
Nuckle T
O'Connor J. T.
O'Connor M.
O'Keane J
O'Loghlin Martin
Odell Chas.
Ogilvie Mrs
Olscamps L. C.
Osen Mrs.
Orkney Miss
Ouimet Léandre.
Owens John B.
Paddon H
Page C
Painchaud E. A
Palmer A
Palmer J. & Son
Paquette M.
Paquin Cyrille.
Paquin Mrs.
Pardellian J. B., jun
Parker S. H
Parkin C. W.
Patterson Wm., jun.
Paure J. Bte.
Payette E
Payette Louis
Payette Philiss
Payment E

Payment L. L.
Pearce Miss F. L.
Pelletin J. J
Pelletier & Brosseau
Pelletier Jos.
Pelletier F.
Pelletier P.
Perrault Alphonse
Perrault H.
Perreault Sophie
Perrio D.
Petitclair Joseph
Peverley C.
Pewsley F.
Phelps M. H
Phelps Geo. F.
Philibert L. E.
Phillips F.
Piché E. U.
Piché Ferd
Picken E.
Picken Mrs. H. B.
Pinsonneault L. D.
Pilon Z.
Pitre J. A
Plamondon H. A.
Plante P. F.
Picardé G. H.
Poirier H.
Poito T.
Poriet H
Portugais Francis
Poudrite Napoleon
Poupart Alphonse
Prevost Armand
Prevost Hector
Price John
Pringle G. H.
Pringle Mrs.
Perugia Thomas
Prand Mrs. W. W
Prudhomme A. & Frères
Prudhomme Mde. F.
Quevillon Joseph
Quinn James
Quintal N. & Fils
Racine Alphonse, & Cie.
Rappat M.
Rastoul F. X
Reed Thomas
Reichling Chas.
Reid H. D.
Reinhardt Mafg. Co.
Reinhold R.
Renhn Rev. H.
Renaud C.
Renaud Isaac
Renaud J. W.
Renoie Samuel
Rhynas John
Ricard A. G. A.
Riddle W.

Riepert C.
Riepert Herman W
Rinpel & Bourdon
Riopelle Jos. Aimé
Ritchot Narcisse, fils
Ritchot Odilon
Ritter J. A
Rivard L. I.
Ruberge Chs.
Roberge & Shepherd
Robert C.
Robert Jos., et Fils
Roberts Miss Alice May.
Robertson Duncan
Robertson W. W
Robertson Wm.
Robillard C., et Co
Roby J. Alph.
Rodrique J.
Rolland A. H.
Relio John
Ross Mrs. W. R.
Rouillard J. B.
Rourke W.
Roussew Arthur
Rousson C.
Roussin Miss L. E.
Rowell Mrs.
Rowell S. P.
Roy Hypolite
Roy G. E
Roy J. A., M.D.
Royer Antoine
Ruffin Chs.
Rutenberg H
Rutherford Wm., et Sons.
Saut Mrs. H. T.
Salle d' Asile de St. Vincent
  de Paul.
Salloway R. G.
Samuel William
Sandilands Andrew
Scaieff Mrs.
Schetague H., N.P.
Schneider Joseph
Schuyte Christophe
Scott Wm.
Seekings George
Semple J. H
Shannon C. M. S.
Sharples Peter.
Shea M.
Shea James.
Shipton F.
Sigouin Alex.
Simon S.
Simonson P.
Simpson D
Sincennes McNaughton
  Line limited.
Singer A.
Sister St. Alphonse

Skeith John
Small H. H.
Smallwood Henry
Smart J.
Smith James.
Smith Jas., Balmoral hotel
Smith Mrs. Mary
Smith W. A.
Smith W. A.
Sobey F.
Somerville William
Sorgius & Kieffer.
Spendlove Dr.
Spindle Thos.
Spring's John A., M.D.
St Amour F. N.
St Cyr A
St George Jos.
St Jean F. N.
St Jean Frères
St Jean Henri
St Jean Louis
St Joseph Asylum
St Louis Rev. Sister
Ste Marie L. P.
St Onge A.
St Onge Olivier
St Pierre Miss O.
St Quentin Jos.
Stancliffe Mrs. F.
Standard Card & Paper Co.
State J. W.
Steel & Campbell
Steel James.
Steel Jas., 1326 Notre Dame
Stenior Mrs. H. W
Stevens F. S
Stevenson Col
Stevenson J. Alex.
Stevenson J. Alex.
Strachan James
Sutprenant Gédeon
Swain W. H.
Faguehoun E.
Tasker E.
Taylor J. & H.
Taylor Wm. T.
Terrien Made.
Tessier E. N.
Tetreault F. X
The Lang Mufg. Co.
The Standard Shirt Co
Theoret Geo. Arthur
Thériault Victor
Therien Rev. J. A
Therien Avila.
Thibaudeau Onésime
Thibeault Z.
Thompson John
Thurnburn H
Tigue Symon
Timbury P.
Towle & Michand

Tremblay J. B.
Tremblay William
Treponier Ferdinand
Treesler R.
Trudeau A.
Trudel Marc.
Truteau M. C.
Tucker John W., B.A.
Tucker Mrs.
Turcot Jos. L.
Turgeon P. M. O.
Turner Mrs. R
Turner W. J. N.
Upton F.
Urquhart Alex.
Vaillancourt J. A.
Valiquet Ph.
Valois Rev. A. L.
Van Allen Mrs. L. A.
Vanier Jos.
Vanier J. Bte.
Vanhos G.
Varin E.
Vasseur T. A
Victoria Rifles Armory
  Association.
Villeneuve Fred. E.
Vincent Stanislas
Vinette Ovide
Vipond J.
Vipond J. J., & Co.
Volkert & Schnaefer.
Walklate Mrs.
Wand C.
Ward Chs.
Warburton John
Ward Mrs. H
Warner Neil.
Watson J. O.
Watson & Pelton
Weir J. & R.
Weld J.
Wermeninger J.
White R.
White W.
Wilks Mrs. A. W.
Wilson F
Wilson Geo. S.
Wilson Mrs. C. J.
Winfindale A. H.
Withers W. G.
Woods Mrs. J. B.
Woodward F.
Wray J. C.
Wright E.
Wright H. B
Wright J. W.
Wright P.
Widil & Co.
Wynde Thomas.
Young G. H.
Young George.

THE CANADIAN PUBLISHING COMPANY,

LIMITED.

CAPITAL $200,000——20,000 SHARES OF $100 EACH.

Head Quarters in Montreal.

OBJECT: To guarantee funds towards cost of publication of LOVELL'S GAZETTEER AND HISTORY OF CANADA, in Eleven Volumes, with Eight Provincial Maps and a Map of the Dominion of Canada.

Funds to be placed in the hands of a Committee of Five, appointed by the Stockholders.

JOHN LOVELL, *to be Manager and Publisher.*

So soon as $150,000 are subscribed, a call of five per cent. will be made, to secure a Canvassing Fund. Whenever $150,000 are subscribed for *Volumes,* for *Lines,* and in procuring *Illustration Contributors,* a meeting of the Shareholders will be called to decide on future action.

Applicants for Stock and further particulars are respectfully requested to apply to

JOHN LOVELL, *Publisher.*

MONTREAL, March, 1891.

LOVELL'S GAZETTEER AND HISTORY OF CANADA.

To be commenced as soon as the subscriptions cover the cost of publication.

THE true history of this magnificent country is yet to be written ; that is, of the places in it. A correct and a truly *National History* would place Canada in a foremost rank. It would record the wonderful progress of this broad Dominion. It would chronicle every leading feature, and especially the wealth which the magnificent Allan Line of Steamships, and now of other Lines of Steamships are bringing to this country. It would show how the Grand Trunk Railway and the Canadian Pacific Railway are opening up our enormous Canada and its billions of acres, too rich to be allowed to remain much longer unknown.

In connection with this great undertaking, of the character and extent of which the Canadian public have been already sufficiently informed through my Prospectus and THE PRESS, the following letter, addressed to me, will afford some idea of the manner in which the project has impressed the mind of an intelligent and disinterested American gentlemen, residing in Plattsburgh, N. Y.

DEAR SIR,—I take pleasure in acknowledging the receipt of your esteemed favor of Sept. 6th, with your revised Prospectus and Sample Backs of the great historical work which you have projected. I find it difficult to speak, write or think about this undertaking without enthusiasm. Such an attempt, to gather in the threads of unwritten history from such a domain as the entire Dominion of Canada, stands without a parallel, certainly in the New World. It seems to me that the carrying out of your plan will add a most valuable characteristic to Canadian history—supplying, in its contributions from real life, what the breathing living organism is to the skeleton.

Large as the task is, which you have undertaken, I believe you will see its accomplishment. I cannot think that business people, and the brainy people of Canada, will allow you to fail of carrying out a plan so vital to the interests of every parish. It is a work which delay renders more and more difficult of accomplishment, as old people pass away. To-day their recollection is clear, but to-morrow they may be gone, and the light they only could supply goes out with them. Regretting that I can do so little beyond wishing you God speed, I remain, yours most sincerely,

GEO. F. BIXBY.

Local records in the work will be thoroughly revised by recognized masters of the subject, before being finally presented to the public. In every case, the Editor's debt to previous writers, to unpublished manuscripts and to *vivâ voce* suggestions will be definitely acknowledged, in order that students, so desiring, may draw instruction from the same sources.

The *origines* of places treated with special fulness, especially when the founders and pioneers are men of moral and intellectual vigor, they impress their characters on their work, and the preservation of their memories must have an inspiring effect on those who come after them. Their association with the great and good of a past day has had a salutary influence on several of our Canadian cities, and on none of them more perceptibly than on Montreal, the story of whose birth and early years is almost without parallel in the annals of civilization.

Although my first attempt failed for want of pecuniary support, I have resolved to make another trial. This time by a Joint Stock Company with a capital of $200,000, in shares of $100 each. After $150,000 are subscribed for, a call of five per cent. will be made to raise a fund, to be applied to a thorough canvass of each Province in the Dominion for subscribers for copies. Should the result amount to $150,000, the matter will at once be made known to the Stockholders, and their decision to put the preparation of the Eleven volumes into my hands by the appointment of the Editor-in-Chief, the Assistant Editor, the Editor of Statistics, of Eight Superintending Revising-Editors, one for each Province, and One Hundred Province Editors will be considered final. By this means the Eleven volumes could be completed and published within two years from date of commencing. Should the Subscription Canvassers fail in their mission, the work will again be abandoned, with a loss to the Shareholders of five per cent. paid in on each share ; but, should the canvass prove favorable, I should have the privilege of re-purchasing subscribed shares, by allowing eight per cent. from time of payment.

The following is a fair sample of how every place, having a name, in the Dominion, would be inserted in LOVELL'S GAZETTEER AND HISTORY OF CANADA :

PROVINCE OF QUEBEC.

THREE RIVERS, founded in 1634, is the third oldest city in this province. It is the capital of the district of Three Rivers and of the counties of St. Maurice, Nicolet, Champlain and Maskinongé. It is at the confluence of the St. Lawrence and St. Maurice Rivers.

[Hereafter a history will be written of this city from the landing of the first white man to time of publication of Lovell's Gazetteer and History of Canada, provided the subscription list covers cost of publication.]

Three Rivers is distant from Montreal 86 miles, from Quebec 86, from Batiscan 21, Sorel 45 miles, Pop. 10,604*—5159 *f*, 5445 *m*, 10,046 *c*, 554 *p*, 4 *jews*—1 *f*, 3 *m*.

Three Rivers has 3 avenues, 3 lanes, 77 streets, 4 squares. 1515 houses—478 brick, 58 stone, 969 wooden.

5 *Churches*—1 Anglican, built in 1852, of stone. First Protestant incumbent, rev. Léger Jean Btc. Noel Veysière; present incumbent, rev. J. H. Jenkins, M.A., rector. Congregation 200

1 Catholic cathedral church, built in 1858, of stone. First bishop, the right reverend monseigneur Thomas Cooke ; present bishop, the right rev. monseigneur Louis François Laflèche ; rev. Louis S. Rhéault, chanoine, procureur ; rev. F. X. Cloutier, care d'office. Congregation 6000.
1 Catholic parish church, built in 1676, of stone. First priest, rev. B. N. Mailloux; present priest, rev. chanoine Napoléon Caron. Congregation 4000.
1 Kirk of Scotland, built in 1845, of stone. First minister, rev. James Thom ; present minister, rev. George R. Maxwell. Congregation 250.
1 Methodist church, built in 1831, of stone. First preacher, rev. Wm. E. Schuetone; present pastor, rev. Richard Eason. Congregation 100.
Providence convent, built in 1864, of stone. First lady superioress, rev. sister Marie de la Charité ; present lady superioress, rev. sister Marie Hypolite. 11 nuns.
1 Ursuline convent, built in 1697, of stone. First lady superioress, rev. mère Marie Drouet de Jésus ; present lady superioress, rev. mère Marie de la Nativité. 66 nuns, 20 novices.
2 telegraph offices, the Canadian Pacific Railway Co.*, and the Great North Western Telegraph Company of Canada*. 1 Bell telephone*.

Professions, Mercantile and other Callings, Trades, etc.

53 *clerical profession*—49 Catholic, 4 Protestant.

31 *legal profession*—1 judge, 20 advocates, 9 notaries, 1 district magistrate.

11 *medical profession*—9 physicians, 1 chemist and druggist, 1 dentist.

78 *mercantile calling*—6 booksellers*, 17 dry goods, retail*, 1 dry goods, wholesale*, 2 fancy goods*, 2 fish dealers*, 2 furniture dealers*, 5 general stores*, 35 grocers, retail*, 2 grocers, wholesale*, 5 hardware, retail*, 1 hardware, wholesale*, 3 stationers*.

95 *other callings*—7 agents*, 1 artist*, 2 billiard rooms*, 9 boarding houses*, 7 commission merchants*, 11 contractors*, 23 carters*, 2 firewood dealers*, 8 hotels*, 5 insurance agents*, 3 land surveyors*, 3 lumber dealers*, 3 printing offices—2 issue newspapers, 1 semi-weekly*, 1 semi weekly*, 1 job*, 6 restaurants*, 1 roller skating rink*, 1 undertaker*.

6 *factories*—1 box*, 1 card*, 1 chair*, 1 furniture,* 1 lath*, 1 marble*.

5 *foundries*—2 iron*, 1 railway car wheels*, 2 stove*

14 *manufactories*—1 broom handles*, 2 cigar*, 1 confectionary*, 1 coffin*, 1 furs and skins*, 1 glove*, 1 hoop-skirts*, 1 silver plating*, 1 snowshoe*, 1 spool*, 1 toboggan*, 1 trunk*, 1 wood shovels*.

5 *mills*—1 carding*, 1 grist*, 1 planing*, 2 saw*.

183 *trades*—9 bakers*, 7 barbers*, 11 blacksmiths*, 1 bookbinder*, 25 boot and shoe makers*, 22 butchers*, 2 bricklayers*, 3 cabinetmakers*, 19 carpenters*, 4 confectioners*, 1 dye-house*, 2 engineers*, 5 hatters*, 5 jewellers*, 4 joiners*, 6 machinists*, 6 masons*, 14 milliners and dressmakers*, 7 painters*, 2 photographers*, 6 plasterers*, 6 saddlers*, 11 tailors*, 8 tinsmiths*, 6 tobacconists*, 2 upholsterers*.

In the matter of the PROSPECTUS of my projected GAZETTEER AND HISTORY OF CANADA, THE PRESS throughout the Dominion were unanimous in putting my object fully and earnestly before their readers, for which I again thank them most cordially.

Editors favorable to my new attempt will please put this important matter before their readers. Prospectus, rates of subscription, etc., will be found on the Cover of this Historic Report of Census of Montreal.

Subscriptions for Stock and for copies of the work will be thankfully received by

JOHN LOVELL, *Publisher.*

23 and 25 St. Nicholas street,
    Montreal, Jan. 31, 1891.

* *f females, m males, c Catholics, p Protestants. Jews to have distinct enumeration.*
† *The superior figures denote the number of persons as inmates or those of hands employed in factories, mills, etc.*
‡ *French Huguenot. Name and year will be satisfactorily accounted for when the history of Three Rivers is written.*

MUNICIPALITIES ADJOINING MONTREAL.

TOWN OF ST HENRY,

Incorporated in 1876 as a Town, adjoining the City limits of Montreal. It was formed by the amalgamation of the Villages of Tannery West and Coteau St Augustin. The Town of St Henry is situated in the Seigniory of Montreal, County of Hochelaga and District of Montreal. The Lachine Canal passes on the south side, and signal stations of the Grand Trunk Railway are situated here at the junctions where the roads branch off east and west, and to Montreal and Lachine. The Grand Trunk Railway Co., with the aid of the Council of the Town, has erected a splendid station at the curve, near the Notre Dame Street bridge. The Municipality of S Henry is governed by a Mayor and Corporation, and a separate permanent Fire and Police force is maintained. The Town contains a Roman Catholic College and Convent, Church and Presbytery, and several important industries, amongst others two extensive tanneries, boot and shoe factory, brick yards, the C. W. Williams Manufacturing Company, a Cotton Manufacturing Company. It has an Abattoir and Stock Yard Company, Town Hall, and a Fire and Police Station. Buildings are being prosecuted briskly, and the Town bids fair to rise into importance, having Fire and Police System of Alarm Telegraph. It is lighted by Gas and Oil Lamps. Distance from Bonaventure Station 2½ miles ; from Lachine 6 miles.

Population:—5995 females ; 5719 males ; 5626 Catholic females ; 5324 Catholic males ; 369 Protestant females ; 395 Protestant males. Total 11,714.

The Town of St Henry has 1983 houses :—912 brick ; 3 dashed ; 3 stone ; 1065 wooden.

ENUMERATION OF PROFESSIONS, BUSINESS HOUSES, TRADES. Etc.

	f	m
Clerical Profession :		
6 Catholic clergymen	5	1
1 Protestant clergyman	1	
Legal Profession :		
3 advocates	3	
1 notary	1	
Medical Profession :		
7 physicians	7	2
Other Professions :		
2 accountants	2	
2 artists	2	
9 agents	9	
3 agents insurance	3	
1 bank director	1	1
12 bookkeepers	12	
40 clerks	40	
1 civil engineer	1	
4 collectors	4	
13 commercial travellers	13	
16 contractors	16	
1 inspector	1	
2 journalists	2	
1 professor	1	
1 receiving clerk	1	
1 revenue officer	1	
2 secretaries	2	
1 stenographer	1	
1 teacher	1	
1 telegraph operator	1	
1 typewriter	1	
Dealers :		
1 crockery dealer	1	
1 fruit dealer		1
11 general dealers	11	
4 grain and hay dealers	2	3

	f	m
Factories :		
1 boot and shoe factory	4	19
1 cotton factory	318	177
1 leather manufacturer		39
9 manufacturers	18	33
1 organ pipe factory		2
1 sewing machine factory	2	144
1 wire manufactory		48
Mills :		
1 iron pipe mill		96
1 sash and planing mill		16
Mercantile Callings :		
7 boot and shoe shops	4	19
1 cutlery	4	48
6 dry goods merchants	8	15
48 grocers retail	19	53
4 hardware shops	1	8
1 ice office		10
8 merchant tailors	4	19
3 tea merchants	3	
1 wine merchant	1	
8 wood and coal dealers	7	4
Different Callings :		
1 abattoir		41
6 baggagemen	6	
1 bank		3
1 billiard and pool room		1
2 boarding houses	2	
5 brakemen	5	
3 bridge keepers	3	
2 captains	2	
1 cashier	1	
2 checkers	2	
1 chief of police	1	
6 conductors	6	
8 councillors	8	
10 drivers	10	

133

DIFFERENT CALLINGS—*Continued.*

		f	m
1	excise officer	1	
1	farmer	1	
39	foremen	39	
14	gardeners	14	
6	gate keepers	6	
1	Grand Trunk Railway depot		2
1	groom	1	
23	hotels	18	10
1	livery stable		2
3	lockmen	3	
3	managers	3	
13	milkmen	13	
1	pedlar	1	
1	pilot	1	
1	police and fire department		8
5	policemen	5	
1	post office		4
76	private residences	76	
2	restaurants	2	
1	road committee		150
4	sailors	4	
1	salesman	1	
1	shipper	1	
1	stevedore	1	
11	storemen	11	
7	switchmen	7	
1	timekeeper	1	
76	unoccupied houses	76	
1	waiter	1	
10	watchmen	10	
1	water works department		3
47	widows	47	

Trades :

		f	m
1	axe maker	1	
22	bakers	22	
4	barbers, master	2	6
9	barbers	9	
1	beer bottler		3
6	blacksmith shops		16
57	blacksmiths	57	
5	boilermakers	5	
1	box maker	1	
3	brass finishers	3	
19	bricklayers	19	
1	broom maker	1	
1	builder	1	
21	butcher shops		28
82	butchers	82	
15	cabinetmakers	16	
95	carpenters	93	
12	carriage makers	12	
3	carters, master	3	
130	carters	130	
3	cigar makers	3	
7	compositors	7	
3	confectioners	3	
8	coopers	8	
13	curriers	13	
4	dressmakers	4	
3	electricians	3	

		f	m
21	engineers	21	
5	file makers	5	
17	finishers	17	
2	firemen	2	
2	goldsmiths	2	
1	grinder	1	
7	hatters	7	
8	heaters	8	
1	iron pipe maker	1	
2	japanners	2	
1	jeweller	1	
114	joiners	114	
675	laborers	675	
1	lead pipe maker	1	
2	leather cutters	2	
49	machinists	49	
33	masons	33	
3	milliner	3	
2	millers	2	
12	millwrights	12	
20	moulders	20	
26	nailers	26	
1	organ builder	1	
1	organ pipemaker	1	
29	painters	29	
1	pattern maker	1	
1	paver	1	
1	photo artist	1	
1	picture framer	1	
16	plasterers	16	
6	plumbers	5	6
8	polishers	8	
2	rollers	2	
1	roofer	1	
7	saddlers	7	
2	saw makers	2	
1	sawyer	1	
1	scale maker	1	
82	shoemakers	82	
1	silversmith	1	
2	stainers	2	
2	steamfitters	2	
5	stonecutters	5	
1	stone polisher	1	
1	sugar refiner	1	
1	tack maker	1	
9	tailors	9	
17	tanners	17	
12	tinsmiths	12	
25	tobacconists	25	
35	traders	35	
2	trunk makers	2	
3	turners	3	
4	undertakers	3	2
1	upholsterer	1	
1	varnisher	1	
4	watchmakers	4	
5	weavers	5	
2	wheelwrights	1	8
1	wire maker	1	

NATIONALITIES.

5249 Catholic Fr. Canadian females.
4929 Catholic Fr. Canadian males.
45 Catholic English females.
11 Catholic English males.
44 Catholic English females b in C.
41 Catholic English males in C.
153 Protestant English females.
171 Protestant English males.
153 Protestant English females b in C.
144 Protestant English males b in C.
103 Catholic Irish females.
99 Catholic Irish males.
106 Catholic Irish females b in C.
114 Catholic Irish males b in C.
10 Protestant Irish females.
9 Protestant Irish males.
4 Protestant Irish females b in C.
8 Protestant Irish males b in C.
3 Catholic Scotch females.
3 Catholic Scotch males.
27 Catholic Scotch females b in C.
26 Catholic Scotch males b in C.
51 Protestant Scotch females.
44 Protestant Scotch males.

30 Protestant Scotch females b in C.
32 Protestant Scotch males b in C.
2 Catholic American females.
1 Catholic American male.
2 Catholic American females b in C.
14 Protestant American females.
14 Protestant American males.
10 Protestant American females b in C.
3 Protestant American males b in C.
19 Catholic French females.
26 Catholic French males.
5 Catholic French females b in C.
2 Catholic French males b in C.
4 Protestant French females.
2 Protestant French males.
1 Catholic Belgian male.
1 Catholic Italian male.
9 Catholic German females b in C.
5 Catholic German males b in C.
5 Protestant German females.
9 Protestant German males.
4 Protestant German females b in C.
7 Protestant German males b in C.
1 Catholic Norwegian female.   Total 11,714.

CATHOLIC CHURCH.

There is one CATHOLIC CHURCH in St Henry. January, 1891.

St Henri Church, built of stone in 1868. First priest

Rev. Father P. Lapierre ; present priest Rev. Fathe. M. R. C. Décarie ; 5 assistant priests ; 3 Catholic Fr Canadian male employees. Notre Dame st.

CONVENT.

There is one CONVENT in St Henry. January, 1891.

St Henry Convent, conducted by the Sisters of St Anne ; built of brick ; for the education of children. It is supported by the Catholic Board of School Commissioners. First Lady Superioress Reverend

Sister Marie Herman ; present Lady Superioress Reverend Sister M. Prudentienne. 25 sisters ; 827 Catholic Fr. Canadian female pupils ; 10 Catholic Irish female pupils ; 1 Catholic Scotch female pupil ; 5 Catholic Fr. Canadian female employees ; 1 Catholic Fr. Canadian male employee. 65 St Pierre st.

CATHOLIC ACADEMY.

There is one CATHOLIC ACADEMY in St Henry. January, 1891.

St Henry Academy, built of brick, in 1871. It is supported by the Catholic Board of School Commis-

sioners. First principal Brother Elphimair ; present principal Bro. Cautian ; 764 Catholic Fr. Canadian male pupils ; 11 Catholic Irish male pupils ; 1 Catholic male employee. 3 St Pierre st.

CATHOLIC ASYLUM.

There is one CATHOLIC ASYLUM in St Henry. January, 1891.

Asile St Henri, built of brick in 1885, by the curate and citizens, for the education of young children and orphans. It is supported by public charity. First

Lady Superioress Reverend Sister M. V. Seguin (St Louis) ; present Lady Superioress Reverend Sister M. B. Dalé ; 8 sisters ; 3 Catholic female pupils ; 100 Catholic male pupils ; 23 orphans ; 4 Catholic Fr. Canadian female employees. St Pierre st.

PROTESTANT CHURCH.

There is one PROTESTANT CHURCH in St Henry. January, 1891.

Ebenezer Methodist Church, built of stone in 1880.

First minister Rev. Hugh Johnston, D.D. ; present minister Rev. William Harris ; 200 congregation. Cor Metcalfe av and St Antoine st.

PROTESTANT SCHOOL.

There is one PROTESTANT SCHOOL in St Henry. January, 1891.

Prince Albert School, built of brick ; founded in 1884. Principal W. Gamble. It is supported by the Protest-

ant Board of School Commissioners ; 12 Catholic female pupils ; 7 Catholic male pupils ; 78 Protestant female pupils ; 88 Protestant male pupils ; 2 Protestant female employees ; 1 Protestant male employee. 3574 Notre Dame st.

SUBSCRIBERS TO LOVELL'S HISTORIC REPORT OF CENSUS OF MONTREAL.
TOWN OF ST HENRY.

Armstrong Walter...... 1
Bissonnette C. A 1
Brodie William 1
Caron & Frère........... 1
Charlebois A 1
Charretier Léon........ 1
Chicoine Frères.......... 1

Corporation 30
Dagenals Ferd....... ....
David O ... .
Decary Rev. R ....
Guay Eugène ....
Henriebon M ....
Labrèche Wilbrod .....

Lafleur Clément 1
Laliberté J. A............
Lanctot Dr..... ....
Larante Pierre ....
Lemieux L............
Lenoir Dr. Joseph.... ...
Longtin Francis ...

Normandin G 1
Papineau A...............
Papineau Joseph ......
Philippe Rev. Brother...
Sanvé Alfred ....
Seneral L, M.............
Thibeault Anthime......

LOVELL'S GAZETTEER AND HISTORY OF CANADA.

Extract from a letter of THE RIGHT HONORABLE SIR JOHN A. MACDONALD, K.C.B., D.C.L., P.M., etc.

I have looked through the Specimen pages of your proposed Gazetteer and History. If carried out, in manner indicated by those pages, it will be a work of the greatest value to the whole Dominion. It ought to be patronized largely by Canadians. Please put me down for a set.

Extract of a letter from HIS LORDSHIP BISHOP LORRAIN, *Vicar Apostolic of Pontiac.*

Please find enclosed my order for a complete set of your Gazetteer and History of Canada. You are 80 years of age ! This is a pretty good old age for a man who purposes to undertake such an immense work as the publication of "The Gazetteer." May the Almighty God keep you to commence and finish such a useful work.

Extract from a letter of J. M. LEMOINE, Esq., *the Historian of Quebec.*

You have my warmest praise for the completion of the literary venture outlined in your Prospectus. None but a veteran like you could dare conceive such a comprehensive project ; none but an indefatigable worker could expect to compass such a task. If I can be of any service to any of your co-adjutors in gathering and sifting information anent old Quebec, please command my services. I can recommend you, from past experience, as an earnest and successful toiler in Canadian annals. I am pleased to find that years have not damped your ardor and that the glow of youth is still yours.

Extract from a letter of GEORGE STEWART, Jun., Esq., *Author of " Canada under the Administration of the Earl of Dufferin," Editor of Stewart's Magazine, etc.*

I have the Prospectus of the Gazetteer and History which you intend publishing. The great enterprise will have my best support. Such a work is needed, and I know no man in Canada better equipped to publish and direct such an undertaking than yourself. I wish you all success.

Extract from a letter of SYDNEY R. BELLINGHAM, Esq., *formerly a resident of Montreal, now residing at Castle Bellingham in Ireland.*

I have the Prospectus of your elaborate National Canadian work. I herewith return a signed order for a complete set. The work merits encouragement.

Extract from a letter of a CANADIAN GENTLEMAN, *now residing in New York.*

I have your letter and Prospectus. I glory in your decision. Put me down for two sets, and for $1500 in case your subscription list does not cover cost of publication. The work must be of great value to the Dominion.

Extract from a letter of a GENTLEMAN *residing in Ottawa.*

I am rejoiced to see that your wonted fires are again blazing up in the Prospectus of the great and comprehensive work it foreshadows.

A Very Great Enterprise.

To the Editor of THE GAZETTE.

SIR,—As an old resident of Montreal who takes a lively interest in its progress and in that of my fellow-citizens, I would beg respectfully to draw the attention of the public to what I term a gigantic enterprise, which is now being carried out by one of the worthiest and most respected men in town—I refer to the veteran publisher, Mr. John Lovell, and his projected Gazetteer and History of Canada. The work is an immense one, particularly for a gentleman of Mr. Lovell's years, and that he should have gone to work upon it demonstrates the enterprising pluck of which he is possessed. The work, when completed, will be a monument to his perseverance and his energy in struggling with difficulties, which to many younger men would be altogether insurmountable. The enterprise is one in which every citizen of Montreal should take an interest. The Gazetteer and History will be invaluable to our business men, and I trust all who can do so will become subscribers, at once, so as to make the project an assured success from the commencement.

Yours truly, W. D. STROUD.

To the Editor of THE GAZETTE.

SIR,—In your issue of yesterday appears a very kind letter from W. D. STROUD, Esquire, in favor of my project. To this estimable citizen, I beg to tender my most sincere thanks, not only for the letter but for the kind way in which he subscribed for nine volumes of my projected Gazetteer and History of Canada. His wish to see such a work issued did not end here. After signing his name, he said : "Mr. Lovell, in case your subscription list does not come up to your expectation, put me down for five additional sets to help your great enterprise." This magnificent offer is worthy of all praise. Every good man will glory in such a citizen. It has my heartfelt thanks. It is a noble contribution towards the issue of one of the greatest works ever attempted in this wonderful and prosperous country.

To Mr. WM. DRYSDALE, publisher, and to other gentlemen, I also beg to offer my thanks for their voluntary subscriptions and for having put my projected Gazetteer and History prominently forward through the Press, and by their strong and forcible advocacy of the true value of the work.

For thirty-five years the thought of being of use to my country, by publishing a true History of every place in it, has cheeringly urged me on. While health and strength are mine I will persevere in my effort.

Yours obediently,

JOHN LOVELL, *Publisher.*

CITY OF ST CUNEGONDE,

Incorporated in 1876, as a city, adjoining the City limits of Montreal, District of Montreal. This Municipality is governed by a Mayor and Corporation. A permanent Fire and Police force is maintained; it is lighted with Incandescent Electric light, and possesses first-class Water Works. The Corporation purchased the old St Jude's Church, which they have converted into a handsome Town Hall with commodious Offices and Court Room, Fire Station and a Large Hall, for public meetings, as well as a private residence for the Chief of Police. The Jacques Cartier Bank has also opened a branch in the building, with Mr. G. N. Ducharme as manager. The Post Office has been lately transferred into the Hall. The City contains two Churches: one Catholic and one Protestant; two Convents, one under the St Ann's Sisters and one under the control of the School Commissioners; an Asylum under the supervision of the Grey Nuns; one College; and two Schools—one Catholic and one Protestant. It possesses some extensive industries, the most important of which are the Montreal Rolling Mills; the Mona Saw Mills; Davidson's Stamping Works; Luttrell's Cracker Factory; Findlay's Foundry; Henault Ice House; Robert Mitchell's Brass Foundry; Leroux's Ice House; T. Prefontaine, Lumber Merchant; Aquin & Itzwere's Door and Sash Factory; Wm. Rutherford & Son, Sash and Door Factory; Dominion Wadding Co.; McCaskill Varnish Factory; Singer Manufacturing Co., Craig & Sons' Electric Works. There is Telegraph and Telephone communication between the Municipal Office and the Water Works.

Population:—4104 females; 4055 males; 3572 Catholic females; 3517 Catholic males; 531 Protestant females; 534 Protestant males; 1 Jewess; 4 Jews. Total 8159.

St Cunegonde has 1277 houses:—1192 brick; 12 stone; 73 wooden.

ENUMERATION OF PROFESSIONS, BUSINESS HOUSES, TRADES, ETC.

Clerical Profession:	f	m
4 Catholic clergymen		4
1 Protestant clergyman		1
Legal Profession:		
3 advocates		3
2 notaries		2
Medical Profession:		
2 physicians		2
3 druggists		3
Other Professions:		
1 agent and collector		1
5 agents		5
1 auditor		1
18 bookkeepers	1	17
67 clerks	32	35
5 collectors		5
6 commercial travellers		6
28 contractors		28
1 journalist		1
3 professors		3
1 sculptor		1
Bank:		
1 bank	1	3
Dealers:		
4 fruit dealers	4	
3 grain dealers		3
2 wood and coal dealers		2
Mercantile Callings:		
5 boots and shoes	1	6
2 clothiers	2	3
3 coal and wood		5
5 dry goods	1	18
2 furniture stores		9
1 fancy goods		4
27 grocery stores	19	24
2 hardware		38
4 ice offices and 2 ice houses		19
2 lumbermen	1	2
1 provision store	1	1
2 tea stores	1	4

Different Callings:	f	m
1 boarding house	1	
2 brakemen		2
1 brass inspector		1
2 bridgemen		2
11 candy shops		9
77 carters		77
1 checker		1
2 civil employees		2
3 conductors		3
1 cook		1
1 custom officer		1
1 dispensary		1
1 electric light company		15
2 engine drivers	2	
14 foremen		14
1 gardener		1
1 gateman		1
25 hotels	16	9
1 lockman	1	
1 lumber yard		21
4 managers		4
9 merchants		9
1 navigator		1
2 night watchmen		2
1 paper carrier		1
1 pedlar	1	6
1 police station		1
67 private residences		67
1 restaurant		1
1 sailor		1
1 shipper		1
11 storemen		11
1 superintendent		1
2 telegraph operators		2
1 time keeper		1
39 unoccupied houses		
4 watchmen		4
27 widows	27	
Factories:		
1 cracker and confectionery factory	8	37
2 door and sash factories		80
1 tinware and stamping works	150	59
1 varnish factory		3
1 wadding factory	4	46

K

	f	m
Foundry:		
1 stove foundry		25
1 brass foundry	12	189
Mills:		
1 rolling mill	17	437
3 saw and planing mills		133
Trades:		
1 artificial stone maker		1
18 baker shops	18	11
13 barbers	13	3
2 beer bottlers		2
1 beltmaker		1
34 blacksmiths	34	2
4 boiler makers		4
8 brass finishers		8
1 brass moulder		1
14 bricklayers	14	7
3 butcher shops	3	3
69 butchers	47	21
11 cabinetmakers		11
86 carpenters	85	4
11 carriagemakers		11
11 compositors		10
3 confectioneries	3	41
8 confectioners		8
2 coopers		2
1 coppersmith		1
4 curriers		4
1 cutter		1
1 decorator		1
11 dressmakers	5	
7 drivers		7
4 electricians		4
29 engineers		29
1 farmer		1
1 file maker		1
6 finishers		6
3 firemen		3
1 founder		1
2 furriers		2
1 gilder		1
1 grinder		1
9 hatters		9
11 heaters		11
1 harness-maker		1
1 jeweller		1
1 jewellery case maker		1
66 joiners		66
329 laborers		329

	f	m
2 locksmiths		2
1 lithographer		1
1 leather cutter		1
2 laundries	11	15
1 lather		1
9 millwrights		9
9 milkmen		9
46 machinists		46
12 masons		12
1 merchant tailor		1
1 marble polisher		1
1 millinery		1
21 moulders		21
1 music teacher		1
36 nailers		36
1 organ builder		1
4 packers		4
27 painters		27
1 paint maker		1
1 paper stainer		1
6 pattern makers		6
2 photographers	1	2
11 plasterers		11
1 plater		1
11 plumbers		11
11 policemen		11
7 polishers		7
1 rope maker		1
1 roofer		1
7 saddlers	8	1
2 safe makers	2	3
1 saw filer		1
1 saw maker		1
2 ship carpenters		2
2 shirt makers		2
32 shoemakers		32
2 silver platers		2
1 spinner		1
1 steam fitters		1
6 stone cutters		6
1 tanner		1
16 tailors	16	4
16 tinsmiths	16	2
37 traders		37
3 truck makers		3
1 tub maker		1
1 undertaker		1
5 upholsterers		5
1 varnish maker		1

NATIONALITIES.

3063 Catholic Fr. Canadian females.
3060 Catholic Fr. Canadian males.
3 Protestant Fr. Canadian females.
3 Protestant Fr. Canadian males.
14 Catholic English females.
19 Catholic English males.
26 Catholic English females b in C.
36 Catholic English males b in C.
392 Protestant English females.
386 Protestant English males.
84 Protestant English females b in C.
90 Protestant English males b in C.
156 Catholic Irish females.
124 Catholic Irish males.
112 Catholic Irish females b in C.
104 Catholic Irish males b in C.
36 Protestant Irish females.
35 Protestant Irish males.
28 Protestant Irish females b in C.
30 Protestant Irish males b in C.
9 Catholic Scotch females.
16 Catholic Scotch males.
8 Catholic Scotch females b in C.
13 Catholic Scotch males b in C.
55 Protestant Scotch females.
65 Protestant Scotch males.
35 Protestant Scotch females b in C.
39 Protestant Scotch males b in C.

3 Protestant Newfoundland females.
5 Protestant Newfoundland males.
4 Protestant Newfoundland females b in C.
3 Protestant Newfoundland males b in C.
2 Catholic Australian males.
9 Catholic American females.
3 Catholic American males.
12 Catholic American females b in C.
18 Protestant American females.
18 Protestant American males.
7 Protestant American females b in C.
2 Protestant American males b in C.
1 Catholic Italian female.
3 Catholic Italian males.
8 Catholic German females.
4 Catholic German males.
1 Catholic German female b in C.
2 Catholic German males b in C.
16 Protestant German females.
13 Protestant German males.
2 Protestant German females b in C.
4 Protestant German males b in C.
2 Protestant Norwegian females.
2 Protestant Norwegian males.
1 Protestant Norwegian male b in C.
3 Catholic Danish females b in C.
1 Protestant Danish male b in C.

CATHOLIC CHURCH.

There is one CATHOLIC CHURCH in St Cunegonde. January, 1891.

St Cunegonde, built of stone in 1880. First and present priest Rev Alphonse Séguin, curate; 2 assistant priests; 2 Catholic Fr. Canadian female employees; 2 Catholic Fr. Canadian male employees. Cor Vinet and St James sts.

CATHOLIC CHAPELS.

There are three CATHOLIC CHAPELS in St Cunegonde. January, 1891.

Chapelle d'Asile St Cunegonde, built of stone in 1889 ; served by the Rev. Vicars of St Cunegonde ; 25 congregation. 124 Duvernay st.

Our Lady of St Ann Chapel, built of brick in 1878. First and present priest Rev. Alphonse Séguin ; 13 congregation. 708 Albert st.

St Ann's Chapel, built of stone in 1887. First and present priest Rev. Alphonse Séguin ; 1 assistant priest. 1466 St Antoine st.

CONVENTS.

There are three CONVENTS in St Cunegonde. January, 1891.

Grey Nuns Convent, built of stone ; founded in 1889, by the Grey Nuns, for orphans. It is maintained by the Citizens Committee. First and present Lady Superioress Reverend Sister Mallepart ; 7 sisters ; 46 Catholic Fr. Canadian female pupils ; 282 Catholic Fr. Canadian male pupils ; 7 Catholic Irish male pupils ; 1 Protestant English male pupil ; 7 Catholic female employees ; 1 Catholic male employee. 124 Duvernay st.

Pensionnat Ste Angèle, built of stone, in 1887 ; founded in 1887, by the Sisters of Ste Anne. First and present Lady Superioress Reverend Sister Marie Pacifique ; 20 sisters ; 150 Catholic Fr. Canadian female pupils ; 2 Protestant English female pupils ; 38 Catholic Irish female pupils. 466 St Antoine st.

St Cunegonde Convent, built of brick in 1878; founded by the Reverend Ladies of the Order of St Anne, for the education of young girls. It is supported by the sisterhood. First Lady Superioress Reverend Sister Marie Pacifique ; present Lady Superioress Reverend Sister Mary Alphonse de Ligouri ; 11 nuns ; 1 Catholic female employee. 708 Albert st.

CATHOLIC ACADEMIES.

There are three CATHOLIC ACADEMIES in St Cunegonde. January, 1891.

St Cunegonde Academy, built of brick in 1884. First principal J. P. Vebert; present principal Rev. Brother Modestus Joseph. It is supported by the Catholic Board of School Commissioners ; 6 brothers ; 5 professors ; 600 Catholic male pupils ; 1 Catholic male employee. 48 Vinet st.

St Cunegonde Academy, built of brick in 1878; founded by the Reverend Sisters of St Anne, in 1878, as a private academy, and also as parish school for girls. It is maintained by the Catholic Board of School Commissioners. First Lady Superioress Reverend Sister Marie Pacifique ; present Lady Superioress Reverend Sister Mary Alphonse de Ligouri ; 11 nuns ; 438 Catholic female pupils ; 2 Protestant female pupils. 1 Catholic female employee ; 1 Catholic male employee. 708 Albert st.

French and English Academy, built of brick ; founded in 1889 by Miss G. Boucher. First and present principal Miss G. Boucher ; self-supporting ; 60 Catholic female pupils ; 33 Catholic male pupils ; 1 Catholic female employee ; 1 Catholic male employee. 2301 Notre Dame st.

CATHOLIC ASYLUMS.

There are two CATHOLIC ASYLUMS in St Cunegonde. January, 1891.

Asile Ste Cunegonde, built of stone ; founded by the Reverend Ladies of the Grey Nunnery, in 1889, as a mixed school for young children. It is supported by a Committee of Ladies and Gentlemen. First and present Lady Superioress Reverend Sister Mallepart ; 5 nuns ; 300 Catholic female pupils ; 257 Catholic male pupils ; 1 Protestant male pupil. 124 Duvernay st.

Maison de Charité Ste Cunegonde, built of stone ; founded by the Reverend Ladies of the Grey Nunnery, in 1889, as an asylum for young children. It is supported by a Committee of Ladies and Gentlemen. First and present Lady Superioress Reverend Sister Mallepart ; 6 nuns ; 5 Catholic female inmates ; 3 Catholic male inmates ; 7 Catholic female employees 1 Catholic male employee. 124 Duvernay st.

PROTESTANT CHURCH.

There is one ANGLICAN CHURCH in St Cunegonde. January, 1891.

St Jude's, built of stone in 1878. First and present minister Rev. J. H Dixon, rector ; 150 congregation ; 1 Protestant male employee. Cor Cours 3 and Vinet sts

PROTESTANT SCHOOL.

There is one PROTESTANT SCHOOL in St Cunegonde. January, 1891.

Stanley School, built of brick in 1875. Principal C. A. Myers. It is supported by the Protestant Board of School Commissioners ; 5 Catholic male pupils ; 35 Protestant female pupils ; 42 Protestant male pupils ; 2 Protestant female employees. 131 Vinet st.

SUBSCRIBERS TO LOVELL'S HISTORIC REPORT OF CENSUS OF MONTREAL.
CITY OF ST CUNEGONDE.

Academie Ste. Cunegonde.	1	Davidson Thos.	1
Asile Ste. Cunegonde	1	Desjardins Ls	1
Bissonnette P. E.	1	Desjardins Paul	1
Bourcier J. B.	1	Dominion Wadding Co....	1
Campeau Henri, M.D	1	Doré Jos. H	1
Campeau S	1	Doucet F. X	1
Chadillos F. X.	1	Dunberry Jas.........	1
Cinq-Mars H A	1	Elliot Henry.........	1
Cité de Ste. Cunegonde.	8	Fabien C. P	1
Collège Ste. Cunegonde...	1	Fauteux Hercule	1
Corran Henry	1	Findlay John, & Son	1
Couillard L	1	Fortin Louis	1
Cypihot T., M.D	1	Gougeon J. A.	1
Greer G. A.	1	Mona Saw Mills.........	1
Grenier J. E.	1	Mongeau L.	1
Izweire Louis.........	1	Nadeau P. O	1
Juneau Joseph	1	Pensionnat Ste. Angèle....	1
Labreche Ovila	1	Perras E.	1
Lamontagne Louis	1	Poirier Joseph	2
Laniel H	1	Portier Chas. F.........	1
Lapierre F. X	1	Préfontaine T.........	1
Laurin L., & Cie.........	1	Rivet J O	1
Louzon R	1	Seguin Rev. A.	1
Laurcell Joseph	1	Soullière E.	1
Marchand E.........	1	Vary Isaie	1
Mathieu L.	1	Wiseman H	1

ST LOUIS DE MILE END.

An incorporated Village near the east end of Mount Royal, Parish of L'Enfant Jésus, Seigniory of Montreal, County of Hochelaga. This Village was formerly united with Coteau St Louis and Côte Visitation in one municipality; but in 1878 it was incorporated as a separate Municipality with a Mayor and seven Councillors. Before the year 1800 the site on which the Village stands was a forest, and mostly belonged to Pierre D. Bélair. An Englishman, named Mountpleasant, purchased it from the former owner, and experimented in orchard culture with a large stock of fruit trees imported from England. His attempt was unsuccessful, and the land passed into the Whitehall and Knapp families. A few years later John and Jacob Wurtele purchased a large portion of it, and in 1816 it was subdivided between Wurtele, Fortier, John Spalding, Richard Smith, and others. Still later Stanley Bagg purchased a tract of about forty acres, on a portion of which the Provincial Exhibition buildings are now erected. In 1805 a clearance was made on the west side of St Lawrence road to the brow of the Mountain, northward from where the Hotel Dieu Convent and Hospital now stands, to the present Mount Royal avenue. The clearance was turned into pasture land and a race course. The course was then the only one in either Lower or Upper Canada. Robert Lovell and family, in 1820 and 1821, occupied what was then known as the Wurtele property, now almost the centre of this prosperous and progressive village, then known as the Mile End. On the outskirts are several farms, among which may be noted that of John Spalding, whose father was one of the first pioneers in this district. All this immense tract of land had originally belonged to the Seminary of St Sulpice and to the Ladies of the Hotel Dieu. A Catholic Church was built in 1857, in connection with which are the Convent of the Sisters of Providence, and an extensive Institution for Deaf Mutes (males), which is under the control of the Cleres de St Viateur. Attached to this Institution is a manufactory where various trades are taught to the afflicted inmates. The Canadian Pacific Railway runs through the village, and near the station is a large Kerosene Oil Refinery. Mail daily. Distance from Montreal Parish Church, 1 mile.

Population:—1723 females; 1726 males; 1660 Catholic females; 1659 Catholic males; 63 Protestant females; 67 Protestant males. Total 3449.

It has 1037 houses:—343 brick; 8 dashed; 15 stone; 671 wooden.

ENUMERATION OF PROFESSIONS, BUSINESS HOUSES, TRADES, ETC.

	f	m
Clerical Profession:		
2 Catholic clergymen	1	
Legal Profession:		
1 notary	1	
Medical Profession:		
2 physicians	2	
1 dentist	1	
1 veterinary surgeon	1	
Other Professions:		
1 artist	1	
2 bailiffs	2	
2 bookkeepers	2	
1 civil engineer	1	
7 clerks	6	2
3 contractors	3	
Mercantile Callings:		
2 bakers shops	2	8
1 barber shop	1	3
17 butchers shops	13	10
1 dry goods store	2	3
2 florists	2	3
1 furniture store	1	
4 grain and hay dealers	3	4
26 grocery stores	25	9
1 hardware and paint store		3
1 lumber merchant	1	1
1 merchant	1	
1 merchant tailor	1	7
1 oil refinery		9
1 wood contractor		2
4 wood dealers	3	9

	f	m
Different Callings:		
1 boiler inspector		1
2 candy stores		2
67 carters		67
3 caretakers		3
1 conductor		1
1 dairyman		1
6 drivers		6
1 farmer		1
3 foremen		3
1 guardian		1
3 hotels	3	2
29 milkmen		29
1 policeman		1
1 police serjant		1
37 private residences		37
1 road master		1
1 school	1	5
1 sexton		1
1 storeman		1
14 unoccupied houses		
1 watchman		1
Trades:		
8 bakers		8
3 barbers		3
1 beer bottler		1
1 belt maker		1
8 blacksmiths		8
1 bookbinder		1
11 bricklayers		11
3 cabinetmakers		3
16 carpenters		16
8 cigar makers		8
7 confectioners		7
4 carriage-makers		4

TRADES—*Continued.*

	f	m			f	m
4 compositors	3		7 plasterers		7	
1 cooper	1		2 plumbers		2	
6 engineers	6		30 quarrymen		30	
1 engraver	1		3 roofers		3	
1 fireman	1		1 saddler		1	
5 gardeners	5	2	1 seamstress	1		
1 gilder	1		29 shoemakers		26	4
1 gunsmith	1		16 stonecutters		16	
6 jewellers	6		1 stone polisher		1	
29 joiners	29	5	4 tailors		4	2
173 laborers	170		3 tinsmiths		3	
2 lime burners	1	3	8 traders		8	
41 masons	41	7	3 upholsterers		3	
9 painters	9	3				

NATIONALITIES.

1632 Catholic Fr. Canadian females.
1614 Catholic Fr. Canadian males.
12 Catholic English females b in C.
5 Catholic English males b in C.
12 Protestant English females.
14 Protestant English males.
39 Protestant English females b in C.
27 Protestant English males b in C.
4 Catholic Irish females.
7 Catholic Irish males.
12 Catholic Irish females b in C.
15 Catholic Irish males b in C.
3 Protestant Irish females.
4 Protestant Irish males.
1 Protestant Irish males b in C.
2 Catholic Scotch females.
2 Catholic Scotch males.
1 Catholic Scotch females b in C.

4 Protestant Scotch females.
6 Protestant Scotch males.
7 Protestant Scotch females b in C.
6 Protestant Scotch males b in C.
1 Protestant Welsh female.
1 Protestant Welsh male.
10 Catholic American females.
11 Catholic American males.
1 Catholic American f. male b in C.
2 Catholic American males b in C.
2 Catholic French females.
3 Catholic French males.
2 Catholic French females b in C.
1 Catholic German male.
2 Protestant German females.
3 Protestant German males.
1 Protestant German female b in C.
1 Protestant German male b in C.

CATHOLIC CHURCH.

There is one Catholic Church in St Louis of Mile End. January, 1891.

St Enfant Jesus Church, built of stone in 1895. First priest Rev. Mr. Tallet; present priest Rev. G. D. Lesage; 4 assistant priests; 3 Catholic Fr. Canadian female employees; 2 Catholic Fr. Canadian male employees; 750 congregation. St Dominique st.

CONVENT.

There is one CONVENT in St. Louis of Mile End. January, 1891.

St Louis of Mile End Convent, built of stone in 1863; founded by Madame Nolan in 1863, under the direction of the Sisters of Providence. 14 sisters; 12 Catholic female employees; 2 Catholic male employees. Nationalities of inmates: 192 Catholic Fr. Canadian females; 22 Catholic Irish females b in C. St Dominique st, St Louis of Mile End.

CATHOLIC SCHOOL.

There is one Catholic School in St Louis of Mile End. January, 1891.

St Louis School, built of brick in 1879; founded in 1879 by Cleres St Viateur. First principal Rev. Bro. Champoux; present principal Rev. Bro. d'Anjou; 298 Catholic male pupils; 1 Catholic female employee; 5 Catholic male employees; Nationalities of inmates: 1 Catholic Fr. Canadian female; 5 Catholic Fr. Canadian males. St Dominique st.

DEAF AND DUMB INSTITUTION.

Ecole d'Agriculture Pratique des Sourds Muets, built of brick in 1861; founded in 1867, by the directors as a school for the deaf and dumb. It is under the direction and control of the Reverend Cleres of St Viateur, and is supported by the Mother House. First principal Rev. Father Manseau; present principal Rev. Father Masse; it has 4 Catholic male instructors; 23 Catholic male pupils; 3 Catholic female employees. Nationalities of inmates: 3 Catholic French Canadian females; 24 Catholic French Canadian males.

PROTESTANT SCHOOL.

There is one PROTESTANT School in St Louis of Mile End. January, 1891.

Dissentient School, built of wood in 1889; founded in 1889 by a Board of Trustees, Miss Laura MacDonald teacher; 18 Protestant female pupils; 13 Protestant male pupils; 2 Catholic female pupils; 2 Catholic male pupils. Stuart st.

SUBSCRIBERS TO LOVELL'S HISTORIC REPORT OF CENSUS OF MONTREAL.
ST LOUIS DE MILE END.

COTEAU ST LOUIS.

AN Incorporated Village near the east end of Montreal, parish of L'Enfant Jésus, seigniory of Montreal, county of Hochelaga. This place, on account of its proximity to Montreal, may be regarded as one of its suburbs. In 1760 it consisted of three or four small houses, erected by Jean Brazeau, who had acquired a tract of what was thought rather poor land from the gentlemen of the Seminary of St. Sulpice, Seigniors of the Island of Montreal. An English settler, James Ross, purchased sixty acres of it, but afterwards resold it to Brazeau. Shortly afterwards the discovery of an immense bed of limestone, suitable for building purposes, gave a great impetus to the prosperity of the locality. Capital was invested, and the first stone extracted in 1773. Among the earlier proprietors of quarries were Benjamin Lapointe, Pascal Comte, John Spalding and Charles Lacroix. The principal buildings in Montreal were built of stone from these quarries. Among the buildings may be cited the old Montreal College, the Church of Notre Dame, Post Office, City Hall, Villa Maria Convent, and most of the Banks. About the year 1800 M. Plessis dit Belair bought a strip of land, extending from the present St Denis street to Robin street, and established a tannery. The district then became known as Tanneries des Belair. Mr. Plessis was the father of Monseigneur Plessis, Bishop of Quebec. The house he then built is still standing, and is now used as a saw mill. Owing to the development of the quarries many small houses were built from time to time. It was incorporated as a village in 1846. In 1855 a Catholic Chapel was erected under the auspices of the Cleres de St. Viateur. Afterwards a Church was built at St Louis de Mile End, and the chapel became a part of the new church. Experiments in orchard culture were at one time made, but proved unsuccessful. The land has been gradually portioned into farms, which are now in a flourishing condition. The quarries, however, form the principal industry, and furnish the bulk of the male population with employment. The village proper is closely built, and during the past year several substantial dwellings have been erected. The Town Hall, which was burned in 1886, has been rebuilt, and presents a fine appearance. In the same year a Free Library was established by the Municipal Council, for the use of the inhabitants. The village has a mayor and six councillors. It possesses one Protestant church, one Catholic school and one Protestant dissentient school. The Catholic church and Convent are at St Louis of Mile End. Mails daily. Distant from the Montreal Parish Church, 1 mile.

Population: 1389 females; 1464 males; 1259 Catholic females; 1311 Catholic males; 130 Protestant females; 123 Protestant males. Total 2853.

Coteau St. Louis has 196 houses:—175 brick, 3 dashed, 69 stone, 249 wooden.

ENUMERATION OF PROFESSIONS, BUSINESS HOUSES, TRADES, ETC.

	f	m		f	m
Clerical Profession :			*Mercantile Callings :*		
1 Protestant Presbyterian clergyman			2 baker shops	2	4
1 Presbyterian church			1 barber shop		
Legal Profession :			1 boot and shoe store	1	
3 advocates	3		2 dry goods dealers	2	
2 notaries	2		16 grocery stores	15	5
Medical Profession :			1 hardware dealer	1	
1 physician	1		1 wood dealer	1	
Other Professions :			*Different Callings :*		
5 agents	5		2 candy stores	2	
1 agent insurance	1		91 carters	91	
1 agent wine	1		1 drivers	1	
2 bailiffs	2		3 foremen	3	
1 bookkeepers	1		1 general store	1	
1 broker	1		1 guardian	1	
1 cashier	1		1 lime company	1	3
11 clerks	11		1 lumber yard		16
3 commercial travellers	3		1 manager	1	
3 contractors	3		11 milkmen	11	
1 customs officer	1		2 policemen	2	
1 mining engineer	1		19 private residences	19	
2 secretaries	2		3 storemen	3	
			33 unoccupied houses		
Dealers :			1 warehouse		
1 coal and wood dealer	1		1 weigher	1	
1 fruit dealer	1		10 widows	10	2
3 grain dealers	2	2			
2 hay and grain dealers	2		*Factory :*		
1 horse dealer	1		1 oil refinery		1
			1 sash and door factory		1

Manufacturers:	f	m
2 brush manufacturers	2	12
2 paint manufacturers	2	3
2 vinegar manufacturers	2	1

Trades:

	f	m
6 bakers	6	3
1 barber	1	
1 basket maker	1	
12 blacksmiths	12	
2 bookbinders	2	
5 bricklayers	5	
1 builder	1	
6 butchers	6	
1 cabinetmaker	1	
11 carpenters	11	
1 cigar maker	1	
2 compositors	2	
1 confectioner	1	
3 engineers	3	
1 farmer	1	
3 firemen	3	
3 furriers	3	
6 gardeners	6	
1 jeweller	1	

	f	m
10 joiners		10
79 laborers		79
2 lathers		2
1 leather cutter		1
3 machinists		3
14 masons		14
7 painters		7
1 paper bag manufacturer		1
1 pattern maker		1
5 plasterers		5
2 plumbers		2
3 printers		3
100 quarrymen		100
1 saddler		1
1 saw filer		1
17 shoemakers		17
1 skin dyer		1
1 steam fitter		1
11 stone cutters		11
1 stove maker		1
4 tailors		4
1 wheelwright		1
4 traders		4
1 trunk maker		1
1 upholsterer		1

NATIONALITIES.

1199 Catholic French Canadian females.
1259 Catholic French Canadian males.
5 Protestant French Canadian females.
2 Protestant French Canadian males.
3 Catholic English females.
3 Catholic English males.
11 Catholic English females b in C.
13 Catholic English males b in C.
14 Protestant English females.
28 Protestant English males.
74 Protestant English females b in C.
67 Protestant English males b in C.
14 Catholic Irish females.
9 Catholic Irish males.
55 Catholic Irish females b in C.
47 Catholic Irish males b in C.
2 Protestant Irish females.
3 Protestant Irish males.
4 Protestant Irish females b in C.
8 Protestant Irish males b in C.

3 Protestant Scotch females.
5 Protestant Scotch males.
13 Protestant Scotch females b in C.
11 Protestant Scotch males b in C.
2 Catholic American females.
2 Catholic American males.
1 Catholic American female b in C.
2 Catholic French females.
2 Catholic French males.
1 Catholic French male b in C.
1 Catholic German female.
1 Catholic German male.
1 Protestant German female.
2 Protestant German males.
5 Protestant German females b in C.
3 Protestant German males b in C.
1 Protestant Polish male.
1 Protestant Swedish male.
1 Protestant Swedish male b in C. Total 2,858.

CATHOLIC SCHOOL.

There is one CATHOLIC SCHOOL in Coteau St Louis. January, 1891.

St Viateur School, built of wood in '87; founded in 1871 by Rev. Father Belanger, Clerc St Viateur. First principal Rev. Father Belanger; present principal Bro. N. T. Leclere. Directed by Catholic School Commissioners; 200 Catholic Fr. Canadian male pupils; 2 Catholic female employees; 5 Catholic male employees. 15 St Louis st.

PROTESTANT CHURCH.

There is one PROTESTANT CHURCH in Coteau St Louis. January, 1891.

Coteau St Louis Presbyterian Church, built of brick in 1887. First minister Rev. Mr. Porter; present minister Rev. Mr. Walker; 200 congregation. Mount Royal av.

PROTESTANT SCHOOL.

There is one PROTESTANT SCHOOL in Coteau St Louis. January, 189.

Coteau St Louis School, built of brick in 1887, founded in 1887 by Protestant School Commissioners. First principal Mr. Trenholm; present teacher Miss Rodrick; 4 Catholic female pupils; 2 Catholic male pupils; 33 Protestant female pupils; 34 Protestant male pupils. Mount Royal ave.

SUBSCRIBERS TO LOVELL'S HISTORIC REPORT OF CENSUS OF MONTREAL.
COTEAU ST LOUIS.

Corporation de Coteau St Louis.....49 | Lafontaine Eng.........1 | Prenoveau C. M. R.....1 | Prenoveau F. X.......1

TOWN OF NOTRE DAME DES NEIGES.

An Incorporated Town, formerly part of the Parish of Montreal, but now of the Parish of Notre Dame de Grace, in the rear of Mount Royal, Seigniory of Montreal, County of Hochelaga. It was first settled in 1869 by the Reverend Sulpicians. The parish being in close proximity to Montreal may be regarded as one of its suburbs. Notre Dame des Neiges is one of the healthy localities in the vicinity of Montreal. Being situate in a pleasant valley in rear of the Mountains, the smoke and vapors arising from the city do not reach it, on account of its position and altitude. In 1760 it consisted of the scattered dwellings of a few settlers. Among the earliest of the proprietors were the Reverend Sulpicians; Pascal Lachapelle; Louis Reichon; Nicolas Desmarchais; Pierre Desmarchais; Pierre Picard; and Charles Picard, uncle of the Rev. E. Picard, S.S., from whom part of the land upon which the Town stands was purchased. It was divided into lots about 1828. The first settlers were mostly tanners, settled on the creek which crosses the Town in four different places. The tanneries have disappeared, with two exceptions, which are now working on a large scale, and are in a flourishing condition. There was formerly a fine quarry here, from which part of the stone used to build the Lachine Canal locks was taken. Owing to the development of these industries many small houses were, from time to time, erected. The inhabitants are now mostly farmers and market gardeners. The first rough stone house in the Town was built about 1776, by Charles Picard, and is still standing. It was incorporated as a village in 1862, Augustin Crevier, now of Ste. Cunegonde, being its first mayor. In 1889 it was incorporated as a town, the first mayor being Pierre Claude, a leather merchant. There is a fine Chapel, built of stone, established by the Reverend Sulpicians in 1696, under the spiritual charge of Missionaries, sent from the Seminary of St. Sulpice. The present curé is the Rev. Napoleon Maréchal, P.P. There is a school established for girls by the Sulpicians in 1853, under the management of the Catholic School Commissioners, and directed by the Reverend Ladies of the Grey Nunnery. Present Lady Superioress Reverend Sister Casgrain. A boys' school, built of stone in 1846, by the Catholic School Commissioners, under the presidency of the late P. Lachapelle. Present president Pierre Claude; superintendent Joseph Germain. Notre Dame College for young boys, directed by the Reverend Fathers of the Holy Cross; Father Joseph Rezé, director. A Protestant dissentient school, under the direction of Miss Noyes. The Novitiate of the Holy Cross, directed by the Rev. Father Guy. The Catholic Cemetery of Notre Dame is situated about half a mile to the south-east of the town, near the ruins of the old capitulation house, where the treaty of surrender of Montreal to the English is supposed to have been signed. The Montreal Athletic Club House, a favorite winter resort for snowshoers and social clubs of all kinds, and summer resort for picnics, is situated here. It has a fine hotel, affording good accommodation; 2 marble works with 30 employees; and 2 tanneries with 50 employees; a post office, mail daily. An omnibus service has recently been started from the Athletic Club House to the city. Distant from Montreal 3 miles.

Population :—385 females ; 388 males ; 316 Catholic females ; 321 Catholic males; 70 Protestant females ; 66 Protestant males. Total 773.

Notre Dame des Neiges has 155 houses :—21 brick, 16 stone, 118 wooden.

ENUMERATION OF PROFESSIONS, BUSINESS HOUSES, TRADES, etc.

Catholic Clerical Profession :		*Mercantile Callings :*	
1 Catholic clergyman		5 grocers	5
		2 marble works	30
Legal Profession :		*Different Callings :*	
2 advocates	2	1 club house	4
		6 farmers	6
Other Professions :		4 florists	4
		1 milkman	1
2 accountants	2	1 policeman	1
2 agents insurance	2	13 private residences	13
1 bookkeeper	1	1 restaurant	1
3 clerks	3	2 tanneries	50
1 secretary	1	1 temperance hotel	1
1 speculator	1	1 toll keeper	1
1 teacher	1	6 unoccupied	

1 weigher.............	1		15 gardeners............	15
10 widows.............	10		1 glove manufacturer....	1
Trades:			34 laborers.............	34
1 master baker........	1		3 marble sculptors......	3
1 barber..............	1		1 printer..............	1
5 blacksmiths.........	5 1		1 sculptor.............	1
3 carpenters..........	3		2 shoemakers...........	2
1 carriage maker......	2 1		2 stonecutters.........	2
2 curriers............	2		1 tailor...............	1
2 engineers...........	2		13 tanners.............	13
2 finishers...........	2		1 tinsmith............	1
			1 trader..............	1

NATIONALITIES.

292 Catholic French Canadian females.
271 Catholic French Canadian males.
  3 Catholic English males.
  6 Protestant English females.
  9 Protestant English males.
 22 Protestant English females b in C.
 15 Protestant English males b in C.
  8 Catholic Irish females.
  7 Catholic Irish males.
 22 Catholic Irish females b in C.
 22 Catholic Irish males b in C.
 2 Protestant Irish females.
 1 Protestant Irish male.
 6 Protestant Irish females b in C.
 6 Protestant Irish males b in C.
 2 Catholic Scotch females b in C.
 3 Protestant Scotch females.
 4 Protestant Scotch males.

17 Protestant Scotch females b in C.
22 Protestant Scotch males b in C.
 2 Protestant Welsh males.
 2 Protestant Welsh females b in C.
 3 Protestant Welsh males b in C.
 2 Catholic Australian females.
 3 Catholic Australian males.
 1 Catholic American female.
 2 Protestant American females.
 2 Protestant American males.
 1 Protestant American female b in C.
 6 Catholic French males.
 2 Catholic French females b in C.
 6 Catholic French males b in C.
 1 Catholic Belgian male.
 1 Catholic German male b in C.
Total 773.

CATHOLIC CHURCH.

There is one CATHOLIC CHURCH in Notre Dame des Neiges.

Notre Dame des Neiges Church, built of stone in 1860, Rev. Father Marechal, priest; 2 assistant priests; 26 congregation.

CONVENT.

There is one CONVENT in Notre Dame des Neiges.

Notre Dame des Neiges, built of stone in 1680; founded in 1653 by the Seminary of St Sulpice; conducted by the Grey Nunnery for class and visiting the sick and poor, maintained by the Government and School Commissioners. First lady superioress Rev. Sister Versailles; present lady superioress Rev. Sister Casgrain; 5 sisters; 3 teachers; 104 Catholic female pupils; 2 Catholic female employees.

CATHOLIC COLLEGE.

There is one CATHOLIC COLLEGE in Notre Dame des Neiges.

College Notre Dame, built of stone in 1869; founded in 1869 by La Congregation Ste. Croix. First principal Rev Father Charles Villandre, present principal Rev. Father L. Geoffrion; self-supporting; 125 Catholic male pupils; 5 Protestant male pupils; 14 Catholic female employees; 50 Catholic male employees. Nationalities of inmates; 140 Catholic French Canadian males; 40 Catholic Irish males.

CATHOLIC SCHOOL.

There is one CATHOLIC SCHOOL in Notre Dame des Neiges.

Village School, built of stone in 1859 by the Catholic Board of School Commissioners of Montreal, Principal Mr. Germain; 58 Catholic French Canadian male pupils; 2 Protestant Irish male pupils.

PROTESTANT DISSENTIENT SCHOOL, UNDER THE DIRECTION OF MISS NOYES.

CLUB HOUSE.

Athletic Club House, built of wood in 1885, in front of the old Gunn residence; incorporated in 1885; established as a resort for snowshoe clubs, driving parties, pedestrians, etc. First president W. T. Costigan; present president James Paton; 100 members; 4 Protestant female employees; 4 Protestant male employees. Archie Fry, manager.

SUBSCRIBERS TO LOVELL'S HISTORIC REPORT OF CENSUS OF MONTREAL. TOWN OF NOTRE DAME DES NEIGES.

OUTREMONT.

AN incorporated village, situated on the north side of Mount Royal, parish of l'Enfant-Jésus, district of Montreal, county of Hochelaga. The site on which the village stands was originally the property of the Reverend Sulpicians, and was known as Côte St. Catherine, in the parish of Montreal. The road had been constructed around the base of the mountain, and served as an outlet to Côte des Neiges and St. Laurent. About ninety years ago Joseph Perrault, legislative councillor and François Descaries, appear to have become proprietors of all the land which comprises Outremont. At this time it was nothing but a bush. Benjamin Hall a few years after purchased a large portion of it, and farms were fairly started. The land which sloped away into the St. Laurent valley proved very fertile, and several gentlemen of means procured farms. Among those were John Gray, who had a large foundry, Colonel Maxwell, Warren Dease, who had made a handsome fortune in the fur trade of the North West, and Doctor Beaubien, father of the Honorable Louis Beaubien. In the course of time, the land became more and more subdivided for farming purposes, and John McMartin, Jean Bouthillier, François Imbault, D. Lorn MacDougall, Sheriff John Boston, John Wiseman, Thomas Wiseman, Dennis Horrigan, Wm. Fraser and William Salter made their homes there.

John Clarke became the purchaser of a valuable site for a country seat, comprising several acres of land. This gentleman had amassed a large fortune in the service of the Hudson Bay Co. He spent a considerable sum here in the erection of a handsome residence, which he named Beaver Lodge. The grounds were beautifully and luxuriantly cultivated. He entertained his friends in a princely manner. He was well known to the writer of this short sketch. His grand physique, fine qualities, commanding appearance, are still fresh in the memory of the writer. He was noted for his bravery, humanity and self-possession on trying occasions. One of his daring acts is worthy of mention here, and the following account of it is from the lips of his eldest daughter, Miss Adele Clarke: While he was in Fort Garry, with his family, a large body of Indians approached the place in their war costume, with painted faces, determined on exterminating the devoted inmates. Mr. Clarke, being a leading citizen, entreated the men of the Fort to stand at their posts and to give fight to their relentless foe. The overwhelming numbers outside the Fort had a disheartening effect on the besieged, most of whom, in their despondency, would have met death without striking a blow. But, fortunately, the cool-headed John Clarke was not so easily cowed. He instantly resolved to meet the fierce Indians, and he accordingly ordered the gate to be opened. He marched out alone, unarmed, and, as he issued forth, ordered the gate to be closed. The brave man, with outstretched arms, walked to where the Indians were encamped. They approached him with awe, believing that a superior being stood before them. They began by feeling his toes, his fingers, his body. The Indian chief put his hand on Mr. Clarke's head, and offered him his *calumet* as a symbol of peace. In fine, his intrepid conduct secured the withdrawal of the Indians, and he returned to the Fort amidst the warmly expressed admiration and gratitude of the fear-stricken occupants. His estimable widow, two of his daughters, and one son are now (1891) residing on Clarke avenue, a delightful locality on the western outskirts of Montreal.

SYDNEY ROBERT BELLINGHAM became the purchaser of a large and valuable tract of land in this place, beautifully situated on the north brow of the Mountain (Mount-Royal). There he built a comfortable house, in which he resided, with his family, for many years. Mr. Bellingham was ever an active and useful citizen. He served this country, as a British subject, faithfully and honorably ; as an able writer, as one of its legislators in the House of Commons, but especially in the trying times of 1837-38, when he rendered signal service during the march of a handful of soldiers to St. Charles, under the command of the valiant Colonel Wetherall. At St. Hilaire it was ascertained that there were at least 3,000 insurgents in arms at St. Charles. The Colonel had only 120 men, all told, under his command. Mr. Bellingham was in command of the movements and actions of the soldiers. On consultation he and the amiable Colonel DeRouville (at whose house Colonel Wetherall, Mr. Bellingham, Captain Glasgow, Captain David, and others, were staying) recommended that a despatch should be sent to Chambly to the brave and noble soldier, Major Ward, who had two companies of the Royals and one of the 32nd Regiment under his command in that place. Not satisfied with merely sending for Major Ward, Mr. Bellingham actually volunteered to carry Colonel Wetherall's despatch himself. A volunteer Montreal Cavalry trooper, of nine years' standing, consented to be his *compagnon de voyage*. At one o'clock on a dark night in November, 1837, both started on their perilous mission, with the understanding that if either fell on the way by the hands of the enemy the other was to ride on as long as the road was free. Fortunately both reached Point Olivier ferry at four o'clock, a.m., aroused the reluctant ferryman from his bed, and compelled him to ferry them across the Richelieu. Shortly afterwards they reached Chambly on jaded horses, which, had they not been well bred, would never have been equal to the fatigue of such a journey over rough and almost impassable roads. Major Ward was soon aroused by the sentinel. After receiving the despatch and exchanging a few words with Mr. Bellingham, the gallant soldier, with two companies of the Royals, one company of the 32nd Regiment, Mr. Sydney R. Bellingham, and the Montreal Cavalry trooper, set out on their way to St. Hilaire. Well might their arrival gladden the heart of the brave Colonel Wetherall and of the loyal DeRouville, for, under Providence, it was the means, not only of saving valuable lives and much treasure, but of preserving this country to their beloved Fatherland. With the additional force the march to St. Charles was begun early on the morning of the following day, and the destination was reached about 12 noon. While nearing St. Charles, Colonel Wetherall noticed a fine-looking old man, with white locks, a picture of goodness—standing at his door. The Colonel was struck with the old man's fine appearance, attitude and carriage, and at once ordered the

Montreal Cavalry trooper to bring him into his presence. The Colonel addressed this aged *habitant* in French, assuring him that he was desirous of meeting his misguided countrymen in a friendly way, and requested him to go up to the breastworks and ask his fellow-countrymen to lay down their arms in order that the Colonel might enter into a parley with them. The venerable man was soon on the way. He was seen entering the breastworks—but not to return. The answer from within was the discharge of such cannon as the insurgents possessed, and a broad-side of small arms, sufficient, if well aimed, to have laid low every British soldier on the field. The gallant and well-meaning Colonel had a few of his men wounded and two killed, but lost no time. In about ten minutes after the action commenced his horse was shot dead under him. In a moment Sydney Robert Bellingham, Esq., was at the side of his dismounted Colonel, placing his own charger at the Colonel's disposal. The latter in a moment was on the powerful horse, ordered his men into line across the field, of course in single file, and placed Major Ward, with a few men, close to the breastworks. For hours the action appeared to be in favor of the insurgents, 3,000 of them stood against 300, but the latter were British soldiers, whose evolutions were directed by an able and experienced commander. The steady fire and courage of the insurgents were certainly worthy of a better cause. The only hope, at this trying moment, for the gallant Colonel was to command a charge on the breastworks. It was done in royal style, and with a shout that raised every man's courage. The breastworks, after severe fighting, were carried at the point of the bayonet. Here Major Ward distinguished himself as a soldier of courage and endurance.

This account of the taking of St. Charles is written as a simple act of justice to a gentleman whose services have never been fully acknowledged. The writer had known him with pride, with pleasure, for upwards of fifty years as a manly defender of right and a hater of oppression. Sydney Robert Bellingham, Esq., was ever a true friend, confiding, generous and noble-hearted. His every act was that of a brave man. Without him the lamented Major Ward and his valiant soldiers would not have been on the field, and positive defeat would have closed the campaign. The writer of this sketch witnessed the battle. He can honestly say that the service rendered to Colonel Wetherall by Major Ward, sword in hand, decided the success of the loyalists in the engagement. The writer counted nineteen bullet holes in the Major's military frock coat, and his horse was riddled with bullets. The fine animal carried his master till his work was accomplished, and died soon after the battle was won. Wonderful to relate—the gallant Major himself escaped without even a flesh wound.

On the day after the battle Mr. Bellingham requested Colonel Wetherall to accept the fine horse which that brave officer had ridden at the battle, as a slight memorial of his signal victory. The gift, so gracefully offered, was, the writer may add, gracefully accepted.

Mr. Bellingham's bravery and foresight throughout the entire march, and especially his valor in risking his life to secure Major Ward's timely and telling help, formed the topic of conversation among the victors of St. Charles. But for his timely aid the effort to reduce so determined and well organized a foe would probably have ended in failure. Mr. Bellingham is now (1891) spending the evening of his days in quiet retirement in his native country—Ireland.

In 1875 the village was incorporated as a municipality, with a mayor and 6 councillors, under the name of Outremont. Several substantial houses were erected and grouped themselves into a village. The farms are well tilled, and the orchards and gardens are among the finest. A small chapel has been erected, where the service of the Church of England is held.

Outremont is destined to become one of the most favorite suburban retreats of Montreal. Its pleasant site and agreeable approach to the city have already induced many prominent business men to take up their residence there. Mail daily; omnibus twice daily. One mile from Montreal.

Population:—173 females; 190 males; 43 Catholic females; 55 Catholic males; 130 Protestant females; 135 Protestant males. Total 363.

Outremont has 65 houses:—26 brick; 2 dashed; 11 stone; 26 wooden.

ENUMERATION OF PROFESSIONS, TRADES, ETC.

Different Professions:

1 accountant	1
1 agent	1
2 agents real estate	2
1 agent manufacturers	1
4 book-keepers	4
2 clerks	2
1 customs officer	1
1 postmaster	1
1 sheriff's officer	1
1 shipping clerk	1

Dealers:

1 flour dealer	1

Different Callings:

1 driver	1
4 farmers	4
1 foreman	1
3 fruit-growers	3
1 manager	1
1 merchant	1

1 milkman	1
2 private residences	2
1 storeman	1
1 tea merchant	1
4 unoccupied	4

Trades:

1 blacksmith	1
1 builder	1
1 carpenter	1
1 compositor	1
1 confectioner	1
1 fancy box maker	1
11 gardeners	11
1 jeweller	1
2 laborers	2
4 machinists	4
1 painter	1
2 plasterers	2
1 saddler	1
1 silversmith	1
2 tailors	2

NATIONALITIES.

56 Catholic French Canadian females.
47 Catholic French Canadian males.
2 Protestant French Canadian males.
1 Catholic English male b in C.
16 Protestant English females.
18 Protestant English males.
15 Protestant English females b in C.
12 Protestant English males b in C.
7 Catholic Irish females.
6 Catholic Irish males.
6 Catholic Irish females b in C.
3 Catholic Irish males b in C.
1 Protestant Irish female.
1 Protestant Irish male.
9 Protestant Irish females b in C.
8 Protestant Irish males b in C.

12 Protestant Scotch females.
9 Protestant Scotch males.
24 Protestant Scotch females b in C.
28 Protestant Scotch females b in C.
3 Protestant Welch females.
1 Protestant Welch male.
1 Catholic American male.
2 Protestant American males.
1 Catholic French male.
3 Catholic French females b in C.
1 Catholic Belgian female.
3 Catholic Belgian males.
1 Protestant German female.
1 Protestant German male.
2 Protestant German females b in C.
1 Protestant Swedish male.

PROTESTANT SCHOOL.

There is one PROTESTANT SCHOOL in Outremont. January, 1891.

Outremont School, built of stone in 1866; founded in 1867. 2 Protestant female teachers ; 25 Protestant female pupils ; 24 Protestant male pupils.

ONE PROTESTANT CHAPEL.

SUBSCRIBERS TO LOVELL'S HISTORIC REPORT OF CENSUS OF MONTREAL. OUTREMONT.

Name		Name		Name		Name	
Ainslie James	1	Dunlop W. W	2	Languedoc Geo. F	1	Reid Robt	1
Beauben L	1	Edward David	1	Lanoix Louis	1	Robson James	1
Cadotte Joseph Treffle	1	Finlay William	1	Loth Robert	1	Russell Wm. H	1
Comte Louis	1	Gorman T. J	1	Masse L. R., C S.V	1	Salter W. R	2
Cooke George, jun	1	Hale Thos	1	Perham L. D	1	Seabrook R. H	1
Cooke George E., sen	1	Holmes Oliver	1	Perry Charles	1	Soultbie Geo. A	1
Cooke Robert	1	Joyce A	1	Perry Mrs. W., jun	1	St Jean Louis	1
Copperthwaite A. F	1	Joyce Horace	1	Peterkin E. H	1	Van Moorhem Theophile	1
David Charles	1	Labelle Gilbert	1	Reid James	1	Wiseman Thos	
Dudley Alfred	1						

www.ingramcontent.com/pod-product-compliance
Lightning Source LLC
Chambersburg PA
CBHW030557270326
41927CB00007B/960